Dynamics of Tradition

Studies in Islamic Law and Society

VOLUME 57

The titles published in this series are listed at *brill.com/sils*

Dynamics of Tradition

Islamic Theology and Law in Relation

Edited by

Idris Nassery
Muna Tatari

BRILL

LEIDEN | BOSTON

This publication is the result of work conducted within the AIWG Short-Term Research Group "The Dynamics of Tradition: Relations between Law and Theology." The Academy for Islam in Research and Society at Goethe University Frankfurt is founded by the Federal Ministry of Research, Technology and Space (BMFTR). This publication was made possible with the support of the BMFTR. Responsibility for the content lies with the respective authors. Funding for copy editing and indexing of this publication was provided by Paderborn University.

The Library of Congress Cataloging-in-Publication Data is available online at https://catalog.loc.gov
LC record available at https://lccn.loc.gov/2025032619

Typeface for the Latin, Greek, and Cyrillic scripts: "Brill". See and download: brill.com/brill-typeface.

ISSN 1384-1130
ISBN 978-90-04-53087-4 (hardback)
ISBN 978-90-04-74688-6 (e-book)
DOI 10.1163/9789004746886

This book is printed on acid-free paper and produced in a sustainable manner.

Contents

PART 3
Perspectives

Preface

Articulating the intricate relationship between Islamic theology and law has always been a scholarly challenge. Yet today—more urgently than ever before—it has become a political and social imperative, especially for Muslim communities living in Europe and North America, and no less for those within Muslim-majority societies. As we began assembling this volume, however, the world was confronted with another urgency—one that disrupted the very rhythms of intellectual exchange that are essential to such collaborative scholarly undertakings.

We therefore express our sincere gratitude to all the authors who, in the uncertain early stages of post-pandemic recovery, made the effort to travel to Paderborn University, navigating new challenges in the cautious return to academic mobility and discourse. We are equally indebted to those who, from afar, enriched our discussions through their online engagement. The combined contributions of all participants—whether present in person or virtually, at the beginning or joining our endeavor at later stages—continue to shape and deepen our thinking in the interrelated domains of Islamic theology, jurisprudence, and legal theory.

This volume represents one of several scholarly outputs produced within the framework of the AIWG Short-Term Research Group *Zur Dynamik der Tradition: Die Beziehungen zwischen Recht und Theologie* (*The Dynamics of Tradition: Relations between Law and Theology*). The research group was a joint project conducted by Paderborn University, Friedrich-Alexander University Erlangen-Nürnberg (FAU), and the Academy for Islam in Research and Society (AIWG) at Goethe University Frankfurt.

The AIWG, a pioneering academic platform dedicated to interdisciplinary research and dialogue on Islamic theological and social questions, has facilitated this work. It supports national research collaborations among scholars in Islamic Theological Studies, affiliated disciplines, and representatives from civil society—including voices from within Muslim communities. Funded by the Federal Ministry of Research, Technology and Space (BMFTR), the AIWG enabled the formation of research groups at Paderborn University, comprising Prof. Dr. Idris Nassery, Prof. Dr. Muna Tatari, and Dr. Abdul Rahman Mustafa, and at Friedrich-Alexander University Erlangen-Nürnberg (FAU), comprising Prof. Dr. Maha El Kaisy-Friemuth and Dr. Mohammed Abdelrahem. We owe special thanks to Dr. Raida Chbib, Managing Director of the AIWG, whose steadfast support was instrumental to the realization of this project.

Our thanks also extend to Nienke Brienen-Moolenaar at Brill, whose generous and timely assistance helped bring this volume to publication. We are honored to see this book included in the *Studies in Islamic Law and Society* series, and we thank the editorial board for their trust in our work.

Figures

Introduction

Idris Nassery and Muna Tatari

Dynamics of Tradition: Islamic Theology and Law in Relation is a carefully curated collection of essays that brings together a multidisciplinary team of scholars to generate new perspectives on the historical and conceptual interplay between Islamic systematic theology (*kalām*) and legal theory (*uṣūl al-fiqh*). By examining the trajectories of these two foundational disciplines, both in their past formations and possible future developments, the volume opens up critical avenues for rethinking their interrelation in light of contemporary challenges.

The interaction between theology and law in Islam has emerged as a focal point of academic inquiry across global contexts, especially as questions of religious authority, ethical normativity, and communal identity have gained prominence. This renewed interest is further spurred by the increasing institutionalization of Islamic theology in higher education frameworks, particularly in Europe, where Muslim communities engage with both inherited traditions and modern pluralistic realities. As the essays in this volume collectively demonstrate, Muslim intellectuals have historically drawn upon both theology and law not only to reinforce but also to critique and reimagine inherited discourses. This dynamic engagement has allowed them to express support for or resistance to various intellectual and legal reforms, thereby shaping the contours of Islamic thought across time and space.

The contributions in this volume delve into the possibilities and limitations of deploying theological and legal frameworks to reassess Islamic history and to envision new pathways for Muslims participating in global conversations on ethics, justice, and civilization. In doing so, the volume underscores the continued relevance of classical disciplines to contemporary debates and demonstrates how these traditions, far from being static, remain vibrant sources of reflection, critique, and renewal.

Contemporary scholars of Islamic theology, law, and society are increasingly confronted with phenomena that are at once deeply rooted and insufficiently explored—phenomena with the potential to fundamentally reconfigure our understanding of Islamic intellectual history. Although *fiqh* and *kalām* developed over time into specialized and distinct fields, they have never ceased to function as interdependent domains. Legal reasoning has consistently been shaped by theological assumptions, just as theology has frequently responded to legal and sociopolitical concerns. The historical record is replete with

 | DOI:10.1163/9789004746886_002

scholars who were thoroughly trained in both areas, capable of navigating the conceptual vocabularies and methodological commitments of each tradition. Yet, precisely because of their historical proximity, the subtle and often reciprocal influences between theology and law have not always received the analytical attention they merit. Uncovering these complex relations allows for a richer understanding of how theological and legal discourses have evolved within a shared interpretive and practical landscape—how legal norms have shaped theological reflection, and how theological frameworks have influenced jurisprudential reasoning.

This volume aims to contribute meaningfully to the study of Islamic intellectual history by bridging past and present, classical foundations and contemporary questions. Situated within a broad range of intellectual traditions, the essays collectively construct a comprehensive framework for analyzing how *kalām* and *uṣūl al-fiqh* have shaped, and continue to shape, the parameters of Islamic thought. The interdisciplinary approach adopted throughout the volume enhances its relevance across fields, offering valuable insights not only for Islamic Studies but also for disciplines such as comparative theology, legal studies, philosophy, political theory, and ethics.

Each chapter adds a unique dimension to the overarching conversation. Readers will find rigorous survey essays on foundational principles in *uṣūl al-fiqh*, detailed case studies of both canonical and underrepresented figures in Islamic theology and jurisprudence, as well as chapters that explore intersections between Islamic thought and modern currents such as phenomenology and secular hermeneutics. This diversity of perspectives allows the volume to capture the depth and breadth of Islamic intellectual traditions and to engage them in new and creative ways.

Intended for scholars, graduate and undergraduate students, and all those engaged in the critical study of religion, law, and theology, this volume offers both depth and accessibility. It will be of particular interest to those working in Islamic history, philosophy, theology, and jurisprudence, as well as to those pursuing comparative legal theory, political theology, linguistics, and intellectual history. By foregrounding the mutual entanglement of law and theology in Islam, and by situating that entanglement within both historical and contemporary frames, the volume advances a deeper understanding of how Islamic traditions have responded—and continue to respond—to the moral, social, and existential questions of our time.

The volume addresses the theme of interdependence between Islamic systematic theology and Islamic legal theory from a variety of perspectives. This topic is especially relevant in Germany, where newly established university-based institutes for Islamic theology are tasked with developing intellectually rigorous content that bridges classical Islamic traditions with contemporary societal challenges—such as rearticulating Muslim identities within secular, pluralistic contexts.

The editing process of this volume was significantly enriched by the careful coordination of the initial draft and the thoughtful contributions of those who generously supported the editorial work throughout. Their commitment, discernment, and attention to detail played a vital role in shaping the final manuscript, and we extend to them our deepest gratitude.

The chapters in this volume were thematically curated by the project board, whose intellectual guidance ensured a coherent and purposeful structure. The volume as a whole was shaped by the rich and sustained academic exchanges among its members—dialogues that proved consistently stimulating and formative for the development of this collective work.

The initial sections outline trajectories that offer new ways of understanding classical debates in the history of Islamic legal theory, reevaluating the ongoing relevance of theology to the field. For example, Ahmad Atif Ahmad's chapter, "*My Name Is Uṣūl al-Fiqh*," addresses a question that particularly confronts Muslim jurists on the cusp of the modern period: What is *uṣūl al-fiqh* for? This chapter moves backward from modernity, narrating the 'life story' of *uṣūl al-fiqh*. Ahmad's thesis suggests that while applying the practical side of the moral-religious law in Islam might appear unfeasible in some contexts, the theoretical legal sciences offer alternative pathways that depend on practitioners' comprehension of the art and its potential.

David Vishanoff's chapter, "*Theologies of Divine Speech and the Human Exigencies of Law: A Conundrum for Classical and Contemporary Islamic Legal Hermeneutics*," illustrates how Muslims desiring to reform the law have revisited theological premises underlying classical legal theory, such as those concerning language, meaning, historicity, and the theocentrism of revelation. By examining historical and contemporary examples, Vishanoff reveals the productive yet challenging conundrum faced by legal hermeneutics as they attempt to balance a coherent theology of divine speech with the practical demands of legal interpretation.

Further exploring the mechanics of interaction, the volume delves into how theology and legal theory were brought together in various traditions shaped by the political, theological, and social climates of their times. Serdar Kurnaz's chapter on epistemology and legal theory in Abū Zayd al-Dabūsī's *Taqwīm al-adilla* demonstrates that epistemology has always been central to *uṣūl*-scholars, who shaped paradigmatic literature for each school of law. Kurnaz critiques contemporary approaches that often overlook the epistemological implications of their methodologies.

Najah Nadi's contribution examines the notion of proof (*dalīl*) in late classical Islamic works of theology, legal theory, logic, and philosophy. She highlights how the interplay between these rationalistic traditions gave rise to the scholarship of verification (*taḥqīq*), characterized by occasionalist and foundationalist tendencies.

Mohammed Abdelrahem's chapter, "Impact of Theological Attitudes on Legal Thinking: Reason and *Maṣlaḥa* in the Legal Thought of Muḥammad ʿAbduh (d. 1323/1905)," considers the influence of rationalist Muʿtazilite theology on ʿAbduh's reformist thinking, particularly his approach to concepts of reason and public welfare (*maṣlaḥa*). Abdelrahem raises the question of whether these vectors can be seen as extensions of Muʿtazilite rational theology, particularly in ʿAbduh's fatwas and Qurʾānic exegesis.

Mohammad Fadel's chapter offers a bold reassessment of al-Shāfiʿī's legal theory by foregrounding its deep theological underpinnings. Challenging conventional readings that frame al-Shāfiʿī's *Risāla* as primarily a juristic intervention, Fadel argues that al-Shāfiʿī was the first major jurist to explicitly ground legal reasoning in a theological conception of divine speech (*kalām Allāh*). The chapter traces how this shift redefined the very nature of Islamic law—from a communal, immanent enterprise exemplified by Mālik's *Muwaṭṭa*ʾ, to a transcendent and divinely anchored system of rules. Through a close engagement with both pre- and post-Shāfiʿī jurisprudential traditions, Fadel explores the doctrinal and ontological stakes of al-Shāfiʿī's theory, particularly the idea that all legal norms are internal to divine speech. The chapter also examines the diverse strategies developed by later jurists to negotiate the theological consequences of this position, including epistemological relativism, procedural objectivity, and the notion of a "most appropriate rule" (*al-qawl bi-l-ashbah*). In articulating how al-Shāfiʿī's theological commitments shaped the development of *uṣūl al-fiqh*, Fadel provides a significant contribution to the volume's overarching aim of rethinking the interdependence of theology and law in Islamic intellectual history.

The volume also engages with contemporary perspectives, focusing on understudied traditions such as the Māturīdīs and Ḥanbalīs, while examining the role of modernity in shaping new theological and legal frameworks. Ramon Harvey's study of al-Māturīdī's treatment of causality (*sabab*) and human agency bridges the gap between *kalām* and *uṣūl*, demonstrating the integrative potential of these disciplines.

Maha El Kaisy-Friemuth's exploration of ʿAbd al-Jabbār's understanding of good and evil highlights how theological concepts fundamentally inform legal reasoning within Muʿtazilite thought. Similarly, Abdul Rahman Mustafa's chapter on the centrality of love in Ashʿarī, Muʿtazilī, and Ḥanbalī discourses connects ethical and theological dimensions with legal theory.

Although each chapter examines specific aspects of the relationship between Islamic systematic theology and law, they collectively illustrate the vibrant and complex scholarship of the past. These contributions go beyond merely reconstructing historical ideas, instead offering insights that resonate with contemporary debates. In exploring possibilities for Muslim identity formation in a secular age, this volume provides substantial paths for meaningful engagement with tradition and modernity.

By weaving together historical, methodological, and contemporary perspectives, this volume articulates a cohesive narrative that underscores the enduring relevance of the dialogue between *kalām* and *uṣūl al-fiqh*. It highlights not only the historical richness of this interplay but also its capacity to address pressing ethical and intellectual questions in the modern world. In doing so, it reaffirms the dynamic and evolving nature of Islamic thought, emphasizing its potential to contribute meaningfully to global discourses on ethics, civilization, and the human condition.

PART 1

Trajectories

CHAPTER 1

My Name Is *Uṣūl al-Fiqh*

Ahmad Atif Ahmad

1 Introducing a Narrative[1]

If it were to speak, as if it were one *homo sapiens*[2] (today an anglophone one, as it happens),[3] *uṣūl al-fiqh* would say, first, that "I am an art and a set of method-statements before being a genre." A resume or short biography of *uṣūl al-fiqh* as a living, evolving being ought not to account for every geographic move and variation of expression by each author, lest an encyclopedia, not a resume, be the result. A resume centers on landmarks.

Before any history, one must attend to 'purpose'. And since the following narrative is Sunni-centric, and no suggestion will be made that Shiʿi jurisprudence or legal epistemology is marginal or that it ought to be excluded, let the

1 To maximize ease of access to the Arabic sources employed here, I used, when possible, the collection of *uṣūl al-fiqh* sources on *al-Maktaba al-shāmila al-ḥadītha* (https://shamela.ws/). Where this collection lacked a source, I needed to indicate, as in the case of Shams al-Dīn al-Iṣfahānī's (d. 688/1289) *al-Qawāʿid al-kulliyya* and ʿAbd al-Wahhāb Khallāf's (d. 1375/1956) *Uṣūl al-fiqh*, I provided additional information to facilitate access to the material quoted. In the latter instance, Khallāf's, I used the edition of al-Daʿwa/al-Azhar Publications, 1375/1956, editorialized by Khallāf's friend Muḥammad Abū Zahra (d. 1394/1974). It is, incidentally, a standard for all editions of the book until the 21st century's commonly circulating editions: ʿAbd al-Wahhāb Khallāf, *Uṣūl al-fiqh*, ed. Muḥammad Abū Zahra (Cairo: al-Daʿwa/al-Azhar, 1375/1956).

2 *Homo sapiens* is singular.

3 English is our means of communication and hence the linguistic garb this narrative takes on, but it is, in the view of the performer of this narrative (the author of the lecture) unnecessary to privilege secondary literature on *uṣūl al-fiqh* (anglophone or not) and turn it into the subject of the narrative. Every contribution needs to acknowledge its limitation, and the limitation of this contribution is both obvious and explicitly stated. We can debate whether the secondary literature as it stands has been the cause of *uṣūl al-fiqh*'s hitherto obscurity to most students of Islamic legal reasoning, which obscurity is not limited to students, but also true of scholars who tried their hand on primary sources of *uṣūl al-fiqh*. The late Bernard G. Weiss, I must add, stands as an exception. But this is not the place to comment on his momentous attempt to speak in the name of Sayf al-Dīn al-Āmidī in *The Search for God's Law* (2010). I also retain the format of a lecture, which is what this piece was presented as, which also goes with the form of a speaker, here *uṣūl al-fiqh*. The lecture, delivered in Paderborn in 2021, appeared in Arabic translation by Dr. Maḥmūd ʿAbd al-ʿAzīz Aḥmad of Cairo University (by the Nohoudh Foundation) and can be accessed (https://nohoudh-center.com/translations).

 | DOI:10.1163/9789004746886_003

great Muḥammad Taqiyy al-Faqīh, of the Ḥārīṣ town of Lebanon's mountains (1911–1999), be the voice of the Shiʿi side only to highlight a basic overlap between a Sunni and a Shiʿi *uṣūl al-fiqh* before the main narrative commences. The note comes in al-Faqīh's preface to *Qawāʿid al-faqīh*, a text in which the author elaborates and offers caselaw for 64 essential principles of *uṣūl al-fiqh*. As advanced scholars move forward and backward from theoretical to practical legal reasoning, doubt arises, al-Faqīh says, as to how the material relates and appeals to authority. The purpose of building an independent intellect (*mujtahid*) is thereby compromised and a mongrel of a 'dependent-independent' mind (*mujtahid muqallid*) arises.[4] The cost of any measure of unclarity on what relationship obtains between *uṣūl* and practical legal reasoning, al-Faqīh asserts, is an inevitable abandonment of the theoretical legal sciences and a search for solace in the subtle atomism of caselaw or in plain literature and semantical quibbles. Al-Faqīh then goes on to say that appeals to authority in the course of an explanation of the reasons of one's judgment is an indication that one is simply 'not quite sure' about these reasons.

Uṣūl al-fiqh is, in other words, a field that trains the mind in explaining one's positions. It is a field of legal and moral epistemology, concerned mostly with action and practical reasoning. We will see, however, that the journey of *uṣūl al-fiqh*, given two long visits by *kalām* (the generalized science of theological speculations from natural and revelatory sources) in the 4–5th/10–11th and again the 7–8th/13–14th centuries turned the *uṣūl al-fiqh* we received into what al-Fārābī would call *ʿilm kullī* ('a science of systemic concerns', analogous to metaphysics and *kalām* itself). In other words, *uṣūl al-fiqh* turned into general epistemology, plain and simple.

The *uṣūl al-fiqh* armamentarium this audience, or any other audience, inherited is an accident of choices by living human beings, i.e., writers. Writers write because they read and want to react to their reading and think aloud. Yet, the field's necessity and purposes, its intersections with adjacent fields, and its potential utility and value all generate, in the eyes of this reader, a unified (positive) energy that went coursing through the veins of human history and is still alive within it. The narrative provided below reflects the narrator's limitation and will appear adequate or not adequate, depending on what you have read, how many times you read it, and what you read first and what you read next.

4 Muḥammad Taqiyy al-Faqīh, *Qawā ʿid al-faqīh* (Beirut: Dār al-Aḍwāʾ, 1407/1987), 7–8. This beautiful statement resonates with a statement by Ibn Rushd (d. 595|1198) as he points to the status of Mālikī scholars in his native Spain, which I cited and discussed in Chapter 4 in Ahmad Atif Ahmad, *The Fatigue of the Sharia* (London: Palgrave Macmillan, 1433/2012).

2 And so *Uṣūl al-Fiqh* Goes

1. I was born circa the end of Islam's second century, not twice:

1a. ʿĪsā b. Abān (d. 221/835) and Muḥammad b. Idrīs, better known as al-Shāfiʿī (d. 204/820) were engaged in the same art and answered the same basic questions on the power of arguments from consensus, analogies and their counters (i.e., counterarguments against arguments from analogy or consensus) in addition to the uncertainty embedded in texts and historical reports. Aside from small pieces of his writing surviving on their own, Ibn Abān's work is Palgrave Macmillan, or an eastern standard and a western one. The eastern standard was attached to the names of al-Qaffāl al-Marwazī (d. 417/1026), a man from Marw, whose teachers and teachers' teachers were also scholars of Marw. The western, or Baghdad-centered, standard brings with it the name of Abū Ḥāmid al-Isfarāyinī (d. 406/1015; himself of eastern origin but moved to Baghdad aged 21). The title Iraqi is sufficient cause for confusion; Iraqi usually means Ḥanafī, and al-Shāfiʿī's short treatise against the two Iraqis was directed at Ibn Abī Layla (d. 83/702) and Abū Ḥanīfa (d. 150/767). In his introduction to al-Juwaynī's (d. 478/1085) *Nihāyat al-maṭlab*, ʿAbd al-ʿAẓīm al-Dīb (d. 1431/2010) draws on much prosopography to rebut distinctions between these two schools based on an assumption that the westerners remained loyal to al-Shāfiʿī's 'old school' views (which he developed in Iraq before settling in Egypt) while the easterners adopted the 'updated' laws he developed in Egypt.[5]

---

5 Abū al-Maʿālī ʿAbd al-Malik al-Juwaynī, *Nihāyat al-maṭlab fī dirāyat al-madhhab*, ed. ʿAbd al-ʿAẓīm al-Dīb (Beirut: Dār al-Minhāj, 1428/2007): In the introduction to his commentary on *Nihāyat al-maṭlab*, ʿAbd al-ʿAẓīm al-Dīb points to the precedence of the ʿIrāqī Shāfiʿīs over the Khurāsānī Shāfiʿīs in their adherence to the old doctrine of the school, while the Khurāsānīs adhered to the new doctrine, vol. 1, 147, in: https://shamela.ws/book/9851/146#p1

"كما ننبه أيضًا لعبارة موهمة وردت في البحث الأصيل لأخينا النبيل الشيخ محمد إبراهيم علي (المذهب عند الشافعية)، فقد جاء عند الحديث عن الطريقتين قوله: وبقيت طريقة العراقيين وحيدة في الميدان الفقهي الشافعي، فقولها هو المعتمد، حتى نبغ القفال الصغير المروزي، واشتهر بالتدوين في الفقه، وتبعه جماعة لا يُحْصَون عددًا ..." فهذه العبارة توحي، بل تُصّرح أن طريقة العراقيين تقدّمت في النشأة عن طريقة الخراسانيين وظلت زمانًا لا يعرف الفقهُ الشافعي غيرَها، حتى ظهرت طريقة الخراسانيين متأخرة عنها بزمانٍ طويل. هذا ما تقول به العبارة. والواقع أن تمايز الطريقتين في رواية المذهب نشأ في وقتٍ واحد، وما قبلهما لم يكن يوصف بأنه عراقي ولا خراساني. والذي يشهد بأنه نشوء الطريقتين كان متزامنًا وفي وقت واحد، بصورة لا تقبل الشك هو النظر إلى ترجمة شَيْخي الطريقتين، الشيخ أبي حامد الإسفراييني، والقفال المروزي، فهما من طبقة زمنية واحدة، بل إن ميلاد القفال شيخ طريقة المراوزة قبل ميلاد أبي حامد شيخ طريقة

1b. Ibn Khaldūn could not have meant that there were two families of *uṣūl al-fiqh* that needed the combiners (*al-jamʿ bayna l-ṭarīqatayn*) to unify the science; his point was essentially heuristic. True, in Chapter 7 of the *Muqaddima* (where he narrates the history of *fiqh*) he jibes at the Iraqis, the Ḥanafīs, as short on Prophetic reports, only to praise them for using 'analogy' operations to fill in the limited Sunna reports they attained. In the same section he dispels a common mistake, which is the assumption that Mālik's reliance on the customs of the Hijaz was an argument from consensus. He clarifies that this is a special case of reliance on a form of Sunna, the living Sunna, rather than reported snippets from the Prophet's life-story (a privilege to be claimed only by the residents of Medina where the Prophet spent the last decade of his life).[6] Ibn Khaldūn comes back to *uṣūl al-fiqh* in Chapter 9, where he makes the familiar distinction between two styles of *uṣūl al-fiqh*. On the face of it, it is

---

العراقيين، فقد ولد القفال سنة 327 هـ على حين ولد أبو حامد سنة 344 هـ، وإذا قيل لنا: إن القفال تأخر اشتغاله بالفقه إلى سن الثلاثين، فالجواب أننا لو قدرنا تأخر ميلاده سبعة عشر سنة مثلاً (وهي فترة الطفولة والصبا) لوقع ميلاده في السنة نفسها التي ولد فيها شيخ طريقة العراق وهي سنة 344 هـ، أو نقول: إن القفال اشتغل بالفقه سنة 357 هـ بعد ما بلغ سنّ الثلاثين، وأفتى بعد نحو عشر سنوات من اشتغاله بالفقه أي في سنة 367 هـ، وقد ذكروا أن الشيخ أبا حامد كان مبكر النبوغ، فأفتى وهو ابن سبع عشرة سنة، أي في سنة 361 هـ. فهذا التدقيق في تواريخ الميلاد والاشتغال بالفقه يضع أمامك الدليل القاطع بأنهما متعاصران تمامًا، وإن تفاوتا بعض التفاوت ميلادًا ووفاةً (القفال 327 – 417 هـ) و (الشيخ أبو حامد 344–406 هـ). وواضح أن هذا الوهم بسَبْق طريقة العراقيين مبنيٌّ على ما هو أكبر منه، وهو أن العراقيين كانوا يروون المذهب القديم فقط، والخراسانيون كانوا يروون المذهب الجديد فقط، حتى مطلع القرن الخامس، حين جمع بينهما الشيخُ أبو علي السنجي المتوفى نحو سنة 430 هـ، وهذا هو نص كلامه الذي أفْهمَ ذلك: "وبظهور هؤلاء العلماء الذين جمعوا بين الطريقتين، بدأ الرافدان الأساسيان الناقلان لفقه الشافعي: قديمة وجديدة يلتقيان في قولٍ موحّد يمثل مذهبَ الشافعي والراجحَ من قوله (1)". وهذا لا قائل به، ولا هو بمعقول، فمنذ قرر الشافعي مذهبه الجديد، ودُوّنت كتبه الجديدة، وهي تُروى في العراق كما كانت تُروى في خراسان. وهذا الوهم جاء الباحثَ من عبارة الشيخ أحمد بك الحسيني -التي هي مصدره-، حيث قال بعد أنِ ذكر طريقة العراقيين: "وحتى جاء القفال الصغير، وتبعه جماعة ..." (2) فأوهم تعبيرُه بـ (حتى) وجودَ (غاية) زمنية، ومدّةٍ بين ظهور الطريقتين. والواقع أن (حتى) في عبارة الحسيني معطوفة على مثلها بالنسبة لطريقة العراقيين، ونص كلامه وهو يتكلم عن تطور المذهب: "... ثم جاء بعدهم بقية أصحاب الوجوه طبقة بعد طبقة، حتى جاء الشيخ أبو حامد الإسفراييني، وتبعه جماعة ... وحتى جاء القفال المروزي وتبعه جماعة ..." فعند التنبه لهذا (العطف) لا توحي العبارة بوجود سبق زمني بين الطريقتين.

6 ʿAbd al-Raḥmān Ibn Khaldūn, *Muqaddima*, ed. A. Khalil Shihada (Beirut: Dār Al-Fikr 1401/1981), vol. 1, 564–70, in https://shamela.ws/book/12320/562

a distinction between *an art that is based on arguments from reason*, the trademark of the *mutakallimūn* ('theologians'), with many examples of authors who follow this path, including the famous four authors of the master-sources: ʿAbd al-Jabbār (d. 415/1025), Abū al-Ḥusayn al-Baṣrī (d. 436/1044), al-Juwaynī (d. 478/1085) and al-Ghazālī (d. 505/1111); *and another that is based on cases and practical scenarios*, with al-Dabūsī (d. 430/1039) as sole example.[7] As the story

---

٥٦٤ وكمل الفقه وأصبح صناعة وعلما فبدّلوا باسم الفقهاء والعلماء القرّاء. وانقسم الفقه فيهم إلى طريقتين: طريقة أهل الرّأي والقياس وهم أهل العراق وطريقة أهل الحديث وهم أهل الحجاز. وكان الحديث قليلا في أهل العراق لما قدّمناه فاستكثروا من القياس ومهروا فيه فلذلك قيل أهل الرّأي. ومقدّم جماعتهم الّذي استقرّ المذهب فيه وفي أصحابه أبو حنيفة وإمام أهل الحجاز مالك بن أنس والشّافعيّ من بعده...

٥٦٥ وأمّا أهل الحجاز فكان إمامهم مالك ابن أنس الأصبحيّ إمام دار الهجرة رحمه الله تعالى واختصّ بزيادة مدرك آخر للأحكام غير المدارك المعتبرة عند غيره وهو عمل أهل المدينة لأنّه رأى أنّهم فيما ينفسون عليه من فعل أو ترك متابعون لمن قبلهم ضرورة لدينهم واقتدائهم، وهكذا إلى الجيل المباشرين لفعل النّبيّ صلّى الله عليه وسلّم الآخذين ذلك عنه. وصار ذلك عنده من أصول الأدلّة الشّرعيّة. وظنّ كثير أنّ ذلك من مسائل الإجماع فأنكره لأنّ دليل الإجماع لا يخصّ أهل المدينة من سواهم بل هو شامل للأمّة. واعلم أنّ الإجماع إنّما هو الاتّفاق على الأمر الدّينيّ عن اجتهاد. ومالك رحمه الله تعالى لم يعتبر عمل أهل المدينة من هذا المعنى وإنّما اعتبره من حيث اتّباع الجيل بالمشاهدة للجيل إلى أن ينتهي إلى الشّارع صلوات الله وسلامه عليه...

7 Ibid., vol. 1, 576, in https://shamela.ws/book/12320/574#p1

وكان أوّل من كتب فيه الشّافعيّ رضي الله تعالى عنه. أملى فيه رسالته المشهورة تكلّم فيها في الأوامر والنّواهي والبيان والخبر والنّسخ وحكم العلّة المنصوصة من القياس. ثمّ كتب فقهاء الحنفيّة فيه وحقّقوا تلك القواعد وأوسعوا القول فيها. وكتب المتكلّمون أيضا كذلك إلّا أنّ كتابة الفقهاء فيها أمسّ بالفقه وأليق بالفروع لكثرة الأمثلة منها والشّواهد وبناء المسائل فيها على النّكت الفقهيّة. والمتكلّمون يجرّدون صور تلك المسائل عن الفقه ويميلون إلى الاستدلال العقليّ ما أمكن لأنّه غالب فنونهم ومقتضى طريقتهم فكان لفقهاء الحنفيّة فيها اليد الطّولى من الغوص على النّكت الفقهيّة والتقاط هذه القوانين من مسائل الفقه ما أمكن. وجاء أبو زيد الدّبّوسيّ من أئمّتهم فكتب في القياس بأوسع من جميعهم وتمّم الأبحاث والشّروط الّتي يحتاج إليها فيه وكملت صناعة أصول الفقه بكماله وتهذّبت مسائله وتمهّدت قواعده وعني النّاس بطريقة المتكلّمين فيه. وكان من أحسن ما كتب فيه المتكلّمون كتاب البرهان لإمام الحرمين والمستصفى للغزاليّ وهما من الأشعريّة وكتاب العهد لعبد الجبّار وشرحه المعتمد لأبي الحسين البصريّ وهما من المعتزلة. وكانت الأربعة قواعد هذا الفنّ وأركانه.

is detailed, one doubts that the point made was anything beyond a heuristic point and a way to account for authorial and juristic styles. *Uṣūl al-fiqh*, in a word, is one art, centered on the question of how the lawgiver or lawgivers make(s) the laws.

1c. True, Ḥanafī authors jump to practical applications when they state rules or principles. In some cases, the application of a 'rule' or a principle is a stretch from the principle, because the principle was made with other ideas in mind. An example? We know that when a *mujtahid* ('a practicing jurist') encounters the unpleasant condition of two opposed arguments of equal power, he may drop both. Al-Shāshī (I mean Niẓām al-Dīn, d. 344/955) applies this, very swiftly and unthinkingly, to the condition faced by a layman forced to make a decision as to whether to perform her ablution or move to dry ablution while in possession of two water-containers, certain that one is appropriate for ablution and one is not. Al-Shāshī's mind also quickly moves to stating analogous cases, including when one has two garments, one a proper prayer garment and one not (for being stained with physical impurities), then moves to other principles with other practical applications.[8] A patient reader will find that all schemata (of *fiqh* and *uṣūl*) are filled up by the end of each *uṣūl* text. The distinction between *ṭarīqat al-mutakallimīn* and *ṭarīqat al-fuqahā'* is not useless, but it may well be misleading.

---

8 Abū ʿAlī al-Shāshī, *Uṣūl al-Shāshī*, ed. Muḥammad Fayḍ al-Ḥasan Gangohi (Beirut: Dār al-Kitāb al-ʿArabī, 1402/1982), 304–5, in https://shamela.ws/book/6302/126

بحث إِذا تعَارض الدليلان مَا يفعل الْمُجْتَهد: ثمَّ اذا تعَارض الدليلان عِنْد الْمُجْتَهد فان كَانَ التَّعَارُض بَين الْآيَتَيْنِ يمِيل الى السّنة وان كَانَ بَين السنتين يمِيل الى آثَار الصَّحَابَة رَضِي الله تَعَالَى عَنْهُم وَالْقِيَاس الصَّحِيح ثمَّ اذا تعَارض القياسان عِنْد الْمُجْتَهد يتحَرَّى وَيعْمل بِأَحَدِهِمَا لأنه لَيْسَ دون الْقيَاس دَلِيل شَرْعِي يُصَار إِلَيْهِ وعَلى هَذَا قُلْنَا اذا كَانَ مَعَ الْمُسَافِر إناءان طَاهِر ونجس لَا يتحَرَّى بَينهمَا بل يتَيَمَّم وَلَو كَانَ مَعَه ثوبان طَاهِر ونجس يتحَرَّى بَينهمَا لَان للْمَاء بَدَلا وَهُوَ التُّرَاب وَلَيْسَ للثوب بدل يُصَار إِلَيْهِ فَثَبت بِهَذَا أَن الْعَمَل بِالرَّأْيِ انما يكون عِنْد انعدام دَلِيل سواهُ شرعا ثمَّ اذا تحرى وتأكد تحريه بِالْعَمَلِ لَا ينْتَقض ذَلِك بِمُجَرَّد التَّحَرِّي وَبَيَانه فِيمَا اذا تحرى بَين الثَّوْبَيْنِ وَصلى الظّهْر بأحدهما ثمَّ وَقع تحريه عِنْد الْعَصْر على الثَّوْب الآخر لَا يجوز لَهُ أَن يُصَلِّي الْعَصْر بِالْآخرِ لَان الأول تَأَكد بِالْعَمَلِ فَلَا يبطل بِمُجَرَّد التَّحَرِّي وَهَذَا بِخِلَاف مَا اذا تحرى فِي الْقبْلَة ثمَّ تبدل رَأْيه وَوَقع تحريه على جِهَة أُخْرَى توجه اليه لَان الْقبْلَة مِمَّا يحْتَمل الانتقال فَأمكن نقل الحكم بِمَنْزِلَة نسخ النَّص وعَلى هَذَا مسَائِل الْجَامِع الْكَبِير فِي تَكْبِيرَات الْعِيد وتبدل رَأْي العَبْد كَمَا عرف.

2. At about age 250 I reached maturity, stimulated by Muʿtazilī–Ashʿarī–Māturīdī *kalām* disputes on human freedom, reason in revelation, and divine responsibilities. Note that Abū al-Ḥusayn al-Baṣrī (d. 436/1044) does not want us to mix *uṣūl* with *kalām* (especially *daqīq al-kalām*, heavy epistemology that does not relate to legal doctrines).

2a. The subject of *uṣūl al-fiqh* remains the sources of judgment. The sources are sometimes words (revelation conveyed), whose historical standing invites inquiries of philosophical and historical nature. To dwell on language and the techniques of interpretation would be alright, but an inquiry on certainty was destined to come center stage: language's uncertainty, coupled with the uncertainty of the human-divine relationship, and the uncertainty embedded in the distance that keeps getting longer between scholar and Prophet. True, once again, Abū al-Ḥusayn al-Baṣrī (d. 436/1044) indirectly notes that the obsession with *kalām*, in particular the definitional and the conceptual, overwhelms the subject and reshapes it. He justifies his authoring of al-Muʿtamad by a sense that his earlier contribution to *uṣūl al-fiqh*, a commentary on ʿAbd al-Jabbār's (d. 415/1025) work, took him too far in the direction of pure religious philosophy.[9]

---

9 Abū al-Ḥusayn al-Baṣrī, *al-Muʿtamad fī uṣūl al-fiqh*, ed. Khalīl al-Mays (Beirut: Dār al-Kutub al-ʿIlmiyya, 1403/1983), vol. 1, 3, in https://shamela.ws/book/6319/2#p1
ثمَّ الَّذِي دَعَانِي إِلَى تأليف هَذَا الْكتاب فِي أُصُول الْفِقْه بعد شرحي كتاب الْعمد واستقصاء الْقَوْل فِيهِ أَنِّي سلكت فِي الشَّرْح مَسْلَك الْكتاب فِي تَرْتِيب أبوابه وتكرار كثير من مسَائِله وَشرح أَبْوَاب لَا تلِيق بأصول الْفِقْه من دَقِيق الْكَلَام نَحْو القَوْل فِي أَقسَام الْعُلُوم وحد الضَّرُورِيّ مِنْهَا والمكتسب وتولد النّظر الْعلم وَنفي توليده النّظر إِلَى غير ذَلِك فطال الْكتاب بذلك وبذكر أَلْفَاظ الْعمد على وَجههَا وَتَأْوِيل كثير مِنْهَا فَأَحْبَبْت أَن أؤلف كتابا مرتبَة ابوابه غير مكررة وَأَعْدل فِيهِ عَن ذكر مَا لَا يَلِيق بأصول الْفِقْه من دَقِيق الْكَلَام إِذْ كَانَ ذَلِك من علم آخر لَا يجوز خلطه بِهَذَا الْعلم وَإِن يعلق بِهِ من وَجه بعيد فَإِنَّهُ إِذا لم يجز أَن يذكر فِي كتب الْفِقْه التَّوْحِيد وَالْعدْل وأصول الْفِقْه مَعَ كَون الْفِقْه مَبْنِيا على ذَلِك مَعَ شدَّة اتِّصَاله بِهِ فبأن لَا يجوز ذكر هَذِه الْأَبْوَاب فِي أُصُول الْفِقْه على بعد تعلقهَا بهَا وَمَعَ أَنه لَا يقف عَلَيْهَا فهم الْغَرَض بِالْكتاب أولى وَأَيْضًا فَإِن القارئ لهَذِهِ الْأَبْوَاب فِي أُصُول الْفِقْه إِن كَانَ عَارِفًا بالْكَلَام فقد عرفهَا على أتم استقصاء وَلَيْسَ يَسْتَفِيد من هَذِه الْأَبْوَاب شَيْئا وَإِن كَانَ غير عَارِف بالْكَلَام صَعب عَلَيْهِ فهمها وَإِن شرحت لَهُ فيعظم ضجره وملله إِذْ كَانَ قد صرف عنايته وشغل زَمَانه بِمَا يصعب عَلَيْهِ فهمه وَلَيْسَ بمدرك مِنْهُ غَرَضه فَكَانَ الأولى حذف هَذِه الْأَبْوَاب من أُصُول الْفِقْه

2b. Al-Zarkashī (d. 794/1392) later distinguished this maturity from birth; the work of the judge of the Muʿtazilīs (ʿAbd al-Jabbār) and the judge of the Ashʿarīs (al-Bāqillānī, d. 403/1012) was only aggregation and development, not *creatio ex nihilo*. Lazy dogmatism, he adds, almost killed the art and limited it to disputations about little fine points.[10]

10 Badr al-Dīn al-Zarkashī, *al-Baḥr al-muḥīṭ fī uṣūl al-fiqh* (Cairo: Dār al-Kutubī 1414/1994), vol. 1, 4, in https://shamela.ws/book/21593/2#p1
أَمَّا بَعْدُ: فَإِنَّ أَوْلَى مَا صُرِفَتْ الْهِمَمُ إلَى تَمْهِيدِهِ، وَأَحْرَى مَا عُنِيَتْ بِتَسْدِيدِ قَوَاعِدِهِ وَتَشْيِيدِهِ، الْعِلْمُ الَّذِي هُوَ قِوَامُ الدِّينِ، وَالْمُرَقِّي إلَى درجَاتِ الْمُتَّقِينَ. وَكَانَ عِلْمُ أُصُولِ الْفِقْهِ جَوَادَهُ الَّذِي لَا يُلْحَقُ، وَحَبْلَهُ الْمَتِينَ الَّذِي هُوَ أَقْوَى وَأَوْثَقُ، فَإِنَّهُ قَاعِدَةُ الشَّرْعِ، وَأَصْلٌ يُرَدُّ إلَيْهِ كُلُّ فَرْعٍ. وَقَدْ أَشَارَ الْمُصْطَفَى - صَلَّى اللَّهُ عَلَيْهِ وَسَلَّمَ - فِي جَوَامِعِ كَلِمِهِ إلَيْهِ، وَنَبَّهَ أَرْبَابُ اللِّسَانِ عَلَيْهِ، فَصَدَرَ فِي الصَّدْرِ الْأَوَّلِ مِنْهُ جُمْلَةٌ سَنِيَّةٌ، وَرُمُوزٌ خَفِيَّةٌ، حَتَّى جَاءَ الْإِمَامُ الْمُجْتَهِدُ مُحَمَّدُ بْنُ إدْرِيسَ الشَّافِعِيُّ - رَضِيَ اللَّهُ عَنْهُ - فَاهْتَدَى بِمَنَارِهِ، وَمَشَى إلَى ضَوْءِ نَارِهِ، فَشَمَّرَ عَنْ سَاعِدِ الِاجْتِهَادِ، وَجَاهَدَ فِي تَحْصِيلِ هَذَا الْغَرَضِ السَّنِيِّ حَقَّ الْجِهَادِ، وَأَظْهَرَ دَفَائِنَهُ وَكُنُوزَهُ وَأَوْضَحَ إشَارَاتِهِ وَرُمُوزَهُ، وَأَبْرَزَ مُخَبَّآتِهِ وَكَانَتْ مَسْتُورَةً، وَأَبْرَزَهَا فِي أَكْمَلِ مَعْنًى وَأَجْمَلِ صُورَةً، حَتَّى نَوَّرَ بِعِلْمِ الْأُصُولِ دُجَى الْآفَاقِ، وَأَعَادَ سُوقَهُ بَعْدَ الْكَسَادِ إلَى نَفَاقٍ. وَجَاءَ مَنْ بَعْدَهُ، فَبَيَّنُوا وَأَوْضَحُوا وَبَسَطُوا وَشَرَحُوا، حَتَّى جَاءَ الْقَاضِيَانِ: قَاضِي السُّنَّةِ أَبُو بَكْرِ بْنُ الطَّيِّبِ وَقَاضِي الْمُعْتَزِلَةِ عَبْدُ الْجَبَّارِ، فَوَسَّعَا الْعِبَارَاتِ، وَفَكَّا الْإِشَارَاتِ، وَبَيَّنَا الْإِجْمَالَ، وَرَفَعَا الْإِشْكَالَ. وَاقْتَفَى النَّاسُ بِآثَارِهِمْ، وَسَارُوا عَلَى لَاحِبِ نَارِهِمْ، فَحَرَّرُوا وَقَرَّرُوا، وَصَوَّرُوا، فَجَزَاهُمْ اللَّهُ خَيْرَ الْجَزَاءِ، وَمَنَحَهُمْ بِكُلِّ مَسَرَّةٍ وَهَنَاءٍ. ثُمَّ جَاءَتْ أُخْرَى مِنْ الْمُتَأَخِّرِينَ فَحَجَرُوا مَا كَانَ وَاسِعًا، وَأَبْعَدُوا مَا كَانَ شَاسِعًا، وَاقْتَصَرُوا عَلَى بَعْضِ رُءُوسِ الْمَسَائِلِ، وَكَثَّرُوا مِنْ الشُّبَهِ وَالدَّلَائِلِ، وَاقْتَصَرُوا عَلَى نَقْلِ مَذَاهِبِ الْمُخَالِفِينَ مِنْ الْفِرَقِ، مَنْ لِهَذَا الْفَنِّ أَصَّلَ، وَإِلَى حَقِيقَتِهِ وَصَّلَ، فَكَادَ يَعُودُ أَمْرُهُ إلَى الْأَوَّلِ، وَتَذْهَبُ عَنْهُ بَهْجَةُ الْمُعَوَّلِ، فَيَقُولُونَ: خِلَافًا لِأَبِي هَاشِمٍ، أَوْ وِفَاقًا لِلْجُبَّائِيِّ، وَتَكُونُ لِلشَّافِعِيِّ مَنْصُوصَةً، وَبَيْنَ أَصْحَابِهِ بِالِاعْتِنَاءِ مَخْصُوصَةً، وَفَاتَهُمْ مِنْ كَلَامِ السَّابِقِينَ عِبَارَاتٌ رَائِقَةٌ، وَتَقْرِيرَاتٌ فَائِقَةٌ، وَنُقُولٌ غَرِيبَةٌ، وَمَبَاحِثُ عَجِيبَةٌ.

2c. Al-Ghazālī (d. 505/1111) picked a brief fight with al-Dabūsī (d. 430/1039) for having too much caselaw (providing a rationale for Ibn Khaldūn's (d. 808/1406) subsequent taxonomy), and al-Samarqandī (d. 539/1144) insisted in his *Mīzān al-uṣūl* on distinguishing Māturīdīs from both Muʿtazilīs and Ashʿarīs. Al-Ghazālī's note[11] about the possibility of expanding *uṣūl al-fiqh* ad infinitum to obey an author's propensity and show off his encyclopedic comprehension may have played a role in a later note by al-Zarkashī (d. 794/1392), aiming to confront the question that *uṣūl al-fiqh* was no independent art; that it was a mix of borrowings from many arts; and that it was best seen as an amalgam or a medley of inquiries of the already established fields of the language sciences, theology, and practical laws.

11 Abū Ḥāmid al-Ghazālī, *al-Mustasfā min ʿilm al-uṣūl*, ed. Muḥammad ʿAbd al-Salām ʿAbd al-Shāfī (Beirut: Dār al-Kutub al-ʿIlmiyya, 1413/1993), 9, in https://shamela.ws/book/5459/7#p1

اعْلَمْ أَنَّهُ لَمَّا رَجَعَ حَدُّ أُصُولِ الْفِقْهِ إِلَى مَعْرِفَةِ أَدِلَّةِ الْأَحْكَامِ اشْتَمَلَ الْحَدُّ عَلَى ثَلَاثَةِ أَلْفَاظٍ: الْمَعْرِفَةُ وَالدَّلِيلُ وَالْحُكْمُ فَقَالُوا: إِذَا لَمْ يَكُنْ بُدٌّ مِنْ مَعْرِفَةِ الْحُكْمِ حَتَّى كَانَ مَعْرِفَتُهُ أَحَدَ الْأَقْطَابِ الْأَرْبَعَةِ فَلَا بُدَّ أَيْضًا مِنْ مَعْرِفَةِ الدَّلِيلِ وَمَعْرِفَةِ الْمَعْرِفَةِ، أَعْنِي الْعِلْمَ. ثُمَّ الْعِلْمُ الْمَطْلُوبُ لَا وُصُولَ إِلَيْهِ إِلَّا بِالنَّظَرِ، فَلَا بُدَّ مِنْ مَعْرِفَةِ النَّظَرِ فَشَرَعُوا فِي بَيَانِ حَدِّ الْعِلْمِ وَالدَّلِيلِ وَالنَّظَرِ وَلَمْ يَقْتَصِرُوا عَلَى تَعْرِيفِ صُوَرِ هَذِهِ الْأُمُورِ، وَلَكِنْ انْجَرَّ بِهِمْ إِلَى إِقَامَةِ الدَّلِيلِ عَلَى إِثْبَاتِ الْعِلْمِ عَلَى مُنْكِرِيهِ مِنْ السُّوفُسْطَائِيَّةِ وَإِقَامَةِ الدَّلِيلِ عَلَى النَّظَرِ عَلَى مُنْكِرِي النَّظَرِ وَإِلَى جُمْلَةٍ مِنْ أَقْسَامِ الْعُلُومِ وَأَقْسَامِ الْأَدِلَّةِ، وَذَلِكَ مُجَاوَزَةٌ لِحَدِّ هَذَا الْعِلْمِ وَخَلْطٌ لَهُ بِالْكَلَامِ، وَإِنَّمَا أَكْثَرَ فِيهِ الْمُتَكَلِّمُونَ مِنْ الْأُصُولِيِّينَ لِغَلَبَةِ الْكَلَامِ عَلَى طَبَائِعِهِمْ فَحَمَلَهُمْ حُبُّ صِنَاعَتِهِمْ عَلَى خَلْطِهِ بِهَذِهِ الصَّنْعَةِ، كَمَا حَمَلَ حُبُّ اللُّغَةِ وَالنَّحْوِ بَعْضَ الْأُصُولِيِّينَ عَلَى مَزْجِ جُمْلَةٍ مِنْ النَّحْوِ بِالْأُصُولِ فَذَكَرُوا فِيهِ مِنْ مَعَانِي الْحُرُوفِ وَمَعَانِي الْإِعْرَابِ جُمَلًا هِيَ مِنْ عِلْمِ النَّحْوِ خَاصَّةً، وَكَمَا حَمَلَ حُبُّ الْفِقْهِ جَمَاعَةً مِنْ فُقَهَاءِ مَا وَرَاءَ النَّهْرِ كَأَبِي زَيْدٍ - رَحِمَهُ اللَّهُ - وَأَتْبَاعِهِ عَلَى مَزْجِ مَسَائِلَ كَثِيرَةٍ مِنْ تَفَارِيعِ الْفِقْهِ بِالْأُصُولِ، فَإِنَّهُمْ وَإِنْ أَوْرَدُوهَا فِي مَعْرِضِ الْمِثَالِ وَكَيْفِيَّةِ إِجْرَاءِ الْأَصْلِ فِي الْفُرُوعِ فَقَدْ أَكْثَرُوا فِيهِ وَعُذْرُ الْمُتَكَلِّمِينَ فِي ذِكْرِ حَدِّ الْعِلْمِ وَالنَّظَرِ وَالدَّلِيلِ فِي أُصُولِ الْفِقْهِ أَظْهَرُ مِنْ عُذْرِهِمْ فِي إِقَامَةِ الْبُرْهَانِ عَلَى إِثْبَاتِهَا مَعَ الْمُنْكِرِينَ، لِأَنَّ الْحَدَّ يُثَبِّتُ فِي النَّفْسِ صُوَرَ هَذِهِ الْأُمُورِ وَلَا أَقَلَّ مِنْ تَصَوُّرِهَا إِذَا كَانَ الْكَلَامُ يَتَعَلَّقُ بِهَا، كَمَا أَنَّهُ لَا أَقَلَّ مِنْ تَصَوُّرِ الْإِجْمَاعِ وَالْقِيَاسِ لِمَنْ يَخُوضُ فِي الْفِقْهِ.

2d. The so-called Ḥanafī/*fuqahā'* way of doing *uṣūl al-fiqh* was in no way isolated from *kalām* debates. If Jaṣṣāṣ's (d. 370/980) *Fuṣūl* is one of their (extant) foundational texts, it is one important place where one finds a crucial distinction between 'disagreements' allowed and 'disagreements' un-allowed in religious and legal doctrines. The disagreement among theologies can be seen as disagreements among religions; hence Basra's judge 'Ubaydullāh b. al-Ḥasan al-'Anbarī (d. 168/784) was confused when he thought that reasonable disagreements would extend to pure religious and theological matters, such as how God is conceptualized.[12]

2e. I borrowed from 'language science' before developing a deep interest in theological debates. Beware: a genre's borders are not only arbitrary; they are accidents of the habits of composition and the arrangement of material; the 3rd/9th century was crucial in cementing the distinctiveness of *uṣūl al fiqh*, which is the outcome of excursus-on-top-of-excursus. Abū 'Ubayd al-Qāsim b. Sallām (d. 224/838) studied with both Abū Yūsuf (d. 184/799) and Muḥammad

12 Abū Bakr al-Jaṣṣāṣ, *al-Fuṣūl fī al-uṣūl* (Kuwait: Wizārat al-Awqāf al-Kuwaytiyya, 1414/1994), vol. 4, 375, in https://shamela.ws/book/676/1254#p1
قَالَ أَبُو بَكْرٍ: زَعَمَ عُبَيْدُ اللَّهِ الْعَنْبَرِيُّ: أَنَّ اخْتِلَافَ أَهْلِ الْمِلَّةِ فِي الْعَدْلِ وَالْجَبْرِ، وَفِي التَّوْحِيدِ وَالتَّشْبِيهِ، وَالْإِرْجَاءِ وَالْوَعِيدِ، وَفِي الْأَسْمَاءِ، وَالْأَحْكَامِ، وَسَائِرِ مَا اخْتَلَفُوا فِيهِ. كُلُّهُ حَقٌّ وَصَوَابٌ. إذْ كُلُّ قَائِلٍ مِنْهُمْ فَإِنَّمَا اعْتَقَدَ مَا صَارَ إلَيْهِ مِنْ جِهَةِ تَأْوِيلِ الْكِتَابِ وَالسُّنَّةِ فَجَمِيعُهُمْ مُصِيبُونَ، لِأَنَّ كُلَّ وَاحِدٍ مِنْهُمْ كُلِّفَ أَنْ يَقُولَ فِيهِ بِمَا غَلَبَ فِي ظَنِّهِ، وَاسْتَوْلَى عَلَيْهِ رَأْيُهُ، وَلَمْ يُكَلَّفْ فِيهِ عِلْمَ الْمُغَيَّبِ عِنْدَ اللَّهِ تَعَالَى، عَلَى حَسَبِ مَا قُلْنَا فِي حُكْمِ الْمُجْتَهِدِينَ فِي أَحْكَامِ حَوَادِثِ الْفُتْيَا. قَالَ أَبُو بَكْرٍ: وَهَذَا مَذْهَبٌ فَاسِدٌ ظَاهِرُ الِانْحِلَالِ. وَالْأَصْلُ فِيهِ: أَنَّ التَّكْلِيفَ مِنْ طَرِيقِ الِاجْتِهَادِ إنَّمَا يَصِحُّ عَلَى الْوَجْهِ الَّذِي يَصِحُّ وُرُودُ النَّصِّ بِهِ، (وَكُلُّ مَا) أَجَزْنَا فِيهِ الِاجْتِهَادَ، وَصَوَّبْنَا فِيهِ الْمُجْتَهِدِينَ عَلَى اخْتِلَافِهِمْ فِيهِ، فَإِنَّمَا أَجَزْنَاهُ عَلَى وَجْهٍ يَجُوزُ وُرُودُ النَّصِّ بِمِثْلِهِ مِنْ الْأَحْكَامِ الْمُخْتَلِفَةِ. فَأَمَّا الْعَدْلُ وَالْجَبْرُ، وَالتَّوْحِيدُ وَالتَّشْبِيهُ وَنَحْوُ ذَلِكَ، فَإِنَّهُ غَيْرُ جَائِزٍ وُرُودُ النَّصِّ فِيهِ بِجَمِيعِ أَقَاوِيلِ الْمُخْتَلِفِينَ. وَالَّذِي كُلِّفَ الْمُخْتَلِفُونَ فِيهِ اعْتِقَادَ كُلِّ شَيْءٍ مِنْهُ عَلَى مَا هُوَ عَلَيْهِ، وَيَسْتَحِيلُ وُرُودُ النَّصِّ بِتَكْلِيفِ بَعْضِ النَّاسِ الْقَوْلَ بِالْعَدْلِ، وَآخَرِينَ الْقَوْلَ بِالْجَبْرِ، وَبِتَكْلِيفِ بَعْضِهِمْ الْقَوْلَ بِالتَّوْحِيدِ، وَآخَرَ الْقَوْلَ بِالتَّشْبِيهِ.

b. al-Ḥasan al-Shaybānī (d. 189/805).[13] His student Ibn Qutayba (d. 276/889) disagreed with Ibn Sallām in his views of *gharīb al-ḥadīth* (how to approach some words in the Prophet's language or even reports of his activities that included uncommon words). In his *al-Ṣāhibī fī fiqh al-lugha,* Ibn Fāris (d. 395/1004) later found much to disagree with Ibn Qutayba. All these discussions are *at the closest margins* of *uṣūl al-fiqh.*

3. I was not dead at age 600: By the time I hit age 600, it was clear that my main obsession was a cluster of questions of legal epistemology. The core is still whether and what knowledge of God's laws are possible. When the great Abū Isḥāq al-Shīrāzī (d. 476/1083) started a summary of *uṣūl al-fiqh* (his *Lumaʿ*), this is how he started it: "Since the goal is to speak of *uṣūl al-fiqh,* I need to start with what 'knowledge' and 'verisimilitude' and surrounds are, because it is by knowing what these are that we get a sense of *fiqh* and its entanglements. We will thus proceed to explain what 'reasoning' and 'fruitful argument' (and related matters) are, because it is these that yield knowledge and verisimilitude. With this we are aided to explain what *fiqh* and *uṣūl al-fiqh* are—God willing."[14]

3a. Textualists (or those who profess to be textualists) such as al-Subkī (d. 756/1355), Ibn Taymiyya (d. 728/1328), and Ibn Ḥajar (d. 852/1448) could only complicate my life, not end it.

The hope that law can be derived from *ḥadīth* is old. ʿAbd al-Ghāfir al-Fārisī (d. 529/1135), author of *al-Siyāq,* a history of Nīsābūr, is quoted by al-Dīb (d. 1431/2010) to have said of al-Juwaynī (d. 478/1085) that he was the one without whom the people of *ḥadīth* would have been a mere story to tell (*lawlāhu*

---

13 Al-Shaybānī's work itself raises questions of how *uṣūl al-fiqh* came to be developed, partly, by Ibn Aban, as I argued in Fifty-Seven Tracts. In this and other instances of referencing early work, I risk appearing to acquiesce to the new fashion of self-referencing for no good reason and on occasions no reason at all, but the difficulty of appearing to take for granted arguments I do not work out here stared me at the other end. Ahmad Atif Ahmad, "Fifty-Seven Tracts: Shaybānī's (d. 189/805) *Aṣl/Mabsūṭ*, Twelve Centuries On," *American Journal of Islam and Society*, 38, nos. 1–2 (2021), 24–64, in: https://ajis.org/index.php/ajiss/article/view/2940/2056.

14 Abū Isḥāq al-Shīrāzī, *al-Lumaʿ fī uṣūl al-fiqh* (Beirut: Dār al-Kutub al-ʿIlmiyya, 1424/2003), 3, in: https://shamela.ws/book/8536/1
ولما كان الغرض بهذا الكتاب أصول الفقه وجب بيان العلم والظن وما يتصل بهما، لأن بهما يدرك جميع ما يتعلق بالفقه، ثم نذكر النظر والدليل وما يتصل بهما، لأن بذلك يحصل العلم والظن، ثم نبين الفقه وأصول الفقه إن شاء الله عز وجل.

la-ṣāra aṣḥābu l-ḥadīthi ḥadīthan)|.[15] Who are these *aṣḥāb al-ḥadīth*? Shāfiʿīs of course.

Al-Shāfiʿī (d. 204/820) is reported to have said: "Were a *ḥadīth* to be established as *ṣaḥīḥ* ('authentic, transmitted by solid means'), its content is the way I go [or is where my view is to be found]." Taqiyy al-Dīn al-Subkī (d. 756/1355) needed to write a short treatise to explain how Shāfiʿī jurists kept their loyalty to their teacher's doctrines as well as to this commitment. This commitment to each valid *ḥadīth* as the final arbiter of what Shāfiʿī law is, in a sense, goes against al-Shāfiʿī's work. If a Shāfiʿī jurist were to find a *ḥadīth* that contradicts al-Shāfiʿī's legal doctrines, that would either mean that al-Shāfiʿī did not do his homework, or that he knew about the *ḥadīth* but thought, against appearances, that it was not worthy of adopting. How would one know which is which?

It is, in fact, treacherous business, al-Subkī says. Employing a statement by Ibn al-Ṣalāḥ (d. 643/1245), he teaches us that

> Authorities that seem to work from this statement of al-Shāfiʿī (i.e., "were a *ḥadīth* to be established as *ṣaḥīḥ* ['authentic'], its content is where my view is to be found.") include Abū Yaʿqūb al-Buwayṭī (d. 231/846), Abū l-Qāsim al-Dārikī (d. 375/985), and this was affirmed by Abū al-Ḥasan Alkiyya al-Ṭabarī (d. 504/1110). This is not simple (*laysa hādhā bi-l-hayyin*)! A jurist has no license to work out legal doctrines from *ḥadīth* he simply considers 'authoritative'. Among al-Shāfiʿī's jurists who followed that path are scholars who derived their legal doctrines from prophetic reports al-Shāfiʿī knew and deliberately ignored, knowing that they were established according to *ḥadīth* standards (*ʿalā ʿilm minhu bi-ṣiḥḥatihi*), due to a consideration others failed to comprehend (*li-maniʿ in iṭṭalaʿ ʿalayhi wa khafiya ʿalā ghayrihi*), such as Abū al-Walīd Mūsā b. Abī al-Jārūd, a student and fellow companion of al-Shāfiʿī.

Well, what should be done then? If a lawyer or scholar of law who follows al-Shāfiʿī's legal logic trusts himself to identify the reasons for an apparent conflict between what al-Shāfiʿī said he would do and what he actually did, this Shāfiʿī lawyer could follow the results of his research. That is to say, he could follow the *ḥadīth* and abandon his own imam, al-Shāfiʿī. If the purported scholar is not at a level that allows him to make that independent decision, he can only work his rule from the *ḥadīth* if, and only if, another independent jurist relied

15 The following section draws on a lecture I wrote for a seminar held by the Institute for Epistemological Studies in Europe, held on April 3, 2021, available in full to the organizers of this conference.

on this *ḥadīth*. This is a very particular and narrow license by which a Shāfiʿī law scholar acts as a follower of another school of law, in order to capture the view of the imam who applied the *ḥadīth*, which al-Shāfiʿī ignored (and we are puzzled as to why he ignored it).

This is a strange conclusion, but it is defensible on two grounds. First, it was al-Shāfiʿī, to begin with, who invited his followers to follow the Prophet and ignore al-Shāfiʿī himself if he failed to do what he professed to do, which is to be a follower of the Prophet. Second, if an independent imam or authority in the law argued from this *ḥadīth* (against al-Shāfiʿī's view), this adds comfort to this follower of al-Shāfiʿī whose juristic techniques do not allow him to understand the matter independent of the views of other imams.

This is Ibn al-Ṣalāḥ's (d. 643/1245) recipe. Did he forget something? Did he say what would happen if the al-Shāfiʿī follower were to find no independent authority that argued from the *ḥadīth*? Ibn al-Ṣalāḥ failed, indeed, to address this case. This al-Subkī notes, following that by a speculation that the reason Ibn al-Ṣalāḥ did not address this possibility was that he may have thought its existence would indicate a case of juristic consensus to essentially ignore the *ḥadīth* in question.

Al-Subkī does not stop here. He says that disagreements about whether a given *ḥadīth* was to lead to a certain conclusion, while the *ḥadīth* was valid and while no independent authority in the law adopted it. Listen to this again: All independent authorities in the law may ignore what seems to be a valid *ḥadīth*, and this would not indicate that this *ḥadīth* is not inherently usable. What would you do then? Al-Subkī concludes with this statement: I would say follow the prophet! Imagine the prophet sitting or standing there asking you to follow him against these other views! Each of us, al-Subkī concludes, is required to only act and live based on his own understanding (*kull*^{u} *wāḥid*^{in} *mukallaf*^{un} *bi-ḥasab*^{i} *fahmih*^{i}). A warning from al-Nawawī (d. 676/1277): Do not forget that an assumption that al-Shāfiʿī neglected to adhere to a *ḥadīth* is not something one can rush to make. Al-Shāfiʿī does appear, al-Nawawī states, to not comply with the apparent content of certain *ḥadīth*s for very good, juristic reasons.

This form of textualism lives on. One may understand its power in certain areas more than in others, however. When a *ḥadīth* relates a matter of ritual, the work of the scholar of religious practice does begin and end with ascertaining what the correct ritual is. This is because, as Ḥanafī legal theorists would have it, there is no reasoning (*qiyās*) in matters of rituals, expiation, or quantifiable punishments (*ʿibādāt, kaffarāt, ḥudūd*). A commentator on the *ḥadīth*s that relate the prophet's worship (e.g., how he did his *tahajjud* or supererogatory night-prayers) would have more to say about the authorities that transmitted the prayer-reports and its exact wording in different versions. *Ḥadīth* 1120 in al-Bukhārī is a perfect example. When Ibn Ḥajar (d. 852/1448) addresses this report, that is what he does, and he does it very well. Reason raises its ugly head, however, once we get to whether this prophetic practice is generalizable to all believers (the issue of the prophet's frequent fasting exercises also comes up), and assuming these rituals are generalizable, whether one should keep the habit of the supererogatory night-prayers when sick and like questions. This section is mostly about getting to know the prophet and his habits, but Zaynab's (d. 8/630) rope (which she hung to cling to so as to avoid falling during long prayers; see *ḥadīth* 1150 in *Fatḥ al-Bārī*, vol. 3, p. 36) comes up to remind us of a general principle: everything in moderation, even worshipping God. Rules such as these come from history and become laws of a universal meaning, subject to interpretations by the scholars of the laws.

The Egyptian genius Aḥmad b. ʿAlī Ibn Ḥajar (d. 852/1448) had the unusual patience needed to aggregate scholarly views of relevance to the limited number of *ḥadīth*s collected by the Uzbeck-Persian Muḥammad b. Ismāʿīl al-Bukhārī (d. 256/870) as *al-Jāmiʿ al-ṣaḥīḥ* (*The Authentic Collection*). Whatever Ibn Ḥajar's intention, this was a major blow to legal reasoning. Ibn Ḥajar paved the way toward a sense that it is reasonable to see law as something made of history/*ḥadīth*. This he accomplished through ample documentation of views that relate to the limited 6,000+ *ḥadīth*s collected by al-Bukhārī, which span all topics, all *madhhab*s, all Islamic geographies.

Al-Shāshī (Niẓām al-Dīn, d. 344/956) was one of the early Ḥanafīs who would say things like "one first looks for the law in God's Book." What could he mean? He certainly means nothing like what the textualists from al-Nawawī and al-Subkī to Ibn Ḥajar meant. He knows the Qur'an will not give him much law and is prepared to move on. The example of how one uses a text to distinguish between two cases of mistaken presumption of permission to cohabit with a concubine, if the mistake of a father or the son, shows that the text places a limit on considering shared property a form of 'community property' given the rank presumed to the father. This does make the case that texts tend to be almost incapable of being standalone sources of the laws.[16]

16 al-Shāshī, *Uṣūl*, 300–1, in: https://shamela.ws/book/6302/124#p1
فصل الْوَاجِب على الْمُجْتَهد: طلب حكم الْحَادِثَة من كتاب الله تَعَالَى ثمَّ من سنة رَسُول الله صلى الله عَلَيْهِ وَسلم بِصَرِيح النَّص أَو دلَالَته على مَا مر ذكره فانه لَا سَبِيل الى الْعَمَل بِالرَّأْيِ مَعَ إِمْكَان الْعَمَل بِالنَّصِّ وَلِهَذَا إِذا إشتبهت عَلَيْهِ الْقبْلَة فَأخْبرهُ وَاحِد عَنْهَا لَا يجوز لَهُ التَّحَرِّي وَلَو وجد مَاء فَأخْبرهُ عدل أَنه نجس لَا يجوز لَهُ التوضي بِهِ بل يَتَيَمَّم وعَلى اعْتِبَار أَن الْعَمَل بِالرَّأْيِ

3b. Documentaries and memorializations such as those of al-Zarkashī are accounts of the diversity of the art, not evidence of its death.

Abū Zahra's (d. 1394/1974) harsh judgment of al-Zarkashī (d. 794/1392) and al-Suyūṭī (d. 911/1505) as collectors, not scholars, if anything, confirms that the growth, diversity, and subject-expansiveness of *uṣūl al-fiqh* did not indicate that it became an overcooked subject (*al-ʿulūm minhā mā lam yandaj wa-minhā mā nadija wa-lam yaḥtariq wa-minhā mā naḍija wa-ḥtaraqa*). There is also an urge to documenting, the writing of encyclopedias (which Europe will witness about three centuries later) that gripped scholars of theoretical and practical jurisprudence in Islam's 8th and 9th centuries and has yet to cease. This urge establishes interest in the cumulative knowledge of the past and a fear that it might be lost, rather than any sense of its end or stagnation.

3c. Expansions of the questions of method of reasoning into philosophy and physics, at the hands of al-Bayḍāwī (d. 685/1285), Abū al-Thanā l-Iṣfahānī (d. 749/1349) &co., are an acknowledgement of a trend, already known in al-Rāzī (d. 606/1210) and al-Āmidī (d. 631/1233), and continued in the works of ʿAḍud al-Dīn al-ʾĪjī (d. 756/1355) and his commentators.

Al-Rāzī's interests started to shape me, *uṣūl al-fiqh*, and move the art into more basic, meta-level questions, which will appear in his followers (al-Urmawī, Abū al-Thanā al-Iṣfahānī, etc.). These questions, to be sure, are not without precedent. And links among questions of language and the reasonability of the law, human freedom and understanding, divine duties, etc. can be found in contemporaries who did not necessarily shop for philosophy as much as al-Rāzī did, such as can be found in al-Khabbāzī's (d. 691/1292) *al-Mughnī*.

A reiteration in the 7th/13th century by the same al-Khabbāzī in his brief theology (*al-Hādī*, Fayzullah 1177, folio. 2) may have been needed that the sources of human judgment remain three in number (functioning senses, verifiable history, and reason). This was an assertion of the basic lesson of *uṣūl al-fiqh*: given a type of 'uncertainty principle' within the confines of which Muslim theologians and jurists have always worked—being embedded in human

---

دون الْعَمَل بِالنَّصِّ قُلْنَا أَن الشُّبْهَة بِالْمحل أقوى من الشُّبْهَة فِي الظَّن حَتَّى سقط اعْتِبَار ظن العَبْد فِي الْفَصْل الأول ومثاله فِي مَا إِذا وطئ جَارِيَة ابْنه لَا يحد وان قَالَ علمت أَنَّهَا عَليّ حرَام وَيثبت نسب الْوَلَد مِنْهُ لَان شُبْهَة الْملك لَا تثبت بِالنَّصِّ فِي مَال الإبن قَالَ عَلَيْهِ الصلوة وَالسَّلَام (أَنْت وَمَالك لأَبِيك) فَسقط اعتبار ظَنّه فِي الْحل وَالْحُرْمَة فِي ذَلِك وَلَو وطئ الابن جَارِيَة أَبِيه يعْتَبر ظَنّه فِي الْحل وَالْحُرْمَة حَتَّى لَو قَالَ ظَنَنْت أَنَّهَا عَليّ حرَام يجب الْحَد

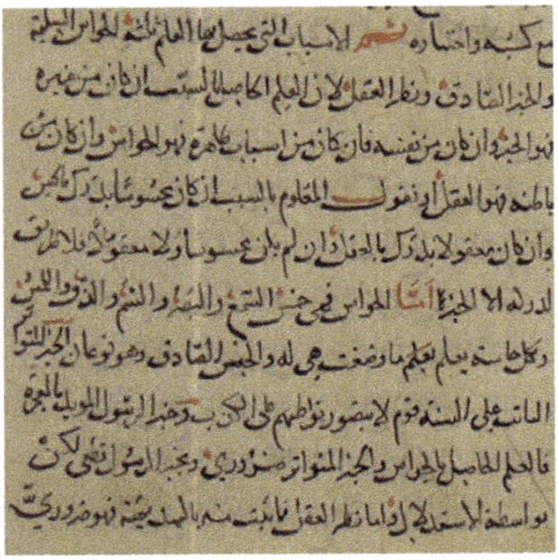

FIGURE 1.1
Illustration highlighting the role of historical reports (*mutawātir* and *āḥād*) and communal belief in legal epistemology
SOURCE: JALĀL AL-DĪN ʿUMAR B. MUḤAMMAD AL-KHABBĀZĪ, *AL-HĀDĪ FĪ UṢŪL AL-DĪN*, ARABIC MANUSCRIPTS IN THE NATIONAL LIBRARY, ISTANBUL, FEYZULLAH EFENDI LIBRARY, MANUSCRIPT NO. 1177, FOL. 2

reasoning, including its sense of what the divine revelation is or amounts to—we are only left with incomplete tests. The purport of revelation, even the one whose authenticity is not in question, is what occupies a Muslim legal philosopher.

This also shows that an offhand remark by Ibn Rushd in his *Kashf*[17] that to know whether a revelation is true or not, or to even understand it to begin with, we need to study its content. When doubt about the historicity of the revelation is overcome, we focus on the content. This leaves us with one more task when it comes to the Sunna of the prophet, a familiar distinction theoretical jurists have always accepted.

It bears reflection whether new elements entered old questions. Here one records Abū al-Thanā's note, in his commentary on Ibn al-Ḥājib's (d. 646/1249) *Mukhtaṣar*, addressing the importance of historical knowledge as foundational to the laws, a question that occupied al-Shāfiʿī in his arguments with Muʿtazilīs and other deniers of the value of both abundantly reported (*mutawātir aw mashhūr*) and sporadically reported (*khabar āḥād*) events, though the status of *tawātur* remained a central assertion in this debate, bringing a balance to a jurist's sense of what is functionally certain within the laws.[18] In the same vein goes any new texture to the question of the possibility that the whole

17 This quote is also included and discussed in detail in Chapter 4 in Ahmad, *The Fatigue*, 57.

18 Shams al-Dīn Abū al-Thanāʾ al-Iṣfahānī, *Sharḥ* Mukhtaṣar Ibn al-Ḥājib, ed. Muḥammad Muẓhir Baqā (Saudi Arabia: Dār al-Madanī, 1406/1986), vol. 1, 640, in https://shamela.ws/book/8156/624
أَكْثَرُ الْعُقَلَاءِ اتَّفَقُوا عَلَى أَنَّ الْمُتَوَاتِرَ يُفِيدُ الْعِلْمَ. وَخَالَفَتِ السَّمَنِيَّةُ - وَهُمْ قَوْمٌ مِنَ الْهِنْدِ - فِي
إِفَادَةِ الْمُتَوَاتِرِ الْعِلْمَ. وَهُوَ بُهْتٌ، أَيْ بَاطِلٌ. فَإِنَّ الْمُتَوَاتِرَ يُفِيدُ الْعِلْمَ، سَوَاءٌ كَانَ إِخْبَارًا عَنْ

Muslim community may hold beliefs that are utterly in contradiction with the foundations of the Muslim religion (*al-umma ʿalā l-kufr ijmāʿ*).[19] (I assume that everyone realizes that this question is far from theoretical at this point; despite counts that claim that Muslims, by heritage and conversion, may amount to something close to two billion people, the possibility of a swift and bold change of beliefs among them is far from unlikely.)

4. *Qawāʿid* and *furūq* are legitimate nephews and nieces of mine.

4a. Works on a variety of types of principles (e.g., al-Qarāfī, Ibn al-Laḥḥām, al-Timurtashī) are not foreign to *uṣūl al-fiqh*; they came with the territory since al-Karkhī (d. 340/950) and al-Dabūsī (d. 430/1039), Abū Muḥammad al-Juwaynī's (d. 438/1047) *al-Jamʿ wa-l-farq* (the notion then solidifies that jurisprudence is a science of understanding what is common and what distinguishes ostensibly similar cases الفقه جمع وفرق).[20]

In an earlier stage, al-Karābīsī (d. 570/1174) had decided to isolate questions of Ḥanafī law where *qiyās* and *istiḥsān* operated, which opened the door for

---

أُمُورٍ مَوْجُودَةٍ فِي زَمَانِنَا، أَوْ أُمُورٍ مَاضِيَةٍ؛ لِأَنَّا نَجِدُ بِالضَّرُورَةِ الْعِلْمَ بِالْبِلَادِ النَّائِيَةِ، كَمَكَّةَ وَبَغْدَادَ وَمِصْرَ، وَالْأُمَمِ الْمَاضِيَةِ، وَالْأَنْبِيَاءِ وَالْخُلَفَاءِ. وَمَا ذَلِكَ الْعِلْمُ إِلَّا مِنَ الْخَبَرِ الْمُتَوَاتِرِ.

19 Fakhr al-Dīn al-Rāzī, *al-Maḥṣūl fī ʿilm uṣūl al-fiqh*, ed. Ṭāhā Jābir Fayyāḍ al-ʿAlwānī (Beirut: Mu'assasat al-Risāla, 1418/1997), vol. 4, 206–8, in https://shamela.ws/book/2022/1299#p1
المسألة الرابعة لا يجوز اتفاق الأمة على الكفر وحكى عن قوم أنه يجوز أن ترتد الأمة لأنها إذا فعلت ذلك لم يكونوا مؤمنين ولا سبيلهم سبيل المؤمنين وإذا كذبت الرسول خرجت من أن تكون من أمته وجه القول الأول أن الله عز وجل أوجب اتباع سبيل المؤمنين واتباع سبيلهم مشروط بوجود سبيلهم وما لا يتم الواجب المطلق إلا به فهو واجب هذا إذا حملنا لفظ المؤمنين على الإيمان بالقلب أما إذا حملناه على التصديق باللسان ظهر أن الآية دالة على أن المصدقين في الظاهر لا يجوز إجماعهم على الخطأ ذلك يؤمننا من إجماعهم على الكفر.
المسألة الخامسة يجوز اشتراك الأمة في عدم العلم بما لم يكلفوا به لأن عدم العلم بذلك الشيء إذا كان صوابا لم يلزم من إجماعهم عليه محذور وللمخالف أن يقول لو اجمعوا على عدم العلم بذلك الشيء لكان عدم العلم به سبيلا للمؤمنين فكان يجب اتباعهم فيه حتى يحرم تحصيل العلم به.

20 Abū Muḥammad ʿAbd Allāh al-Juwaynī, *al-Jamʿ wa al-farq* (*Kitāb al-furūq*), ed. ʿAbd al-Raḥmān ibn Salāma ibn ʿAbd Allāh al-Muzaynī (Beirut: Dār al-Jīl li-l-Nashr wa al-Ṭibāʿa wa al-Tawzīʿ, 1424/2004), vol. 2, 3, in https://shamela.ws/book/14176/674.

an articulation of some principles of distinction.[21] Questions as to the 'level' of the principles (of *furūq* or distinctions) operating in similar works are best left alive, since what an author decides to include in his work is his own decision. Similarly, how a reader sees certain distinctions will tell us something about their prejudicial stance on the matter of which *uṣūl* is made. Take, for example, the distinction (article 328 in our edition)[22] between a vague, undetailed testimony of fornication by four men that can be streamlined but explained away (where both alleged violators and witnesses walk away; i.e., no punishment for either fornication or defamation is suffered) and a vague, undetailed testimony that show disagreeing witnesses.

Whether there is an order ranking of *kalām–uṣūl–fiqh* as al-Samarqandī stated in his *Mīzān al-uṣūl* (where *kalām* is foundational to *uṣūl* and the later to *fiqh*) may end up being a question of our use of the words and end in a verbal, rather than a substantive, disagreement. A view of *uṣūl* as foundational to *fiqh* and *fiqh* as foundational to *qawāʿid* (Alī l-Nadwī adopts in his *al-Qawāʿid al-fiqhiyya*) also goes in the same direction. In Tāj al-Dīn al-Subkī's (d. 771/1370) *Ashbah* one finds a short section on *kalām* principles that directly lead to

21 Jamāl al-Islām Asʿad al-Karābīsī, *al-Furūq*, ed. Muḥammad Ṭamūm (Kuwait: Wizārat al-Awqāf al-Kuwaytiyya, 1402/1982), vol. 1, 33, in https://shamela.ws/book/8182/1.

هَذِهِ الْمَسَائِلُ الْتَقَطْتُهَا مِنَ الْكُتُبِ لَيْسَ فِيهَا قِيَاسٌ وَاسْتِحْسَانٌ إِلَّا خِلَافٌ مَشْهُورٌ بَيْنَ أَصْحَابِنَا - رَضِيَ اللَّهُ عَنْهُمْ - وَسَمِعْتُ الْقَاضِيَ الْإِمَامَ أَبَا الْعُلَا صَاعِدَ بْنَ مُحَمَّدٍ - أَنَارَ اللَّهُ بُرْهَانَهُ وَثَقَّلَ بِالْخَيْرَاتِ مِيزَانَهُ - أَظْهَرَ الْفُرْقَانَ بَيْنَهَا فَاسْتَحْسَنْتُهَا، وَأَرَدْتُ أَنْ أُفْرِدَهَا لِيَسْهُلَ حِفْظُهَا...

22 Ibid., vol. 1, 287, in https://shamela.ws/book/8182/255

أَرْبَعَةٌ شَهِدُوا عَلَى رَجُلٍ بِالزِّنَا، فَسَأَلَهُمْ الْقَاضِي عَنْ مَاهِيَّتِهِ فَقَالُوا: لَا نَزِيدُكَ عَلَى هَذَا؛ لَمْ تُقْبَلْ شَهَادَتُهُمْ، وَلَا حَدَّ عَلَيْهِمْ وَكَذَلِكَ لَوْ وَصَفَهُ بَعْضُهُمْ دُونَ بَعْضٍ. وَلَوْ شَهِدَ ثَلَاثَةٌ بِالزِّنَا وَوَصَفُوهُ وَقَالَ الرَّابِعُ أَشْهَدُ أَنَّهُ زَانٍ، فَسُئِلَ عَنْ صِفَتِهِ فَلَمْ يَصِفْهُ وَجَبَ الْحَدُّ. وَالْفَرْقُ أَنَّهُ يَجُوزُ أَنَّهُمْ لَوْ فَسَّرُوا إِنَّمَا يُوجَبُ الْحَدُّ عَلَيْهِ، وَلَا يَجِبُ عَلَيْهِمْ وَيَجُوزُ بِخِلَافِ ذَلِكَ، فَالِاتِّفَاقُ عَلَى الشَّهَادَةِ بِالزِّنَا وُجِدَ، وَالْخِلَافُ مُمْكِنٌ فَلَا يَبْطُلُ الْمُتَعَيَّنُ بِهِ بِالْمُمْكِنِ. وَلَيْسَ كَذَلِكَ إِذَا شَهِدَ ثَلَاثَةٌ أَوَّلًا، وَوَصَفُوا وَلَمْ يَصِفْ الرَّابِعُ؛ لِأَنَّ الْخِلَافَ قَدْ ظَهَرَ، وَيَجُوزُ أَنْ يُفَسِّرَ الرَّابِعُ، وَيَجُوزُ أَنْ لَا يُفَسِّرَ فَلَا يَبْطُلُ الظَّاهِرُ بِخِلَافِ الْمُمْكِنِ كَالْعَدَالَةِ الظَّاهِرَةِ لَا تَبْطُلُ بِفِسْقٍ مُمْكِنٍ.

ramifications in *fiqh*[23] and another on *uṣūl* principles that have direct applications in *fiqh*.[24]

---

23 Tāj al-Dīn al-Subkī, *al-Ashbāh wa-l-naẓāʾir*, ed. ʿĀdil Aḥmad ʿAbd al-Mawjūd and ʿAlī Muḥammad Muʿawwaḍ (Beirut: Dār al-Kutub al-ʿIlmiyya, 1411/1991), vol. 2, 3–4, in https://shamela.ws/book/8634/474#p1

أصل: قال الشيخ أبو الحسن رضي الله عنه: السعادة والشقاوة لا يتبدلان. ومعنى ذلك أن الاعتبار في الأعمال بالخواتيم. فلا ينفع من مات على الكفر تقدم قناطير من إيمان ولا يضر من مات على إيمان قناطير من كفران.

وقال أبو حنيفة رضي الله عنه: يتبادلان، وتحرير المسألة في كتب الكلام وقد ذكرناها محررة في كتاب منع الموانع.

وألفاظ الشافعي رضي الله عنه وفروعه تدل على القول، بما قاله أبو الحسن...

أصل: العلم: "الاعتقاد الجازم المطابق لموجب" فما لا مطابقة فيه – من الاعتقادات الجازمة ليس بعلم، فلا علوم لأرباب الضلالات وذوي الجهالات. وهو بخلاف الظن؛ إذ لا تشترط المطابقة فيه[2]. فلو قال لآخر: أنت تعلم أن هذا الإنسان – الذي في يدي – حر حكم بعتقه. بخلاف ما لو قال: أنت تظن. نقله الرافعي عن الروياني عن بعض الأئمة.

ولو قيل [أطلقت] [3] امرأتك؟ فقال: اعلم أن الأمر على ما تقوله. ففي كونه إقرار بالطلاق وجهان. حكاهما الرافعي في فروع الطلاق من حكاية الروياني عن جده أصحهما: ليس بإقرار، لأنه أمره أن يعلم ولم يحصل هذا العلم. قلت: ويمكن تخريج هذا الفرع على أن الأمر لا يستلزم الإرادة، فإنه طلب منه أن يعلم هذا الأمر ولم يرده؛ إذ لو أراده لأنشأ إيقاع الطلاق.

ثم أقول: أمره أن يعلم ولم يحصل هذا العلم. فيه نظر، لأنه لما أمره أن الأمر على ما يقول، ومراده بما يقول قوله: الآن طلقت امرأتك، لأن يقول: "فعل مضارع حقيقة في الحال" وأيضًا فلا قول له إلا ذلك؛ وإنما يكون الأمر [على] ما قال الآن إذا كانت الآن طالقًا. فظاهر العبارة أن هذا إقرار.

وقد يقال: ليس قوله إلا الاستفهام عن أنه هل طلق امرأته؟ فكأنه قال: اعلم أن الأمر على الاستفهام الذي نقوله على أنه لو قال: له علي ألف – فيما أعلم [أو أشهد] [5] لزمه الألف، بخلاف ما لو قال: فيما أحسب أو أظن. ذكره أبو سعد الهروي وشريح الروياني في "أدب القضاء" قال أبو سعد: "لا انفصال للعلم عن الظن عند علماء الأصول". وذكر الرافعي المسألة الأولى في آخر الباب الأول من الإقرار.

24 Ibid., vol. 2, 77, in https://shamela.ws/book/8634/550#p1

[مسائل أصولية يتخرج عليها فروع فقهية]

أعلم أنا لنا في أصول الفقه مصنفات اشتملت على قدر كبير من الفروع المخرجة على الأصول، من نظره عرف أنا لم نسبق إليه، ومن أحاط بما في كتبنا الأربعة وهي: "شرح مختصر ابن

4b. This connection in no way cancels my (*uṣūl al-fiqh*'s) deeper connections with *kalām* or, for that matter, with the art of disputation and the foundational principles governing juristic disagreement and debating. Take Shams al-Dīn al-Iṣfahānī's (d. 688/1289) *Foundational Principles* (*al-Qawāʿid al-kulliyya*), which places together the basics of logic, the two *uṣūl*s, and disputation. This short manual reminds us of the connections sustained in these fields, as the summation and recounting of basic principles show the deep connections of the four fields. This al-Iṣfahānī was interested in cross-referencing the material within the metaphysics of law, theoretical jurisprudence, legal logic, and legal disputes. This was not only in regards to the tools of reasoning from *qiyās* and its structural components *talāzum*/*dawarān*/*naqd*/etc, but all the way down to basic tools such as *istiṣḥāb* and its overlap with *al-akhdh bi-l-aqall*, let alone the multilayered (i.e., theologico-legal) questions of *taklīf*/answerability and the nature of the reasoning soul (*al-nafs al-nāṭiqa*), which makes a formidable appearance in arguments for resurrection after death.[25]

4c. The rise of discussions on *maṣlaḥa* and *ʿurf* (and to an extent *maqāṣid*) culminating in early modern and modern discussions of these two also run deep in a shared territory that brings *uṣūl* and other theoretical legal sciences

---

الحاجب" و"شرح منهاج البيضاوي" و"المختصر المسمى" و"جمع الجوامع" والأجوبة على الأسئلة التي أوردت عليه المسمى "منع الموانع" من الفروع المخرجة على الأصول أحاط بسفر كامل "من ذلك" ونحن نذكر هنا مشيرًا بما ينبغي أن يدخل في الأشباه والنظائر ومما بعضه غير مذكور في كتبنا المشار إليها ونورده على ترتيب جمع الجوامع مستعينين بالله متوكلين مصلين على نبيه محمد صلى الله عليه وسلم.

أصل: التكليف إلزام ما فيه كلفة ومشقة ومن ثم يختص بالواجب والمحرم، وقيل: طلبه، فيشمل معهما المندوب والمكروه وهذان القولان لأئمتنا وسلكت الحنفية طريق سبيل آخر فقالوا: التكليف ينقسم إلى وجوب أداء وهو المطالبة بالفعل إيجادًا أو إعدامًا سواء خصصنا تلك المطالبة بالحكمين أم قلنا بدخول الأربعة، وإلى وجوب في الذمة سابق عليه، وعنوا بهذا القسم من الوجوب اشتغال الذمة بالواجب وإن لم يصلح صاحب الذمة للإلزام كالصبي إذا أتلف مال إنسان فإن ذمته تشتغل بالعوض ثم إنما يجب الأداء على الولي، وزعموا أن استدعاء التكليف الأول عقلاً وفهمًا للخطاب الأول، بخلاف الثاني.

قالوا: والأول يتلقى من الخطاب والثاني من الأسباب.

25 Shams al-Dīn al-Iṣfahānī, *al-Qawāʿid al-kulliyya fī jumlat min al-funūn al-ʿilmiyya*, ed. Manṣūr Kūshinkāgh and Bilāl Tāshqīn (Istanbul: Markaz al-Buḥūth al-Islāmiyya, 1438/2017), 55, 89, 264, 303, 306, 364.

together. In other words, while basic tools of legal reasoning, such as *qiyās* and *istiḥsān* (or arguing based on a direct, obvious rationale for a ruling or, alternatively, based on subtle considerations that also fulfill an imagined purpose for the laws) is old and both a) rooted in practical legal reasoning and b) undergirded by *kalām*, i.e., theological considerations, these became (at this stage and afterwards) *explicit means* of the derivation of legal norms, supported by *uṣūl al-fiqh* reasoning. This is an easy one. No need to dwell on it.

5. Just as my pre-colonial death was an optical illusion, so is an alleged death at the hand of colonialism: Ibn ʿĀbidīn's doctrine on social standards and law paves the way for ʿAbd al-Wahhāb Khallāf's (d. 1375/1956) expansion of *uṣūl al-fiqh* to rule on modern laws in the middle east. Al-Sanhūrī's sense of *ʿurf* as a mechanism of generating and interpreting law is of a piece with these developments. If you plan to question the faithfulness of these 20th-century figures to their tradition, be prepared to question the Ibn ʿĀbidīn who put the three conditions for *ʿurf* to affect laws. The same Ibn ʿĀbidīn struggled with extending the logic of *qiyās* by applying it to cases emanating from previous *qiyās* (he arbitrarily set the border at the year 400, out of helplessness if anything). All these quarrels are simply a function of the length of time that has elapsed since the tradition's founding. But Ibn ʿĀbidīn's lesson was that peace with one's tradition can only mean engagement with it, rather than stopping at condemning its detractors.

6. Not unlike my 1,200-year long past, my future will be tied with reason and its innovations, not texts.

No art or system is without its weak points or flops. Even some of my classics (e.g., al-Samʿānī's *Qawāṭiʿ*, vol. 2, 367–69, Beirut 1999, where the author argues that the Prophet's statement "Imams come from Quraysh" builds a point of preference for al-Shāfiʿī, the author's final affiliation, after decades of being a Ḥanafī) include silly factionalist bias. There is very, very little of that in my sources. The theoretical legal sciences end up reaching the modern line with much clarity and integrity, little known in most other branches of knowledge, whether it is grammar or philosophy, literature or history.

On the cusp of the modern, practicing Muslim jurists focused on questions of the practical side of the moral-religious law, but not all paid attention to the theoretical legal sciences (*uṣūl, qawāʿid, furūq*, etc.). Those among them who were forced to teach at modern law schools (e.g., Khallāf and Abū Zahra in Cairo) asked a question that will turn out to be more productive: What is *uṣūl al-fiqh* for? One needs to know something about its history to answer. Yet, one better start from the modern and move backward, which invites this conclusion: If applying the practical side of the moral-religious law in Islam sounds unfeasible, the theoretical legal sciences offer a different answer: It might work, and it would depend on the practitioners' comprehension of the art and its potential.

In the 1942 preface to his book on *uṣūl al-fiqh*, Abd al-Wahhāb Khallāf insisted that *uṣūl al-fiqh* was a method; hence the positive laws (*aḥkām*) derived in *fiqh* may be inappropriate for times other than those in which they were devised but the methods of reasoning in *uṣūl al-fiqh* would survive the changing times. Khallāf dedicates multiple notes in his work (the ones we used to hate when we first read the book, before studying modern law) pointing out some basic convergences between old and new principles of legal reasoning. These span the gamut from principles that 'knowledge of the law simply means its knowability or accessibility to those who seek to know them' (whether you read Ashʿarī/Muʿtazilī debates on the matter or jump to a practical conclusion stated in article 2 (the book's common edition has it as article 22) of the June 1883 'laws of procedure' for the national courts, *lā'iḥat tartīb al-maḥākim al-ahliyya*) to the nitpicking principles of inferences from texts, considering the general and the particular, the direct and the metaphorical, the straightforward and the ambiguous, and like matters.[26]

---

26 Khallāf, *Uṣūl*, 129 a. 141.

وثانيها: أن يكون معلوما أن التكليف به صادر ممن له سلطان التكليف، وممن يجب على المكلف اتباع أحكامه لأنه بهذا العلم تتجه إرادته إلى امتثاله، وهذا هو السبب في أن أول بحث في أي دليل شرعي هو حجيته على المكلفين، أي أن الأحكام التي يدل عليها أحكام واجب على المكلفين تنفيذها. وهو السبب أيضا في أن كل قانون وضعي يتوجب بالديباجة الخاصة التي تدل على أن الحاكم أصدر القانون بناء على عرض مجلس الوزراء وموافقة البرلمان، ليعلم المكلفون أن القانون صادر ممن لهم سلطان التشريع، وممن يجب عليهم امتثال تكاليفهم؛ فيتجهوا للتنفيذ. ويلاحظ أن المراد بعلم المكلف بما كلف به إمكان علمه به، لا علمه به فعلا، فمتى بلغ الإنسان عاقلا قادرا على أن يعرف الأحكام الشرعية بنفسه أو بسؤال أهل الذكر عنها، اعتبر عالما بما كلف به، ونفذت عليه الأحكام وألزم بآثارها ولا يقبل منه الاعتذار بجهلها. ولهذا قال الفقهاء: لا يقبل في دار الإسلام عذر الجهل بالحكم الشرعي، لأنه لو شرط لصحة التكلف علم المكلف فعلا بما كلف به ما استقام التكليف، واتسع المجال للاعتذار بجهل الأحكام. وعلى هذا التقنين الوضعي، فالناس يعتبرون عالمين بالقانون بتيسير إمكان علمهم به، وذلك بنشره بالطريق القانوني بعد إصداره. ولا اعتبار لأن كل فرد من المكلفين علم به فعلا أو لا، ولذا جاء في مادة (22) من لائحة ترتيب المحاكم الأهلية: لا يقبل من أحد أن يدعي بجهله القانون. وكذلك المراد بعلم المكلف بأن تكليفه بما كلف به صادر ممن يجب

Taking al-Sanhūrī's employment of *ʿurf* as a companion to living sharia to be legitimate, one may go even farther and call for an employment of the notion of individual consent as a foundation to the future life of Islamic norms. An individual's consent to follow a religion, to follow a law, to follow a moral system, and to enter into contracts—all serve as sources of law. An individual could always bind herself or himself (*nadhr*, *yamīn*), and the result is a duty. An aggregation and a confluence of these may be theorized as an instance of collective consent (or *ʿurf*). This will help practitioners draw a realistic sense of where a living sharia may be found and developed.

3 After the Narrative

Uṣūl al-fiqh goes forward, then, having taught one of the most basic lessons in the history of human reasoning. That is, that doubt need not prevent action. If boxed in within the confines of an impoverished Islamic studies, *uṣūl al-fiqh* is vulnerable to imported flat historicism and critique (the news that a post-critique, post-historicist age has dawned may not have arrived yet to some). What eliminates *uṣūl al-fiqh* is to be subjected to extraneous assumptions, assuming that all possibilities of what *uṣūl al-fiqh* meant may be true, except of course those that arise from within *uṣūl al-fiqh*'s own self-understanding.

Uṣūl al-fiqh started with simple primary components, questions about language, history, and legal and theological logic, which yielded secondary tools that continue to be needed today. The resulting set of method-statements included reflections on answerability (*ahliyya*) to legal and moral obligations, which summarizes important elements of jurisprudence. The exceptions, one learns, to the normal state of answerability include traveling (which allows the traveler to perform their daily prayers in aggregated and truncated form) just as they include puerperium (which removes the obligation altogether).[27]

عليه امتثال أحكامه، وإمكان علمه بهذا لا علمه به فعلا. فكل حكم شرعي يمكن للمكلف أن يعرف دليله، وأن يعرف أن دليله حجة شرعية، على المكلفين إتباع ما يستمد منه، سواء أكان هذا بنفسه أم بواسطة سؤال أهل الذكر عنه.

27 Muḥammad Ibn Amīr al-Ḥājj, *al-Taqrīr wa-l-taḥbīr* (Beirut: Dār al-Kutub al-ʿIlmiyya, 1403/1983), vol. 2, 172, in https://shamela.ws/book/21605/510

(وَهَذَا فَصْلٌ آخَرُ اخْتَصُّوا) أَيْ الْحَنَفِيَّةُ (بِهِ فِي بَيَانِ أَحْكَامِ عَوَارِضِ الْأَهْلِيَّةِ أَيْ أُمُورٌ لَيْسَتْ ذَاتِيَّةً لَهَا طَرَأَتْ أَوَّلًا) أَيْ خِصَالٌ أَوْ آفَاتٌ لَهَا تَأْثِيرٌ فِي الْأَحْكَامِ بِالتَّغْيِيرِ أَوْ الْإِعْدَامِ سُمِّيَتْ بِهَا

Discussions of statutory interpretation in modern legislation are enriched by visits to *uṣūl al-fiqh* manuals' sections on the interpretation of authoritative language. Modern debates in analytic philosophy, the relationship between word and world, and the limits of what can be said are enlightened and expanded when juxtaposed to similar debates of the past.

This would be a conclusion, or an afterword, unless it is understood more deeply. On a deep reading, this was, in fact, a prologue to a better relationship with an open world that does not need to be limited by art's inherited instances. This, then, is an introduction to the study of *uṣūl al-fiqh*, unburdened by the deep misunderstanding of its history and value as a contribution to the human mind.

If the performer of this narrative, the author of this paper, were a student of any other field within the many intellectual contributions of ancient, medieval, and modern minds, I would have (make that might have) been vulnerable to the despair vented by post-colonial postures in scholarship, which leaves a contemporary scholar of this type with only one of two options: either

---

لِمَنْعِهَا الْأَحْكَامَ الْمُتَعَلِّقَةَ بِأَهْلِيَّةِ الْوُجُوبِ أَوْ الْأَدَاءِ عَنْ الثُّبُوتِ إِمَّا؛ لِأَنَّهَا مُزِيلَةٌ لِأَهْلِيَّةِ الْوُجُوبِ كَالْمَوْتِ أَوْ لِأَهْلِيَّةِ الْأَدَاءِ كَالنَّوْمِ وَالْإِغْمَاءِ أَوْ مُغَيِّرَةٌ لِبَعْضِ الْأَحْكَامِ مَعَ بَقَاءِ أَصْلِ الْأَهْلِيَّةِ لِلْوُجُوبِ وَالْأَدَاءِ كَالسَّفَرِ وَلِذَا لَمْ يَذْكُرْ الْكُهُولَةَ وَالشَّيْخُوخَةَ وَنَحْوَهُمَا فِي جُمْلَتِهَا؛ لِأَنَّهَا لَيْسَتْ بِإِحْدَى هَذِهِ الْأَقْسَامِ (فَدَخَلَ الصِّغَرُ) لِعَدَمِ اشْتِرَاطِ الطُّرُوءِ وَالْحُدُوثِ بَعْدَ الْعَدَمِ فِيهَا أَوْ كَوْنُهُ لَيْسَ مِنْ الْأُمُورِ الذَّاتِيَّةِ لِلْإِنْسَانِ وَمِنْ ثَمَّةَ كَانَ الْكَبِيرُ إِنْسَانًا كَالصَّغِيرِ وَإِنْ كَانَ ثَابِتًا فِي أَصْلِ الْخِلْقَةِ لَا يَخْلُو عَنْهُ إِلَّا نَادِرًا كَآدَمَ وَحَوَّاءَ - عَلَيْهِمَا السَّلَامُ - وَمُلَخَّصُهَا أَحْوَالٌ مُنَافِيَةٌ لِأَهْلِيَّتِهِ غَيْرُ لَازِمَةٍ لَهُ (وَهِيَ) أَيْ الْعَوَارِضُ (نَوْعَانِ: سَمَاوِيَّةٌ أَيْ لَيْسَ لِلْعَبْدِ فِيهَا اخْتِيَارٌ) فَنُسِبَتْ إِلَى السَّمَاءِ بِمَعْنَى أَنَّهَا نَازِلَةٌ مِنْهَا بِغَيْرِ اخْتِيَارِهِ وَإِرَادَتِهِ، وَهِيَ أَحَدَ عَشَرَ (الصِّغَرُ وَالْجُنُونُ وَالْعَتَهُ وَالنِّسْيَانُ وَالنَّوْمُ وَالْإِغْمَاءُ وَالرِّقُّ وَالْمَرَضُ وَالْحَيْضُ وَالنِّفَاسُ وَالْمَوْتُ) قَالُوا وَإِنَّمَا لَمْ يَذْكُرْ الْحَمْلَ وَالْإِرْضَاعَ وَالشَّيْخُوخَةَ الْقَرِيبَةَ إِلَى الْفَنَاءِ وَإِنْ تَغَيَّرَ بِهَا بَعْضُ الْأَحْكَامِ لِدُخُولِهَا فِي الْمَرَضِ وَأَوْرَدَ الْإِغْمَاءَ وَالْجُنُونَ مِنْ الْمَرَضِ وَقَدْ أُفْرِدَا بِالذِّكْرِ وَأُجِيبَ لِاخْتِصَاصِهِمَا بِأَحْكَامٍ كَثِيرَةٍ يَحْتَاجُ إِلَى بَيَانِهَا بِخِلَافِ تِلْكَ (وَمُكْتَسَبَةٌ أَيْ كَسَبَهَا الْعَبْدُ أَوْ تَرَكَ إِزَالَتَهَا)، وَهِيَ سَبْعَةٌ سِتَّةٌ مِنْهُ، وَهِيَ الْجَهْلُ وَالسَّفَهُ وَالسُّكْرُ وَالْهَزْلُ وَالْخَطَأُ وَالسَّفَرُ وَوَاحِدٌ مِنْ غَيْرِهِ وَهُوَ الْإِكْرَاهُ.

celebrating or complaining about modern conditions. *Uṣūl al-fiqh*, read as the performer suggests, does lead in a different direction, one of confidence that a student of this field can engage comfortably with modern (including materialist) philosophy, the history of laws and of science, and whatever the next stage in reasoning and scholarship may be. One may even grant that ours is a world that stipulates that there is no rhyme or reason in the world but one must then recoil and assert that *uṣūl al-fiqh* remains a resource for both rhyme and reason. (*Uṣūl al-fiqh* is a product of the world; something to ponder.) *Uṣūl al-fiqh* brings together a feast of tools, from reflections on language and history to debates on the nature of certainty and argument. These tools do not vie for supremacy; they cooperate. In modern philosophy things are different. A linguistic turn in modern philosophy, to give one final example, was a shift in focus, almost a trivialization of one pursuit (metaphysics, including the metaphysics of mathematics) for the benefit of ordinary language analysis. In *uṣūl al-fiqh*, these questions coexist, rather than compete.

Bibliography

Ahmad, Ahmad Atif, "Fifty-Seven Tracts: Shaybānī's (d. 189/805) *Aṣl/Mabsūṭ*, Twelve Centuries On," *American Journal of Islam and Society*, 38, nos. 1–2 (2021), 24–64, online at https://ajis.org/index.php/ajiss/article/view/2940/2056.

Ahmad, Ahmad Atif, *The Fatigue of the Sharia* (London: Palgrave Macmillan, 1433/2012).

al-Baṣrī, Abū al-Ḥusayn, *al-Muʿtamad fī uṣūl al-fiqh*, ed. Khalīl al-Mays (Beirut: Dār al-Kutub al-ʿIlmiyya, 1403/1983).

al-Faqīh, Muḥammad Taqiyy, *Qawāʿid al-faqīh* (Beirut: Dār al-Aḍwāʾ, 1407/1987).

al-Ghazālī, Abū Ḥāmid, *al-Mustasfā min ʿilm al-uṣūl*, ed. Muḥammad ʿAbd al-Salām ʿAbd al-Shāfī (Beirut: Dār al-Kutub al-ʿIlmiyya 1413/1993).

al-Ḥājj, Muḥammad Ibn Amīr, *al-taqrīr wa-l-taḥbīr* (Beirut: Dār al-Kutub al-ʿIlmiyya 1403/1983).

Ibn Khaldūn, ʿAbd al-Raḥmān, *Muqaddima*, ed. A. Khalil Shihada (Beirut: Dār Al-Fikr 1401/1981).

al-Iṣfahānī, Shams al-Dīn Abū al-Thanāʾ, *Sharḥ* Mukhtaṣar Ibn al-Ḥājib, ed. Muḥammad Muẓhir Baqā (Saudi Arabia: Dār al-Madanī, 1406/1986).

al-Iṣfahānī, Shams al-Dīn Abū al-Thanāʾ, *al-Qawāʿid al-kulliyya fī jumlat min al-funūn al-ʿilmiyya*, ed. Manṣūr Kūshinkāgh and Bilāl Tāshqīn (Istanbul: Markaz al-Buḥūth al-Islāmiyya, 1438/2017).

al-Jaṣṣāṣ, Abū Bakr, *al-Fuṣūl fī al-uṣūl* (Kuwait: Wizārat al-Awqāf al-Kuwaytiyya, 1414/1994).

al-Juwaynī, Abū al-Maʿālī ʿAbd al-Malik, *Nihāyat al-maṭlab fī dirāyat al-madhhab*, ed. ʿAbd al-ʿAẓīm al-Dīb (Beirut: Dār al-Minhāj 1428/2007).

al-Juwaynī, Abū Muḥammad ʿAbd Allāh, *al-Jamʿ wa-l-farq* (*Kitāb al-furūq*), ed. ʿAbd al-Raḥmān ibn Salāma ibn ʿAbd Allāh al-Muzaynī (Beirut: Dār al-Jīl li-l-Nashr wa-l-Ṭibāʿa wa-l-Tawzīʿ, 1424/2004).

al-Karābīsī, Jamāl al-Islām, Asʿad, *al-Furūq*, ed. Muḥammad Ṭamūm (Kuwait: Wizārat al-Awqāf al-Kuwaytiyya, 1402/1982).

Khallāf, ʿAbd al-Wahhāb, *Uṣūl al-fiqh*, ed. Muḥammad Abū Zahra (Cairo: al-Daʿwa/ al-Azhar, 1375/1956).

al-Rāzī, Fakhr al-Dīn, *al-Maḥṣūl fī ʿilm uṣūl al-fiqh*, ed. Ṭāhā Jābir Fayyāḍ al-ʿAlwānī (Beirut: Muʾassasat al-Risāla, 1418/1997).

al-Shāshī, Abū ʿAlī, *Uṣūl al-Shāshī*, ed. Muḥammad Fayḍ al-Ḥasan Gangohi (Beirut: Dār al-Kitāb al-ʿArabī, 1402/1982).

al-Shīrāzī, Abū Isḥāq, *al-Lumaʿ fī uṣūl al-fiqh* (Beirut: Dār al-Kutub al-ʿIlmiyya, 1424/2003).

al-Subkī, Tāj al-Dīn, *al-Ashbāh wa-l-Naẓāʾir*, ed. ʿĀdil Aḥmad ʿAbd al-Mawjūd and ʿAlī Muḥammad Muʿawwaḍ (Beirut: Dār al-Kutub al-ʿIlmiyya, 1411/1991).

al-Zarkashī, Badr al-Dīn, *al-Baḥr al-muḥīṭ fī uṣūl al-fiqh* (Cairo: Dār al-Kutubī 1414/1994).

CHAPTER 2

Theologies of Divine Speech and the Human Exigencies of Law: A Conundrum for Classical and Contemporary Islamic Legal Hermeneutics

David R. Vishanoff

1 Introduction

The ideal of a comprehensive and coherent theological vision sometimes comes into productive tension with the practical exigencies of legal interpretation. This tug of war between theology and law has shaped and reshaped the discipline of Islamic legal theory (*uṣūl al-fiqh*), and more particularly the analysis of language that I will call legal hermeneutics, from its formative period until today. This essay presents examples from both classical and modern Islamic theology and legal theory, and concludes that constructing a theologically consistent and practically adequate legal hermeneutic is possible but may come at a price that few are willing to pay.

How a Muslim theologian imagines God's speech has (or logically ought to have) crucial implications for how he or she understands and interprets the Qur'an's legal and ethical injunctions. The practical human concerns of law, however, often lead interpreters to prefer more flexible and powerful hermeneutical theories that seem less than perfectly consistent with their theological premises. This tension between the theological coherence of one's legal hermeneutic and its practical adequacy for the exigencies of lived human experience has been apparent throughout the history of Islamic legal theory, and continues to present a daunting and thrilling intellectual challenge today.

Some contemporary thinkers would question whether theology and metaphysics really need to govern epistemology and hermeneutics, and would suggest instead that practical concerns like social justice, and lived experiences like economic deprivation, have existential priority over theological reflections on the nature of God and his attributes, and therefore should be given priority, in the search for God's will, over purely theoretical concerns like philosophical coherence.[1] Others would argue that legal theory should indeed follow

1 Farid Esack, for example, strives for theoretical coherence while giving priority to lived experience and the pursuit of justice. Farid Esack, *Qur'an, Liberation & Pluralism: An Islamic Perspective of Interreligious Solidarity against Oppression* (Oxford: Oneworld, 1997).

 | DOI:10.1163/9789004746886_004

from theological premises, but that a theologically principled legal theory need not impede the interpretive practice of jurists because legal theory is not what actually constrains the law; the law's adaptability depends not so much on hermeneutics and legal theory as on the maxims and institutional mechanisms by which the law is handed down and applied.[2] Nevertheless, many Muslim intellectuals do aspire to a full theoretical convergence between the theology of revelation, legal theory, and legal interpretation; and for them it may be instructive to explore some historical and modern examples of the relationship between theories of divine speech and theories of legal interpretation. I will not address the question of how law actually does or should adapt to changing historical circumstances, or the question of whether those adaptations are or should be governed by hermeneutical theories. Instead I will address myself mainly to those readers who do believe that some adaptations of Islamic law are required by the circumstances of modern life, and that these should be justified by a principled legal hermeneutic which, in turn, should follow from a coherent conception of divine revelation.

I will begin with three examples from the formative period of Islamic legal theory, starting with the Muʿtazilī Qāḍī ʿAbd al-Jabbār (d. 415/1025), who argued that the doctrines of divine justice and God's created speech entailed a minimalist and relatively rigid approach to interpretation, at least in law. In contrast, the Ashʿarī Mālikī Qāḍī Abū Bakr al-Bāqillānī (d. 403/1013) argued for greater ambiguity and flexibility on the basis of his theory of God's eternal speech. I will argue that while these hermeneutical approaches were principled and theologically coherent, both of them complicated, in principle, the task of finding in the language of revelation a secure grounding for the details of law as it existed and evolved in legal thought and practice. In the 5th/11th century, therefore, a more pragmatic, law-oriented, and theologically less principled hermeneutical paradigm, which I will illustrate by reference to the Ḥanbalī Abū Yaʿlā Ibn al-Farrāʾ (d. 458/1066), came to dominate legal hermeneutics across all the Sunni schools of law. Despite centuries of sophisticated further developments in *uṣūl al-fiqh*, that basic set of powerful and flexible interpretive rules for the analysis of language endures largely unchanged in mainstream Sunni works of legal theory today. I will argue that this law-oriented hermeneutic makes it easier for interpreters to claim that their interpretations, whether conservative or novel, constitute the most obvious and authentic readings of scripture.

2 See for example Wael B. Hallaq, *Authority, Continuity, and Change in Islamic Law* (Cambridge: Cambridge University Press, 2001), xi–xii, 166, 174, 188–89, 208, 233–35, 239–41; Samy A. Ayoub, *Law, Empire, and the Sultan: Ottoman Imperial Authority and Late Ḥanafī Jurisprudence* (Oxford: Oxford University Press, 2020), 109–13, 140–42, 150–56.

However, since novel interpretations face higher barriers to acceptance, many modern Muslims who desire to reform the law have not been satisfied with this powerful and flexible hermeneutic, but have instead revisited some of the basic theological premises of classical Sunni legal theory, including its views on the language, meaning, historicity, and theocentrism of revelation, in order to justify novel legal and ethical interpretations. I will offer two principal examples. Aksin Wijaya (b. 1974), a creative and prolific thinker little known outside of Indonesia, has drawn upon classical Ashʿarī views about God's speech (as well as a wide range of medieval and modern Muslim and non-Muslim thinkers) to support a flexible, contextually sensitive, and anthropocentric approach to interpretation that allows him to support his modern liberal reading of Islamic law; but his theology of revelation appears to be constructed in a somewhat ad hoc manner to suit his hermeneutical goals rather than forming a principled starting point for his hermeneutical reflection, as was the case with the early theologians. A more philosophically consistent and thoroughly anthropocentric reimagining of the doctrine of revelation and the theory of law was proposed by Hasan Hanafi (1935–2021), who transposed the entirety of classical legal theory into the vocabulary of European phenomenology; but his radical reconceptualization of revelation encountered stiff resistance, and his revolutionary hermeneutic did not find acceptance as a practical method for legal interpretation. All these historical and modern examples illustrate a troubling but productive conundrum still faced by legal hermeneutics today: how can interpretation be grounded simultaneously in a coherent theology of divine speech and the messy human exigencies of law?

2 The Baṣra Branch of the Muʿtazila

In a groundbreaking book titled *Divine Discourse: Philosophical Reflections on the Claim that God Speaks*, the Christian philosopher Nicholas Wolterstorff developed a theory of what it would mean for God to speak, and then worked out the hermeneutical implications of that model of divine speech. Building on the speech act theory of J. L. Austin and others, he proposed that God performs various illocutionary actions such as promising and commanding by means of the locutionary actions—the verbal utterances or writings—of various human beings whom God deputizes to speak on God's behalf, or whose speech God appropriates. By means of such human utterances, which include canonized scriptural texts, God takes on the same kinds of moral relationships and obligations as human speakers who engage in acts of asserting, promising, or commanding—though the kind of illocutionary act God performs by way of a particular scriptural text is not always the same illocutionary act its human author performed in writing it. Starting from this model of divine speech, Wolterstorff then proposed the outlines of a hermeneutic in which God should not be taken as asserting everything that the human authors of scripture are found to assert. In this hermeneutic, it is the interpreter's goal to discern just what kinds of illocutionary stance God intends to take toward each of the assertions, commands, entreaties, promises, threats, and other speech acts performed by the human authors of scripture.[3]

To focus in this way on the nature of divine speech (as distinct from revelation) was surprisingly novel for a Western philosopher, but this kind of exercise has a long history in Islamic theology, where God's attribute of speech has been a major focus of debate, and in legal theory, where the hermeneutical implications of various theories of divine speech have been worked out in much more detail than in Wolterstorff's proposal. The Muʿtazila, for example, famously held that God's speech is an action, and thus part of the temporal created order. ʿAbd al-Jabbār, the best-known representative of the Baṣran branch of that school, identified the act of speaking with the sentences, words, letters, and sounds that are produced by a speaker—not, as Wolterstorff did, with illocutionary actions like promising.[4] And of course he considered the original production of the letters and sounds of the Qurʾan to be an act of God, not the act of any human author. But by declaring the Qurʾan to be an act of God, he subjected it to the requirements of God's attribute of justice, so that like Wolterstorff he considered that God's speech takes place within a web of moral obligations between speaker and hearer—though we will see that in his legal theory he downplayed the idea that by speaking God performatively takes upon himself any new obligations. Like Wolterstorff, ʿAbd al-Jabbār considered his theory of divine speech to have important hermeneutical implications, which he worked out with remarkable consistency in his legal theory.

His view that God's speech is an act created in time and space did not lead ʿAbd al-Jabbār to treat the Qurʾan as a historical document to be interpreted contextually[5]—though there is one intriguing passage in his monumental work *al-Mughnī fī abwāb al-tawḥīd wa-l-ʿadl* that points tantalizingly in this

3 Nicholas Wolterstorff, *Divine Discourse: Philosophical Reflections on the Claim that God Speaks* (Cambridge: Cambridge University Press, 1995).

4 ʿAbd al-Jabbār ibn Aḥmad, *Sharḥ al-Uṣūl al-khamsa*, with the commentary of Aḥmad ibn al-Ḥusayn ibn Abī Hāshim [Mānkdīm], ed. ʿAbd al-Karīm ʿUthmān (Cairo: Maktabat Wahba, 1965), 528–29; Omar Farahat, *The Foundation of Norms in Islamic Jurisprudence and Theology* (Cambridge: Cambridge University Press, 2019), 99–106.

5 See Abū al-Ḥasan ʿAbd al-Jabbār al-Asadābādī, *al-Mughnī fī abwāb al-tawḥīd wa-l-ʿadl*, ed. Ṭāhā Ḥusayn, et al. (Cairo: Wizārat al-Thaqāfa wa-l-Irshād al-Qawmī, 1960–1969), 17:127.

direction.[6] Neither did it diminish the authority or importance of revelation in Muʿtazilī epistemology, as both opponents and admirers of the Muʿtazila have often too hastily assumed.[7] On the contrary, ʿAbd al-Jabbār argued that it was his Ashʿarī opponents who were undermining the value of revelation by making God's speech one of his eternal attributes, thus putting it beyond the reach of human knowledge and leaving no way to prove its truth and reliability as a source of knowledge.[8] To his mind, to know for sure that God's speech was trustworthy, one had to know that God cannot speak deceitfully or even ambiguously, and we only know that because we know, rationally, that God must be just. But justice is a characteristic of a person's actions, not of a person's attributes. If God's speech were an eternal attribute, it would be a category mistake to say that it was subject to God's justice and therefore must be good and true. That is why, in his theological works, ʿAbd al-Jabbār discussed God's speech not in the section on *tawḥīd* (God's oneness) but in the section on *ʿadl* (justice).[9] God's speech is only good, beneficial, and trustworthy if it is an action; and an action is something produced in time. That is why God's speech has to be part of the temporal created realm.

The idea that God's speech is one of his good, just, and beneficial actions had two important consequences for ʿAbd al-Jabbār's legal hermeneutic. First, ʿAbd al-Jabbār reasoned that to be good God's speech must have a purpose. That purpose can only be to benefit human beings, since God himself needs nothing and does not stand to gain anything from his own actions.[10] The only benefit that God's speech can possibly impart to humans, ʿAbd al-Jabbār reasoned, is to inform them of God's law. The Qur'an cannot really inform people

---

6 See ʿAbd al-Jabbār, *al-Mughnī*, 7:78–80, where ʿAbd al-Jabbār argues that God would have been speaking falsely if he had spoken about historical events, such as his sending of the prophet Noah, in eternity past or at any time before those events took place. God's speech must have been created after, and thus in some sense in response to, the events it narrates. I thank Khalil Andani for pointing me to this passage.

7 See, for example, Abū al-Ḥasan al-Ashʿarī, *al-Ibāna ʿan uṣūl al-diyāna*, ed. Fawqiyya Huṣayn Maḥmūd (Cairo: Dār al-Anṣār, 1977), 70; William Montgomery Watt, "Early Discussions about the Qur'ān," *The Muslim World* 40 (1950), 99–104; Christopher Melchert, *The Formation of the Sunni Schools of Law, 9th–10th Centuries* C.E. (Leiden: Brill, 1997), 15 n. 69; Farahat, *Foundation of Norms*, 97–98.

8 ʿAbd al-Jabbār, *al-Mughnī*, 7:19–20, 106–9; ʿAbd al-Jabbār, *Sharḥ al-Uṣūl al-khamsa*, 527–37; J. R. T. M. Peters, *God's Created Speech: A Study in the Speculative Theology of the Muʿtazilī Qāḍī l-Quḍāt Abū l-Ḥasan ʿAbd al-Jabbār bn Aḥmad al-Hamadhānī* (Leiden: E. J. Brill, 1976), 59–60, 65–68.

9 See ʿAbd al-Jabbār, *Sharḥ al-Uṣūl al-khamsa*, 527; ʿAbd al-Jabbār, *al-Mughnī*, 17:30–80.

10 ʿAbd al-Jabbār, *al-Mughnī*, 7:182, 224; Margaret Larkin, *The Theology of Meaning: ʿAbd al-Qāhir al-Jurjānī's Theory of Discourse* (New Haven: American Oriental Society, 1995), 31.

about God's own nature, or about the basic principles of reason, because one has to know all those things before one can be sure that God is just and that the Qur'an is, therefore, a trustworthy source of knowledge.[11] Consequently, ʿAbd al-Jabbār regarded God's speech as purely informative, as a set of statements about the law,[12] and not as a performative speech act that brings about new moral relationships between people, as in Wolterstorff's theory. This informative view of God's speech has been taken for granted by many Muslim thinkers, but one could also imagine a performative theology of revelation in which the Qur'an functions primarily to create new moral relationships.[13] After all, the Qur'an itself presents God's speech as performative and even creative.

A second consequence of God's speech being an action characterized by justice is that it must always be clear. If God's purpose is to communicate his law, he would fail completely—which, of course, is impossible—if he were ever to create words that did not express exactly what he meant. His speech, therefore, is necessarily always clear when read in light of the other evidence God makes available.[14] The Ashʿariyya could offer no such guarantee, so ʿAbd al-Jabbār considered that their theology undermined revelation as a source of knowledge. In his eyes the Muʿtazila were the real champions of revelation.[15]

This principle of clarity led ʿAbd al-Jabbār and other Baṣran Muʿtazilī theologians to formulate interpretive rules that were remarkably literalist. In the domain of theology they were known for metaphorical interpretation, but in their view theology was not the point of the Qur'an. For ʿAbd al-Jabbār the Qur'an could not actually be an independent source of theological knowledge; at best it could only supplement or encourage rational knowledge of God, and must always be reinterpreted if necessary to accord with that prior knowledge.[16] But in the field of law, which was the real subject matter of the Qur'an, the Muʿtazila were not proponents of metaphorical interpretation at all. Modern Muslim reformers looking for a flexible Qur'anic hermeneutic

---

11 ʿAbd al-Jabbār, *al-Mughnī*, 16:354, 17:93; ʿAbd al-Jabbār ibn Aḥmad al-Hamadhānī, *Mutashābih al-Qurʾān*, ed. ʿAdnān Muḥammad Zarzūr (Cairo: Dār al-Turāth, 1969), 1–5.

12 ʿAbd al-Jabbār, *al-Mughnī*, 17:23–24, 94–95; David R. Vishanoff, *The Formation of Islamic Hermeneutics: How Sunni Legal Theorists Imagined a Revealed Law* (New Haven: American Oriental Society, 2011), 135–37, 143–45.

13 See further David R. Vishanoff, *Islamic Legal Theory: A Critical Introduction Based on al-Juwayni's* Waraqat fi usul al-fiqh (Indianapolis: Hackett, 2022), 18–20, 49–52.

14 ʿAbd al-Jabbār, *al-Mughnī*, 7:182–83, 185, 16:347–58, 17:30–86; ʿAbd al-Jabbār, *Sharḥ al-Uṣūl al-khamsa*, 531.

15 See ʿAbd al-Jabbār, *Mutashābih al-Qurʾān*, 2, 5; ʿAbd al-Jabbār, *Sharḥ al-Uṣūl al-khamsa*, 531.

16 See ʿAbd al-Jabbār, *Mutashābih al-Qurʾān*, 4–5, 34–39; ʿAbd al-Jabbār, *al-Mughnī*, 16:354, 360.

should not look to the Muʿtazila! In the domain of legal hermeneutics (*uṣūl al-fiqh*) they expressed a strong preference for taking the Qur'an literally and at face value.[17] If an expression is general (or unrestricted), it must be meant to apply unrestrictedly to everything it linguistically denotes, unless God previously or simultaneously provides clear evidence narrowing its scope to refer to just some of the things it denotes.[18] Likewise a command cannot be taken to imply anything more than what ʿAbd al-Jabbār's definition of command entails, which is that God desires the act to be performed; so commands only entail recommendation, not obligation.[19] Commands do not require immediate obedience,[20] or more than one act of obedience.[21] They do not imply, in and of themselves, that if one fails to obey one will have to make up the duty later.[22] A command does not prohibit the opposite of what is commanded,[23] nor does a prohibition make an act legally invalid.[24] If God specifically prohibits an action in certain circumstances, this does not imply anything about whether it is permitted in other circumstances,[25] as many other scholars held. God can mean only exactly what he says, or else he has to provide clarifying evidence, and he must make that evidence available at the very moment of his speech; he cannot delay clarifying it (*ta'khīr al-bayān*)[26] as most other legal theorists said he could.

The Baṣra Muʿtazila were not as rigid as the strictest members of the Ẓāhiriyya, a literalist movement that was sparked in part by members of the Baghdād school of the Muʿtazila.[27] Some early proponents of Ẓāhirism adhered so literally to the words of revelation that if two revealed texts seemed to conflict one of them would be discarded before either would be

17 See generally Vishanoff, *Formation of Islamic Hermeneutics*, 110–16, 123–33, 141, 150.
18 ʿAbd al-Jabbār, *al-Mughnī*, 17:27–29, 54–58, 72–73.
19 ʿAbd al-Jabbār, *al-Mughnī*, 17:107–9, 113–14, 116.
20 ʿAbd al-Jabbār, *al-Mughnī*, 17:119–20.
21 ʿAbd al-Jabbār, *al-Mughnī*, 17:124.
22 ʿAbd al-Jabbār, *al-Mughnī*, 17:121.
23 ʿAbd al-Jabbār, *al-Mughnī*, 17:112.
24 ʿAbd al-Jabbār, *al-Mughnī*, 17:136.
25 ʿAbd al-Jabbār appears to endorse negative implication by a condition in *al-Mughnī*, 17:86, but he is clearly said to have rejected it by Muḥammad ibn ʿAlī ibn al-Ṭayyib Abū al-Ḥusayn al-Baṣrī in *al-Muʿtamad fī uṣūl al-fiqh*, ed. Khalīl al-Mays (Beirut: Dār al-Kutub al-ʿIlmiyya, [1983]), 1:142, and by Badr al-Dīn Muḥammad ibn Bahādur ibn ʿAbd Allāh al-Zarkashī in *al-Baḥr al-muḥīṭ fī uṣūl al-fiqh*, ed. ʿAbd al-Qādir ʿAbd Allāh al-ʿĀnī, ʿUmar Sulaymān al-Ashqar, and ʿAbd al-Sattār Abū Ghudda (Kuwait: Wizārat al-Awqāf wa-l-Shu'ūn al-Islāmiyya, 1988), 4:47.
26 ʿAbd al-Jabbār, *al-Mughnī*, 17:65–73.
27 On the connections between the Baghdād Muʿtazila and the Ẓāhiriyya, see Vishanoff, *Formation of Islamic Hermeneutics*, ch. 3.

reinterpreted.[28] The Ẓāhiriyya did not think there was any coherent moral meaning or rationale behind God's speech or law; they believed that the law consisted solely of the words of God's speech, which must therefore be followed to the letter. That approach was theologically principled, but it turned out to be practically unsustainable: there were too many apparent conflicts between revealed texts, and too many texts that had to be reinterpreted to accommodate the evolving legal discourse and lived practice of the Muslim community. Already by the time of Ibn Ḥazm (d. 456/1064) the Ẓāhiriyya had been slowly giving way to the more flexible interpretive theory of mainstream jurists, and Ibn Ḥazm's own legal hermeneutic ended up looking remarkably similar to that of the Mālikīs around him. Pure Islamic literalism died out long ago.[29]

The Baṣra Muʿtazila were not that strict. They engaged in the mainstream juristic practice of reconciling conflicting evidence through reinterpretation, and of extrapolating from the available evidence by means of analogy when necessary, because they were convinced that God's law must be coherent, reasonable, and good, and that if his speech did not fit what was known from other revealed evidence and from reason then it must be interpreted to fit the available evidence. In practice Qāḍī ʿAbd al-Jabbār's legal interpretations were presumably not radically different from that of his Shāfiʿī colleagues, notwithstanding the minimalist and literalist tendency of his hermeneutic. But at least in principle, in the chapters on legal theory in his *Mughnī*, ʿAbd al-Jabbār remained quite attached to the plain literal meaning of revelation, and avoided any deviation from it that was not absolutely required by the other evidence God had provided.

This theory of interpretation was principled, and it flowed from ʿAbd al-Jabbār's theological premises, but it was not a very powerful, flexible, or practical legal hermeneutic. It was cautious and even minimalist, assigning to the Qur'an only those meanings that could be justified by clear evidence. Such certainty is hard to maintain in Islamic law, and ambiguity is hard to avoid, so ʿAbd al-Jabbār's hermeneutic did not survive for long even among

28 Abū al-Walīd al-Bājī, *Iḥkām al-fuṣūl fī aḥkām al-uṣūl*, ed. ʿAbd al-Majīd Turkī (Beirut: Dār al-Gharb al-Islāmī, 1986, reprint 1995), 266 ¶181; Abū Muḥammad ʿAlī ibn Aḥmad ibn Saʿīd Ibn Ḥazm, *al-Iḥkām fī uṣūl al-aḥkām*, based on the edition of Aḥmad Muḥammad Shākir (8 vols. in 2, Beirut: Dār al-Āfāq al-Jadīda, 1983), 2:38–39, 3:147.

29 See Vishanoff, *Formation of Islamic Hermeneutics*, 67, 84–88, 93–101, 104–7. For an illuminating survey of aspects of literalism that can be found throughout Islamic intellectual history, see Robert Gleave, *Islam and Literalism: Literal Meaning and Interpretation in Islamic Legal Theory* ([Revised] paperback edition, Edinburgh: Edinburgh University Press, 2013).

the Muʿtazila. By the early 5th/11th century even his own pupil Abū al-Ḥusayn al-Baṣrī (d. 436/1044) was shying away from such a theologically grounded legal hermeneutic and adopting the much more pragmatic hermeneutic of those legal theorists, referred to as the *fuqahāʾ*, who were more oriented toward law than theology.[30]

3 The Ashʿariyya

Before turning to the *fuqahāʾ*, however, it is worth describing the alternative hermeneutic of Abū al-Ḥasan al-Ashʿarī (d. 324/935) and his second-generation follower al-Qāḍī Abū Bakr al-Bāqillānī (d. 403/1013), whose theology supported a more flexible but still impractical hermeneutic. They shared ʿAbd al-Jabbār's concern to ground hermeneutics in the theology of revelation, but they believed God's speech to be eternal, so their hermeneutic was necessarily quite different. Al-Bāqillānī in particular developed very explicitly the hermeneutical implications of the Ashʿarī doctrine that God's speech is an eternal attribute subsisting in God's essence, while the letters and words that make up the Qurʾan are just a created expression of that eternal attribute. That attribute, technically called a *maʿnā*, is also the meaning (*maʿnā*) that is expressed by the words of the Qurʾan. God's speech is both an eternal attribute and an eternal command, prohibition, statement, and all the other meanings that make up God's revelation.[31]

---

30 For example, Abū al-Ḥusayn al-Baṣrī, *al-Muʿtamad*, 1:3, 5, 43–51, 69–75, 315–16; George Makdisi, *Ibn ʿAqīl: Religion and Culture in Classical Islam* (Edinburgh: Edinburgh University Press, 1997), 80–81.

31 See Abū Bakr Muḥammad ibn al-Ṭayyib al-Bāqillānī, *al-Taqrīb wa-l-irshād* (*al-ṣaghīr*), ed. ʿAbd al-Ḥamīd ibn ʿAlī Abū Zunayd (3 vols., Beirut: Muʾassasat al-Risāla, 1998), 1:316–17, 335, 2:5, 25, 88, 198, 318; Abū Bakr ibn al-Ṭayyib al-Bāqillānī, *al-Inṣāf fī mā yajibu iʿtiqāduhu wa-lā yajūzu al-jahl bih*, ed. Muḥammad Zāhid ibn al-Ḥasan al-Kawtharī (2d ed., [Cairo:] Muʾassasat al-Khānjī, 1382/1963), 26, 71–143; Daniel Gimaret, *La doctrine d'al-Ashʿarī* (Paris: Cerf, 1990), 201–2; Gregor Schwarb, "Capturing the Meanings of God's Speech: The Relevance of *Uṣūl al-Fiqh* to an Understanding of *Uṣūl al-Tafsīr* in Jewish and Muslim *Kalām*," in *A Word Fitly Spoken: Studies in Mediaeval Exegesis of the Hebrew Bible and the Qurʾān presented to Haggai Ben-Shammai*, ed. Meir M. Bar-Asher et al. (Jerusalem: Ben-Zvi Institute, 2007), 122*–23*, 129*; Alexander Key, *Language between God and the Poets:* Maʿnā *in the Eleventh Century* (Oakland: University of California Press, 2018), 132–37; Farahat, *Foundation of Norms*, 107–15, 151–59; Bernard G. Weiss, *The Search for God's Law: Islamic Jurisprudence in the Writings of Sayf al-Dīn al-Āmidī*, revised edition (Salt Lake City: University of Utah Press / Herndon, Va.: International Institute of Islamic Thought, 2010), 65–68.

This theory of speech introduced an ontological gap between God's speech itself, which consists of meanings, and the words of the Qur'an that express those meanings. Al-Bāqillānī made of that ontological gap a hermeneutical gap. The goal of interpretation is to know the Qur'an's meaning, but that meaning does not reside in words; it resides in God. All we have access to is words, so we have to use those words as evidence from which to infer the hidden meaning of God's speech. In ordinary human speech we can often grasp the speaker's meaning immediately, without any reflective process, because contextual cues like facial expressions, tone of voice, and the physical setting make it obvious what the speaker is trying to say; but since we cannot perceive God directly we do not get those same contextual cues along with his speech, so we have to sit down and think: if God chose these words to express his meaning, then he must have meant such and such. Interpreting divine speech requires a process of rational deliberation to move us from the words the speaker utters to the inner meanings the speaker intends to express.[32]

Our knowledge of the Arabic language, of course, gives us a lot of clues about what meanings each word might be used to express, but al-Bāqillānī said that many important words and verbal forms, including, for example, the imperative form of a verb, can express many different meanings. Interpreting an imperative verb, therefore, requires more evidence than just the word itself. Unless we can find additional evidence from which to infer what was meant by a particular imperative—a command or an authorization, an obligation or a recommendation—we have to suspend judgment and admit that we do not know the word's meaning. Al-Bāqillānī and the few legal theorists who followed him were therefore known as the *wāqifiyya*, the suspenders of interpretive judgment.[33]

This appears to leave the meaning of revelation woefully underdetermined, and to leave interpreters in a quandary. Uncertainty, however, presents an opportunity. The biggest interpretive challenge in Islamic law is not usually a lack of evidence but a superabundance of evidence that often seems to point in several directions at once. The groundbreaking legal theorist Muḥammad ibn Idrīs al-Shāfiʿī (d. 204/820) showed how that superabundance of evidence can be reconciled into a coherent picture of the law: some evidence can be designated as unclear, and other conflicting evidence can then be used to

---

32 Al-Bāqillānī, *al-Taqrīb*, 1:429–36, 3:285; Vishanoff, *Formation of Islamic Hermeneutics*, 181–83.

33 See for example al-Bāqillānī, *al-Taqrīb*, 1:423–24, 427, 2:7, 15, 33, 60, 73; Farahat, *Foundation of Norms*, 177–87; cf. Weiss, *The Search for God's Law*, 341, 346–54, 360–62, 380–81, 396, 399–400.

reinterpret it. Al-Bāqillānī's hermeneutic justifies this solution by making it possible to claim that almost any evidence is unclear, and that virtually any other evidence, no matter how weak, can be used as evidence from which to infer its intended meaning. The pieces of revelation can therefore be fitted together in nearly endless combinations to produce almost unlimited interpretive possibilities. For al-Shāfiʿī and for al-Bāqillānī ambiguity was not a problem but an opportunity that gave interpreters great flexibility in determining the hidden meaning of God's speech.[34]

Nevertheless, in principle al-Bāqillānī's hermeneutic called for an enormous amount of interpretive labor. Very little could be taken for granted; many crucial interpretations had to be justified by appeal to additional pieces of evidence. Like ʿAbd al-Jabbār's hermeneutic, al-Bāqillānī's was theologically principled but practically unwieldy. It offered numerous avenues for exploring alternative interpretations in response to social changes and the variable pressures of daily life, but it complicated the task of giving those interpretations the sanction of divine revelation. His hermeneutic was laudably consistent with his theology of divine speech, but it left a daunting task to any interpreter who wished to show that his chosen interpretations followed naturally from the application of his hermeneutic to God's speech.

4 The Jurists

Few legal theorists, therefore, followed either al-Bāqillānī or ʿAbd al-Jabbār beyond the early 5th/11th century. Most adopted a more pragmatic hermeneutic that retained the flexibility of the Ashʿariyya but also provided the interpretive power to claim that certain interpretations were obvious without having to justify them by appeal to evidence beyond the words themselves. They might say, for example, that imperative verbs have a strong and definite default meaning—they impose an obligation of immediate and repeated obedience and simultaneously prohibit and render invalid any action contrary to the commanded act—but that this default meaning can easily be set aside in favor of a less stringent meaning on the basis of the slightest evidence. I call this hermeneutic the law-oriented hermeneutical paradigm because it was adopted across the Sunni schools of law by legal theorists whose main concern was the elaboration or justification of law, not philosophical coherence or theological

34 Vishanoff, *Formation of Islamic Hermeneutics*, 152–89; cf. Weiss, *The Search for God's Law*, 341–42, 441.

consistency.[35] Many of these thinkers did not make any attempt to articulate explicitly the theological conception of divine speech that lay behind their hermeneutic, but I want to introduce briefly one particularly strong proponent of this hermeneutical paradigm, the Ḥanbalī Abū Yaʿlā Ibn al-Farrāʾ (d. 458/1066), whose definitions and arguments reveal that his powerful and flexible hermeneutic came at the cost of theological coherence.[36]

When we look at how Abū Yaʿlā defined commands, for example, and how he defended his rules for their interpretation, we can see that he (much like Wolterstorff) considered God's speech a kind of performative illocutionary act that brings about a moral relationship between God and humanity. In his theological writing he asserted that God's speech is eternal,[37] but in his work on legal theory he asserted just as clearly that a command is a kind of action: an act of verbally demanding or requesting that a person of inferior status perform some action.[38] This conception of commands had profound hermeneutical consequences. If a command were just a word—an imperative verb uttered with a certain intent under certain conditions, as the Muʿtazila held—then its meaning would be closely tied to the linguistic meaning of the imperative. That was why the Muʿtazila ascribed only minimal legal meaning to commands. If, on the other hand, a command is an act of requesting somebody to do something, then it can be imagined to include all sorts of implications that follow from a superior's instructions to a subordinate. If a master asks his slave to bring him a drink, for example, we might normally suppose that he wants the drink now, not at some unspecified time before the slave's death, and that if the slave continues to just sit there he will be punished. These things are not part of the linguistic meaning of an imperative verb, but they are part of the social meaning of a master's instructions to a slave.[39]

This view of speech as a socially embedded act made it possible for Abū Yaʿlā to maximize the legal force of revealed language, and to claim that the strong meanings he assigned to commands and other utterances were obvious from the words of revelation alone, without appeal to additional evidence. At the same time, however, Abū Yaʿlā retained all the flexibility of al-Shāfiʿī's and al-Bāqillānī's hermeneutics, justifying departures from his strong default

35 Cf. Farahat's "theology-averse jurists" (*Foundation of Norms*, 187).

36 See generally Vishanoff, *Formation of Islamic Hermeneutics*, ch. 6.

37 Abū Yaʿlā Ibn al-Farrāʾ, *Kitāb al-Muʿtamad fī uṣūl al-dīn*, ed. Wadīʿ Zaydān Ḥaddād (Beirut: Dār al-Mashriq, 1974), 44, 86–93; see also Abū Yaʿlā Muḥammad ibn al-Ḥusayn al-Farrāʾ, *al-ʿUdda fī uṣūl al-fiqh*, ed. Aḥmad ibn ʿAlī Sīr al-Mubārakī (5 vols., Riyadh: n.p., 1990), 2:388.

38 Abū Yaʿlā, *al-ʿUdda*, 1:157, 214–24, 2:387.

39 See Abū Yaʿlā, *al-ʿUdda*, 1:141, 224, 238, 247, 281, 288, 292, 2:368–74.

meanings, whenever these seemed necessary, by appeal to even the weakest of evidence. This was the thrust of the law-oriented hermeneutical paradigm, and that explains why it was adopted so quickly and so widely, even among the theologians and the Ẓāhiriyya, by the middle of the 5th/11th century. The law-oriented hermeneutic was practically adequate for dealing with a large and complex body of revealed evidence, and for interpreting that evidence in a way that was responsive to the interpreter's human experience and social context.

This pragmatism, however, came at the price of theological coherence. Would Abū Yaʿlā really have affirmed, if pressed, that God's speech was an eternal action performed upon created beings from eternity past? I doubt he would have, but in the 5th/11th century theological grounding was becoming less and less of a concern; theology was being excised from books of legal theory and from the curriculum of the Islamic sciences.[40] Law and legal theory could be based, at least implicitly, on a notion of revelation that was incoherent or, at best, paradoxical. This lack of attention to theological consistency also seems characteristic of modern Sunni textbooks on *uṣūl al-fiqh*, which continue to uphold the essentials of the law-oriented hermeneutical paradigm without revisiting the theology of divine speech that undergirds it.

5 The Danger of Authoritarianism

This turn from theological principle to interpretive pragmatism is not innocent. It poses the moral danger of what Khaled Abou El Fadl calls authoritarianism: the arrogation of authority that often occurs when an interpreter identifies his or her interpretation as the obvious and indisputable meaning of God's speech, without disclosing her presuppositions, values, or interpretive choices, and thus effectively substitutes her own interpretation for the text of revelation.[41] The law-oriented hermeneutical paradigm embraced by the Sunni schools of law permitted exactly that, at least in principle, because it allowed jurists to find a great deal of legal meaning in revelation, and to claim that it was the plain literal meaning of the text, while reserving the flexibility to

40 See Abū al-Ḥusayn al-Baṣrī, *al-Muʿtamad*, 1:3; George Makdisi, "The Juridical Theology of Shâfiʿî: Origins and Significance of *Uṣûl al-Fiqh*," *Studia Islamica* 59 (1984), 14–17, 21, 26–30, 33–39; George Makdisi, "Ashʿarī and the Ashʿarites in Islamic Religious History, Part I," *Studia Islamica* 17 (1962), 44–46.

41 Khaled Abou El Fadl, *Speaking in God's Name: Islamic Law, Authority, and Women* (Oxford: Oneworld, 2001), 5, 7, 53–56, 92–93, 141–45, 158–61, and *passim*.

deviate from that default meaning whenever they felt it necessary to do so. The law-oriented paradigm concealed the jurists' interpretive labor, making their conclusions seem more obvious than they were—something that theologians like ʿAbd al-Jabbār and al-Bāqillānī would have denounced.

The jurists were not free to employ their powerful and flexible hermeneutic at will. The constraints of the scholarly tradition limited quite severely their ability to propose whimsical new interpretations and claim revealed authority for them, even if they might have been hermeneutically justifiable. In the modern world, however, where the scholarly tradition no longer controls the framework or the limits of legal interpretation, the law-oriented hermeneutic has become a more powerful and dangerous tool. Modernists, Salafis, and reformers of all stripes frequently employ the principles and mechanisms of classical legal theory, wittingly or unwittingly, to justify interpretations that would never have been accepted within the classical interpretive tradition. More often than not they do so without any apparent awareness of the theological underpinnings of that hermeneutic.

It is significant, therefore, that some recent and contemporary Muslim thinkers have proposed explicit and creative theologies of revelation. One example is Muhammad Shahrur (1938–2019), who developed at great length a distinction between a suprahistorical *qur'ān* and a historical *umm al-kitāb*.[42] That metaphysical distinction had a definite hermeneutical purpose: it allowed Shahrur to classify Qur'anic teachings that fit his own modern liberal values as eternal and objective, while declaring other parts of the Qur'an to be historically contingent and subject to human reasoning. His theology appears to have been driven by his hermeneutical objectives, rather than the other way around as with ʿAbd al-Jabbār and al-Bāqillānī. Nevertheless, having identified his hermeneutical goal, Shahrur did make a serious attempt to ground it in a coherent theology of revelation.

---

42 See Andreas Christmann, "'The Form Is Permanent, but the Content Moves': The Qur'anic Text and Its Interpretation(s) in Mohamad Shahrour's *al-Kitab wal-Qur'an*," in *Modern Muslim Intellectuals and the Qur'an*, ed. Suha Taji-Farouki (Oxford: Oxford University Press, 2004), 263–95; Andreas Christmann, "'Read the Qur'an as if It Was Revealed Last Night': An Introduction to Muhammad Shahrur's Life and Work," in *The Qur'an, Morality and Critical Reason: The Essential Muhammad Shahrur* (Leiden: Brill, 2009), xxxv; Muḥammad Shaḥrūr, *al-Kitāb wa-l-qur'ān: Qirā'a muʿāṣira* (Damascus: al-Ahālī, [1990]), 51–61.

6 Aksin Wijaya

Another remarkably elaborate and creative Qur'anic metaphysics is that proposed by Aksin Wijaya (b. 1974), Professor and Director of Graduate Studies at the State Institute of Islamic Religion (IAIN) in Ponorogo, East Java. Like the Ashʿariyya, he thinks it important to distinguish between God's eternal inner speech and its temporal verbal expression,[43] but rather than focusing on the metaphysical properties of God's attribute of speech he analyzes the communicative process through which that speech ends up on the pages of the Qur'an.[44] In addition to differentiating between the heavenly and earthly dimensions of revelation, he draws a distinction between the oral and written forms of the Qur'an, and thus ends up with a tripartite model consisting of God's direct revelation to the Prophet (*wahyu*), the oral Qur'an (*al-Qur'an*), and the ʿUthmānic Codex (*Mushaf Usmani*).[45]

Wijaya defines *wahyu*, the first dimension of revelation, as an act of communication[46] that took place when the Prophet, by virtue of his extraordinarily spiritual orientation, transcended the physical dimension of his human nature and entered the realm of spirit and divinity.[47] This communication took place, he argues, in a private language or sign system that was not Arabic and was independent of any specific culture.[48] This communication involved no intermediary; the stories about Gabriel conveying God's messages were just the Prophet's way of explaining his claim of revelation to an audience who conceived of supernatural inspiration as coming through intermediaries such as jinn.[49] Nor did it require any interpretation; rather, it yielded immediate,

---

43 See Aksin Wijaya, *Arah Baru Studi Ulum Al-Qur'an: Memburu Pesan Tuhan di Balik Fenomena Budaya* (Yogyakarta: Pustaka Pelajar, 2009), 59–63 and 68–69, where he says approvingly that this view resolves the conflict over the created or eternal nature of God's speech by distinguishing aspects of God's speech that had been conflated. He attributes to Abū al-Ḥasan al-Ashʿarī the view that God's speech has only an eternal dimension, and attributes to Ibn Rushd the distinction, usually associated more broadly with the Ashʿariyya, between the meaning that constitutes God's inner speech and the verbal form in which it is expressed.

44 See Wijaya, *Arah Baru*, 74–95.

45 Summarized in Wijaya, *Arah Baru*, vii, 94. This tripartite model is independent of the similar-sounding one put forward by Mohammed Arkoun; Aksin Wijaya, interview by author, 18 August 2015, Ponorogo, Indonesia.

46 Wijaya, *Arah Baru*, 54.

47 Wijaya, *Arah Baru*, 27–29, 74–77, 80–81. Wijaya also says that God simultaneously entered the human dimension and took on some kind of human attribute (*nasut*).

48 Wijaya, *Arah Baru*, 54–55, 64–67, 76–78, 85.

49 Wijaya, *Arah Baru*, 78–84, 100 n. 67.

unreflective, and perfect understanding of the divine message (*pesan*) by the Prophet. It is this original message, which cannot be explained as the product of Arab culture, that constitutes the principal miraculous feature of the Qur'an[50] and that God has promised to protect from corruption.[51] Because it is free of cultural trappings and is therefore relevant to any social context,[52] only this part of the Qur'an's message is authoritative for all. It is, therefore, the sole object of the interpreter's quest.[53]

The words of the oral Qur'an (*al-Qur'an*) Wijaya regards as a second act of communication that took place between the Prophet and his original Arab audience. This required transferring the divine message from the private language in which the Prophet had received it into clear Arabic.[54] The Arabic words of the Qur'an did not exist in the heavenly realm; they were chosen by the Prophet himself.[55] In his initial prophetic experience in the cave of Ḥirā' the Prophet had been commanded to read—not to recite particular words that were given to him, but to read or diagnose the social reality of his time and place in light of the universal revelation he was to receive.[56] He did so using the existing medium of Arabic which, following Naṣr Ḥāmid Abū Zayd (1943–2010), Wijaya regards as a carrier of its own cultural message.[57] The Prophet responded to pagan Arab society in its own terms, mimicking cultural concepts such as the notion of a charismatic figure who receives otherworldly messages through intermediaries and expresses them in poetic form.[58] The result was that God's message became "trapped" in an Arabic linguistic and cultural system, so that it could not speak directly to all God's servants across the face of the whole earth.[59] The oral Qur'an proclaimed by the Prophet carried both a divine message and a human cultural message in approximately equal proportions.[60] Wijaya does not say how he reaches his figure of fifty percent, but by giving a specific number he goes beyond vague assertions about the ability of a language to carry its own implicit message and offers a clear idea of just how

---

50 Wijaya, *Arah Baru*, 38–42; 48–51. Wijaya also recognizes a literary dimension to its miraculous nature.

51 Wijaya, *Arah Baru*, 162.

52 Wijaya, *Arah Baru*, 53.

53 See Wijaya, *Arah Baru*, 158, 160.

54 Wijaya, *Arah Baru*, 85–89.

55 Wijaya, *Arah Baru*, viii, 64–65, 86, 87 n. 48, 164. Wijaya attributes such a view to Abū Ḥanīfa.

56 Wijaya, *Arah Baru*, 42–48.

57 Wijaya, *Arah Baru*, viii, 8–9, 73 n. 31, 105, 159, 160, 163, 218.

58 Wijaya, *Arah Baru*, 97–102, 105; see also 118–19.

59 Wijaya, *Arah Baru*, 163.

60 Wijaya, *Arah Baru*, vii.

radical his interpretive project is: he will consider himself at liberty to dismiss about half of the Qur'an's content as Arab cultural baggage that need not be imported into Indonesia.

The third communicative event occurred after the death of the Prophet, when his Companions passed on the Qur'an's message in writing. In order to avoid conflict over the oral Qur'an's seven variant recitations (which Wijaya seems to regard as irretrievably lost), they reduced it to a single written text, the ʿUthmānic Codex (*Mushaf Usmani*).[61] In this way God's message was further entrapped, this time by the linguistic and cultural system of one particular tribe, the Quraysh, and also by the act of writing itself.[62] Wijaya argues that the very act of fixing the Qur'an as a written text broke the direct connection between speaker and hearer that had previously allowed the Companions to understand the oral Qur'an immediately and unreflectively.[63] The ʿUthmānic Codex, which is the only form in which we now have access to God's message, can be understood only through a process of linguistic analysis, which by its nature tends to highlight the cultural messages that are embedded in the Arabic language.[64] Equally problematic is the hegemony accorded to specifically Qurashī language and culture. The seven variant readings were intended to address the linguistic and cultural diversity of the Prophet's Arab audience, but the ʿUthmānic codification further narrowed both the cultural relevance and the cultural message of revelation,[65] so that the message of the text we read today is about twenty percent Qurashī ideology. That leaves only thirty percent of the text's message that can be attributed to God himself. The task of hermeneutics is to identify and extract that thirty percent from behind the veil of Arab and Qurashī culture so that revelation can speak to all societies past and present, across the face of the whole earth including Indonesia, without subjecting them to Arab cultural imperialism.[66]

This is a splendid example of an explicit theology of revelation put forward in the service of Qur'anic hermeneutics. Wijaya reworks the classical Ashʿarī doctrine of God's eternal speech in terms of modern communication theory, and ends up with a justification for a hermeneutic of recovery that sounds like a slightly more sophisticated, Indonesianized version of the hermeneutic of Fazlur Rahman (1919–1988). The hermeneutical dimension of Wijaya's project,

61 Wijaya, *Arah Baru*, 89–93.
62 Wijaya, *Arah Baru*, 165.
63 Wijaya, *Arah Baru*, 2–3, 165–68, 180, 220.
64 Wijaya, *Arah Baru*, 168.
65 Wijaya, *Arah Baru*, 169–72.
66 Wijaya, *Arah Baru*, 173–75.

however, remains underdeveloped in his book on the Qur'anic sciences. He says that "exegesis" (*tafsīr*), which considers only the language of the text, can only discover the Qur'an's Arab cultural message,[67] and so calls for it to be supplemented with "hermeneutics"[68] so as to consider both the internal linguistic and external contextual dimensions of the text.[69] He calls for analysis of Qur'anic vocabulary after the manner of Toshihiko Izutsu (1914–1993),[70] as well as isolation of the divine elements of the Qur'anic message from its Arab cultural elements[71] along the general lines taken by Fazlur Rahman[72] and Naṣr Ḥāmid Abū Zayd.[73] Following Maḥmūd Muḥammad Ṭāhā (1909–1985), he suggests that God's universal message is more readily apparent in the Meccan portions of the ʿUthmānic Codex.[74] It remains unclear, however, how the narrowing from seven oral to one written version of the Qur'an is to be undone in the process of "hunting for God's message behind the phenomenon of culture."[75] The sample exegetical problem to which he applies his hermeneutic by way of illustration—the Qur'anic term *islām*—is even less developed than his hermeneutical theory: he never gets beyond internal vocabulary analysis before leaping to a predictable list of modern liberal values which, he concludes, must be the universal values that form the genuine revealed core of the Qur'anic message.[76] It is his theology of revelation that is most detailed and suggestive; indeed one hardly needs an explicit statement of hermeneutical method, or a specific example of interpretation, to see the kinds of interpretive moves that his theory of revelation suggests and supports. His theology allows him to depart radically from the explicit language of scripture, in order to address the concrete particulars of his contemporary Indonesian context, while still claiming to anchor his interpretations in the authority of an imagined suprahistorical act of divine communication.

In Wijaya's hermeneutic, as in al-Bāqillānī's and Shahrur's, the doctrine of an eternal or suprahistorical heavenly message plays a central role: it is the

67 Wijaya, *Arah Baru*, viii, 168–69.

68 Wijaya, *Arah Baru*, viii, 175–82.

69 Wijaya, *Arah Baru*, 5, 12–14 (following Amīn al-Khūlī's distinction between *mā ḥawla al-Qur'ān* and *mā fī al-Qur'ān*).

70 Wijaya, *Arah Baru*, 216, 221–22, 230–33.

71 Wijaya, *Arah Baru*, 158, 218–21.

72 Wijaya, *Arah Baru*, 142–43, 218–19, 224–27.

73 Wijaya, *Arah Baru*, 216–19, 227.

74 Wijaya, *Arah Baru*, 124–35, 138, 234–36.

75 This phrase is from the subtitle of Wijaya's book *Arah Baru Studi Ulum Al-Qur'an: Memburu Pesan Tuhan di Balik Fenomena Budaya*.

76 Wijaya, *Arah Baru*, 228–37.

object of interpretive inquiry. The concept of a transcendent and ahistorical divine discourse behind the timebound Arabic words of the Qur'an is not just a pious affirmation of the transcendent nature of revelation; it is an imagined locus of pure meaning untainted by the processes of human communication and interpretive reasoning. If the Qur'an is a historical and literary text comparable to other historical and literary artifacts, in a linguistic medium that reflects a particular human society, then the desire to find in it a divinely authoritative norm that transcends human cultures requires the positing of some suprahistorical revelation that transcends the words of the Qur'an yet is somehow reflected in them. The interpretive mechanisms that would guarantee recovery of that pure divine message may be difficult to define with any precision, or to carry out in any objective manner, but this does not trouble Aksin Wijaya. It is enough to believe that there is gold beneath the dross of Arab culture. This justifies not a certain method but a certain attitude toward the Qur'an, and toward those who would try to impose its foreign values and customs on Indonesian Muslims.

Indeed, the Indonesian context is crucial for understanding the relationship between Wijaya's theology of revelation and his hermeneutic. The state-supported drive for indigenization or "Indonesianization" of Islam[77] is a driving force behind much Indonesian Qur'anic hermeneutics. For Wijaya and his circle, the interpretive outcome is not in doubt. Even the historicizing hermeneutic is already largely a given. What is needed is legitimacy: an updating of the Qur'anic sciences that shows how traditional concepts like the occasions of revelation, the distinction between Meccan and Medinan verses, and above all the Ashʿarī doctrine of God's eternal speech actually support modern historicizing hermeneutical theories. Wijaya undertakes a similar project in a book on Islamic epistemology[78] where he draws on an assortment of western and classical Islamic theories, including the Aristotelean-inflected "bottom-up" epistemology of Ibn Rushd (1126–1198)[79] and the Illuminationist epistemology of Mulla Sadra,[80] to legitimate his argument that Islamic epistemology and hermeneutics should be anthropocentric, driven by the particulars of local

77 See Wijaya, *Arah Baru*, 114–15; Carool Kersten, *Islam in Indonesia: The Contest for Society, Ideas and Values* (Oxford: Oxford University Press, 2015), 182–87, 202–20; Carool Kersten, *A History of Islam in Indonesia: Unity in Diversity* (Edinburgh: Edinburgh University Press, 2017), 151–53.

78 Aksin Wijaya, *Satu Islam Ragam Epistemologi: Dari Epistemologi Teosentrisme ke Antroposentrisme* (Yogyakarta: Pustaka Pelajar, 2014).

79 Wijaya, *Satu Islam*, 95–109, 158.

80 Wijaya, *Satu Islam*, 131–46.

human needs and experiences,[81] rather than theocentric and governed by a certain conception of God's will or speech, as most of classical theology and legal theory were.[82] As with Shahrur, therefore, I think that Wijaya's theology of revelation, while explicit and creative, is not what drives his hermeneutic. Rather, his contextually sensitive hermeneutic is motivated by the drive for practically adequate and locally relevant interpretation, and his rather ad hoc theological bricolage is motivated by his need to legitimate that hermeneutic.

Despite Wijaya's remarkably systematic attempt to ground his hermeneutic in a coherent theology of revelation, his principled theological grounding does not entirely shield him from the danger of authoritarianism. Although he does not claim to discover by his method a single divinely intended meaning in the Qur'an, but only one of several meanings that fall within the range or limits of God's intended meanings,[83] his hermeneutic is such that he could easily use it to foist his own liberal values on the Qur'an as though they were its only universal, transcultural message. And his hermeneutic itself seems to have been foisted onto his theological reflection on God's speech, for like Shahrur he seems to have started from the hermeneutical imperatives he felt were dictated by the exigencies of his modern context, and then to have mined the history of Islamic theology and philosophy to find notions of revelation that would suit his hermeneutic. Nevertheless, like Shahrur, Wijaya has at least been explicit about his hermeneutic's theological foundations, however novel and precarious those may be. And he has amply demonstrated that the Islamic intellectual tradition is a rich resource that can be rethought and redeployed in the service of contemporary legal hermeneutics.

7 Hasan Hanafi

For a more thorough, principled, and theologically consistent rethinking of Islamic legal hermeneutics, I know of no better example than Hasan Hanafi (1935–2021), whose radical reconstruction of the discipline of *uṣūl al-fiqh* was motivated not only by the interpretive exigencies of modern life but also by his encounter with the anthropological turn in modern European theology. His early work, written in French during his time at the Sorbonne,[84] set the course

81 Wijaya, *Satu Islam*, 157–58, 313–15, 322–37.
82 Wijaya, *Satu Islam*, 3, 66, 147–48, 156–57, 356–59.
83 Aksin Wijaya, interview by author, 18 August 2015, Ponorogo, East Java, Indonesia.
84 His three doctoral theses were published as Hassan Hanafi, *Les méthodes d'exégèse: Essai sur la science des fondements de la compréhension "ʿilm uṣul al-fiqh"* (Cairo: Conseil

for his life's work[85] by showing how to bring classical Islamic thought into dialogue with the philosophical environment of mid-20th-century Europe, which was steeped in the phenomenology of Heidegger and Husserl. In order to make Islamic thought meaningful in phenomenological terms, and vice versa, he rethought Islamic legal theory and hermeneutics, and indeed the very notions of revelation and divinity, in terms of human experience. In *Les méthodes d'exégèse*, an opaque but brilliant work, he transposed the entire edifice of classical legal theory into the vocabulary of phenomenology.[86]

The result was a completely anthropocentric theory of interpretation in which the quest for meaning begins with the particular experiences of daily life, which are brought into relation with the received truths of revelation. As each person grasps his[87] own experiences in the light of revelation,[88] and brings his interpretation into conversation with the experiences of others,[89] the law—which is to say, human understanding (*fiqh*) of the natural drives and motivations that are the fount of all human action[90]—emerges as an increasingly unified collective grasp of what is most universal about human experience.[91] The goal of interpretation is not to arrive at a knowledge of God's transcendent will, but to bring our actions more and more into alignment with what is most fundamentally, universally, and ideally true about human nature.[92] The process of legal interpretation takes place entirely within the domain of human experience, beginning with particular human experiences and ending with a conceptual grasp and a practical implementation of universal human nature. This hermeneutic meets the need felt by Hanafi, Wijaya, and

---

Supérieur des Arts, des Lettres et des Sciences Sociales, 1965); Hassan Hanafi, *L'exégèse de la phénoménologie: L'état actuelle* [sic] *de la méthode phénoménologique et son application au phénomène religieux* (Cairo: Dar al-Fikr al-Arabi, [1980s]); and Hassan Hanafi, *La phénoménologie de l'exégèse: Essai d'une herméneutique existentielle à partir du Nouveau Testament* (Paris, 1966; Cairo: Anglo-Egyptian Bookshop, 1988).

85 See Carool Kersten, "Bold Transmutations: Rereading Hasan Hanafi's Early Writings on *Fiqh*," *Comparative Islamic Studies* 3 (2007), 23, 25; Carool Kersten, *Cosmopolitans and Heretics: New Muslim Intellectuals and the Study of Islam* (London: Hurst, 2011), 106, 128.

86 See Hanafi, *Méthodes d'exégèse*, i–iii, lxxxix–cxxxix, 540–43; Kersten, "Bold Transmutations," especially 28, 30, 33; Kersten, *Cosmopolitans and Heretics*, 130–33.

87 Since medieval legal theorists and Hasan Hanafi invariably take for granted a male interpreter, I will use masculine pronouns when representing their views.

88 See Hanafi, *Méthodes d'exégèse*, ccvi, 58–59, 71–72, 106–7, 238, 262.

89 Hanafi, *Méthodes d'exégèse*, cci–ccii, ccviii–ccix, cclxiii–cclxv, 107, 244, 292–93.

90 Hanafi, *Méthodes d'exégèse*, cxx, 214–15, 332, 359, 369–70, 382, 384, 392, 403–6, 416–18, 443, 451–52.

91 Hanafi, *Méthodes d'exégèse*, civ–cvi, clxxxix, ccviii–ccix, 57, 84–96, 107, 291–93, 384; Kersten, *Cosmopolitans and Heretics*, 134, 137.

92 Hanafi, *Méthodes d'exégèse*, 75–77, 213–14, 218, 313–14, 397–400, 419–25, 543.

so many other contemporary Muslims for a law that addresses current human concerns and responds to the particulars of time and place without degenerating into relativism.[93]

This hermeneutic, however, comes at the cost of a complete humanization of revelation. Indeed, Hanafi does not see this as a cost or a drawback; it is his goal to transpose not just legal hermeneutics but the concept of revelation itself onto the plane of human experience—the only plane that phenomenology claims to elucidate. Accordingly, he redefines the four main sources of law: the Qur'an becomes "anonymous experience," the Sunna "privileged experience," consensus "intersubjective experience," and reasoning by analogy "individual experience."[94] Even the Qur'an, though it has no particular human author, is an articulation of human experience—an idealized, anonymous experience representing what is best and most universal about human life.[95] Hanafi insists that the most fundamental source of revelation is actually the fourth, *qiyās* (analogy) or *ijtihād* (legal reasoning), which he understands as the process of grasping one's own personal experience and relating it (by analogy) to the other sources that have been handed down or agreed upon as universally true of all human experience.[96] In phenomenological terms, *ijtihād* is simply the eidetic process of grasping reality.

This implies—or follows from—Hanafi's radical assertion that the Qur'an is not the speech of a transcendent God that has been sent down into the human world, but simply an articulation of human experience, at a highly universalized level, from one of those great figures of human history known as Enunciators who include heroes, artists, poets, and in the Qur'an's case a prophet[97]—though Hanafi prefers to avoid such religious terminology.[98] The Prophet did not experience or communicate about anything transcendent; that is by definition impossible, since the noumenal realm is not the object of phenomenal experience.[99] Rather, the Prophet simply did what all human

93 See Hanafi, *Méthodes d'exégèse*, cci–ccii, ccxxxvii, 86, 126, 134, 238, 249, 292–93, 433–34.

94 Hanafi, *Méthodes d'exégèse*, 7–8, 63–64, 106–7.

95 Hanafi, *Méthodes d'exégèse*, cxc–cxci, 65–77, 218, 310, 314; Hasan Hanafi, "What Does the Qur'ān as Sacred Text Mean? Some Preliminary Observations," in *Al-Kitab: La sacralité du texte dans le monde de l'Islam*, ed. D. De Smet, G. de Callataÿ, and J. M. F. van Reeth (Brussels: Peeters, 2004), 55.

96 Hanafi, *Méthodes d'exégèse*, clxviii, cxciv, cxcvii–cxcviii, ccxxxviii–ccxxxix, 57–59, 104–7, 262, 297, 311, 319–20, 433, 542.

97 Hanafi, *Méthodes d'exégèse*, cxc–cxci, ccliv–cclv, 7, 53, 63, 65–67, 73, 75–77, 79, 84, 310–11, 313–14, 375–76.

98 See Hanafi's comments in *Méthodes d'exégèse*, xxxi n. 1, cxxxv–cxxxviii, 7 n. 2, 7 n. 4, 30 n. 2, 66, 78–79, 88, 167, 313.

99 Hanafi, *Méthodes d'exégèse*, 166, 309–14, 358, 487, 521–23.

beings do, seeking to grasp his own experience in light of the handed-down wisdom of the ages that reflects the experience of past generations.[100] That he did so in an unusually incisive and objective way—that is, in a way that reflects what is truly universal about human nature[101]—does not give his "privileged experience" (the Sunna) or the "anonymous experience" that he articulated (the Qur'an) a qualitatively different character from the experiences (*ijtihād*) of other individuals.[102] Consequently, when discussing *ḥadīth* (Prophetic reports), Hanafi argues that the most genuine reports are not those that are most reliably attributed to the Prophet but, on the contrary, those that are fabricated by later "transmitters," because the spontaneous and undistorted articulation of each person's own experience is the very essence of revelation.[103]

This radical reconceptualization of revelation leaves God out of the picture, and in fact we may be forgiven for asking (as some of his critics have) whether Hanafi has not become in effect an atheist.[104] Hanafi would respond that this misses the point of his project, which is not to deny God but rather to give him a place in the phenomenological domain of human experience. That his French dissertation largely avoids the religious term "God," and speaks instead of a "universal human consciousness,"[105] is not a denial of the claims of Islamic theology but an attempt to make them relevant to the situation of modern Muslims, and also to render them meaningful in the terms of modern European philosophy, which has already transposed Christian theology onto the plane of anthropology. If Islamic discourse about God and revelation is to have any significance in the contemporary social, political, and philosophical context, it must be recast in terms of human experience and action.[106]

This will seem to many Muslims an unacceptable price to pay for the holy grail of a theologically coherent but practically adequate legal hermeneutic. Some would argue that Hanafi has simply given up on the tension between the particular realities and exigencies of legal interpretation in the modern world, on the one hand, and the goal of a theocentric religious discourse

---

100 Hanafi, *Méthodes d'exégèse*, ccxxxix, 76, 161.

101 Hanafi, *Méthodes d'exégèse*, 65–66, 73–84.

102 Hanafi, *Méthodes d'exégèse*, cxci, cxcvii, cclxiv–cclxv, 7–8, 53, 55, 106–7, 292, 406–8.

103 Hanafi, *Méthodes d'exégèse*, cxcvii, 32, 49–59.

104 See Hanafi, *Méthodes d'exégèse*, cxi–cxii, cxxxvi, 72, 529; Hasan Hanafi, "Théologie ou anthropologie?" in *Renaissance du monde arabe: Colloque interarabe de Louvain*, ed. Anouar Abdel-Malek, Abdel-Aziz Belal, and Hasan Hanafi (Gembloux: Duculot, 1972), 264.

105 See, e.g., Hanafi, *Méthodes d'exégèse*, cxxxvi, 179, 293, 313, 421.

106 Hanafi, *Méthodes d'exégèse*, xxi–xxii, lxviii, cclxiii, cclxvi, 110–11, 313, 418–19, 421–24, 521–30; Hanafi, "Théologie ou anthropologie?" 233–43, 246–51, 256–58, 264; Kersten, *Cosmopolitans and Heretics*, 133, 157, 165.

and a life lived in submission to a transcendent authority on the other: in his quest for relevance, Hanafi has completely sacrificed transcendence. Others might appreciate the point of a theology articulated entirely in terms of human experience, but might find that Hanafi's notion of universal human experience—which seems to take the place of God in his hermeneutic—is too homogenizing and insufficiently postmodern; it runs the risk of a different kind of authoritarianism in which the experience of one person or group, without claiming any transcendent authority, is nevertheless deemed a human universal and therefore takes on the authority of "revelation" for everyone else. But whatever one's objections to the theology behind Hanafi's reconstruction of Islamic legal theory, it must be admitted that his project has set a high bar for theological consistency in the quest for a practically adequate legal hermeneutic, and that it has illustrated just how great a challenge that quest presents to contemporary Muslim intellectuals working at the interface between theology and law.

8 Conclusion

Hanafi has done, in effect, just what Nicholas Wolterstorff did in his book on *Divine Discourse*: he has shown how a scriptural hermeneutic adequate to the modern world can be grounded in a coherent philosophy of revelation or divine speech. Many contemporary Muslim scholars have likewise turned their attention to hermeneutics, seeking a theory of scriptural interpretation adequate for the concrete demands of living faithfully in the modern world. Devising a powerful and flexible hermeneutic, in and of itself, is not especially difficult; medieval legal theorists did that long ago, inspired by al-Shāfiʿī and building on the insights of Ashʿarī theologians. In so doing, however, the law-oriented theorists lost sight of the theological paradoxes or contradictions that were at least implicitly demanded by their increasingly pragmatic hermeneutic. Perhaps some such theological paradoxes are a necessary part of any religious thought that aspires to adequately capture the complex experience of religious life. Aksin Wijaya and Hasan Hanafi, however, like al-Bāqillānī and ʿAbd al-Jabbār, were willing to make their theologies of revelation explicit, and spell out their consequences for interpretation, rather than just putting forward a hermeneutic and then assuming (or pretending) that it made theological sense. For those who aspire to theoretical coherence, Wijaya and Hanafi offer two starkly different but equally creative models of explicit reflection on the connections between the theology of revelation and legal hermeneutics, grounded in both classical Islamic and modern European thought. Neither model, however, provides an easy solution to the tension between the desire for a comprehensive and coherent theological vision and the practical exigencies of legal interpretation.

Bibliography

ʿAbd al-Jabbār al-Asadābādī, Abū al-Ḥasan, *al-Mughnī fī abwāb al-tawḥīd wa-l-ʿadl*, ed. Ṭāhā Ḥusayn et al. (Cairo: Wizārat al-Thaqāfa wa-l-Irshād al-Qawmī, 1960–1969).

ʿAbd al-Jabbār al-Asadābādī, Abū al-Ḥasan, *Mutashābih al-Qurʾān*, ed. ʿAdnān Muḥammad Zarzūr (Cairo: Dār al-Turāth, 1969).

ʿAbd al-Jabbār al-Asadābādī, Abū al-Ḥasan, *Sharḥ al-Uṣūl al-khamsa*, with the commentary of Aḥmad ibn al-Ḥusayn ibn Abī Hāshim [Mānkdīm], ed. ʿAbd al-Karīm ʿUthmān (Cairo: Maktabat Wahba, 1965).

Abou El Fadl, Khaled, *Speaking in God's Name: Islamic Law, Authority, and Women* (Oxford: Oneworld, 2001).

Abū al-Ḥusayn al-Baṣrī, Muḥammad ibn ʿAlī ibn al-Ṭayyib, *al-Muʿtamad fī uṣūl al-fiqh*, ed. Khalīl al-Mays (Beirut: Dār al-Kutub al-ʿIlmiyya, [1983]).

al-Ashʿarī, Abū al-Ḥasan, *al-Ibāna ʿan uṣūl al-diyāna*, ed. Fawqiyya Huṣayn Maḥmūd (Cairo: Dār al-Anṣār, 1977).

Ayoub, Samy A., *Law, Empire, and the Sultan: Ottoman Imperial Authority and Late Ḥanafī Jurisprudence* (Oxford: Oxford University Press, 2020).

al-Bājī, Abū al-Walīd, *Iḥkām al-fuṣūl fī aḥkām al-uṣūl*, ed. ʿAbd al-Majīd Turkī (Beirut: Dār al-Gharb al-Islāmī, 1986, reprint 1995).

al-Bāqillānī, Abū Bakr ibn al-Ṭayyib, *al-Inṣāf fī mā yajibu iʿtiqāduhu wa-lā yajūzu al-jahl bih*, ed. Muḥammad Zāhid ibn al-Ḥasan al-Kawtharī (2d ed., [Cairo:] Muʾassasat al-Khānjī, 1382/1963).

al-Bāqillānī, Abū Bakr ibn al-Ṭayyib, *al-Taqrīb wa-l-irshād* (*al-ṣaghīr*), ed. ʿAbd al-Ḥamīd ibn ʿAlī Abū Zunayd (Beirut: Muʾassasat al-Risāla, 1998).

Christmann, Andreas, "'Read the Qurʾan as if It Was Revealed Last Night': An Introduction to Muhammad Shahrur's Life and Work," in *The Qurʾan, Morality and Critical Reason: The Essential Muhammad Shahrur* (Leiden: Brill, 2009).

Christmann, Andreas, "'The Form Is Permanent, but the Content Moves': The Qurʾanic Text and Its Interpretation(s) in Mohamad Shahrour's *al-Kitab wal-Qurʾan*," in *Modern Muslim Intellectuals and the Qurʾan*, ed. Suha Taji-Farouki (Oxford: Oxford University Press, 2004), 263–95.

Esack, Farid, *Qurʾan, Liberation & Pluralism: An Islamic Perspective of Interreligious Solidarity against Oppression* (Oxford: Oneworld, 1997).

Farahat, Omar, *The Foundation of Norms in Islamic Jurisprudence and Theology* (Cambridge: Cambridge University Press, 2019).

Gimaret, Daniel, *La doctrine d'al-Ash'arī* (Paris: Cerf, 1990).

Gleave, Robert, *Islam and Literalism: Literal Meaning and Interpretation in Islamic Legal Theory* ([Revised] paperback edition, Edinburgh: Edinburgh University Press, 2013).

Hallaq, Wael B., *Authority, Continuity, and Change in Islamic Law* (Cambridge: Cambridge University Press, 2001).

Hanafi, Hasan, "Théologie ou anthropologie?" in *Renaissance du monde arabe: Colloque interarabe de Louvain*, ed. Anouar Abdel-Malek, Abdel-Aziz Belal, and Hasan Hanafi (Gembloux: Duculot, 1972).

Hanafi, Hasan, "What Does the Qur'ān as Sacred Text Mean? Some Preliminary Observations," in *Al-Kitab: La sacralité du texte dans le monde de l'Islam*, ed. D. De Smet, G. de Callataÿ, and J. M. F. van Reeth (Brussels: Peeters, 2004).

Hanafi, Hasan, *L'exégèse de la phénoménologie: L'état actuelle* [sic] *de la méthode phénoménologique et son application au phénomène religieux* (Cairo: Dar al-Fikr al-Arabi, [1980s]).

Hanafi, Hasan, *La phénoménologie de l'exégèse: Essai d'une herméneutique existentielle à partir du Nouveau Testament* (Paris, 1966; Cairo: Anglo-Egyptian Bookshop, 1988).

Hanafi, Hasan, *Les méthodes d'exégèse: Essai sur la science des fondements de la compréhension "'ilm uṣul al-fiqh"* (Cairo: Conseil Supérieur des Arts, des Lettres et des Sciences Sociales, 1965).

Ibn al Farrā', Abū Ya'lā, *al-'Udda fī uṣūl al-fiqh*, ed. Aḥmad ibn 'Alī Sīr al-Mubārakī (Riyadh: n.p., 1990).

Ibn al Farrā', Abū Ya'lā, *Kitāb al-Mu'tamad fī uṣūl al-dīn*, ed. Wadī' Zaydān Ḥaddād (Beirut: Dār al-Mashriq, 1974).

Ibn Ḥazm, Abū Muḥammad 'Alī ibn Aḥmad ibn Sa'īd, *al-Iḥkām fī uṣūl al-aḥkām*, based on the edition of Aḥmad Muḥammad Shākir, 8 vols. in 2 (Beirut: Dār al-Āfāq al-Jadīda, 1983).

Kersten, Carool, "Bold Transmutations: Rereading Hasan Hanafi's Early Writings on *Fiqh*," *Comparative Islamic Studies* 3 (2007), 22–38.

Kersten, Carool, *A History of Islam in Indonesia: Unity in Diversity* (Edinburgh: Edinburgh University Press, 2017).

Kersten, Carool, *Cosmopolitans and Heretics: New Muslim Intellectuals and the Study of Islam* (London: Hurst, 2011).

Kersten, Carool, *Islam in Indonesia: The Contest for Society, Ideas and Values* (Oxford: Oxford University Press, 2015).

Key, Alexander, *Language between God and the Poets:* Ma'nā *in the Eleventh Century* (Oakland: University of California Press, 2018).

Larkin, Margaret, *The Theology of Meaning: 'Abd al-Qāhir al-Jurjānī's Theory of Discourse* (New Haven: American Oriental Society, 1995).

Makdisi, George, "Ashʿarī and the Ashʿarites in Islamic Religious History, Part I," *Studia Islamica* 17 (1962), 37–80.

Makdisi, George, "The Juridical Theology of Shâfiʿî: Origins and Significance of *Uṣûl al-Fiqh*," *Studia Islamica* 59 (1984), 5–47.

Makdisi, George, *Ibn ʿAqīl: Religion and Culture in Classical Islam* (Edinburgh: Edinburgh University Press, 1997).

Melchert, Christopher, *The Formation of the Sunni Schools of Law, 9th–10th Centuries C.E.* (Leiden: Brill, 1997).

Peters, J. R. T. M., *God's Created Speech: A Study in the Speculative Theology of the Muʿtazilī Qāḍī l-Quḍāt Abū l-Ḥasan ʿAbd al-Jabbār bn Aḥmad al-Hamadhānī* (Leiden: E. J. Brill, 1976).

Schwarb, Gregor, "Capturing the Meanings of God's Speech: The Relevance of *Uṣūl al-Fiqh* to an Understanding of *Uṣūl al-Tafsīr* in Jewish and Muslim *Kalām*," in *A Word Fitly Spoken: Studies in Mediaeval Exegesis of the Hebrew Bible and the Qur'ān presented to Haggai Ben-Shammai*, ed. Meir M. Bar-Asher et al. (Jerusalem: Ben-Zvi Institute, 2007), 111*–156*.

Shaḥrūr, Muḥammad, *al-Kitāb wa-l-qur'ān: Qirā'a muʿāṣira* (Damascus: al-Ahālī, [1990]).

Vishanoff, David R., *Islamic Legal Theory: A Critical Introduction Based on al-Juwayni's* Waraqat fi usul al-fiqh (Indianapolis: Hackett, 2022).

Vishanoff, David R., *The Formation of Islamic Hermeneutics: How Sunni Legal Theorists Imagined a Revealed Law* (New Haven: American Oriental Society, 2011).

Watt, William Montgomery, "Early Discussions about the Qur'ān," *The Muslim World* 40, nos. 1–2 (1950), 27–40, 96–105.

Weiss, Bernard G., *The Search for God's Law: Islamic Jurisprudence in the Writings of Sayf al-Dīn al-Āmidī*, revised edition (Salt Lake City: University of Utah Press / Herndon, Va.: International Institute of Islamic Thought, 2010).

Wijaya, Aksin, *Arah Baru Studi Ulum Al-Qur'an: Memburu Pesan Tuhan di Balik Fenomena Budaya* (Yogyakarta: Pustaka Pelajar, 2009).

Wijaya, Aksin, *Satu Islam Ragam Epistemologi: Dari Epistemologi Teosentrisme ke Antroposentrisme* (Yogyakarta: Pustaka Pelajar, 2014).

Wolterstorff, Nicholas, *Divine Discourse: Philosophical Reflections on the Claim that God Speaks* (Cambridge: Cambridge University Press, 1995).

al-Zarkashī, Badr al-Dīn Muḥammad ibn Bahādur ibn ʿAbd Allāh, *al-Baḥr al-muḥīṭ fī uṣūl al-fiqh*, ed. ʿAbd al-Qādir ʿAbd Allāh al-ʿĀnī, ʿUmar Sulaymān al-Ashqar, and ʿAbd al-Sattār Abū Ghudda (Kuwait: Wizārat al-Awqāf wa-l-Shu'ūn al-Islāmiyya, 1988).

PART 2

Mechanics

CHAPTER 3

Epistemology and Legal Theory in al-Dabūsī's *Taqwīm al-adilla*: A Case Study on the Interplay between Legal Theory, Law and Theology

Serdar Kurnaz

1 Introduction

Epistemological questions were a major concern in Islamic law and legal theory. If we look back at the first centuries of the development of Islamic law, we see different concurring understandings of law with reference to epistemology.[1] Epistemology, on the other hand, was related to theology; theological works discussed epistemological terms like 'knowledge' (*ʿilm*), 'conjecture' (*ẓann*), and 'ignorance' (*jahl*). These categories influenced legal theory as well. Furthermore, the dominant understanding of the law, at least from the 4th/10th century onwards, that it should be derived from the scriptural sources, i.e., the Qur'an and the Hadith, had lasting influence on legal epistemology. Especially during the 5th/11th and 6th/12th centuries, there was a noticeable increase in debates about Islamic legal theory with respect to varying theologies and epistemologies.

This article is dedicated to drawing attention to an example from the Transoxanian tradition during the aforementioned period. It focuses on Abū Zayd al-Dabūsī's (d. 430/1039) epistemology and its effects on his legal theory as articulated in his *Taqwīm al-adilla*, which later became an influential Ḥanafī text. Al-Dabūsī has an epistemological approach different from the standard epistemology articulated in theological writings and later (especially Shāfiʿī) *uṣūl* works. His approach, therefore, demands special attention. This article first outlines al-Dabūsī's epistemology and his core theological assumptions and traces their impacts on his legal theory. To trace these impacts, I focus on

1 See, for example, Wael B. Hallaq, *The Origins and Evolution of Islamic Law* (Cambridge: Cambridge University Press, 2005); David Vishanoff, *The Formation of Islamic Hermeneutics: How Sunni Legal Theorists Imagined a Revealed Law* (New Haven, CT: American Oriental Society, 2011).

 | DOI:10.1163/9789004746886_005

an example from his works on legal theory and substantial law: the question of *fasād al-manhī ʿanh*, that is, the question whether a prohibited action has legal efficacy if someone conducts a prohibited action. Subsequently, I will present ʿAlāʾ al-Dīn al-Samarqandī's (d. 539/1144) reinterpretation of al-Dabūsī's view on *fasād al-manhī ʿanh*, which stemmed from his particular theological concerns. This reinterpretation will illustrate how differing theological assumptions can lead to different approaches to legal questions and arguments. The article will end with an outlook for a contemporary Islamic legal theory in lieu of summarizing the main results, since premodern theological debates can establish potential trajectories for developments in contemporary Islamic law.

2 Abū Zayd al-Dabūsī's Epistemology and Its Influence on His Legal Theory

Abū Zayd ʿAbdallāh (ʿUbaydallāh) b. Muḥammad b. ʿUmar b. ʿĪsā al-Dabūsī was born in the town of Dabūsiyya, near Samarqand. He died in 430/1039 in Bukhara. While little is known about his life,[2] it is widely acknowledged that al-Dabūsī is one of the most influential Ḥanafī scholars, especially in the development of the Ḥanafī *uṣūl* terminology. Fortunately, only a few of al-Dabūsī's works have survived, including his two major books, *Taʾsīs al-naẓar* (*The Foundation of Inquiry*) on legal points of disagreements (*khilāf*) and *Taqwīm al-adilla fī uṣūl al-fiqh* (*The Assessment of Proofs in Legal Theory*) on legal theory. One of al-Dabūsī's other surviving works is a book on Sufism titled *al-Amad al-aqṣā* (*The Utmost Limit/Goal*).[3]

In the course of my analysis of al-Dabūsī's epistemology in *Taqwīm al-adilla*, I will also incorporate his epistemological views as found in *al-Amad al-aqṣā* and will point to the overlaps between his theological and mystical conception of knowledge. The title of the last chapter of his *Taqwīm*, where al-Dabūsī discusses the definition of knowledge and other related terms, already suggests his interest in Sufism: "Concerning the States of the Human Heart before and after

2 Brannon M. Wheeler, "al-Dabūsī, Abū Zayd," in *Encyclopaedia of Islam Three Online*, ed. Kate Fleet, Gudrun Krämer, Denis Matringe, John Nawas, and Devin J. Stewart (available online at https://doi.org/10.1163/1573-3912_ei3_COM_25771).

3 Carl Brockelmann, *Geschichte der arabischen Litteratur* (2nd edition, Leiden: Brill, 1943), vol. 1, 184; Fuat Sezgin, *Geschichte des arabischen Schrifttums* (Leiden: Brill, 1967), vol. 1, 456. About this book in particular, see Murteza Bedir, "Interplay of Sufism, Law, Theology and Philosophy: A Non-Sufi Mystic of 4th–5th/10th–11th Centuries," in *El Sufismo y las normas del Islam*, ed. and transl. Alfonso Carmona (Murcia: Editora Regional de Murcia Colección de Ibn ʿArabī, 2006), 253–70 (with a Spanish translation on pp. 15–34).

Knowledge."[4] As the title of the chapter indicates, al-Dabūsī links knowledge to the "states of the human heart" (*aḥwāl qalb al-ādamī*) and taste (*ladhdha*), which is a Sufi terminology.[5] In his treatise on Sufism, in *al-Amad*, al-Dabūsī has the idea "that the locus of both the divine light that constitutes the basis of Sufi epistemology and of reason, being the ground of theological elaboration, is the same, namely the heart."[6] Therefore, both in his jurisprudential work, *Taqwīm*, and in his treatise on Sufism, *al-Amad*, he describes reason as the light with which the heart can perceive and discover truths.[7] Thus, al-Dabūsī makes use of Sufi terminology in his legal theoretical work, to which I will return at a later stage of the analysis. First, I want to present how al-Dabūsī defines technical terms related to epistemology in *Taqwīm*. Subsequently, I will address the impact of his epistemology on the question if conducted prohibited actions have legal efficacy or not.

2.1 *Definition of Knowledge and Related Terms*

Before presenting his epistemology, al-Dabūsī mentions the four states of the heart of human beings before obtaining knowledge. His emphasis lies on the heart, since, as we will see below, for al-Dabūsī, reason (*ʿaql*) is the light through which the heart sees when it looks at proofs and gains knowledge.

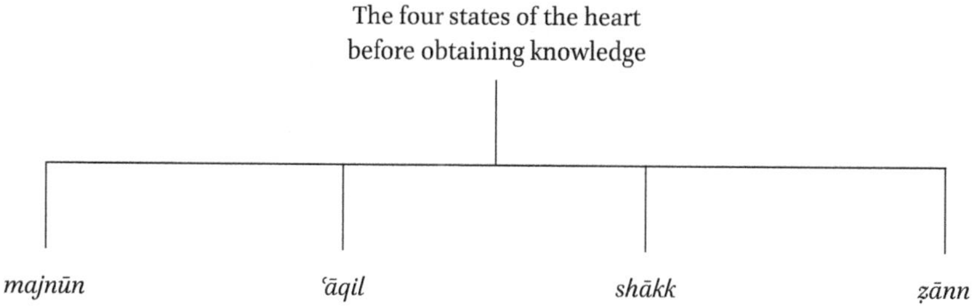

FIGURE 3.1 Visualization of the four epistemological states of the human heart before knowledge: *majnūn*, *ʿāqil*, *shākk*, and *ẓānn*

4 Abū Zayd al-Dabūsī, *Taqwīm al-adilla*, ed. Khalīl Muḥyi al-Dīn al-Mays (Beirut: Dār al-kutub al-ʿilmiyya, 1421/2001), 465.

5 'Taste' (*ladhdha*) is often related to the major Sufi concept of *dhawq*, which also means 'taste'; see Denis Gril, "Dhawq," in *Encyclopaedia of Islam Three Online*, ed. Kate Fleet, Gudrun Krämer, Denis Matringe, John Nawas, and Devin J. Stewart (available online at https://doi.org/10.1163/1573-3912_ei3_COM_26001).

6 Bedir, "Interplay," 270. Bedir also draws attention to the fact that al-Dabūsī sometimes refers to the brain when he speaks about reason. For the interplay between reason and divine light, see also ibid., p. 264.

7 Al-Dabūsī, *Taqwīm*, 465; Abū Zayd al-Dabūsī, *al-Amad al-aqṣā*, ed. Muḥammad ʿAbd al-Qādir ʿAṭā' (Beirut: Dār al-kutub al-ʿilmiyya, 1436/2015), 37. On the description of reason as divine light in Sufi literature, see Bedir, "Interplay."

According to al-Dabūsī, at birth, the individual human being is like a *majnūn* ('a "foolish" one') who does not have the skills for reasoning: a *majnūn* cannot grasp what he/she is told. The opposite of *majnūn*, al-Dabūsī remarks, is *ʿāqil* ('capable of reason') that is the person who possesses reason. After being *majnūn*, humans become *ʿāqil*.[8] Al-Dabūsī, however, does not describe this transition. Since the human being becomes *ʿāqil* after being *majnūn*, al-Dabūsī defines 'reason' (*ʿaql*) as the light through which the heart sees when it looks at 'proofs' (*ḥujaj*), like the lamp providing light for the eye.[9] With this light, the heart can see things hidden to the senses. Being capable of reason does not mean that one is always reasonable. When humans cannot or do not want to see with their heart, then they are *jāhil* ('ignorant'), since the opposite of knowledge, according to al-Dabūsī, is 'ignorance' (*jahl*). Thus, being *ʿāqil*, humans' hearts begin to see. If the heart sees weakly, then one becomes a 'doubter' (*shākk*). For al-Dabūsī, doubt is the opposite of 'certainty' (*yaqīn*); the knowledge object appears for the seeing in a state that contradicts its actual nature.[10] If the heart sees stronger than in this first state of human beings, even though still not in the needed entirety of the knowledge object, the heart becomes something that only presumes or assumes that something exists

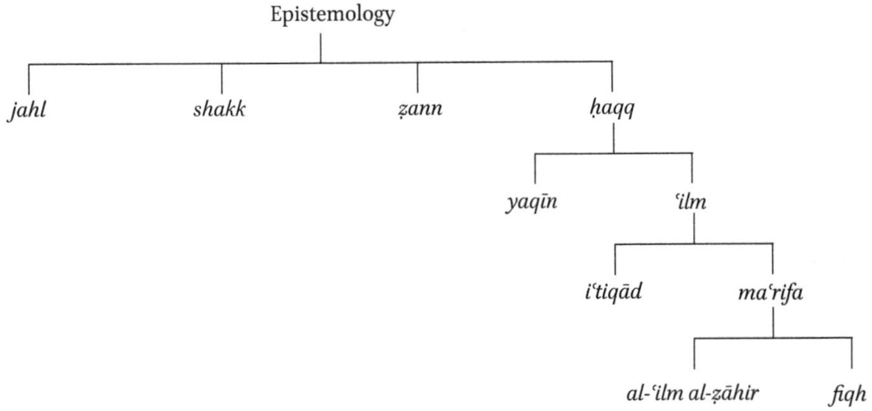

FIGURE 3.2 Diagram showing the flow from theological and epistemological foundations to legal conclusions in al-Dabūsī's Ḥanafī legal theory

8 Al-Dabūsī, *Taqwīm*, 465.

9 Al-Dabūsī, *Taqwīm*, 465. For the same description in his Sufi work, see *al-Amad*, 37. In both works, he says that it is *ka-l-shihāb li-l-ʿayn*. There is, however, a difference between these two works. In *al-Amad*, the condition "when it looks on evidence" is missing.

10 Al-Dabūsī, *Taqwīm*, 465.

in the incompletely recognized form. Al-Dabūsī calls those who do not recognize the knowledge object in its entirety 'speculators' (*ẓānn*). After having discussed the four states of the heart before 'knowing', namely being *majnūn*, *ʿāqil*, *shākk* and *ẓānn*, al-Dabūsī turns towards knowledge and the relevant terms that refer to epistemology. Figure 3.2 above summarizes these technical terms.

Starting with speculation, or conjecture, it is, for al-Dabūsī, a kind of doubt: one does prefer a meaning that occurs in the mind; however, there is no solid proof that justifies this preference. The preference is arbitrary. If, on the other hand, one has a solid proof for that preference, al-Dabūsī calls this type of knowledge 'truth' (*ḥaqq*), which results in 'certainty' (*yaqīn*). He finds the basis for this juxtaposition between truth and speculation in Q 53:28: "Indeed speculation is no substitute for the truth" (*inna l-ẓanna lā yughnī mina l-ḥaqqi shayʾan*). Although al-Dabūsī regards speculation as the opposite of truth, he makes an exception to this negative connotation: speculation can be regarded as knowledge in a metaphorical sense. The condition for its validity in return is that it must be based on 'evidence' (*dalīl*); knowledge must always be based on a valid proof. In this case, al-Dabūsī differentiates this kind of speculation from doubt and names it 'preponderant view' (*ghālib al-raʾy*). For this type of knowledge, al-Dabūsī gives the example of knowledge acquired through 'analogical reasoning' (*qiyās*) and *ijtihād*, since both for analogical reasoning and *ijtihād*, one has always to refer to a valid proof for the knowledge obtained, like a reference to Qur'an and/or Sunna. Although this type of knowledge, i.e., preponderant view, is falsifiable, he understands it as being part of the above-mentioned term of 'truth' (*ḥaqq*).[11]

Al-Dabūsī defines knowledge as the result of eager reflection on something and the successful attainment of the correct outcome, which is the recognition of the knowledge object as it actually is. If through this process one can definitely exclude doubt, then this is for al-Dabūsī 'knowledge' (*ʿilm*). Knowledge, however, becomes 'belief/conviction' (*iʿtiqād*), if one is convinced of the attained knowledge, which is based on solid proof. It seems that in al-Dabūsī's view belief has a stronger epistemic status than mere knowledge. To underline this, he uses the following picture: People 'link' (*ʿaqada*) their heart to what they see. If they do not, the result would be 'dissolution' (*ḥall*) from knowledge which leads to ignorance. Al-Dabūsī shows this with reference to the Qur'anic passage about Satan's refusal to obey God's command to prostrate before

11 Al-Dabūsī, *Taqwīm*, 465–66.

Adam:[12] although Satan knew God's existence (he was *ʿālim bi-llāh*), he did not sincerely believe (*ghayr muʿtaqid*) in Him.[13]

Al-Dabūsī distinguishes further states of knowledge. The first state of knowledge, he says, is subject to a type of 'confusion' (*iḍṭirāb*). He describes this confusion as the first moment of occurrence of the knowledge, which means that it comes into mind for the first time; the term *iḍṭirāb* possibly emphasizes a certain pain of challenge. Al-Dabūsī tries to explain how we can understand this state as follows: Think of someone who enters a city for the first time in his/her life. He/she is a stranger in this city and needs guidance, as long as he/she does not establish friendships with locals that lead to mutual knowledge and familiarity. This familiarity with the city allows to overcome this state of confusion. For al-Dabūsī the same is true for knowledge: If one can remove this confusion, the obtained knowledge persists with certainty and it reaches the next stage, which al-Dabūsī calls *maʿrifa*. *Maʿrifa* is the heart's reflection and reasoning on the available proofs, which are not merely based on sense perception. Its opposite is *fikra*, an idea or a conception; since for an idea there is a lack of persistence of certainty—it is always subject to revision—it does not hold as a wholesome argument. *Maʿrifa*, however, is a degree above knowledge because of the additional attribute of what al-Dabūsī calls 'company' (*ṣuḥba*); with this term, al-Dabūsī intends the above-mentioned persistence of knowledge. *Maʿrifa*, therefore, is the highest degree of knowledge; it is not a mere idea, a speculation, rather an irrefutable, permanent knowledge based on solid proof.

In several passages al-Dabūsī uses *maʿrifa*, *ʿilm*, and *yaqīn* synonymously, which makes it unclear whether al-Dabūsī creates here a hierarchy or even sees them as being synonyms for solid knowledge in general.[14] However, al-Dabūsī further divides *maʿrifa* into two types: first, *ẓāhir* or outward knowledge without knowledge about the inner/deeper meaning (lit. *bāṭin*) of the knowledge object; discovering the deeper/inner meaning of the knowledge object,

12 Al-Dabūsī does not refer to a specific passage. He probably has passages of the Qur'an like Q 2:34 in mind.

13 Al-Dabūsī, *Taqwīm*, 466.

14 Al-Dabūsī, *Taqwīm*, 466. We can observe that al-Dabūsī places a stronger emphasis on certainty than is generally found in Islamic legal theory. Whereas many scholars consider most types of knowledge in the realm of *fiqh* as being *ẓannī*, al-Dabūsī locates knowledge in the realm of certainty. This could be the reason why he classifies *ẓāhir*-statements in the religious sources as being a *qaṭʿī* evidence (since *qaṭʿī* evidences lead to *yaqīn*) and not *ẓannī*. See Serdar Kurnaz, *Methoden zur Normderivation im islamischen Recht: Eine Rekonstruktion der Methoden zur Interpretation autoritativer textueller Quellen bei ausgewählten islamischen Rechtsschulen* (Berlin: EB-Verlag, 2016), 268–69.

however, can lead to 'wisdom' (*ḥikma*). It is this second type of *maʿrifa* which allows to obtain the inner meaning of the knowledge object, which al-Dabūsī calls *fiqh*. *Fiqh* is a complete understanding of the knowledge object through which the heart reaches its deeper, inner meaning alongside the outward knowledge. With this deep knowledge 'the heart can enjoy' the knowledge obtained (*yaltadhdh al-qalb bihi*). In this case, *maʿrifa* becomes *fiqh*. However, here again, al-Dabūsī equates *fiqh* with *ʿilm*, which could be understood in the sense of al-Dabūsī's attempt to underline that all of what he discusses about *maʿrifa*, *iʿtiqād*, and *fiqh* is part of the notion of 'knowledge' (*ʿilm*).[15] Unlike the definitions of *fiqh* offered by his contemporaries, which are narrower in their scope as being juristic knowledge,[16] al-Dabūsī sees *fiqh* as knowledge in general, going so far as to include the inner dimensions of the knowledge object.

So far, al-Dabūsī did not define what a solid proof for obtaining knowledge is. Now, he defines 'proof' (*dalīl*) as a necessary requirement for gaining knowledge. Proof for him has two types: sensually 'perceptible' (*ḥissī*) and 'rational' (*ʿaqlī*) proofs. For al-Dabūsī, human beings and animals share the ability to obtain knowledge about actual events in daily life based on sense perception, whereas only human beings are able to grasp rational proofs through reflection. Al-Dabūsī now turns towards the question regarding how to gain knowledge with respect to these proofs. One can obtain knowledge through either 'memorizing' (*ḥifẓ*) the proofs, which are 'conclusive arguments' (*ḥujaj*, sg. *ḥujja*), like the 'revealed texts' (*nuṣūṣ*) in the Qur'an and Sunna, or through a (full) 'understanding' (*fahm*) of the proofs. For al-Dabūsī one can only obtain knowledge at the highest level (which is *fiqh*) through reflection and deeper understanding of the proofs; memorizing is not sufficient for obtaining the inner meaning of the knowledge object. Thus, for him, *fiqh* is 'understanding and reflection' (*fahm*). In contrast, animals enjoy their knowledge according to their sense perception and enjoy it in each moment; they have no way to profound understanding. For humans, however, the highest degree of joy is to act according to knowledge based on (rational?) proofs.[17] Rational proofs for al-Dabūsī can be divided in four different types: a priori knowledge, 'reflection, inquiry' (*taʾammul*, *naẓar*), 'experience' (*tajriba*), and sense

15 Al-Dabūsī, *Taqwīm*, 467.

16 See for example Abū al-Maʿālī al-Juwaynī, *al-Waraqāt*. He describes *fiqh* as being more specific than knowledge: *al-fiqh akhaṣṣ min al-ʿilm*, see https://waraqat.vishanoff.com/a/a3/ (consulted online on 19 February 2022). Likewise, most definitions of *fiqh* attempt to distinguish *fiqh* as a specific type of knowledge from general knowledge.

17 Al-Dabūsī, *Taqwīm*, 467–68.

perception[18]—here we see again an overlap in his basic taxonomy of proofs in sensually perceptible and rational.

Once al-Dabūsī established that reflection and reasoning on proofs and their inner meaning lead to a full understanding (*fiqh*) of the knowledge object, he focuses on the rational grounds on which the law is based, as we will see in the next section.

2.2 *Al-Dabūsī's Epistemological Frame of Law*

In *Taqwīm*, the order of the respective chapters is the opposite of presented here: al-Dabūsī discusses first the epistemological frame of his understanding of law and then defines knowledge and categorizes it. However, it is safe to assume that he had the definition of *fiqh* and knowledge in mind while writing the chapters on epistemology before finishing his book with the definition of knowledge, *fiqh*, and the other related terms that we already discussed above. It is possible, however, to conclude that 'law' (*sharʿ*) according to al-Dabūsī emerges within the epistemological frame that we find in *Taqwīm*. The following chart gives an overview how al-Dabūsī frames his understanding of law:

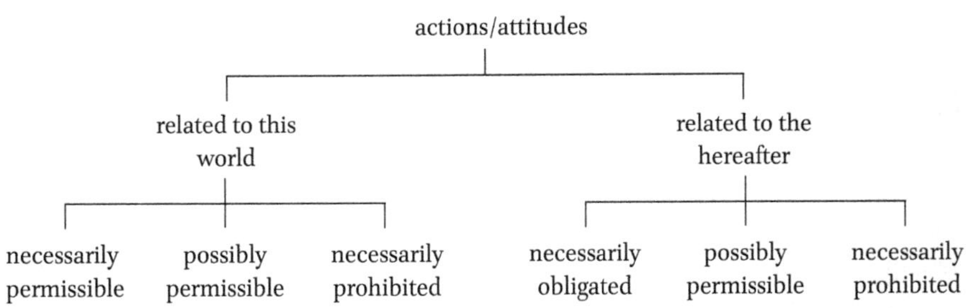

FIGURE 3.3 Diagram showing al-Dabūsī's six-part typology of law: necessarily/possibly permissible, obligated, and prohibited actions across worldly and religious domains

18 Al-Dabūsī, *Taqwīm*, 448. Bedir shows that al-Dabūsī always attempts to distinguish four categories, including in *al-Amad*, which at times leads him to artificial categorizations. A possible reason for the continuous fourfold division of categories may be the Neoplatonic influence, especially the influence of the *Brethren of Purity* (*Ikhwān al-ṣafāʾ*), who "shared the Pythagorean insistence on numbers, especially on the number four, due to the importance of the latter in their view of spiritual realm (for spiritual principles)." Bedir, "Interplay," 265–66; cf. Ian Richard Netton, *Muslim Neoplatonism: An Introduction to the Thought of the Brethren of Purity* (Ikhwān al-Ṣafāʾ) (Edinburgh: Edinburgh University Press, 1991), 9–12.

Al-Dabūsī distinguishes systematically between two dimensions of law regarding (1) actions (and attitudes) concerning this life and (2) those related to the hereafter. Regarding these two dimensions, in al-Dabūsī's system, the law has two outward borders: (1) obligations and necessarily permissible actions and (2) necessarily prohibited actions. In between these two borders, there are actions that are facultatively permissible.[19] The epistemological frame, then, consists according to al-Dabūsī of six elements all of which are determined based on rational argumentation:

(1) Necessarily permissible actions related to worldly matters;
(2) Necessary religious obligations;
(3) Necessarily prohibited actions related to worldly matters;
(4) Necessary religious prohibitions;
(5) Possibly permissible actions related to worldly matters;
(6) Possibly permissible religious actions.

It is noteworthy that al-Dabūsī makes use of a *fiqh*-value language by using the following three technical terms: 'obligation' (*wujūb*), 'prohibition' (*taḥrīm*), and 'permission' (*ibāḥa*).[20] This already indicates a correlation between rational reasoning and the *fiqh*'s value system of actions.

2.2.1 Necessarily Permissible Actions Related to Worldly Matters

For al-Dabūsī, there are certain actions that fall under the rubric of necessarily permissible actions:

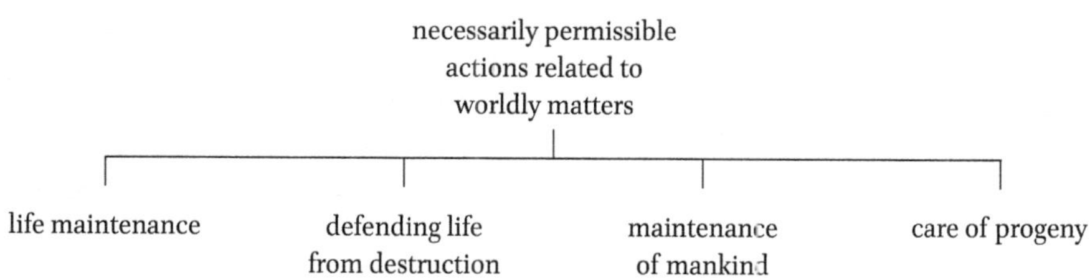

FIGURE 3.4 Depiction of actions such as eating, protection, procreation, and child-rearing as rationally and legally necessary

Al-Dabūsī states, that the Sharia (i.e., revelation) should not ignore these actions; furthermore, it cannot prohibit them. Since there is full accordance between law (revelation) and rational arguments, these actions should be permissible. The performance of these actions is necessary for the existence

19 Al-Dabūsī, *Taqwīm*, 449, 451, 455–56, 458, 462.

20 Murteza Bedir, "Reason and Revelation: Abū Zayd al-Dabbūsī on Rational Proofs," *Islamic Studies*, 43 (2004), 227–45, here 235.

of people, which is why their permissibility is argued rationally. Since the law should be based on these necessities, these actions should be deemed as definitively permissible. These actions for al-Dabūsī are of four kind, although this fourfold division could be narrowed down to two:[21] (1) actions necessary for life maintenance, (2) actions defending life from destruction, (3) actions necessary for maintenance of mankind (lit. *mā yaqūmu bihi l-jins*), and (4) actions which enable the care of progeny (lit. *mā taqūmu bihi l-tarbiya*). As Bedir summarizes it, necessarily permissible acts are thus "eating and drinking, protecting the body from external harm, having sexual intercourse, and rearing children."[22] These actions are all good in their very nature, which is why they should be permissible.

2.2.2 Necessary Religious Obligations

In the same way, al-Dabūsī argues that there are actions and attitudes that are rationally argued to be obligatory; the law should contain these obligations, the opposite is impossible. Al-Dabūsī uses here the word *maʿrifa* for this type of knowledge, since *maʿrifa* refers to more than merely knowing something; it rather refers to a full understanding of an object or an idea. We can summarize these actions as follows:[23]

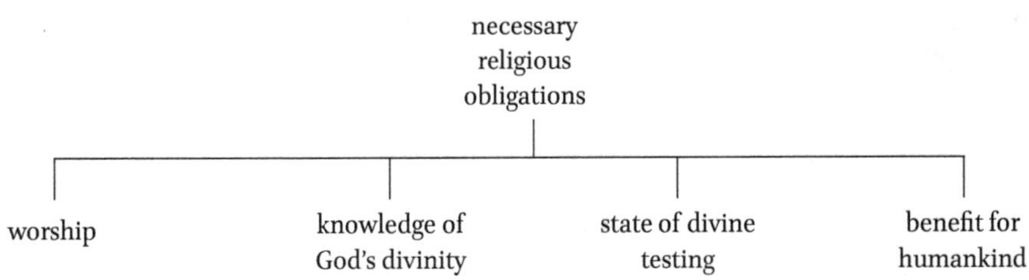

FIGURE 3.5 Diagram showing core obligations like worship, knowledge of divine testing, and acknowledgment of divine creation

For al-Dabūsī, human beings must necessarily have knowledge about the obligation for worship, which results from the knowledge of God's divinity. This again leads to the necessary obligation to know that human beings were created to be tested; they are in a state of divine testing in this world that has an impact on the life in the hereafter. Further, human beings are obligated by knowledge of the fact "that the creation of the world is conducive to worldly

21 Al-Dabūsī, *Taqwīm*, 449–50.
22 Bedir, "Reason and Revelation," 236.
23 Al-Dabūsī, *Taqwīm*, 451.

and other-worldly benefits for mankind."[24] Al-Dabūsī combines rational arguments with proofs from the Qur'an to show the necessarily obligatory nature of these four types of knowledge. For example, if one knows that he/she is created, then he/she necessarily should know that a creator exists. Again, since 'pointlessness' (*ʿabath*) is impossible for God, the creation must have a meaningful objective, which is to test people so that they will be rewarded or punished in the hereafter. This correlates for al-Dabūsī with Qur'anic verses like Q 51:56.[25] For al-Dabūsī this type of religious obligation is not an obligation to perform, but rather a pure obligation related to knowledge, that means the knowledge of being obliged to do something as opposed to be obliged to act in a specific way.[26]

2.2.3 Necessarily Prohibited Actions Related to Worldly Matters

After having established the rationally argued obligations and necessarily permissible actions for worldly and religious matters, al-Dabūsī discusses definitive prohibitions related to worldly matters. For him, this category of actions has again four types:[27]

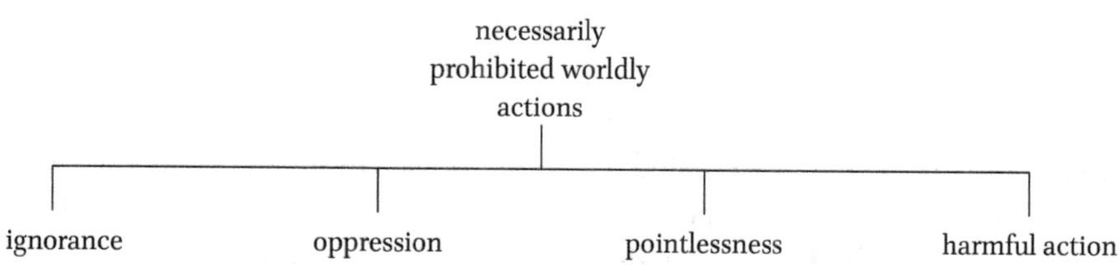

FIGURE 3.6 Diagram showing *jahl*, *ẓulm*, *ʿabath*, and *safah* as rationally prohibited actions

For al-Dabūsī, 'ignorance' (*jahl*) is prohibited, as it is an action or an attitude that manifests itself as a lack of use of one's ability to think in light of the reason. It is as if someone closed his/her eyes to avoid daylight and walked in darkness although light was available not to go astray. 'Oppression' (*ẓulm*) is *a fortiori* forbidden when it is already the case for *jahl*, because oppression or unrighteousness is to put something not in its proper place on purpose. 'Pointlessness/absurdity' (*ʿabath*) is forbidden, since pointlessness for al-Dabūsī is to do something without benefit and is therefore forbidden. Harmful action (*safah*, 'foolishness') is again doing something without benefit;

24 Bedir, "Reason and Revelation," 238.

25 Al-Dabūsī, *Taqwīm*, 451–54.

26 Bedir, "Reason and Revelation," 238.

27 Al-Dabūsī, *Taqwīm*, 455.

furthermore, it leads to harm. Accordingly, since *ʿabath* is forbidden then *safah* is as well, since *safah* is worse than *ʿabath*.

2.2.4 Necessary Religious Prohibitions

Al-Dabūsī defines four kinds of rationally argued definitive religious prohibitions. However, he explicitly says that the following four prohibitions are not the opposite of what he presented earlier as religious obligations (see above 2.2.2). Further, they are prohibited because they are 'intrinsically evil' (*qabīḥ li-ʿaynihi*).

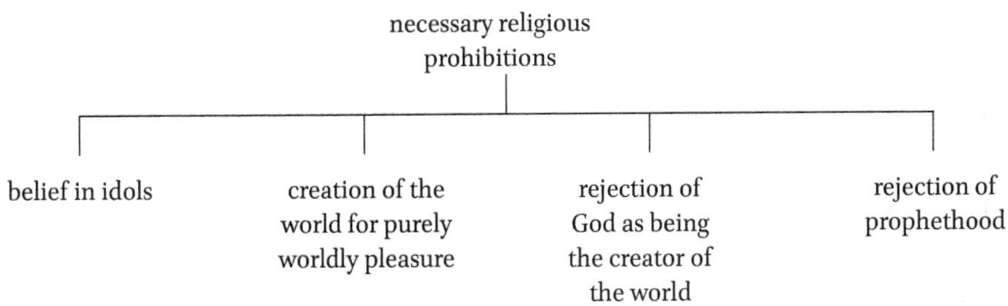

FIGURE 3.7 Diagram showing belief in idols, denial of God or prophets, and the creation of the world for merely worldly pleasure as forbidden

For al-Dabūsī, it is rationally forbidden to believe in idols, since idols are created just as human beings are created; created beings cannot share divinity with God. Thus, believing in created things as objects of worship is forbidden.[28] It is also forbidden to believe in the idea that creatures have merely been created for the purposes of worldly pleasure in this life. Additionally, for al-Dabūsī, it is forbidden to pursue only worldly desires. The next two categories of religious prohibitions that are definitively proven and cannot be overruled by any law are the rejection of God as the 'creator' (*ṣāniʿ*) or 'the rejection of God's existence' (*al-kufr bi-llāh*) and the rejection of the prophethood, which is the channel to declare human beings that they are in a state of 'trial' (*jazāʾ*) by God with regard to reward or punishment in the hereafter.[29] The latter means that prophets proclaim the existence of the Day of Judgement and therefore one must accept the prophethood of prophets; its rejection is prohibited.

2.2.5 Possibly Permissible Actions Related to Worldly Matters

So far, al-Dabūsī established the outward borders of the law (obligations–prohibitions) on a rational basis. The law cannot contradict these obligations

28 In this regard he refers here to Q 7:194.

29 Al-Dabūsī, *Taqwīm*, 456–57.

and prohibitions, and cannot override them. Now, al-Dabūsī focuses on the sphere of law in between these two borders. He marks this sphere as being the sphere of permissible actions. For him, 'permissible' (*jā'iz*) in this context means that something can be 'rationally facultative' (*mubāḥan 'aqlan*) and is not necessarily obligatory, so that it is possible to prohibit it, if there is a revelatory or rational proof for its prohibition. Thus, he follows—while knowing that scholars argue here differently—the principle of the fundamental permissibility of actions unless there is proof for a prohibition (*al-ibāḥa ḥattā yaqūmu l-dalīlu al-ḥaẓri*). Al-Dabūsī notes that reason and Sharia (revelation) do not contradict each other in this sphere; they are both *ḥujja* and confirm each other. If Sharia prohibits something on this level, then this is a proof for the fact that reason allows its prohibition. This prohibition was so far hidden due to the lack of sufficient reflection and reasoning.

Again, al-Dabūsī finds four categories for rationally argued facultatively permissible actions related to worldly matters, which again could have been summarized in fewer categories: (1) means for existence beyond essential needs, (2) saving of property of one or more than one kind (e.g., accumulating wealth), (3) improvement of life, which is not directly related to surviving or to the necessities of existence, and (4) sexual intercourse for mere pleasure without the wish for procreation.[30] Al-Dabūsī lists several reasons for the prohibition of adultery, wine, gambling, etc., since these prohibitions fall under the category of possibly permissible actions; in times of necessity, one is allowed to do something prohibited of this kind, like eating pork when in danger of starving. For al-Dabūsī, rejecting such concessions could even lead to a sinful decision.[31]

Al-Dabūsī underlines that the principle of the fundamental permission of actions (*al-aṣl al-ibāḥa*), which he follows here, can be derived from the Qur'an; he refers to Q 6:145: "Say, 'I do not find in what has been revealed to me that anyone is forbidden to eat anything except carrion or spilt blood, or the flesh of swine—for that is indeed unclean—or an impiety offered to other than God.' But should someone be compelled, without being rebellious or aggressive, indeed your Lord is all-forgiving, all-merciful." Al-Dabūsī states that the precept of permissibility is, however, speculative, thus not a definitive, rather an 'evident' (*ẓāhir*) proof. Because it is *ẓāhir*, Sharia can show that actions of this kind are prohibited—there is no definitive reason that hinders Sharia to rule other than permissibility. Here, al-Dabūsī refers to the method of *takhṣīṣ*, the specification of a general rule or utterance: the Sharia renders a permissible

30 Al-Dabūsī, *Taqwīm*, 458; cf. Bedir, "Reason and Revelation," 239.

31 Al-Dabūsī, *Taqwīm*, 459.

action as being prohibited specifically, although reason considered it to be permissible in general terms. Thus, the revelation can specify permissible actions; where it does not, one can apply this general rule of permissibility.[32]

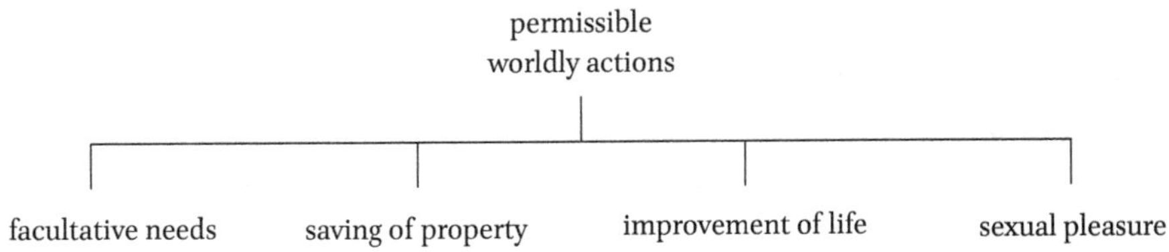

FIGURE 3.8 Diagram showing facultative needs like wealth accumulation, luxury, and sexual pleasure as conditionally permitted

2.2.6 Possibly Permissible Religious Actions

Finally, al-Dabūsī presents four positions in order to illustrate how to deal with religious permissible actions—this typology differs from the above-mentioned categories and does not describe different types of actions, rather four different views on permissible religious actions; it is not clear, why al-Dabūsī deviates from his approach: (1) permissible religious activities are nonsense since God did not obligate us to do so; (2) all of them are rationally good; (3) they are all obligatory as far as it is possible to pursue them (an opinion held by mystics, the Ṣūfiyya, as al-Dabūsī informs us); the immediate punishment for ignorance, however, needs a 'revelatory' (*sharʿī*) proof. (4) The fourth position is al-Dabūsī's: it is obligatory to believe in God and to obey His commands; one has to wait until He commands a religious obligation, knowing, however, that permissible religious actions are rationally good and not bad.[33]

2.2.7 Concluding Remarks on al-Dabūsī's Epistemology

Al-Dabūsī has a holistic understanding of *fiqh* and bases the 'law' (*sharʿ*) on rational grounds. Interestingly, he makes use of Sufi terminology in articulating his legal epistemology. This holistic understanding can be proven with respect to Bedir's study of al-Dabūsī's *al-Amad*. Bedir observes that al-Dabūsī seeks to establish a juristic spiritualism where rationality is an important aspect of it.[34] It leads al-Dabūsī to reflect on esoteric (*bāṭin*) knowledge in close relation to 'exoteric' (*ẓāhir*) knowledge.[35] In *al-Amad*, 'knowledge/cognition' (*maʿrifa*) is essential for salvation. In *Taqwīm*, *maʿrifa* is also important and comprises

32 Al-Dabūsī, *Taqwīm*, 460–61.
33 Al-Dabūsī, *Taqwīm*, 462–64.
34 Bedir, "Interplay," 258.
35 Bedir, "Interplay," 260–61.

fiqh, which, as we have seen above, bears two types of knowledge: *ẓāhir* and *bāṭin*. Al-Dabūsī's reliance on Sufism can be explained through the historical circumstances under which he wrote his work. He lived within the struggle of traditionalism, rationalism and Sufism: al-Dabūsī attempts to underline that the Ḥanafī tradition is compatible with the Sunni tradition, respects both traditionalist tendencies and Sufi approaches, which became increasingly predominant under Sunni circles.[36] However, he attempts to adhere to the rationalistic framework within the Ḥanafī school, although there was no one specific Ḥanafī theory of rationalism.

To sum up: al-Dabūsī tries to synthesise these three approaches in his epistemology. Doing so, he was aware of the fact that he could be seen as a Muʿtazilī scholar, which he, if we follow Bedir's analysis,[37] tried to avoid. We can observe this effort in his discussion of the question, whether reason is able to know God without the existence of revelation. Here al-Dabūsī once again presents four different opinions: (1) God cannot be known by reason without the aid of revelation, (2) reason can perceive God independently from revelation, but there is no obligation to argue, that this knowledge obliges humans to believe in God, unless the revelation necessitates it, (3) reason can know God independently from revelation and one is obliged to recognize God before revelation, and (4) the question is absurd, since humankind was never left without revelation.[38] Al-Dabūsī suggests his preference for the second option,[39] although his approach to this issue seems contradictory.[40] He attempts to find a middle way between a traditionalist approach and the rationalistic approach of the Muʿtazila, since he is unwilling to ignore rational proofs, because they are important for him in jurisprudential and Sufi matters alike.

In his writings on legal theory and epistemology, al-Dabūsī argues for the outward borders of the law on rational bases and establishes the idea that revelation and reason do not contradict. The revelation cannot cross these borders and does not override them; it takes shape within them.[41] When revelation

36 Bedir, "Interplay," 256–58; see for historical circumstances as well Bedir, "Reason and Revelation," 234–35.

37 Bedir, "Interplay;" Bedir, "Reason and Revelation."

38 Al-Dabūsī, *Taqwīm*, 442; Bedir, "Reason and Revelation," 233.

39 Al-Dabūsī, *Taqwīm*, 446.

40 Bedir, "Reason and Revelation," 233–34.

41 We know that Abū Manṣūr al-Māturīdī (d. 333/944), a key figure for Central Asian Ḥanafī scholars, held a similar position, where reason and revelation do not contradict. They are not related to each other in hierarchy; cf. Ulrich Rudolph, "Ratio und Überlieferung in der Erkenntnislehre al-Ašʿarī's und al-Māturīdī's," *Zeitschrift der Deutschen Morgenländischen Gesellschaft*, 142/1 (1992), 72–78, here 84–85. For a new approach to al-Māturīdī's

forbids something, it correlates with reason. Reason, however, has primacy over revelation, since if something is necessarily permissible, obligatory or prohibited on rational grounds, the revelation cannot override it. Consequently, al-Dabūsī's epistemological framework affects his legal theory, which we can see, for instance, in the discussion about the following question: If an action is forbidden by law, does it have any legal efficacy if someone performs a forbidden action? In the next section, I will examine al-Dabūsī's discussion on this question with a particular attention to his overall epistemology.

2.3 *Al-Dabūsī on the Question of* fasād al-manhī ʿanh

Al-Dabūsī discusses the question that, if one commits a prohibited action, for instance concludes a sales contract with interest (*ribā*), whether this action, this sales contract in the example, is legally effective (*mashrūʿ*)? To answer this question, al-Dabūsī divides prohibitions into different categories—his categorization here correlates with the one for commands.[42]

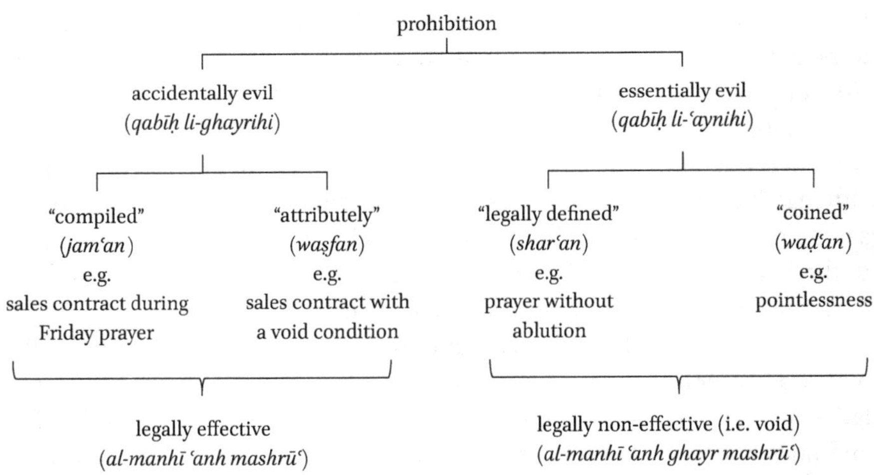

FIGURE 3.9 Taxonomy of four types of prohibitions: essential by nature or law, and accidental by attribute or proximity—with legal consequences

The first category of prohibitions is subject to evil actions that are evil in themselves, e.g., essentially evil actions. The second category is subject to evil actions because of other factors; they are accidentally evil. Al-Dabūsī further divides essential evil actions into two subcategories: first, evil as it was coined

epistemology, see Hureyre Kam, *Das Böse als Gottesbeweis: Die Theodizee al-Māturīdīs im Lichte seiner Epistemologie, Kosmologie und Ontologie* (Berlin: EB-Verlag, 2019), 29–97.

42 Al-Dabūsī, *Taqwīm*, 44–46.

(lit. *waḍʿan*) as such and, secondly, evil defined as such through law. The second category also has two subcategories: First, evil can occur as an attribute of the action, and secondly, it can be in close proximity with an evil action and can therefore be compiled with it (lit. *mā jāwarahū jamʿan*).[43]

Examples for evil actions, which are coined as such, are foolishness, or harmful actions respectively (*safah*) and pointlessness (*ʿabath*). We have already seen that *safah* and *ʿabath* are two of the four types of rationally argued definitively prohibited actions related to worldly matters. This means that these actions are evil actions, which we can grasp as such on rational bases. This is for al-Dabūsī the reason why they are called *safah* and *ʿabath*: Even their names show their evil nature, or the other way around: because they are evil, we use words with negative connotations for them. Because such actions are essentially evil, they are void and have no legal efficacy. An example for the second category of essentially evil actions through law is the sale of semen before the animal was created by God since the law shows that semen is not to be classified as property (*māl mutaqawwim*) which can be subject to sales contracts. These types of actions are void as well.[44]

The third category, the accidental evil, which has evilness not as an essential feature, is for example a sales contract with a void condition (*sharṭ fāsid*) like interest (*al-ribā*). It is not that the sales contract is evil essentially; rather, it has to be regarded as an evil action only because of a *ribā*-clause, i.e., having a void condition. It is evil, because it does not fulfil the required condition of equivalence (*mumāthala*) in sales contracts, as al-Dabūsī underlines. An example for the fourth category is sales contracts during the time of the Friday prayer, which is forbidden according to Q 62:9. Al-Dabūsī says that there is no essential linkage between sales contracts and Friday prayer; they are completely independent from each other, neither of them is part of the other. There is a proximity between them only if someone wants to engage in trade during the Friday prayer time that makes this action evil. The reason is that trade distracts from the prayer; according to al-Dabūsī, one cannot pray and engage in trade at the same time.[45]

Al-Dabūsī's conclusion is that the first two types of actions are void. They are essentially evil, therefore prohibited and do not have any legal effects (they are *ghayr mashrūʿayn*). Therefore, if revelation and reason show that something is essentially evil, the prohibited action is void. The other two types, however, are, although being prohibited, legally effective, because these actions are

43 Al-Dabūsī, *Taqwīm*, 52.

44 Al-Dabūsī, *Taqwīm*, 52.

45 Al-Dabūsī, *Taqwīm*, 52.

not essentially evil rather linked to something else, which is evil. Thus, it is a sinful action to engage in trading during the Friday prayer, however, the sales contract that was concluded at that time is valid and legally effective.[46] In al-Dabūsī's epistemological framework, such actions fall under the category of possibly permissible actions related to worldly matters, therefore they are not directly void.

Al-Dabūsī subsumes these four categories into two kinds of actions: actions grasped through senses (*ḥissan*) as evil. These categories are void, since they are equal with the essentially evil actions. On the other hand, there are actions prohibited through law (*sharʿan*). They are accidentally evil; the evil aspect of the action is not essential, it is an accidental attribute.[47] We can conclude that al-Dabūsī locates this legal theoretical question within the framework of his epistemology. Since the first two categories correlate with the rationally proven prohibited actions, they are legally ineffective and thus void. Since the other two categories fall in the sphere of possibly permissible actions, their prohibition is not due to their essential evilness but other factors. Therefore, they are not void and have legal efficacy despite being prohibited.

This distinction of evil actions was highly influential in the Ḥanafī tradition, as al-Dabūsī played a significant role in shaping Ḥanafī legal theory.[48] Shams al-A'imma al-Sarakhsī (d. 483/1090), for example, argues for the same distinction. He differentiates forbidden actions similar to al-Dabūsī's four- and two-fold taxonomy in order to answer the question whether a prohibited action is void or not.[49] We will see in the next section that another Central Asian Ḥanafī scholar, ʿAlā' al-Dīn al-Samarqandī (d. 539/1144),[50] discussed this categorization as well. He referred to al-Dabūsī's categorisation of prohibitions but

46 Al-Dabūsī, *Taqwīm*, 53.

47 Al-Dabūsī, *Taqwīm*, 54.

48 Bedir, "Reason and Revelation," 230–31.

49 Shams al-A'imma al-Sarakhsī, *Uṣūl al-Sarakhsī*, ed. Abū al-Wafā' al-Afghānī (Beirut: Dār al-kutub al-ʿilmiyya, 1413/1993), vol. 1, 80–82. The same is true for Abū al-ʿUsr al-Bazdawī (d. 482/1089), see ʿAbd al-ʿAzīz al-Bukhārī, *Kashf al-asrār ʿan Uṣūl Fakhr al-Islām al-Bazdawī*, ed. ʿAbd Allāh Maḥmūd Muḥammad ʿUmar (Beirut: Dār al-kutub al-ʿilmiyya, 1417/1997), vol. 1, 376–78. Hacer Yetkin says that al-Dabūsī was the first one who made such a distinction; Hacer Yetkin, *Hanefî Usûlünün Kurucularından Debûsî ve Usûl Anlayışı* (Istanbul: IFAV, 2017), 229–31.

50 On al-Samarqandī's life, see Wilferd Madelung, "ʿAlā'-al-Dīn Samarqandī," in *Encyclopaedia Iranica*, vol. 1/7, pp. 782–83 (an updated version is available online at: https://www.iranicaonline.org/articles/ala-al-din-samarqandi-abu-bakr-mohammad-b/); Angelika Brodersen, "ʿAlā' al-Dīn al-Samarqandī," in *Encyclopaedia of Islam Three Online*, ed. Kate Fleet, Gudrun Krämer, Denis Matringe, John Nawas and Devin J. Stewart (available online at https://doi.org/10.1163/1573-3912_ei3_COM_26318).

reinterpreted it according to a Māturīdī theological framework. I will now turn to this interpretation of al-Dabūsī's categorization of prohibitions to give another example of the correlation between law and theology.

3 'Alā' al-Dīn al-Samarqandī's (d. 539/1144) Reinterpretation of the Categories of Prohibition

Al-Samarqandī reinterprets al-Dabūsī's fourfold division of prohibitions due to his theological concerns. He is the first scholar to overtly mention that he tries to find a way to delineate a Māturīdī framework for Ḥanafī legal theory. This is not a coincidence; already his master, Abū al-Muʿīn al-Nasafī (d. 508/1115), was committed to giving the Māturīdī *kalām* a systematic shape and defending it against competing theological schools.[51]

We have some historical evidence for an explanation why al-Samarqandī sought to establish a Māturīdī *uṣūl*. We know that by the 5th/11th century Muʿtazilī literature and ideas were suppressed, and that the Ashʿarī views and ideas dominated the field of *kalām* and *uṣūl*. The rare survival of Muʿtazilī *uṣūl* ideas were those of al-Qāḍī ʿAbd al-Jabbār (d. 415/1025, Shāfiʿī in *fiqh*) and Abū al-Ḥusayn al-Baṣrī (Ḥanafī in *fiqh*), highly conserved in Shāfiʿī (additionally in Mālikī and Ḥanbalī), as well as in Zaydī literature.[52] During that period, Shāfiʿī and Mālikī scholars were predominantly Ashʿarīs. Ḥanafīs, however, held mixed theological views: many of them were either Muʿtazilī in their theological views, e.g. Abū al-Ḥasan al-Karkhī (d. 340/952) and Abū Bakr al-Jaṣṣāṣ (d. 370/981), or were influenced by Muʿtazilī views, like al-Dabūsī. Al-Dabūsī and other like-minded scholars were aware that some of their theological positions were Muʿtazilī in their origins and acknowledged this fact in their writings. Other scholars, like Shams al-A'imma al-Sarakhsī (d. 483/1090), were looking for Sunni positions, but were not insisting on them—they did not insist on them at all costs and were clearly non-Muʿtazilī but not anti-Muʿtazilī. There were also those scholars who adopted positions similar to

51 Ulrich Rudolph, "Das Entstehen der Māturīdīya," *Zeitschrift der Deutschen Morgenländischen Gesellschaft*, 147 (1997), 394–404.

52 For ʿAbd al-Jabbār's jurisprudential principles see al-Qāḍī ʿAbd al-Jabbār, *al-Mughnī fī abwāb al-tawḥīd wa-l-ʿadl*, vol. 17. *al-sharʿiyyāt*, ed. Ṭaha Ḥusayn (Cairo: Wizārat al-thaqāfa wa-l-irshād al-qawmī al-mu'assasa al-miṣriyya al-ʿāmma, without date). For Abū al-Ḥusayn al-Baṣrī see his *al-Muʿtamad fī uṣūl al-fiqh*, ed. Khalīl al-Mays (Beirut: Dār al-kutub al-ʿilmiyya, 1426/2005). On Zaydi literature, see Hassan Ansari and Sabine Schmidtke, "The Muʿtazilī and Zaydī Reception of Abū l-Ḥusayn al-Baṣrī's *Kitāb al-Muʿtamad fī Uṣūl al-fiqh*: A Bibliographical Note," *Islamic Law and Society*, 20/1 (2013), 90–109.

Ashʿarī theology as well as those who advocated Murjiʾī theological positions. Thus, there was a vacuum for Ḥanafīs in their theological views, even though they belonged to the Sunni tradition. They could not regard Ashʿarī *kalām* as their own, since they were always in struggle with the Shāfiʿī tradition, who were almost entirely Ashʿarī. In these centuries, we see increasing attempts to underline the specifically Māturīdī nature of Ḥanafī legal theory and emphasis on a geographically marked scholarly tradition, i.e., scholars from Samarqand or Transoxania (*mā warāʾ al-nahr*), as we see it in the writings of al-Nasafī, al-Samarqandī, and Abū al-Thanāʾ Maḥmūd b. Zayd al-Lāmishī (d. in the first half of the 6th/12th century).[53]

This vacuum could be avoided with reference to another Sunni scholar beside Abū al-Ḥasan al-Ashʿarī (d. 324/935–6).[54] Abū Manṣūr al-Māturīdī (d. 333/944) was a highly influential Sunni scholar whose theological views attracted the attention of Ḥanafis early on. While he was a contemporary of al-Ashʿarī, his theology was revived and made more prominent through the efforts of Abū al-Muʿīn in his *Tabṣirat al-Adilla* (*Elucidation of proofs*).[55] Al-Māturīdī was *the* eponym, who fitted perfectly to fulfil the gap of theological systematization for *uṣūl al-fiqh* since he fiercely criticized Muʿtazilī principles in his *opus magnum*, *Kitāb al-Tawḥīd.* Since the Muʿtazilīs were in decline, al-Māturīdī was the perfect authority who distanced himself from them and at the same time was different enough from al-Ashʿarī to be regarded as the eponym of an independent theological school. Be it as it may, if we consider later Ḥanafī sources, we can conclude that al-Samarqandī was only partially successful with his project.[56]

For al-Samarqandī, *uṣūl al-fiqh* is a branch of *uṣūl al-dīn* and, therefore, every *uṣūl al-fiqh* should be based on *kalām* presuppositions. He is concerned about Ḥanafī literature written until his lifetime: he complains about

53 On the theological developments during the fourth and fifth centuries, see Murteza Bedir, “Mâtürîdî Fıkıh Usûlü: Gerçek mi Kurgu mu?” in *Büyük Türk Bilgini İmâm Mâtürîdî ve Mâtürîdîlik*, ed. İlyas Çelebi (Istanbul: M. Ü. İlahiyat Fakültesi Vakfı Yayınları, 2012), 412–20; Aron Zysow, “Muʿtazilism and Māturīdism in Ḥanafī Legal Theory,” in *Studies in Islamic Legal Theory*, ed. Bernard Weiss (Leiden: Brill, 2002), 235–65; Dale J. Correa, “Taking a Theological Turn in Legal Theory: Regional Priority and Theology in Transoxanian Ḥanafī Thought,” in *Locating the Sharīʿa: Legal Fluidity in Theory, History and Practice*, ed. Sohaira Siddiqui (Leiden: Brill, 2019), 111–26.

54 On al-Ashʿarī and the theological school named after him, see Daniel Gimaret, *La doctrine d'al-Ashʿarī* (Paris: Les Éditions du Cerf, 1990).

55 On al-Māturīdī and his reception, see Rudolph, *Sunnī Theology in Samarqand*; Angelika Brodersen, *Der unbekannte* kalām: *Theologische Positionen der frühen Māturīdīya am Beispiel der Attributenlehre* (Münster: LIT, 2014).

56 Bedir, “Mâtürîdî Fıkıh Usûlü,” 412–20; Correa, “Taking a Theological Turn in Legal Theory.”

the purely juristic style of argumentation in these *uṣūl*-books.[57] In contrast to al-Dabūsī, al-Samarqandī does not have a holistic understanding of *fiqh*, rather, he relates *fiqh* to knowledge based on reasoning that does not ignore revelation. Reasoning in this sense is then inferential (*istidlālī*) and revelatory (*samʿī*). This type of knowledge can be certain or presumptive.[58] Thus, al-Samarqandī does not relate to law on purely rational bases as al-Dabūsī did before; he is more concerned about the theological bases of law (*sharʿ*). Therefore, he reinterprets some *uṣūl*-related discussions theologically, for instance, the above-mentioned fourfold division of prohibitions that goes back to al-Dabūsī.

Al-Samarqandī quotes al-Dabūsī nearly word by word. He says that there are two categories (*qismayn*) of prohibitions and that each of them has two further forms (*nawʿān*). They are four in total, and all correspond to al-Dabūsī's categories.[59] Following up, al-Samarqandī says that their *mashāyikh*, i.e., Māturīdī scholars in Central Asia,[60] saw in this description of prohibitions difficulties concerning its wording (he says: *fī hādhā l-kalām khalal*). For him, al-Dabūsī's statement that prohibitions have different categories can only be regarded as correct when we interpret it properly. The wording of al-Dabūsī's statement is, however, problematic because, for al-Samarqandī, it is not allowed to say that actions can be evil in their very essence. This would lead to the problem that God does evil deeds since actions could be evil in their essence, which is impossible according to al-Samarqandī. Further, if actions were essentially evil, people would have no dissent about the meaning of *safah* and *ʿabath*; two examples quoted by al-Dabūsī earlier. Since reasonable people (*ʿuqalāʾ*) disagree on what these two words mean, they cannot be essentially evil. For al-Samarqandī, the correct interpretation of the statement that something can be evil, however, is that actions are evil because of an additional meaning (*maʿnā zāʾid*), which is related to the one who acts (e.g. the *fāʿil*) or to something or to someone else. In terms of *safah*, it is essentially evil because of an additional meaning, which is the lack of "a commendable result [of the action] or alike" (*al-ʿāqiba al-ḥamīda wa-naḥwa dhālika*). The additional meaning cannot be related to the action, it does not exist with the action, since an attribute

---

57 ʿAlāʾ al-Dīn al-Samarqandī, *Mīzān al-uṣūl fī natāʾij al-ʿuqūl*, ed. Muḥammad Zakī ʿAbd al-Barr (Doha: Matbaʿat ad-Dawḥa, 1404/1984), 1–5.

58 Al-Samarqandī, *Mīzān*, 9–10. Al-Samarqandī follows the common taxonomy with knowledge being *ḍarūrī*, and *istidlālī* (which is the same as *al-ʿilm al-muktasab*), having three sources: reason, sense perception and transmission: al-Samarqandī, *Mīzān*, 8–11.

59 Al-Samarqandī, *Mīzān*, 226.

60 Correa, "Taking a Theological Turn in Legal Theory," 122.

and an action are both accidents (*aʿrāḍ*, sg. *ʿaraḍ*), and an accident cannot exist in combination with an accident only.

To understand this argument, we have to make a short excursus about what *ʿaraḍ* is, which again is part of a natural philosophy on which theologians based their theology: the *kalām* atomism. According to this theory, the world consists of substances (*jawāhir*, sg. *jawhar*, or *ʿayn*) and accidents. Bodies (*ajsām*) and matter can only exist as a combination of both. The indivisible smallest part in this realm is the atom. Theologians discuss how many atoms constitute a body. "Since bodies are composed of substances and accidents, scholars ask how to differentiate between substances and accidents. Accidents, for them, are attributes (*ṣifāt*, sing. *ṣifa*) of substances like colour, smell, and movement. They cannot exist without being connected to a substance."[61] Al-Samarqandī makes use of this argument of *kalām* atomism to negate the idea that actions can have an attribute of being good or evil. According to *kalām* atomism, accidents need substances (*jawhar*) or bodies (*ajsām*) in order to exist; however, actions and being good or evil are both accidents, so that it is not possible that two accidents can be combined and exist on their own.[62] Here, we see two theological arguments, which enables al-Samarqandī to criticize al-Dabūsī's definition. The first is the famous discussion about *taḥsīn* and *taqbīḥ*, whether good and bad exist independently from God's command and humans can grasp it independently.[63] The second is remarkable: al-Samarqandī argues according to *kalām* atomism, since his teacher al-Nasafī introduced it to Māturīdī *kalām* explicitly.[64] Thus, al-Samarqandī tries to avoid inconsistencies between theology and legal theory with regard to established theological views during his time.

We can see the same line of argumentation in al-Samarqandī's interpretation of the abovementioned four categories. According to al-Samarqandī, prohibitions, in reality, cannot have four different types. Prohibition is of one kind, and it declares that something is prohibited (it refers to *taḥrīm*). He states

61 Serdar Kurnaz, "Substances (*jawāhir*), Accidents (*aʿrāḍ*), and Rental Agreements: The Relation between Atomism in Islamic Theology (*kalām*) and Islamic Law (*fiqh*)," *Journal of Islamic Philosophy*, 15/2 (2024), 102–35, here 105.

62 Al-Samarqandī, *Mīzān*, 227–28. For a detailed analysis of the relationship between atomism and Islamic law, see Kurnaz, "Substances (*jawāhir*), Accidents (*aʿrāḍ*), and Rental Agreements."

63 For a detailed analysis of al-Samarqandī's approach to this question, see Hisashi Obuchi, "ʿAlāʾ al-Dīn al-Samarqandī's Non-Realist Approach to Good (*Ḥasan*) and Bad (*Qabīḥ*): Moral Ontology in Sixth/Twelfth-Century Māturīdī Theology and Legal Theory," *Journal of Islamic Ethics*, 8 (2024), 71–98.

64 Rudolph, *Sunnī Theology in Samarqand*, 249–53.

that this is the general rule among most *uṣūlī* scholars.[65] For al-Samarqandī, al-Dabūsī's fourfold division is only true if we interpret the sentence as follows: not the prohibition itself, rather its form (*ṣīghat al-nahy*) has four different kinds.[66]

The four categories that al-Samarqandī presents are more or less the same as al-Dabūsī's: the first category of prohibition is related to actions that are rationally-essentially evil (like *safah*, *ʿabath*, disbelief, and oppression); the second is related to essentially evil actions according to the law (e.g., prayer without ablution); the third is the same as al-Dabūsī's fourth category: the prohibited action is not evil, neither rationally nor according to the law. Rather, it is a good action and legally valid itself, but is in close proximity to something evil, be it defined as evil rationally or through the law. An example is the abovementioned sales contract during the Friday prayer. The fourth category is different with regard to al-Dabūsī's concept: the prohibition is related to something good in itself, but the prohibited action is different from it (*ghayr*) and not permissible (*ghayr mashrūʿ*), so that it is possible to imagine both as independent from each other. In other words, one action is valid with the absence of the other; al-Samarqandī defines this condition as *ghayrān/ghayrayn*. An example is the prohibition of fasting during the days of the Feast of Sacrifice (*ʿīd al-aḍḥā, ayyām al-tashrīq*). Fasting is an acceptable action, it is worship; the prohibition, however, is related to fasting, but the prohibited action differs from fasting itself. Put differently, fasting on the day of the Feast of Sacrifice would lead to the rejection of God's invitation to eat and drink. This rejection, which occurs through fasting, is forbidden. Under these circumstances, fasting would constitute a cause of being disobedient to God. If someone does not eat and drink without having fasting in mind, this is not a sin and is different from the latter case, since fasting prohibits eating and drinking, which is not the case if someone freely decides not to eat.[67]

We can conclude that al-Samarqandī, although being generally in line with al-Dabūsī's views on prohibition, tries to reinterpret his approach according to Māturīdī theological presumptions. Two of his criticisms are ontological and one is hermeneutical. In contrast, al-Dabūsī's concern by dividing prohibitions into four categories was of epistemological interest and for the sake of epistemological coherence. He deals with an epistemological question: an evil action can be grasped as such through reason or revelation/law (*sharʿ*). Then one must decide whether the prohibition is related to an evil action or is in

65 Kurnaz, *Methoden*, 103–5.

66 Al-Samarqandī, *Mīzān*, 229.

67 Al-Samarqandī, *Mīzān*, 229–34.

close proximity to it. Thus, al-Dabūsī does not ask whether an action can be essentially evil or not. The same is true for his epistemological framework. He is instead concerned with the rationally graspable obligatory and prohibited actions. Al-Samarqandī, on the other hand, has ontological concerns in mind. He insists that actions cannot have an evil essence or cannot be essentially good or bad; the evilness of an action results from an additional meaning, which is, as he states, related to the actor or to something else, but not to the action itself. With a second ontological/cosmological argument in mind, he stresses that the additional meaning cannot be related to the action itself, since actions and attributes are both accidents. Accidents need a substance or a body to exist with, since according to *kalām* atomism an accident cannot exist only in connection with accidents. Al-Samarqandī discusses later a related question from an epistemological point of view, namely, whether actions can be grasped rationally and/or through revelation as being evil or not, and then proceeds to quote the established positions on this issue among various scholars.[68] The second part of al-Samarqandī's criticism is again hermeneutical. According to the general hermeneutical rule that every prohibition leads to the normative status of *ḥarām*, there can be only one category of prohibition for him. However, if we consider the different modes of prohibition, we find four types of it. Unlike al-Dabūsī, al-Samarqandī does not directly discuss the question of *fasād al-manhī ʿanh* in his *Mīzān al-Uṣūl* (*The Balance of the Fundamentals*) when he quotes al-Dabūsī at this particular point; rather, he is interested in the different types of prohibitions.

The crucial point is that al-Samarqandī does not want to break completely with al-Dabūsī or the Ḥanafī tradition to give the Ḥanafī *uṣūl* a different theological shape according to Māturīdī *kalām* convictions. Although he sees problems in the wording of al-Dabūsī's views, he corrects the wording by giving interpretations of his own. Hence, he does not break with the Ḥanafī lineage by arguing that the wording of al-Dabūsī's view is problematic; instead, he interprets al-Dabūsī's statement in order to resolve some of its perceived defects.

4 Concluding Remarks

Core theological assumptions have direct effects on legal theory as well as on substantive law. Al-Dabūsī, for instance, bases law on purely rational grounds while not ignoring the Qurʾan and Sunna. He sees the needs of people as a

68 Al-Samarqandī, *Mīzān*, 236–41.

major factor for his understanding of law. This approach also affects his legal theory. On the other hand, al-Samarqandī bases his legal theory on specifically Māturīdī theology. Thus, in two different contexts within the same school of law, the Ḥanafī school, scholars' approaches to legal theory and law could vary.

This can provide us with hints how to think about contemporary approaches to the relationship between religious law and theology. A contemporary Islamic legal theory should therefore be aware of its own context in order to tackle the question of (religious) law and theology. If we, for example, ask for the relationship between Islamic law and Islamic theology today, we should be aware of different contexts. If we look at the recent developments in Germany and the ongoing establishment of Islamic Theology at state universities, we have to be aware of the secular space at the universities in which Islamic Theology started to be implemented. For instance, doing theology at universities requires specific understandings of knowledge, a particular taxonomy of scientific disciplines, following a specific scientific language and particular epistemologies. Furthermore, theology should be in close connection with disciplines like law, philosophy, and sociology, since traditional Islamic law also engaged with different theories as an adaptive system. It included, for instance, atomism, which had its origins possibly in Greek philosophy.[69]

Although offering highly interesting approaches, as we have seen in al-Dabūsī's and al-Samarqandī's writings, it is not sufficient to rely only on premodern literature to engage with the question of the relation between law and theology. Both authors directly discussed the subject of philosophy of law within their given contexts and disciplines they engaged with. We could also see the changes in their legal writings with changing theological assumptions

69 Harry Austryn Wolfson, *The Philosophy of the Kalam* (Cambridge, Mass./London: Harvard University Press, 1976), 466–95; Otto Pretzl, "Die frühislamische Atomenlehre," *Der Islam*, 19 (1931), 117–30; Alnoor Dhanani, *Physical Theory on Kalām* (Leiden: Brill 1994), 191–92; Tzvi Langermann, "Islamic Atomism and the Galenic Tradition," *History of Science: An Annual Review of Literature, Research and Teaching*, 47 (2009), 277–95. Scholars discussed whether the origins lie rather in Indian philosophy (Pines, *Atomenlehre*, 94–124) or in the Iranian tradition (Josef van Ess, "60 Years After Shlomo Pines's Beiträge and Half a Century of Research on Atomism and Islamic Theology," in Josef van Ess, *Kleine Schriften*, ed. Hinrich Biesterfeldt (Leiden: Brill, 2018), pp. 1121–44, here 1134–36). Be it as it may, we can conclude with Langermann: "However that may have been, the final products the atomistic philosophies developed by the different schools of the kalam and their individual representatives—were distinct, original creations. (…) [A]tomism was transformed and embedded in a distinctly Islamic world-view. All of the 'sources' that have been proposed so far (…) comprise definitions or concepts of atoms and an atomist physics that were at the disposal of the *mutakallimūn* when they embarked upon their project." Langermann, "Islamic Atomism," 277–78.

and contexts. For a contemporary Islamic legal theory, in order to deal with the relationship between law, theology and philosophy, a philosophy of law could serve as a new discursive field. It would allow studying Islamic law and legal theory within both intra- and interdisciplinary frameworks. Here, one could discuss issues pertaining to epistemology, authority, ethics, hermeneutics, linguistic philosophy, and (religious) law since these subjects are directly and systematically addressed in the field of philosophy of law, as it has developed in the past two centuries. Thus, related discussions in various fields of Islamic studies could be brought together in this new setting. This task, however, needs time and much work, which goes beyond the scope of this paper.

Bibliography

ʿAbd al-Jabbār, al-Qāḍī, *al-Mughnī fī abwāb al-tawḥīd wa-l-ʿadl*, ed. Ṭaha Ḥusayn (Cairo: Wizārat al-thaqāfa wa-l-irshād al-qawmī al-muʾassasa al-miṣriyya al-ʿāmma, n.d.).

Abū al-Ḥusayn al-Baṣrī, *al-Muʿtamad fī uṣūl al-fiqh*, ed. Khalīl al-Mays (Beirut: Dār al-kutub al-ʿilmiyya, 1426/2005).

Ansari, Hassan and Sabine Schmidtke, "The Muʿtazilī and Zaydī Reception of Abū l-Ḥusayn al-Baṣrī's *Kitāb al-Muʿtamad fī Uṣūl al-fiqh*: A Bibliographical Note," *Islamic Law and Society*, 20, no. 1 (2013), 90–109.

Bedir, Murteza, "Interplay of Sufism, Law, Theology and Philosophy: A Non-Sufi Mystic of 4th–5th/10th–11th Centuries," in *El Sufismo y las normas del Islam*, ed. and transl. Alfonso Carmona (Murcia: Editora Regional de Murcia Colección de Ibn ʿArabī, 2006), 253–70 (with a Spanish translation on pp. 15–34).

Bedir, Murteza, "Mâtürîdî Fıkıh Usûlü: Gerçek mi Kurgu mu?" in *Büyük Türk Bilgini İmâm Mâtürîdî ve Mâtürîdîlik*, ed. İlyas Çelebi (Istanbul: M. Ü. İlahiyat Fakültesi Vakfı Yayınları, 2012), 412–20.

Bedir, Murteza, "Reason and Revelation: Abū Zayd al-Dabbūsī on Rational Proofs," *Islamic Studies*, 43 (2004), 227–45.

Brockelmann, Carl, *Geschichte der arabischen Litteratur* (2nd edition, Leiden: Brill, 1943).

Brodersen, Angelika, "ʿAlāʾ al-Dīn al-Samarqandī," in *Encyclopaedia of Islam Three Online*, ed. Kate Fleet et al. (available online at https://doi.org/10.1163/1573-3912_ei3_COM_26318).

Brodersen, Angelika, *Der unbekannte* kalām: *Theologische Positionen der frühen Māturīdīya am Beispiel der Attributenlehre* (Münster: LIT, 2014).

al-Bukhārī, ʿAbd al-ʿAzīz, *Kashf al-asrār ʿan Uṣūl Fakhr al-Islām al-Bazdawī*, ed. ʿAbd Allāh Maḥmūd Muḥammad ʿUmar (Beirut: Dār al-kutub al-ʿilmiyya, 1417/1997).

Correa, Dale J., "Taking a Theological Turn in Legal Theory: Regional Priority and Theology in Transoxanian Ḥanafī Thought," in *Locating the Sharīʿa: Legal Fluidity in Theory, History and Practice*, ed. Sohaira Siddiqui (Leiden: Brill, 2019), 111–26.

al-Dabūsī, Abū Zayd, *al-Amad al-aqṣā*, ed. Muḥammad ʿAbd al-Qādir ʿAṭāʾ (Beirut: Dār al-kutub al-ʿilmiyya, 1436/2015).

al-Dabūsī, Abū Zayd, *Taqwīm al-adilla*, ed. Khalīl Muḥyi al-Dīn al-Mays (Beirut: Dār al-kutub al-ʿilmiyya, 1421/2001).

Dhanani, Alnoor, *Physical Theory on Kalām* (Leiden: Brill 1994).

Gimaret, Daniel, *La doctrine d'al-Ashʿarī* (Paris: Les Éditions du Cerf, 1990).

Gril, Denis, "Dhawq," in *Encyclopaedia of Islam Three Online*, ed. Kate Fleet et al. (available online at https://doi.org/10.1163/1573-3912_ei3_COM_26001).

Hallaq, Wael B., *The Origins and Evolution of Islamic Law* (Cambridge: Cambridge University Press, 2005).

al-Juwaynī, Abū al-Maʿālī, *al-Waraqāt*, online at https://waraqat.vishanoff.com/a/a3/ (accessed 19 February 2022).

Kam, Hureyre, *Das Böse als Gottesbeweis: Die Theodizee al-Māturīdīs im Lichte seiner Epistemologie, Kosmologie und Ontologie* (Berlin: EB-Verlag, 2019).

Kurnaz, Serdar, "Substances (*jawāhir*), Accidents (*aʿrāḍ*), and Rental Agreements: The Relation between Atomism in Islamic Theology (*kalām*) and Islamic Law (*fiqh*)," *Journal of Islamic Philosophy*, 15, no. 2 (2024), 102–35.

Kurnaz, Serdar, *Methoden zur Normderivation im islamischen Recht: Eine Rekonstruktion der Methoden zur Interpretation autoritativer textueller Quellen bei ausgewählten islamischen Rechtsschulen* (Berlin: EB-Verlag, 2016).

Langermann, Tzvi, "Islamic Atomism and the Galenic Tradition," *History of Science: An Annual Review of Literature, Research and Teaching*, 47 (2009), 277–95.

Madelung, Wilferd, "ʿAlāʾ-al-Dīn Samarqandī," in *Encyclopaedia Iranica*, vol. 1, 782–83 (updated version online at: https://www.iranicaonline.org/articles/ala-al-din-samarqandi-abu-bakr-mohammad-b/).

Netton, Ian Richard, *Muslim Neoplatonism: An Introduction to the Thought of the Brethren of Purity* (Ikhwān al-Ṣafāʾ) (Edinburgh: Edinburgh University Press, 1991).

Obuchi, Hisashi, "ʿAlāʾ al-Dīn al-Samarqandī's Non-Realist Approach to Good (*Ḥasan*) and Bad (*Qabīḥ*): Moral Ontology in Sixth/Twelfth-Century Māturīdī Theology and Legal Theory," *Journal of Islamic Ethics*, 8 (2024), 71–98.

Pretzl, Otto, "Die frühislamische Atomenlehre," *Der Islam*, 19 (1931), 117–30.

Rudolph, Ulrich, "Das Entstehen der Māturīdīya," *Zeitschrift der Deutschen Morgenländischen Gesellschaft*, 147 (1997), 394–404.

Rudolph, Ulrich, "Ratio und Überlieferung in der Erkenntnislehre al-Ašʿarī's und al-Māturīdī's," *Zeitschrift der Deutschen Morgenländischen Gesellschaft*, 142, no. 1 (1992), 72–78.

al-Samarqandī, 'Alā' al-Dīn, *Mīzān al-uṣūl fī natā'ij al-'uqūl*, ed. Muḥammad Zakī 'Abd al-Barr (Doha: Matba'at ad-Dawḥa, 1404/1984).
al-Sarakhsī, Shams al-A'imma, *Uṣūl al-Sarakhsī*, ed. Abū al-Wafā' al-Afghānī (Beirut: Dār al-kutub al-'ilmiyya, 1413/1993).
Sezgin, Fuat, *Geschichte des arabischen Schrifttums* (Leiden: Brill, 1967).
van Ess, Josef, "60 Years After Shlomo Pines's Beiträge and Half a Century of Research on Atomism and Islamic Theology," in Josef van Ess, *Kleine Schriften*, ed. Hinrich Biesterfeldt (Leiden: Brill 2018), 1121–44.
Vishanoff, David, *The Formation of Islamic Hermeneutics: How Sunni Legal Theorists Imagined a Revealed Law* (New Haven, CT: American Oriental Society, 2011).
Wheeler, Brannon M., "al-Dabūsī, Abū Zayd," in *Encyclopaedia of Islam Three Online*, ed. Kate Fleet et al. (available online at https://doi.org/10.1163/1573-3912_ei3_COM_25771).
Wolfson, Harry Austryn, *The Philosophy of the Kalam* (Cambridge, Mass./London: Harvard University Press, 1976).
Yetkin, Hacer, *Hanefî Usûlünün Kurucularından Debûsî ve Usûl Anlayışı* (Istanbul: IFAV, 2017).
Zysow, Aron, "Mu'tazilism and Māturīdism in Ḥanafī Legal Theory," in *Studies in Islamic Legal Theory*, ed. Bernard Weiss (Leiden: Brill, 2002), 235–65.

CHAPTER 4

The Late Classical Concept of Proof (*dalīl*) and Its Foundationalist and Occasionalist Features

Najah Nadi

1 Introduction

The scholarship of the prominent Persian polymath, Saʿd al-Dīn al-Taftāzānī (d. 792/1390) has suffered from neglect in contemporary academic works.[1] This is partially due to the general neglect suffered by the contributions of the late classical Islamic scholarship, and partially due to the perceived difficulty of his highly philosophical and philological works.[2] This paper is an attempt to highlight the merits of examining such neglected scholarship in enhancing our understanding of core conceptions within the Islamic tradition, one of which is the concept of proof (*dalīl*). What constitutes a sound proof producing new knowledge and whether a sound proof necessarily causes knowledge of its conclusion to occur in all cases are two significant questions that occupied those working in legal and theological traditions within Islamic intellectual history. These two questions are inadequately associated in academic works with the theories of occasionalism and foundationalism, though such association can transform our understanding of the relationship between legal and theological disciplines, and of epistemology in general. This paper suggests that late classical Sunni scholars' occasionalist commitments have not posed an epistemological challenge when determining the epistemic value or function of their proofs; it is the foundationalist approach to knowledge that dominated their evaluation of those *adilla* (pl. of *dalīl*). Put differently, they found occasionalism and foundationalism compatible. We have endeavoured to explain how.

There has been no systematic evaluation of how the concept of *dalīl* developed in classical or late classical works to correspond to the Sunni theological

1 This neglect has also extended to traditional *madrasas*. See Ahmed El Shamsy, "Islamic Book Culture through the Lens of Two Private Libraries, 1850–1940," *Intellectual History of the Islamicate World*, 4 (2016), 61–81, at 76.

2 The well-known Azharī reformer, Muḥammad ʿAbduh criticised the Azhar syllabus for its heavy reliance on al-Taftāzānī's commentaries. One of his concerns was its complex philosophical content. See the discussion in Maḥmūd Shākir's introduction to *Asrār al-balāgha* by ʿAbd al-Qāhir al-Jurjānī (Jadda: Dār al-Madanī, 1417/1996), 17–24.

 | DOI:10.1163/9789004746886_006

view of occasionalism. Further, no work has been done on whether these Sunni scholars' commitment to a foundationalist conception of knowledge has challenged their theological inclinations. As such, my paper addresses several questions in the hope of arriving at a satisfying understanding of the complex nature of the late classical conception of *dalīl*. These questions include: Can a foundationalist epistemology be based on occasionalist theology? What are the underlying theological principles guiding the relationship between proofs and conclusions? What is the foundation(s) for the 'truth' claim carried by classical scholars addressing the above questions? To answer these questions, I divide my paper into three main sections: I begin with an overview of the classical and late classical forms of occasionalism and foundationalism, noting major developments toward the formation of the verification (*taḥqīq*) scholarship.[3] I then move to outline the conception and typology of *dalīl* and highlight its occasionalist and foundationalist features. Lastly, I present al-Taftāzānī's original approach to understand the comparability of the cause-effect relationship to the proof-conclusion relationship, concluding that the epistemological inquiry into *dalīl* is best seen as an inferential rather than causative method of reasoning. It thus becomes clear that Taftāzānī offers a creative solution to dealing with occasionalist concerns.

2 Classical Foundationalism

The term foundationalism most commonly refers in contemporary scholarship to a Cartesian or other similar searches for basic foundations or justifications.[4] The foundationalism deployed by classical and late classical Islamic traditions and referred to in this paper is more Aristotelian and Peripatetic than Cartesian; the foundations in Peripatetic foundationalism are a set of undeniable and self-evident (*badīhī*) principles. These principles or starting points inform the search for knowledge in a manner that avoids infinite regress and circular reasoning. This is not a rationalist enterprise; sense-data plays a role, and even sense-data requires principles such as the law of non-contradiction to lead to knowledge. In addition to this notion of

3 Elsewhere I show that the *taḥqīq* tradition is the main feature of late classical scholarship, and that Saʿd al-Dīn al-Taftāzānī is himself a participant in this *taḥqīq* tradition. See Najah Nadi, *Theorising the Relationship between* Kalām *and* Uṣūl al-Fiqh*: The Theological-Legal Epistemology of Saʿd al-Dīn al-Taftāzānī* (*d.* 792/1390) (PhD diss., University of Oxford, 2018).

4 See Ali Hasan and Richard Fumerton, "Foundationalist Theories of Epistemic Justification," in *The Stanford Encyclopedia of Philosophy*, ed. Edward N. Zalta and Uri Nodelman (fall 2022 edition), online at https://plato.stanford.edu/archives/fall2022/entries/justep-foundational/.

principles, classical Islamic foundationalism centres around the following thesis: some knowledge must (logically) be immediately known—serving as the foundations from which thinking may begin, and some must be acquired through inquiry. A lack of such foundations logically entails either circular reasoning (A is derived from B and B is derived from A) or an infinite regress (A is derived from B, B from C, C from D, *ad infinitum*). Circular reasoning is nonsense (like explaining that you went to the store in order to go to the store), while an infinite regress entails that we would in fact know nothing (while this is not the case), as the prerequisite of traversing these infinite steps would never actually occur (because they are infinite).

Perhaps the locus classicus explaining foundationalism in the Islamic tradition is that of the pioneer logician al-Kātibī (d. 675/1277) in his widely circulated logical manual, *al-Risāla al-Shamsiyya*. He states, after dividing knowledge into conceptions and assents:

> Not all from each [type of knowledge, i.e., conceptions and assents] is self-evident (*badīhiyyan*)—lest we would have never been ignorant of anything (in the first place)—nor is all of each speculative (*naẓariyyan*)—lest it [knowledge] entail a vicious circle or infinite regress. Rather, some of each [type] is immediately known and some is speculative, acquired through thought.[5]

In the above passage, al-Kātibī states explicitly the foundationalist notion of principles: that there exist a set of conceptions and assents that require no speculative thinking in their establishment. Further, he states the foundationalist thesis: these principles are required so that they may act as *foundations* for other conceptions and assents which are not immediately known. He goes on to explain that the modes of logical thinking required for obtaining speculative knowledge are also of two types, immediate non-inferential, and speculative.[6] As such, al-Kātibī's, and the late classical foundationalist's thesis is twofold in nature: a) humans can obtain knowledge through speculative inquiry (*naẓar*) and b) such inquiry must rely on an undeniable set of conceptions and assents, which are also called first principles (*awwaliyyāt*). Speculative inquiry is the realm where natural human disagreements occur in arriving at knowledge. In *al-Shamsiyya*, al-Kātibī does not entertain any disagreements in accepting that

5 Shams al-Dīn al-Quzwīnī al-Kātibī, *al-Risāla al-Shamsiyya*, ed. Jād Allāh Ṣāliḥ (Amman: Dār al-Nūr al-Mubīn, 1432/2011), 53.

6 An example of non-inferential mode of logical thinking is the first syllogistic form (AAA); an example of inferential logical thinking is all other syllogistic forms.

speculative knowledge is preceded by a non-inferential set of conceptions and assents which act as foundations for speculative inquiry. Therefore, he does not address sceptical critics, at least not in *al-Shamsiyya*.

In his commentary on al-Kātibī's text, al-Taftāzānī tackles a few possible objections, one of which is most relevant here. One objection may be framed through asking the question: Does the need for first principles merely reflect the human, finite attempt to gain knowledge within a finite time? In other words, if we imagined an infinite being performing an infinite inquiry, would first principles still be needed? Al-Taftāzānī first reiterates al-Kātibī's point that if every single conception and every single judgement requires a proof, we inevitably find ourselves either in a vicious circle or an infinite regress. Circularity is materially impossible, meaning a thing will never precede itself in existence (if A is true because of B and B is true because of A, then A must exist before itself to justify B, because B is *itself* a justification for A). Infinite regress is, materially and rationally impossible, as it implies that every instance of knowledge is justified by previous knowledge, itself justified by what precedes it, infinitely. Al-Taftāzānī then presents a crucial epistemological problem[7] with accepting infinite regress: if you imagine the line of speculative thinking to go infinitely, and assume you have an infinite being to carry on this infinite inquiry, such a being would never reach a complete conclusion, and thus can never claim knowledge of a thing. Why? He answers:

> as this necessitates our inability to obtain any knowledge in finite [moments of] time [i.e. times that are themselves finite and have an ending, even though existing within a span of time imagined to be infinite]. This is because obtaining any knowledge requires the presence of all needed [premises] for such obtainments. It is impossible for the intellect to perceive infinite ordered premises in finite [moments of] time. Indeed, each perception requires a time.[8]

Hence, the late classical Islamic form of foundationalism embodies an emphasis on the human capacity to acquire knowledge, through inquiry, in their own finite moments of time. This acquisition necessitates the existence of reliable and stable foundations to begin with. Those foundations along with

7 Of course, infinite regress is mainly an ontological concern, as discussed in *kalām*, but it impacts many theological discussions such as pre-eternity and the necessity of the Creator to bring forth the existence of finite, possible, beings.

8 Saʿd al-Dīn al-Taftāzānī, *Sharḥ* al-Risāla al-Shamsiyya, ed. Jād Allāh Ṣāliḥ (Amman: Dār al-Nūr al-Mubīn, 1432/2011), 104.

newly acquired conceptions and assents will act as evidence, i.e., proofs, for unknown objects of knowledge. It is thus important for those working on epistemological theories in Islam to note the complex relationship between the intelligibility of the world, the human capacity to reason, as well as the problem of creation—a point I will turn to shortly—in understanding the classical form of foundationalism. It comes as no surprise that the most famous statement from the most famous theological manual in the classical tradition, *al-ʿAqāʾid al-nasafiyya* by Abū al-Muʿīn al-Nasafī (d. 508/1114), announces, "the realities of things are established (*thābita*); the knowledge of them is realized (*mutaḥaqqiq*), contra sophists,"[9] offering a realist view of the world and a foundationalist view of its knowability. In his commentary, ubiquitously studied in late classical circles, al-Taftāzānī explains that what we mean by establishment (*thubūt*) of the realities here is their correspondence to things in themselves (*nafs al-amr*), while what is meant by the realization of its knowledge is that their knowledge is obtainable for the human mind, not that we actually know all of them. He also notes that 'realities' here encompasses conceptions, or simple realities, and assents, or propositional realities, i.e., judgements.[10]

The necessity of first principles for human acquisition of knowledge is even more explicitly stated by al-Taftāzānī's younger contemporary, al-Sayyid al-Sharīf al-Jurjānī (d. 816/1413), in his famous commentary on al-Ījī's *Mawāqif*. Al-Jurjānī writes, "all speculative knowledge, religious and otherwise, return to them (i.e., necessary knowledge [*ḍarūriyyāt*]), as they are the first principles. If it were not for these [first principles], we would never have been able to obtain any knowledge."[11] ʿAbd al-Ḥakīm al-Siyalkūtī (d. 1067/1657), in his commentary on al-Jurjānī's commentary on same text, further clarifies that it is not sufficient for these first principles to be true in and of themselves, but they must be realized in the soul such that they become an attribute of this soul.[12] In other words, not their existence, but *knowledge of them in the inquirer* is what suffices as the condition for gaining further knowledge.

9 Abū al-Muʿīn al-Nasafī, "al-ʿAqāʾid al-Nasafiyya," in *Majmūʿat al-ḥawāshī al-bahiyya ʿalā sharḥ al-ʿAqāʾid al-Nasafiyya* (Cairo: Maṭbaʿat Kurdistān al-ʿIlmiyya, 1329/1911), 1:26, 32.

10 See Saʿd al-Dīn al-Taftāzānī, "Sharḥ *al-ʿAqāʾid al-nasafiyya*," in *Majmūʿat al-ḥawāshī al-bahiyya ʿalā sharḥ al-ʿaqāʾid al-nasafiyya* (Cairo: Maṭbaʿat Kurdistān al-ʿIlmiyya, 1329/1911), 1:27, 33–34.

11 Sayyid al-Sharīf ʿAlī ibn Muḥammad al-Jurjānī, *Sharḥ* al-Mawāqif (on the margins of al-Ījī's *al-Mawāqif*; Cairo: al-Maktaba al-Azhariyya li-l-Turāth, 1432/2011), 1:123.

12 ʿAbd al-Ḥakīm ibn Shams al-Dīn al-Siyalkūtī, *Ḥāshiya ʿalā* Sharḥ al-Mawāqif (on the margins of al-Jurjānī's *Sharḥ* al-Mawāqif; Cairo: al-Maktaba al-Azhariyya li-l-Turāth, 1432/2011), 1:123.

3 Ashʿarī–Māturīdī Occasionalism

Occasionalism is broadly defined as the theological doctrine asserting "God's absolute power by negating any kind of natural causality,"[13] commonly attributed to the Ashʿarī–Māturīdī theological schools in opposition to the Muʿtazilites and the philosophers. The two Ashʿarī–Māturīdī[14] theological principles that caused this doctrine to come to prominence are: a) contingent beings' (*mumkināt*) utter dependence on the Necessary Existent (*wājib al-wujūd*), and b) the Necessary Existent is all-powerful and has ultimate choice (*qādiran mukhtāran*). Such a dependence was understood to deny humans'—and all other existent things'—creation of acts, or capacity to act freely, in the created world. A fire does not have an independent capacity to burn, and a human does not have an independent capacity to walk, for example. Similarly, a proof does not have the independent capacity to lead to conclusions, i.e., to cause knowledge to occur in one's mind. Thus, existence depends on God directly, and causation of any new thing or state that comes about also depends directly on God's will.

The term occasionalism originates in English in relation to the notion that what appear to be causes are in fact occasions for God to bring about effects. It is worth noting that the Ashʿarī–Māturīdī schools still upheld "that God is in the habit of creating burning in us when we touch fire, and that for all practical purposes we can be confident that this will happen the next time this occurs."[15] Thus, the separation between cause and effect is not expected or normal, and would be considered a miracle. Put another way, the effect will follow

---

13 For a brief overview of the development of the theory of occasionalism from the 3rd/9th to the 5th/12th century, see Ulrich Rudolph, "Occasionalism," in *The Oxford Handbook of Islamic Philosophy*, eds. Khaled El-Rouayheb and Sabine Schmidtke (Oxford: Oxford University Press, 2016), 347–63. For later developments of the concept, see Khaled El-Rouayheb, *Islamic Intellectual History in the Seventeenth Century: Scholarly Currents in the Ottoman Empire and the Maghreb* (New York, NY: Cambridge University Press, 2015), 294–304.

14 There is a tendency in contemporary writings on occasionalism being associated with the Ashʿarī rather than the Māturīdī theological school. I contend that this differentiation is inaccurate or outdated. While it is true that the formulation of the theological principles underpinning occasionalism slightly differed in both traditions in the classical periods, it does not justify eliminating Māturīdīs as participants in such a tradition. In addition, the late classical works have demonstrated that these concepts have developed in a very similar language in Ashʿarī–Māturīdī theological manuals. See, for example, the Māturīdī theological manual al-Nasafī, "al-ʿAqā'id al-Nasafiyya," 1:142–45.

15 Khaled El-Rouayheb, *Islamic Intellectual History in the Seventeenth Century*, 294.

the cause unless there is a miracle. The two said occasionalist schools use the term 'divine habit' (*ʿāda ilāhiyya*) to refer to what determines the relationship between causes and effects in the universe. Hence, classical occasionalism does not completely deny causality; instead, the classical Ashʿarī–Māturīdī scholars assert that causality is 'conventional' (*ʿādī*), i.e., the relationship between causes and effects are of conventional entailment. They distinguish themselves from the philosophers who hold that causality is 'necessary' (*ḍarūrī*) because causes necessitate effects to come into existence, and the Muʿtazilites who hold that contingent beings have the power 'to engender' (*tawlīd*) effects in this world. These three positions were the main reported positions in the classical period.

Later scholars have explicitly defended the classical Ashʿarī–Māturīdī doctrine of causality against those who claimed it removed human agency by denying their causal power. For example, our author, al-Taftāzānī reports in his *Sharḥ* al-ʿAqāʾid al-Nasafiyya a Muʿtazilī objection to the theological doctrine of human actions that, if true, there would be no point of 'legal responsibility' (*taklīf*), reward and punishment. He responds by saying that this objection is not valid as we accept human 'choice' (*ikhtiyār*) and 'acquisition' (*kasb*) of actions.[16] Even more explicitly, Jalāl al-Dīn al-Dawānī (d. 908/1502) in his treatise dedicated to the question of creation of actions, *Risālat khalq al-aʿmāl*, claims that misunderstandings have led opponents of Ashʿarīs to claim they negated power and will as attributes of human beings. He clarifies that, in fact, Ashʿarīs accept human will and power as occasions or 'causes' (*asbāb*) for the actions to come to existence.[17]

These later defences and their like could justifiably be understood as elaborations or adaptations of the classical occasionalist positions inherited from the early Ashʿarī–Māturīdī works to answer increasing dissatisfactions with the early formulations of the doctrine. This practice of re-formulating doctrines is not strange to Islamic intellectual history and should not be eliminated as suspicious. More pertinent to my aims here is to show how the Ashʿarī–Māturīdī conception of occasionalism split into two distinct positions in later works.

16 Al-Taftāzānī continues to clarify that this objection is applicable to *jabriyya* as they deny human choice and acquisition. See al-Taftāzānī, "*Sharḥ* al-ʿAqāʾid," 144.

17 Jalāl al-Dīn al-Dawānī, "Risālat khalq al-aʿmāl," in *al-Rasāʾil al-mukhtāra* (Amman: Dār al-Aṣliyīn, 1439/2018), 71–72.

4 Late Classical Development: Rational Entailment Instead of Conventional Entailment

In addition to the above three views on the relationship between causes and effects, a fourth came to prominence in the later traditional works. This fourth position emerged from within the Ashʿarī–Māturīdī schools and appropriated aspects of the Islamic 'philosophical tradition' (*ḥikma*) into what was later claimed to be the *taḥqīq* position on the question of causality. This fourth position argues that the relationship between causes and effects is that of 'rational entailment' (*luzūm ʿaqlī*). Those supporting this doctrine held the view that it does not involve 'necessary entailment' (*ḍarūrī ījābī*) nor an entailment of engenderment.

ʿAbd al-Raḥmān al-Akhḍarī (d. 953/1546), the author of the famous didactic poem on logic, *al-Sullam al-murawnaq*, reports that the sound opinion on the question of the relationship between premises and conclusions is that of rational entailment. He states:

> Regarding how premises signify
> Conclusions, there is the following difference of opinion:
> Rational (signification), 'conventional' (*ʿādī*), 'engenderment' (*tawlīdī*),
> Or necessary (causation), the first being the endorsed opinion.

His Egyptian commentator, the Grand Shaykh of al-Azhar, Ḥasan al-ʿAttār (d. 1250/1835) associated this view with Imām al-Ḥaramayn al-Juwaynī (d. 478/1085) and supported al-Akhḍarī's endorsement for this view. Al-ʿAttār also repeats this assertion in his commentary on al-Maḥallī's (d. 864/1459) *uṣūl al-fiqh* text but attributing this view to Fakhr al-Dīn al-Rāzī, and explaining that this view has become that of the later tradition of 'verification' (*taḥqīq*).[18]

The prominent Ottoman late classical logician *cum* philosophical theologian, Ismāʿīl Gelenbevī (d. 1205/1791), the author of the widely studied manual of the art of dialectic, *Risālat al-ādāb*, states four positions for the relationship between proofs and conclusions: a) Ashʿarīs who insist it is 'a conventional entailment' (*luzūm ʿādī*), b) the wise 'philosophers' (*ḥukamāʾ*) who claim it is 'an entailment of preparation' (*luzūm iʿdādī*) by which they mean it is an obligation upon God to create the knowledge of the conclusion upon the knowledge of the premises as those premises fully prepare the mind to arrive to the conclusions, c) Muʿtazilites who say it is 'an entailment of engenderment' (*luzūm*

18 See Ḥasan al-ʿAttār, *Ḥāshiya ʿalā* Matn al-Sullam, ed. ʿAbd al-Ghaffār Ḥasan (Cairo: Dār al-Imām al-Rāzī, 1443/2022), 330–35.

tawlīdī), meaning that the knowledge of the premises engenders, or creates, the knowledge of the conclusion by merit of its generative power, and d) Imām Fakhr al-Dīn al-Rāzī (d. 606/1209) who suggests it is a rational entailment, by which he means the separation (*infikāk*) between the knowledge of the premises and the knowledge of the conclusion is rationally impossible, although all knowledge is created by God. Al-Rāzī's opinion, Gelenbevī continues, is based on the 'verified view' (*taḥqīq*) that indeed there is rational entailment between some of God's actions. It is simply impossible to create some parts of things without others, just as it is impossible to create accidents (like walking) without a substance (like an individual human).

The Kurdish theologian and logician ʿAbd al-Raḥmān al-Pinjwīnī (d. 1319/1900) in his commentary on the above treatise clarifies that al-Rāzī's view is not in opposition to his Ashʿarī school's two core theological principles, namely 1) that contingent beings depend on God and 2) that God has the ultimate power and choice to act in this universe. It is merely that al-Rāzī contends that knowledge of the conclusion is created in the person necessarily when knowledge of the premises is created in them. The two must go together; it is rationally impossible to have one without the other. Al-Pinjwīnī reports al-Dawānī's scholarly verification on this matter. How could al-Rāzī remain within the theological principles of his school while maintaining that the causality in the relationship between proof and the conclusion is one of rational entailment? This raises the crucial question of whether the two theological principles of the Ashʿarī school mentioned earlier in this section do necessarily entail the view of conventional causation, commonly understood to define occasionalism.

Before answering this question, the related position of the wise philosophers needs to be made clear. Al-Dawānī claims that the *taḥqīq* understanding of the *ḥukamāʾ* position is that they too uphold one of the two main theological principles of the Ashʿarīs, namely, that God is the only 'true actor' (*fāʿil ḥaqīqī*) in this universe and that all other actors are merely conditions and instruments. Yet they still uphold a view of causation that is different from the classical Ashʿarīs and the late tradition's *taḥqīq*. Al-Dawānī reports this *taḥqīq*-position of the *ḥukamāʾ* on the authority of Avicenna's philosophical *magnum opus*, *al-Shifāʾ*, as well as the writings of Avicenna's two students, the prominent philosopher and direct pupil of Avicenna, Abū al-Ḥasan Bahmanyār (d. 458/1067), in his famous *al-Taḥṣīl*, and the philosopher and court physician to the Seljuk court in the time of al-Ghazālī, Omar Khayyam (d. 525/1131), best known to English speakers for his quatrains.[19] It is worth noting that Naṣīr al-Dīn al-Ṭūsī's

19 Jalāl al-Dīn al-Dawānī, "Risālat khalq al-aʿmāl," 75.

(d. 672/1274) commentary on Avicenna's *Ishārāt* makes a similar claim concerning the position of the *ḥukamāʾ*.[20] This shows a lineage of this interpretation of the *ḥukamāʾ* position referring back to Avicenna as their teacher.

This is important, as bringing the theological position of the *ḥukamāʾ* regarding the question of creation and human agency closer to the theological principles of the Ashʿarī–Māturīdī schools may have served a purpose in creating a late classical *taḥqīq* position on causality joining elements of the early Ashʿarī–Māturīdī and the position of the *ḥukamāʾ*. We may propose an answer to the question raised above regarding the two Ashʿarī–Māturīdī theological principles thought to have led to their view of conventional causality (contingent beings' dependence on God and God's ultimate power to act): they do not logically necessitate conventional causality. We have already seen that late Ashʿarī–Māturīdī scholars who hold these two principles opted for a rational view of causality and we have seen that the *ḥukamāʾ* hold the second of these principles yet opted for a necessary view of causality. The difference between the late classical Ashʿarī–Māturīdī view of causality and that of the *ḥukamāʾ* is that the former still insisted that there is no necessary causal power for the causes to bring forth their effects; they must be created by God. The *ḥukamāʾ* attached necessary causal powers to causes. This is a conceptual and theological difference but in reality both agree that disassociation between causes and effects is impossible.[21] This impossible disassociation (or necessary entailment) is particularly stressed when discussing epistemological assessments of proofs, as we will see below. Therefore, the present article sets out to explain the relationship between causality and proofs: on one side is the necessary entailment between causes and effects, and proofs and conclusions on the other.

In addition to clarifying the classical Ashʿarī–Māturīdī understanding of occasionalism as a theological doctrine that offers a particular conception of causality, this section also shows the emergence of a fourth late classical *taḥqīq* position of occasionalism that merges the Ashʿarī–Māturīdī position on one side and the *ḥikma* position on another, while holding that this new position remains consistent with the theological principles of the Ashʿarī–Māturīdī schools.

This late classical commitment to a foundationalist approach to knowledge and an occasionalist approach to theology, specifically concerning the nature of human agency and its relationship to an all-powerful God has implications on the late classical typology of 'proof' (*dalīl*). This typology, as

20 Naṣīr al-Dīn al-Ṭūsī, *Talkhīṣ al-Muḥaṣṣil*, 518.

21 One may argue that the late classical view is specific to the case of *dalīl* while they still maintain that disassociation between natural causes and their effects remain possible.

I will show, is based on an interpenetration produced between the concerns of the logical, legal, theological, and philosophical traditions and exhibits occasionalist and foundationalist characteristics.

5 The Concept and Typology of *Dalīl* in Classical and Late Classical Scholarship

The previous section outlined the two classical principles of al-Imām al-Ashʿarī and the late classical conceptions of occasionalism. It concluded that the scholarship encompasses two distinct positions concerning the relationship between causes and effects and that the two positions are true to the occasionalist theological principles of the two Sunni schools (Ashʿarī and Māturīdī). The first, and early classical position, argues that the relationship between causes and effects is that of conventional entailment, while the second, and late classical, position argues that the relationship is that of rational entailment. Both positions insist that the causes and the effects are both created by God. This relationship is indeed relevant to our understanding of *dalīl* as it defines the relationship between proofs and conclusions, causes and effects, respectively.

The significance of the concept of *dalīl* lies in its centrality in most, if not all, disciplines within the Islamic intellectual traditions. Although each classical Islamic discipline offered its own guidelines for what it deemed an acceptable *dalīl*, it would be reasonable to say that the late classical tradition has standardized a typology of *dalīl* that we see reproduced in works of various disciplines, with minor modifications made to fit the objective of their specific subject matter. A classical Muslim scholar may argue that this typology was developed within one particular subject, namely theology (*kalām*), and then spread to other subjects.[22] But, as I will show, it was rather the synthesizing

---

22 The reason for such a classical claim is the organization and hierarchical structure of the sciences, or what is known as the classification of the sciences (*tartīb al-ʿulūm*). This concept, which the Muslims inherited from their Greek precedents, ranks disciplines according to their subject matter; insisting that the most universal and honourable discipline is the one responsible for offering the ontological and epistemological framework for all other subjects. Al-Ghazālī (d. 505/1111) explicitly identifies this higher discipline with the subject of *kalām*. He terms *kalām* "the most-honourable science" (*ashraf al-ʿulūm*) and ascribes to it the task of establishing "the postulates of all religious sciences" (*mabādiʾ al-ʿulūm al-dīniyya kullihā*). All other subjects are particular (*juzʾī*) and are dependent on *kalām* for their establishment. See Abū Ḥāmid al-Ghazālī, *al-Mustaṣfā min ʿilm al-uṣūl*, ed. Muḥammad ʿAbdul Salam ʿAbdul Shāfī (Beirut: Dār al-Kutub al-ʿIlmiyya, 1413/1993), 1:17. This view is not novel or restricted to al-Ghazālī but is rather held by generations after him.

of the intra-disciplinary works of these authors that led to this typology. The appropriation and naturalization of the rationalist disciplines into the fabric of late classical Islamic scholarship played a significant role in motivating such a standardization.[23] Below I first introduce the late classical *dalīl*-typology and then show its occasionalist and foundationalist features.

Perhaps the clearest indication of the late classical typology of *dalīl* is its standardized definition, which is often repeated in the introductions of the texts we have received from this period. This definition simply states that a *dalīl*[24] is that through which, upon sound speculative inquiry, it becomes possible to arrive at certain or preponderant propositional knowledge of a certain or a preponderate propositional conclusion (*mā yumkinu al-tawaṣṣul bi-ṣaḥīḥ al-naẓari fīhi ilā al-ʿilm aw al-ẓann bi-maṭlūb khabarī*).[25] This definition itself brings forth the aforementioned interconnectedness of the logical, legal, theological, and philosophical concerns of the *taḥqīq* tradition. First, the definition makes clear the logical distinction between two types of knowledge: propositional conclusions, that is, assented knowledge, and simple apprehension, that is, conceptual knowledge, restricting the need for a *dalīl* to the first type of knowledge. Second, it presents the theological question of creation and its dependence on the Creator through attaching the philosophical term 'possibility' or (*imkān*) as the attribute of attaining knowledge from the *dalīl*. Third, it makes the possible arrival to knowledge from a *dalīl* conditional upon the performance of speculative inquiry (*naẓar*), a process of logical and epistemological significance in the Islamic tradition. Finally, the definition sets out a clear distinction between two epistemic values for knowledge: the merely probable

---

23 For an overview of such a naturalization project see Asad Q. Ahmed and Robert Gleave, "Rationalist Disciplines and Postclassical Islamic Legal Theories: Introduction," *Oriens*, 46/1–2 (2018), 1 (online at https://doi.org/10.1163/18778372-04601001). Mehmet Kadri also shows the rule of the arts of argumentation (*munāẓara*) in synthesizing and standardizing specific scholarly elements in the late classical scholarship. See Mehmet Kadri, *The Development of Dialectic and Argumentation Theory in Post-Classical Islamic Intellectual History* (PhD diss., McGill University, 2011).

24 Linguistically, the term *dalīl* means guide (*murshid*), which may either refer to the one who sets up a sign for guidance, the sign which has been set for guidance, or the one who offers such a sign in guidance. For example, if we ask what the *dalīl* for the existence of God is, the answer may be the Creator, the universe, or the scholar who studies the universe. See Zayn al-Dīn Abū ʿAbdullah al-Rāzī, *Mukhtār al-Ṣiḥāḥ* (Beirut: al-Maktaba al-ʿAṣriyya, 1999), s.v. *d-l-l*, 106.

25 See for example, ʿAḍud al-Dīn al-Ījī, *Sharḥ* Mukhtaṣar al-muntahā al-uṣūlī, ed. Fadī Naṣīf and Ṭāriq Yaḥiyā (Beirut: Dār al-Kutub al-ʿIlmiyya, 1421/2000), 1:40–43; Sayf al-Dīn al-Āmidī, *al-Iḥkām fī uṣūl al-aḥkām* (Beirut: Dār al-Fikr, 1424/2003), 1:13; Saʿd al-Dīn al-Taftāzānī, *Ḥāshiya ʿalā* Sharḥ al-Mukhtaṣar (Cairo: al-Maṭbaʿa al-Amīriyya/Bulāq, 1403/1983), 1:39–40; Ismāʿīl Gelenbevī, *Risālat al-ādāb* (Istanbul, al-Maktaba al-Hāshimiyya, 2018), 33.

and the certain. Each of these five claims embodied in the definition of *dalīl* requires further elaboration in order for us to fully understand the established conception of *dalīl* in the late classical tradition and how it is sought to be applicable to the various Islamic disciplines.

6 The Logical Concern

Quṭb al-Dīn al-Rāzī (also known as al-Quṭb al-Taḥtānī; d. 766/1365), a famous commentator on al-Kātibī's *al-Shamsiyya* and an eminent figure of the late logical and philosophical traditions, dedicates a small treatise to the logical classification of knowledge into 'conception' (*taṣawwur*) and 'assent' (*taṣdīq*), titled *Risāla fī al-taṣawwur wa-l-taṣdīq* or *al-Risāla al-maʿmūla*.[26] He explains that a conception (*taṣawwur*) is 'the occurrence of a [simple] form of a thing in the mind' such as lion, book, the universe, and so on. The term 'assent' (*taṣdīq*), however, is a synonym of the term 'judgement' (*ḥukm*). Assent may be either directed to the affirmation of a propositional relation (e.g., 'Zaid is standing') or the denial of a propositional relation (e.g., 'Zaid is not standing'.)[27] To further explain the distinction between the two, al-Taftāzānī quotes Ibn Sīnā's seminal work, *al-Shifāʾ*:

> When you say, 'whiteness is an accident', the conception (of this 'relation' [*nisba*]) is that an image (both) of this composition and that of which it is composed—i.e., whiteness and accident—is imprinted in your intellect. But an assent (to this relation) is when the relation between this image and the objects themselves occurs in the intellect with correspondence (*muṭābaqa*) (between them).[28]

Hence, the definition of *taṣdīq* confines it to propositional knowledge and ties it to correspondence with reality. The late classical definitions of *dalīl*, as a method of attaining those assents, i.e., judgements (*aḥkām*), were adapted

26 For details, see Maḥmūd ibn Muḥammad al-Rāzī, *Risālatān fī al-taṣawwur wa-l-taṣdīq*, ed. Mahdī Sharīʿatī (Beirut: Dār al-kutub al-ʿIlmiyya, 2004), 98.

27 Al-Taḥtānī cites notable differences in the methods of defining *taṣdīq* but the scope of this paper does not allow delving into such a debate. Much of his discussion is found in al-Rāzī's treatise. (See *supra*.)

28 Saʿd al-Dīn al-Taftāzānī, *Sharḥ* al-Maqāṣid (Istanbul: Maṭbaʿat al-Ḥājj Muḥarram al-Busnawī, 1887), 1:20.

to reflect this requirement.[29] The equation of *ḥukm* and *taṣdīq* in logical and philosophical texts interested those working in Islamic legal theory (*uṣūl al-fiqh*) in particular to define their conception of *dalīl* as a requirement to arrive at legal judgements to align to this logical classification of knowledge. In turn, logical and philosophical texts had to accommodate probabilistic conclusions in their standard definitions of *dalīl* so as to encompass the reasoning employed by jurists. The 12th/17th-century key logicians, including Mīr Zāhid (d. 1101/1689–90) and al-Bahārī (d. 1119/1707–8), present the *taḥqīq* view equating *ḥukm* and *taṣdīq*. They also emphasized that *taṣdīq* encompasses only those arguments that lead to either certainty (*yaqīn*) or preponderance (*ẓann*), both of which require the prior existence of a proof (*dalīl*). Further, the two logicians do in fact cite *uṣūl* works for their explication of these *taḥqīq* views on *taṣdīq*.

7 The Philosophical and Theological Concerns

The definition of *dalīl* quoted above uses the philosophical term possibility (*imkān*) to explain the way through which *dalīl* leads to a conclusion. This raises the question: which of the previously discussed theological positions align with this definition? To answer, we must first understand this philosophical conception of *imkān* to show how late classical scholars widened the definition of *dalīl* to include the two occasionalist conceptions of causality, while they continue to support the second, i.e. that of rational entailment, as the *taḥqīq*-position.

It is worth noting that while the concept of possibility (*imkān*) is a philosophical concept, the definition of *dalīl* led theologians, logicians, and legal theorists to unpack its delicate features in their commentaries, in order to ground their understanding of *dalīl* in philosophy. Let's take the following example to illustrate the meaning of *imkān*: when I say 'the table is broken is a possible proposition', the term 'possible' has one of three different meanings, according to late classical texts of 'Islamic philosophy' (*ḥikma*). The first is 'specific possibility' (*imkān khāṣṣ*): that neither the proposition nor its contradictory are necessary. Affirmation and negation are each merely possible: just as it is possible that the table is broken, so is it merely possible that it is not broken. There is no ontological necessity or impossibility at play here. The second is the 'general positively qualified possibility' (*imkān ʿāmm muqayyad bi-jānib al-wujūd*), that the proposition is either possible or necessary, and its

29 This almost created a 'blind spot' in the classical theory of knowledge; that is, conceptual knowledge.

contradictory (not X) is possible but not necessary. This type eliminates the necessity of the table *not* being broken. The third type is the 'general negatively qualified possibility' (*imkān ʿāmm muqayyad bi-jānib al-ʿadam*), that this proposition is either possibly true, or possibly false, or necessarily false, but it cannot be necessarily true. This type eliminates the necessity of the table being broken.[30]

If we apply the three types of *imkān* on the relationship between proofs and their conclusions, we will understand that the classical Ashʿarī-Māturīdī conception of *dalīl* is in accordance with the first type of possibility, that is, proofs *possibly* lead to its conclusion but not *necessarily*. As for the late Ashʿarī–Māturīdī Imām al-Ḥaramayn al-Juwaynī, al-Rāzī, the *ḥukamāʾ*, as well as the Muʿtazilites, their conception of *dalīl* accords with the second type of possibility; that is, proofs lead to their conclusion possibly or necessarily. Such a necessity, as explained, is conditioned on the successful performance of speculative inquiry as well as the Divine creation of the premises (in the case of the late Ashʿarī–Māturīdī and the *ḥukamāʾ* conception only) in so far as the intellect has complete capacity to arrive at the conclusion, or in so far as the premises have the capacity to produce conclusions through engenderment (*tawlīd*; in the case of the Muʿtazilites). Most commentators, including those supporting the early Ashʿarī–Māturīdī view, support interpreting *imkān* in the definition of *dalīl* as a general positively qualified possibility because it logically validates the definition as inclusive of the four theological views concerning causality while the first interpretation, as specific possibility, would exclude all but the early classical view of causal relations between proofs and conclusions.

8 Between Inferential Reasoning (*istidlāl*) and Causal Reasoning (*taʿlīl*): Is There a Difference?

The preceding discussion on varying conceptions of the relationship between a proof and the knowledge of its conclusion assumes this relationship's comparability to the relationship between causes and effects. In this section, I offer al-Taftāzānī's creative insight into this discussion. I show that while he supports an occasionalist view of correlation between proofs and conclusions that accords with the early Ashʿarī–Māturīdī position, he cleverly notes a distinction between the proof-conclusion relationship on the one hand, and the cause-effect relationship on another. He shows awareness that some logicians, theologians, and legal theorists understand the concept of *dalīl* as a causative

30 See Ismāʿīl Gelenbevī, *Risālāt al-ādāb*, 38.

type of reasoning, meaning: the proof is the cause for the knowledge of its conclusion to occur. The classical and late classical scholars discussed appear to have adopted a similar view. Therefore, they refined their theological principles to align with their epistemological methods. This is exemplified in the shift in understating the proof–conclusion relationship that has become the *taḥqīq* view on the matter. Reading al-Taftāzānī's explicit statements in support of the early classical Ashʿarī–Māturīdī view of causality was an unexpected turn as someone familiar with his strong inclinations toward supporting *taḥqīq* positions. For example, in his *uṣūl al-fiqh* commentary, *Ḥāshiya ʿalā* Sharḥ al-Mukhtaṣar, al-Taftāzānī explains the implication of this occasionalist principle on the epistemic value of *dalīl*. He writes:

> Contingent beings are, essentially, dependent upon God. Hence, necessary and probable knowledge (which are [both] contingent beings) correlate in their occurrence to the necessary and probable proofs through the creation of God, the Exalted. They have no efficacy or obliging (power) in themselves (*min ghayr taʾthīr lahumā aw-ījāb*).[31]

This passage makes it clear that al-Taftāzānī advocates an early Ashʿarī–Māturīdī occasionalist view of correlation between proofs and their conclusions, in a conventional and not a rational manner. It is also clear that he is responding to the philosophers who claim that proofs have obliging powers to necessitate conclusions and Muʿtazilites who argue that proofs have actual causal or generative efficacy. Notably, he does not mention—nor does he appear to consider—the later classical view of rational entailment (without necessitation or causation), a position that arguably emerged a few centuries before his time. Al-Taftāzānī goes on to explain how this conventional entailment relationship works in arriving at conclusions:

> The meaning of 'the *dalīl*'s entailment of knowledge' (*istilzām al-dalīl al-ʿilm*) is their correlation; that is, the *dalīl* correlates to necessary knowledge 'in a conventional manner' (*ʿādatan*). Correspondingly, it is not strange to say that the 'probable proof' (*amāra*) is also correlating to probable knowledge in the same (conventional) manner ... This correlation prevents dissociation (between proofs and knowledge) conventionally, although it permits it rationally.[32]

31 Al-Taftāzānī, *Ḥāshiya ʿalā* Sharḥ al-Mukhtaṣar, 1:42–43.

32 Al-Taftāzānī, *Ḥāshiya ʿalā* Sharḥ al-Mukhtaṣar, 1:43–44; Similarly, in Saʿd al-Dīn al-Taftāzānī, *al-Talwīḥ ʿalā* al-Tawḍīḥ (Beirut: Dār al-Kutub al-ʿIlmiyya, 1996), 16–18.

Furthermore, and more directly relevant to the argument of this section, the following passage from al-Taftāzānī's magnum opus, *Sharḥ* al-Maqāṣid, illustrates how a *dalīl* leads to knowledge of a conclusion:

> By saying that a *dalīl* leads to something or entails something, we do not mean that it brings such a thing into existence, as in the case of causes (*ʿalā mā huwa shaʾnu al-ʿilal*). Rather, (we mean) that whenever it (the *dalīl*) is existent, such a thing (i.e., its conclusion) is existent, and whenever it is speculated, such a thing becomes known. In summary, (the *dalīl*'s) existence entails the (conclusion's) establishment; performing speculative inquiry of such a *dalīl* entails the knowledge of (its conclusion) (*wa-ḥāṣiluhu anna wujūdahu mustalzimun li-thubūtihi wa-l-naẓar fīhi mustalzimun li-l-ʿilmi bih*).[33]

To understand this complex passage, let us consider the classical example of fire and burning: fire is said to be the cause of burning because it brings about the effect of burning—i.e., it causes burning to come into existence.[34]

Can this causal relationship be applied to the connection between a proof and its conclusion? In other words, can we say that a proof is the cause of its conclusion in the sense that it brings the conclusion into existence? If so, then when we assert that the Qurʾanic command *aqīmū al-ṣalāh* "perform prayer" serves as a proof for the obligation of prayer, we would be implying that this command is what brought the obligation itself into existence. In other words, the Qurʾanic command is the legal cause (*ʿilla*) for the legal obligation. This comparability, to my knowledge, is fine to most logicians, theologians, and legal theorists of the classical and late classical period. Al-Taftāzānī, however, suggests that *dalīl*-based reasoning, known as inferential reasoning (*istidlāl*), operates in the opposite manner to *ʿilla*-based reasoning, or common causality. To go back to our examples: for al-Taftāzānī, *dalīl* is more comparable to 'burning' rather than 'fire.' When we speculate about(?) 'burning' we come to *know* that 'fire' exist. Similarly, when we speculate about the above command to perform the prayer, we come to know that the obligation to pray exists. So 'burning' and 'religious commands' are effects that lead us to find out their causes.

Explicitly, in his *Talwīḥ ʿalā al-tawḍīḥ*, al-Taftāzānī asserts that all of what we call religious causes (*ʿilal sharʿiyya*) are within the realm of inferential reasoning, rather than causal reasoning. Namely, religious causes are the effects

33 Al-Taftāzānī, *Sharḥ al-Maqāṣid*, 1:41.

34 Whether or not such 'causing' is by fire being an occasion for God to create burning or by its own obliging and engendered capacity.

of 'divine judgements' (*aḥkām*), not vice versa.[35] As such, al-Taftāzānī clearly distinguishes between *istidlāl* (lit. 'seeking or offering the *dalīl*') and *taʿlīl* (lit. 'seeking or offering the *ʿilla*') as two different methods of reasoning. This distinction between *dalīl* and *ʿilla* serves as an elevation of the epistemic value of *dalīl* against the early classical occasionalist view of possibility he upholds. Al-Taftāzānī in fact responds to what we may call an extremist occasionalist who is denying any epistemic value of proofs based on their understanding of *istidlāl* as a form of causality. The opponent, al-Taftāzānī reports, claims that saying speculative inquiry leads to necessary knowledge (*ʿilm*) when a *dalīl* is contemplated would result in us saying that the existence of 'the Necessary Existent' (*wājib al-wujūd*) is necessitated through the contemplation of the appropriate *dalīl*. This saying, the opponent continues, means that if such a *dalīl* is absent or not investigated, it would entail the non-existence of the Necessary Existent, which is rationally absurd.[36] Al-Taftāzānī's response to this opponent was simply to clarify that what is described in this objection is not the proof–conclusion relationship, it is the cause–effect relationship. The opponent is assuming that the universe, as a proof for the Necessary Existent, is the cause rather than the effect for the Necessary Existent, and hence claims that the non-existence or non-speculation of the universe entails the non-existence of the Necessary Existent. In other words, al-Taftāzānī asserts that what is entailed from the *dalīl* is the *knowledge* of the judgement, *not* the existence of the judgement itself, as is the case in *ʿilla* where fire entails the existence of burning.[37]

In the process of *istidlāl*, al-Taftāzānī explains, we seek to attain knowledge of *aḥkām* through performing speculative inquiry onto the *dalīl*. Since the *dalīl* is understood not as the cause but as the *effect* of the *ḥukm*, it must nevertheless possess a mode of signification that facilitates access to that *ḥukm*. This distinction between causal and inferential reasoning is so fundamental to al-Taftāzānī that he repeats it on different occasions in his major *kalām* and *uṣūl* texts. Whether this distinction is novel to him and the *mutakallimūn* of late classical *uṣūlī–kalām* scholarship or not is an inquiry which requires further investigation. But later commentators, such as al-Siyalkūtī (d. 1067/1657),

35 Al-Taftāzānī, *al-Talwīḥ ʿalā* al-Tawḍīḥ, 18.

36 To simplify this objection, take the example of a human voice in a vacant space. If A hears a human voice, they will be certain there exists a cause for this voice and that this cause is a human being, because the voice is an effect for this cause. This means that the voice necessitated the existence of the human being. If the voice never existed or A did not hear it, the opponent debating al-Taftāzānī claims that this, for A, means that the human being never existed.

37 Al-Taftāzānī, *al-Talwīḥ ʿalā* al-Tawḍīḥ, 16.

suggests that this distinction created two types of demonstrative syllogisms in logical treaties. The first is the inferential demonstrative syllogism (*al-burhān al-innī*) and the second is the causative demonstrative syllogism (*al-burhān al-limmī*). The first is an attribution to the Arabic particle *inna*, which indicates the affirmation of the sentence after it, while the second is an attribution to the particle *lima* which indicates the cause of the sentence which is used to ask for the cause of something. The first type is described thus because it signifies the affirmation of a judgement but not its cause, the second because it offers the cause of the judgement.[38]

9 The Epistemological Concern: Speculative Inquiry

I showed in the first section above that the foundationalist approach in classical Islamic scholarship combines the need for first principles and the human capacity to obtain certain and probable knowledge. This form of foundationalism was preserved conceptually within late classical scholarship. What was changed then was to add occasionalist features to the concept of *dalīl*. This was expressed in late classical works by modifying the standard definition of *dalīl* to explicitly include the conditional nature of arriving at knowledge—that is, knowledge resulting from a proof and the successful performance of speculative inquiry (*naẓar*). *Naẓar* remains the standard scholarly method for arriving at certain and probable conclusions within this late classical system. The terms *naẓar* and *istidlāl* are used interchangeably in most of the central works of theology, logic, and legal theory. However, the lengthy discussion of these terms in *Sharḥ al-Maqāṣid* allows us to conclude that the following adjectival terms are synonyms: speculative (*naẓarī*) and inferential (*istidlālī*). Though *naẓar* and *dalīl* (the etymological bases of the two, previous terms) are distinct, they must come together. When knowledge is not self-evident, it requires *both naẓar* and *dalīl*. *Naẓar* is an action (the specific type of investigation or seeking knowledge) and *dalīl* is the evidence which is investigated.

---

38 Al-Siyalkūtī, *Ḥāshiya ʿalā* Sharḥ al-Mawāqif, 2:4. It is important to note that the distinction between *taʿlīl* and *istidlāl* also impacted al-Taftāzānī's views on the other types of *adilla* and not only of syllogisms. For example, in his *Sharḥ* al-Shamsiyya, al-Taftāzānī indicates that in juristic analogy, the *ʿilla* is not the cause (*sabab*) for the *ḥukm*; rather, it is the shared quality (*al-jāmiʿ*) under which the principle-case and branch-case are included. He acknowledges that the *jāmiʿ* is either the *dalīl* or the *ʿilla*; it is not restricted to *ʿilla*. See al-Taftāzānī, *Sharḥ* al-Risāla al-Shamsiyya, 366–67.

The earliest and perhaps the most circulated definition of *naẓar* within the classical works of *kalām*, *uṣūl*, and logic is that of Abū Bakr Muḥammad ibn al-Ṭayyib al-Bāqillānī (d. 403/1013). Al-Bāqillānī states that *naẓar* is 'the thought through which necessary knowledge or firm probability is sought'[39] (*al-fikr alladhī yuṭlabu bihi ʿilm aw ghalabat ẓann*). He further explains that *naẓar* leads to certain and probable knowledge, meaning that knowledge necessarily occurs in the mind upon the sound performance of *naẓar*, not that *naẓar* generates or engenders such a knowledge, as said by Muʿtazila and Qadariyya.

Several scholars, including Imām al-Ḥaramayn al-Juwaynī, al-Ījī, al-Āmidī, and al-Taftāzānī raised questions regarding the applicability of this definition to, and its inclusiveness of, all types of *naẓar*. For instance, later definitions added the requirement of intentionality in the process, namely, that the thought process begins with the intention of arriving at conclusions rather than mere coincidental thinking such as self-dialogue and intuitions.[40] Further, al-Taftāzānī states that the real essence of *naẓar* includes the search for and assigning of the appropriate material of a proof. *Naẓar* thus consists of two intellectual movements: one is related to the material, and the second arranges this material in a form indicating its connection to the desired conclusion. Both movements of *naẓar* are mentioned at the very beginning of this chapter and are further elaborated in the following passage from al-Taftāzānī's *Sharḥ al-Maqāṣid*:

> If we attempt to acquire a sought-after conception or judgement—and no doubt it (this sought-after conclusion) must have already been noticed in a way (*mashʿūran bihi min wajh*)—the intellect makes a movement through its stored images and starts shifting from one image to another image until it (i.e., the intellect) attains the material for (this sought-after's) its premises (*mabādiʾ*), such as its essences and accidents, as well as middle terms. Hence it (i.e., the intellect) may comprehend them as specific and distinguishable (as they are). Then, it moves within these (premises) to arrange them in a special order (i.e. form) that leads to A conceptualizing a sought-after conclusion by its reality, or B by a way that distinguishes it from anything else. Or C, (to lead to) accepting it with certainty, or D,

39 Abū Bakr Muḥammad ibn al-Ṭayyib al-Bāqillānī, *al-Taqrīb wa-l-irshād*, ed. ʿAbd al-Ḥamīd ibn ʿAlī Abū Zunayd (Beirut: Muʾassasat al-Risāla, 1419/1998), 1:173. For a defence of the translation of *iʿtiqād* as opinion (and *doxa* [Gr.] and *opinio* [Lat.]), see Alexander Treiger, *Inspired Knowledge in Islamic Thought: Al-Ghazālī's Theory of Mystical Cognition and Its Avicennian Foundation* (London and New York: Routledge, 2012), 30.

40 See Shams al-Dīn Muḥammad al-Fanārī, *Fuṣūl al-badāʾiʿ fī uṣūl al-sharāʾiʿ* (Beirut Dār al-Kutub al-ʿIlmiyya, 2006).

> (accepting it) without certainty. Here, we have two movements: by the first, we acquire the material (*mādda*; for *naẓar*, i.e., the investigated proofs), and by the second we acquire the form (*ṣūra*; of these proofs). … The reality of *naẓar* is the combination of these two movements.[41]

This indicates that the reality of *naẓar* is the two steps: obtainment of the suitable material for the argument and ordering them in an acceptable logical form. This detailing of the procedure of *naẓar* allows latter discussions to refer to these 'parts' of *naẓar* and their respective role.

10 *Dalīl*-Typology

The discussed late classical conceptualisation of *dalīl* has influenced the typology of its classification in two ways: the classification of formal proofs as well as the classification of material proofs. By formal proofs, I refer to the logical form of proofs which shows the relationship between the *dalīl*'s premises and conclusions. By material proofs here I refer to the sources that can be used in formulating a *dalīl*, namely, rational or revelational material.

11 The Formal Typology

As we explained, every *dalīl* requires a suitable mode of signification (*wajh al-dalāla*) which connects their premises to their conclusion through a relationship of entailment. The epistemic value and suitability of this connection is what determines the validity and epistemic value of *dalīl*: if *wajh al-dalāla* is certain, the conclusion is certain, and if probable, the conclusion is probable.[42] Jalāl al-Dīn al-Maḥallī states that for such a process to lead to its desired conclusion, one must investigate the mode of signification (*wajh al-dalāla*), which he defines as the way (*jiha*) through which the intellect is enabled to move from the premises to the conclusion, in a certain or probable manner. *Wajh al-dalāla* is thus 'an attribute in the proof (*ṣifa fī al-dalīl*)', not a mere rational preceptive (*amr iʿtibārī ʿaqlī*).[43] According to al-Ījī, a proper *dalīl* must include an element that necessarily entails the conclusion (*mustalzim*); otherwise,

41 Al-Taftāzānī, *Sharḥ al-Maqāṣid*, 1:30–31.

42 This is to leave aside for the moment the manner in which the material of a *dalīl* factors into its epistemic value.

43 Al-Taftāzānī, *Sharḥ al-Maqāṣid*, 1:43–44.

the intellect will not reach the conclusion through the *dalīl*. This necessary entailment must be established in the subject (of the premise), so that the conclusion becomes propositional (i.e., contains a judgement). This is the reason why a *dalīl* must contain two premises, so that one of them tells us about the entailed connection (*luzūm*), and the other tells us about the occurrence/existence of such a connection (in the subject) (*ḥuṣūl al-malzūm*).[44]

In classical *kalām* and *uṣūl* works, *adilla* (sg. *dalīl*) are restricted into three types: 'syllogisms', 'juristic analogies', and 'inductive reasoning' (*qiyās, istiqrā', and tamthīl*). It is important to explain the classical rationale behind such a restriction and how these *adilla* lead to their conclusions. Al-Taftāzānī explains that the reason for restricting the *adilla* in these three types is that a *dalīl* leads to its conclusion through establishing a proper connection between its premises and its 'sought-after' conclusion (*maṭlūb*) or 'judgement' (*ḥukm*). What makes a connection (*wajh dalāla*) proper according to him is that both elements, the *dalīl* and the judgement, include a shared meaning which justifies the inclusion of the latter to the subject of the former. He explains that this inclusion may occur in three cases: (A) when the sought-after conclusion or the judgement is contained in the *dalīl*; (B) when the *dalīl* is contained in the sought-after conclusion; and (C) when the *dalīl* and the sought-after conclusion are contained in a third object which they share. These three types of connection between the judgement and its *dalīl* create the tripartite typology of *dalīl*. Al-Taftāzānī states:

> This is because there must be a suitable connection between the *dalīl* and the sought-after conclusion to produce the latter from the former. This suitable connection is either through the inclusion (*ishtimāl*) of one of them in the other, or otherwise. If the *dalīl* includes the sought-after conclusion, then this is the case of syllogism, because the conclusion is contained in the two premises (of the syllogism). If the sought-after conclusion includes the *dalīl*, this is the case of inductive reasoning, because the sought-after conclusion is the general principle established through its existence within its particulars. As for the second case (where neither contains the other), there must be a third (object) for both (i.e., the *dalīl* and the sought-after conclusion) to share so that the knowledge of one of them produces the knowledge of the other. This is the case of juristic analogy, because the judgement of the branch-case (*far'*), which is the sought-after conclusion, is produced through the judgement of the

44 al-Ījī, *Sharḥ* Mukhtaṣar, 1:44.

> principle-case (*aṣl*), through their inclusion in a shared third, which is the legal cause (*ʿilla*).[45]

Al-Taftāzānī explained the cases in which the three *adilla* lead to conclusions that are certain or preponderate and suggested that only demonstrative syllogism leads to necessary knowledge. On the other hand, all other types are, practically, probabilistic in the way they indicate their conclusions. In theory, he contends that juristic analogy and inductive reasoning may lead to necessary knowledge. This conclusion of al-Taftāzānī's is based on his view that the connection between proofs and their conclusions needs to be a connection of inclusion (*ishtimāl*), not necessary entailment (*iltizām*). Al-Taftāzānī maintains that the fulfilment of the condition of *wajh al-dalāla* is what matters for a legal theorist or a theologian. Al-Taftāzānī, consequently, states that a proof only leads to its conclusion on the presumption that the scholarly investigation (*naẓar*) has taken place, rather than, as some may think, through the premises themselves or through their arrangement in one form of proof or the other.[13]

We have seen that *dalīl* refers to three different types of argumentative structure. The relation between all three is not entailment, so new categories and nuances of definition were required to set out the rules for these argumentative structures. It should also be noted that the emphasis on *wajh al-dalāla* and its role is more significant in al-Taftāzānī's theory of signification than it is in the works of his contemporaries and predecessors, and it certainly merits further investigation.

12 The Reason–Revelation Typology

Classically, scholars have offered a bipartite classification of *dalīl* into reason (*ʿaql*) and revelation (*naql*). Late classical scholarly authors, al-Taftāzānī included, have problematised this classification, arguing that *adilla* are of three types: 'purely rational' (*ʿaqlī maḥḍ*), purely revelational, and a composite of revelational and rational. They rendered the purely revelational type inconceivable and made the newly crafted type, the composite, its replacement. The reasoning behind this alternation, they argue, is that revelation depends on

45 Al-Taftāzānī, *Sharḥ al-Maqāṣid*, 1:50; al-Rāzī makes a similar remark on the comparison between these three types of *adilla*, but not on the basis of inclusion; rather, on the basis of rational entailment (*luzūm*). This entailment method is also the explanation al-Ījī gives in his *al-Mawāqif*. See Fakhr al-Dīn Muḥammad ibn ʿUmar al-Rāzī, *Muḥaṣṣal afkār al-mutaqaddimīn wa-l-mutaʾakhkhirīn* (Cairo: al-Maṭbaʿa al-Ḥusayniyya, 1323/1905), 32.

reason in its existence; the veracity of revelation has been established through the judgement of the intellect.

The first scholar to initiate this view is Fakhr al-Dīn al-Rāzī in his *Muḥaṣṣal*. Al-Rāzī states that the existence of the purely revelational *dalīl* is impossible (*muḥāl*) because, he explains, unless the intellect establishes the veracity of the reporter (the Prophet), the report itself does not entail necessary knowledge.[46] This explanation is similar to the explanation of al-Taftāzānī, his teacher, al-Ījī, as well as his contemporary al-Jurjānī. Al-Ījī states (with al-Jurjānī's commentary between brackets):

> *Dalīl* is either rational throughout its premises (be it immediate or mediated premises), or revelational throughout all of them (in the same manner), or a composite of the two. The first is the (purely) rational (*dalīl* which does not depend on revelation). The second (which is the purely revelational *dalīl*) is inconceivable because the veracity of the Prophet is essential [for the revelational *dalīl*] (to entail knowledge), and such [a veracity] is only known by reason (through investigating the miracle that proves his veracity. For if you would try to prove this through revelation, [your argument] would be circular or infinitely regress). The third (which is the composite) is what we call revelational (because of its dependence upon revelation in general. Thus, *dalīl* is restricted to two types: the rational and the composite of rational and revelational [premises]. This is the 'verified opinion' [*taḥqīq*]).[47]

Rejecting the existence of the purely revelational *dalīl* became a feature of the late Ashʿarī–Māturīdī tradition.[48] This view should not be seen as a result of a commitment to a rationalist approach, though it certainly is used to secure the rather fragile epistemic value of prophetic reports (including the Qur'an) while engaging with rationalist opponents. This security stems from claiming that revelational judgements *have been* authenticated by rational premises in the distant line of their reasoning. The idea of considering the long line of immediate and distant premises of a particular judgement is a keen feature

46 Al-Rāzī, *Muḥaṣṣal afkār al-mutaqaddimīn wa-l-muta'akhkhirīn*, 31.

47 Al-Jurjānī, *Sharḥ* al-Mawāqif, 2:49; al-Ījī, *al-Mawāqif*, 2:49. Also see al-Taftāzānī, *Sharḥ al-Maqāṣid*, 1:52–53.

48 The origins of this view may be traced to Imām Ḥaramayn al-Juwaynī's classification of the objects of knowledge into those which can only be obtained by the intellect, those which can only be obtained by revelation, and those which can be obtained by both. See Abū al-Maʿālī ʿAbd al-Malik b. ʿAbd Allāh al-Juwaynī, *al-Shāmil fī uṣūl al-dīn*, ed. ʿAlī Sāmī al-Nashshār (Alexandria: al-Maʿārif, 1389/1969).

of foundationalist epistemology and does not stand in opposition of the late classical scholars' understanding of occasionalist theology. The debate on the compatibility of reason and revelation[49] could then find an easier pathway to follow; since both, *ʿaql* and *naql*, cannot be contraries and true simultaneously. In other words, submitting to al-Rāzī's view on the impossibility of purely revelational indicants may strengthen, rather than weaken, the epistemic value of what he termed composite indicants (*dalīl murakkab*).

13 Conclusion

In this paper, I offered an overview of the main discussions concerning occasionalism and foundationalism in classical and late classical scholarship as well as their most important implications on the development of the concept of *dalīl*. I showed that the classical foundationalist approach to knowledge remained the same in the late classical *taḥqīq* tradition, while the classical occasionalist approach to theology has undertaken notable shifts, without deviating from the core principles. The occasionalist theological principles of the early classical Ashʿarī–Māturīdī schools spurred fruitful discussions in the late classical periods that led to a reformulation of the Sunni schools view on occasionalism. This newly formulated view remained in line with the said theological principles while benefiting from the philosophical precision of Avicenna's treatment of epistemology, specifically inquiry and knowledge acquisition. Al-Taftāzānī's critical assessment of *istidlāl*'s comparability to *taʿlīl* has offered a new insight onto on the applicability of the early occasionalist concerns to the epistemic value of proofs, and the foundationalist approach to knowledge as a whole. As such, foundationalism is compatible with occasionalism within different and variant understandings of its theological principles in the classical and late classical traditions; and within the different and variant understanding of the relationship between *adilla* and conclusions being inferential entailment or conventional entailment. Several modern writers have attempted to align *kalām* with dialectical reasoning and philosophy with the demonstrative. One may be tempted to read ontological contingency into epistemological contingency. However, in these great thinkers, we do not see

49 For an overview of the problem, see for example Binyamin Abrahamov, *Islamic Theology: Traditionalism and Rationalism* (Edinburgh: Edinburgh University Press, 1998) and Carl Sharif El-Tobgui, *Revelation and the Reconstitution of Rationality: Taqī al-Dīn Ibn Taymiyya's (d. 728/1328)* Darʾ taʿārud al-ʿaql wa-l-naql *or* The Refutation of the Contradiction of Reason and Revelation (PhD. diss., McGill University, 2013).

Ashʿarī–Māturīdī contingency rendering proofs to be merely probabilistic nor dialectic, nor do they see demonstrative proof as an affront to the Divine prerogative nor power. Thus, interpreting the occasionalism of the present late classical thinkers as necessarily undercutting demonstrative knowledge would be gratuitous and anachronistic.

Bibliography

Abrahamov, Binyamin, *Islamic Theology: Traditionalism and Rationalism* (Edinburgh: Edinburgh University Press, 1998).

Ahmed, Asad Q. and Robert Gleave, "Rationalist Disciplines and Postclassical Islamic Legal Theories: Introduction," *Oriens*, 46, nos. 1–2 (2018), 1–5 (online at https://doi.org/10.1163/18778372-04601001).

al-Āmidī, Sayf al-Dīn, *al-Iḥkām fī uṣūl al-aḥkām* (Beirut: Dār al-Fikr, 1424/2003).

al-ʿAttār, Ḥasan, *Ḥāshiya ʿalā* Matn al-Sullam, ed. ʿAbd al-Ghaffār Ḥasan (Cairo: Dār al-Imām al-Rāzī, 1443/2022).

al-Bāqillānī, Abū Bakr Muḥammad ibn al-Ṭayyib, *al-Taqrīb wa-l-irshād*, ed. ʿAbd al-Ḥamīd ibn ʿAlī Abū Zunayd (Beirut: Muʾassasat al-Risāla, 1419/1998).

al-Dawānī, Jalāl al-Dīn, "Risālat khalq al-aʿmāl," in *al-Rasāʾil al-mukhtāra* (Amman: Dār al-Aṣliyīn, 1439/2018).

El Shamsy, Ahmed, "Islamic Book Culture through the Lens of Two Private Libraries, 1850–1940," *Intellectual History of the Islamicate World*, 4 (2016), 61–81.

El-Rouayheb, Khaled, *Islamic Intellectual History in the Seventeenth Century: Scholarly Currents in the Ottoman Empire and the Maghreb* (New York, NY: Cambridge University Press, 2015).

El-Tobgui, Carl Sharif, *Revelation and the Reconstitution of Rationality: Taqī al-Dīn Ibn Taymiyya's (d. 728/1328)* Darʾ taʿārud al-ʿaql wa-l-naql *or* The Refutation of the Contradiction of Reason and Revelation (PhD. diss., McGill University, 2013).

al-Fanārī, Shams al-Dīn Muḥammad, *Fuṣūl al-badāʾiʿ fī uṣūl al-sharāʾiʿ* (Beirut Dār al-Kutub al-ʿIlmiyya, 2006).

Gelenbevī, Ismāʿīl, *Risālat al-ādāb* (Istanbul, al-Maktaba al-Hāshimiyya, 2018).

al-Ghazālī, Abū Ḥāmid, *al-Mustaṣfā min ʿilm al-uṣūl*, ed. Muḥammad ʿAbdul Salam ʿAbdul Shāfī (Beirut: Dār al-Kutub al-ʿIlmiyya, 1413/1993).

Hasan, Ali and Richard Fumerton, "Foundationalist Theories of Epistemic Justification," in *The Stanford Encyclopedia of Philosophy*, ed. Edward N. Zalta and Uri Nodelman (fall 2022 edition), online at https://plato.stanford.edu/archives/fall2022/entries/justep-foundational/.

al-Ījī, ʿAḍud al-Dīn, *Sharḥ* Mukhtaṣar al-muntahā al-uṣūlī, ed. Fadī Naṣīf and Ṭāriq Yaḥiyā (Beirut: Dār al-Kutub al-ʿIlmiyya, 1421/2000).

al-Jurjānī, ʿAbd al-Qāhir, *Asrār al-balāgha* (Jadda: Dār al-Madanī, 1417/1996).

al-Jurjānī, Sayyid al-Sharīf ʿAlī ibn Muḥammad, *Sharḥ* al-Mawāqif (on the margins of al-Ījī's *al-Mawāqif*; Cairo: al-Maktaba al-Azhariyya li-l-Turāth, 1432/2011).

al-Juwaynī, Abū al-Maʿālī ʿAbd al-Malik b. ʿAbd Allāh, *al-Shāmil fī uṣūl al-dīn*, ed. ʿAlī Sāmī al-Nashshār (Alexandria: al-Maʿārif, 1389/1969).

Kadri, Mehmet, *The Development of Dialectic and Argumentation Theory in Post-Classical Islamic Intellectual History* (PhD diss., McGill University, 2011).

al-Kātibī, Shams al-Dīn al-Quzwīnī, *al-Risāla al-Shamsiyya*, ed. Jād Allāh Ṣāliḥ (Amman: Dār al-Nūr al-Mubīn, 1432/2011).

Nadi, Najah, *Theorising the Relationship between* Kalām *and* Uṣūl al-Fiqh*: The Theological-Legal Epistemology of Saʿd al-Dīn al-Taftāzānī (d. 792/1390)* (PhD diss., University of Oxford, 2018).

al-Nasafī, Abū al-Muʿīn, "al-ʿAqā'id al-Nasafiyya," in *Majmūʿat al-ḥawāshī al-bahiyya ʿalā sharḥ al-ʿAqā'id al-Nasafiyya* (Cairo: Maṭbaʿat Kurdistān al-ʿIlmiyya, 1329/1911).

al-Rāzī, Fakhr al-Dīn Muḥammad ibn ʿUmar, *Muḥaṣṣal afkār al-mutaqaddimīn wa-l-muta'akhkhirīn* (Cairo: al-Maṭbaʿa al-Ḥusayniyya, 1323/1905).

al-Rāzī, Maḥmūd ibn Muḥammad, *Risālatān fī al-taṣawwur wa-l-taṣdīq*, ed. Mahdī Sharīʿatī (Beirut: Dār al-kutub al-ʿIlmiyya, 2004).

al-Rāzī, Zayn al-Dīn Abū ʿAbdullah, *Mukhtār al-Ṣiḥāḥ* (Beirut: al-Maktaba al-ʿAṣriyya, 1999).

Rudolph, Ulrich, "Occasionalism," in *The Oxford Handbook of Islamic Philosophy*, eds. Khaled El-Rouayheb and Sabine Schmidtke (Oxford: Oxford University Press, 2016), 347–63.

al-Siyalkūtī, ʿAbd al-Ḥakīm ibn Shams al-Dīn, *Ḥāshiya ʿalā* Sharḥ al-Mawāqif (on the margins of al-Jurjānī's *Sharḥ* al-Mawāqif; Cairo: al-Maktaba al-Azhariyya li-l-Turāth, 1432/2011).

al-Taftāzānī, Saʿd al-Dīn, "Sharḥ *al-ʿAqā'id al-nasafiyya*," in *Majmūʿat al-ḥawāshī al-bahiyya ʿalā sharḥ al-ʿaqā'id al-nasafiyya* (Cairo: Maṭbaʿat Kurdistān al-ʿIlmiyya, 1329/1911).

al-Taftāzānī, Saʿd al-Dīn, *al-Talwīḥ ʿalā* al-Tawḍīḥ (Beirut: Dār al-Kutub al-ʿIlmiyya, 1996).

al-Taftāzānī, Saʿd al-Dīn, *Ḥāshiya ʿalā* Sharḥ al-Mukhtaṣar (Cairo: al-Maṭbaʿa al-Amīriyya/Bulāq, 1403/1983).

al-Taftāzānī, Saʿd al-Dīn, *Sharḥ* al-Maqāṣid (Istanbul: Maṭbaʿat al-Ḥājj Muḥarram al-Busnawī, 1887).

al-Taftāzānī, Saʿd al-Dīn, *Sharḥ* al-Risāla al-Shamsiyya, ed. Jād Allāh Ṣāliḥ (Amman: Dār al-Nūr al-Mubīn, 1432/2011).

Treiger, Alexander, *Inspired Knowledge in Islamic Thought: Al-Ghazālī's Theory of Mystical Cognition and Its Avicennian Foundation* (London and New York: Routledge, 2012).

CHAPTER 5

Impact of Theological Attitudes on Legal Thinking: Reason and *Maṣlaḥa* in the Legal Thought of Muḥammad ʿAbduh (d. 1323/1905)

Mohammed Abdelrahem

1 Introduction

Islamic sciences are characterized by a dynamic interplay of themes and methodologies, fostering an interdisciplinary relationship that shaped their development over centuries. This interaction often leads to the emergence of new disciplines, as evidenced by the integration of *ḥadīth* and *fiqh* ('Islamic jurisprudence'), which gave rise to *ʿilm ḥadīth al-aḥkām* ('the study of legal *ḥadīth*').[1] Similarly, the relationship between *tafsīr* ('Qurʾānic exegesis') and *fiqh* prompted jurists to interpret Qurʾānic verses containing legal provisions, leading to the field of *tafsīr āyāt al-aḥkām* ('exegesis of legal Qurʾānic verses').[2] Among the most significant intersections is the relationship between *ʿilm al-kalām* ('Islamic theology') and *uṣūl al-fiqh* ('Islamic legal theory'), where theological principles have historically influenced the foundational methodologies of juristic reasoning. In the 4th/10th and 5th/11th centuries, Muslim theologians made notable contributions to *uṣūl al-fiqh*, adopting a distinctive methodological framework known as 'the approach of theologians'. This approach contrasted with the juristic method favored by Ḥanafī scholars, reflecting the broader intellectual debates of the period.[3]

1 One of the early and most prominent scholars who wrote on this science is Jamāl al-Dīn al-Zaylaʿī (d. 762/1360) and al-Ḥāfiẓ al-ʿIrāqī (d. 806/1403). The former wrote his book, *Naṣb al-rāya fī takhrīj aḥādīth* al-Hidāya (*Raising the Flag for Studying the Chains of Transmission of the* aḥādīth *of* The Guidance), as a commentary on the Ḥanafī book *al-Hidāya* (*The Guidance*) by the Ḥanafī jurist al-Mirghiyānī (d. 593/1197). The latter wrote *Takhrīj aḥādīth* al-Iḥyāʾ (*Studying the Chains of Transmission of the* aḥādīth *of* The Revival) as a commentary on al-Ghazālī's *Iḥyāʾ ʿulūm al-dīn* (*The Revival of the Religious Sciences*).

2 Many *fuqahāʾ* (sg. *faqīh*, 'a Muslim jurist') wrote commentaries on the Qurʾānic verses containing legal provisions. The first to contribute to this genre was al-Shāfiʿī (d. 204/820), the Ḥanafī jurist al-Jaṣṣāṣ (d. 370/981), and the Mālikī jurist Ibn al-ʿArabī (d. 543/1148), with all their works entitled *Aḥkām al-Qurʾān* (*Legal Provisions of the Qurʾān*).

3 In an earlier study, I explored the contributions of al-Qāḍī ʿAbd al-Jabbār al-Muʿtazilī (d. 415/1025) to *uṣūl al-fiqh*, particularly in the 17th section of his *al-Mughnī fī abwāb*

 | DOI:10.1163/9789004746886_007

While the Muʿtazilī emphasis on reason distinguished their approach from the Ashʿarīs and the Māturīdīs, discussions around the concept of *ʿilal al-aḥkām* ('causes behind legal rulings') during the 5th/11th and 6th/12th centuries reveal a shared reliance on rational methodologies across these theological schools. However, differences persisted regarding the precedence of reason over textual sources. These differences became less pronounced in the 5th/11th and 6th/12th centuries, as scholars sought to reconcile rational and textual approaches within a unified framework for *uṣūl al-fiqh*.

This dynamic interaction between theology and law, which has always been a cornerstone of Islamic intellectual history, finds a particularly distinctive expression in the works of prominent Islamic scholars of the modern era, most notably Imām Muḥammad ʿAbduh (1266–1323/1849–1905), a leading figure among reformist thinkers in modern Islam. In his thought, theological attitudes such as the role of 'reason' (*ʿaql*) and the principle of 'public welfare' (*maṣlaḥa*) serve as the foundation for re-evaluating traditional legal rulings. ʿAbduh's project reflects an integrated approach where theology, ethics, and law converge to address both spiritual and societal needs, offering a framework for reform that remains deeply rooted in Islamic principles while responding to contemporary challenges.

2 Subject and Methodology

This study explores the impact of theological attitudes on legal thinking in ʿAbduh's work, focusing on two core concepts: reason and *maṣlaḥa*. These concepts not only inform his methodology but also serve as tools for interpreting Islamic law in a manner that prioritizes justice, accountability, and the evolving needs of society. Concepts of reason and *maṣlaḥa* were not employed arbitrarily; instead, they were integral to his efforts to critically assess traditional legal provisions that had remained static for centuries. This methodological rigor reflects a notable parallel between ʿAbduh's thought and Muʿtazilī principles, particularly in his reliance on rational criteria for

---

al-tawḥīd wa-l-ʿadl, where he addressed the Muʿtazilī perspective on the sources of legislation, including the Qurʾān, *ijmāʿ* ('consensus'), Prophetic acts, and *qiyās* ('analogical reasoning'). That study raised a central question about the extent to which Muʿtazilī theological principles shaped their contributions to *uṣūl al-fiqh*, particularly given al-Qāḍī ʿAbd al-Jabbār's role as Supreme Judge during the Buwayhid dynasty; see Mohammed Abdelrahem, "Auswirkung der Theologie auf das rechtsphilosophische Denken der Muʿtazila: Lektüre bei al-Qāḍī ʿAbd al-Ǧabbār," *Zeitschrift für Recht & Islam*, 13/14 (2022), 57–80, http://zri.gair.de/index.php/en/contents/current-issue.

addressing theological and legal issues. This influence is evident in many of his legal opinions and fatwas, inspiring subsequent scholars and intellectuals, including ʿAbd al-Ḥalīm Maḥmūd (d. 1328/1978), Ḥasan Ḥanafī (d. 1443/2021), al-Ṭāhir Ibn ʿĀshūr (d. 1393/1973), and ʿAlī ʿAbd al-Rāziq (d. 1386/1966), who similarly adopted rationalist approaches to Qurʾānic and Sunna texts.

The study adopts a critical-analytical methodology, focusing on ʿAbduh's writings that emphasize the role of reason in understanding Islamic provisions. It explores the theological discussions presented in *Risālat al-tawḥīd* and compares ʿAbduh's perspectives with those of classical schools of jurisprudence. It further examines the influence of these theological positions on ʿAbduh's legal interpretations, particularly in his analysis of family law, where his religious discourse is distinctly reflected, as he consistently employed the concept of *maṣlaḥa* as a guiding legal principle. This emphasis underscores his dual commitment to religious reform and societal progress.

By re-evaluating traditional rulings through the lens of ethical considerations and contemporary societal realities, ʿAbduh challenged established interpretations that, in his view, failed to uphold the core Islamic principles of justice and equality. His critiques of polygamy and oral divorce, for instance, demonstrate his ability to reconcile classical jurisprudential frameworks with a modern understanding of social dynamics, particularly in advocating for women's rights and human dignity.

To provide a comprehensive analysis, the study draws on primary sources such as *Risālat al-tawḥīd*, articles from *al-Manār* magazine, co-published with Jamāl al-Dīn al-Afghānī (d. 1315/1897), and *al-Aʿmāl al-kāmila*, compiled by Muḥammad ʿImāra (d. 1441/2020). These are supplemented with secondary sources—Arabic and non-Arabic—that explore ʿAbduh's reformist thought and legal opinions. This analysis revolves around three key dimensions. First: Abduh's conception of reason as a theological and epistemological tool, examining its role in understanding and interpreting religious doctrines. Second: the application of reason in matters of belief, exploring how he utilized reason to address theological questions. Third: the application of reason and the concept of *maṣlaḥa* in his jurisprudential thought, with a particular focus on his positions on the definition of marriage, the permissibility of polygamy, and the validity of oral divorce, which have figured prominently in ʿAbduh's reform project.[4]

4 Yusra Khreegi, *Women in the Writings of Muhammad ʿAbduh* (School of Oriental and African Studies, University of London, 2014; PhD thesis), 137, https://eprints.soas.ac.uk/20318/.

3 Imām Muḥammad ʿAbduh

Muḥammad ʿAbduh was born around 1849 and received his early traditional religious education at al-Azhar Mosque in Cairo, earning the *ʿālimiyya* degree in 1877, which qualified him to teach at al-Azhar University. In 1880, ʿAbduh became the editor-in-chief of Egypt's official journal *al-Waqāʾiʿ al-miṣriyya* (*Egyptian Affairs*), where he voiced progressive views on social, moral, and legal issues, including polygamy, which he would later explore in his Qurʾānic commentary. His involvement with the ʿUrābī movement, which sought constitutional reform and opposition to foreign control, led to his arrest and subsequent exile to Paris. There, he collaborated with the prominent reformer Jamāl al-Dīn al-Afghānī to publish the influential journal *al-ʿUrwa al-wuthqā* (*The Firmest Bond*), a platform for advocating political and social reform across the Muslim world. Following his exile, ʿAbduh taught theology, history, and Arabic literature at a progressive school in Beirut before returning to Egypt in 1888. Under the reign of Khedive ʿAbbās Ḥilmī II (r. 1892–1914), he held several prestigious positions, reflecting his influence and status as a reformer. In 1894, he was appointed to the al-Azhar Administrative Council, and in 1899, he became the Grand Mufti of Egypt. As Grand Mufti, ʿAbduh was not confined to issuing fatwas but actively engaged in intellectual discourse through newspaper publications, lectures, and books, including works on Qurʾānic exegesis. Despite his widespread influence, ʿAbduh faced increasing criticism from traditional scholars at al-Azhar for his non-conventional views, which were reflected in several controversial fatwas. On July 11, 1905, ʿAbduh passed away from cancer in Alexandria, leaving behind a rich legacy as a pioneer of Islamic modernism and a key figure in the intellectual revival of the Muslim world.[5]

ʿAbduh's most significant work, *Risālat al-tawḥīd* (*Theology of Unity*, first edition published in 1897), presents an in-depth exploration of key theological concepts and issues, positioning reason as central to understanding faith and belief.[6] In addition to *Risālat al-tawḥīd*, ʿAbduh contributed a partial commentary on the Qurʾān, which was later completed by his disciple Muḥammad Rashīd Riḍā (d. 1354/1935). Riḍā published the full commentary under the title *al-Manār*, a seminal work of modern Qurʾānic exegesis that reflects ʿAbduh's

5 For more information see Johanna Pink, "ʿAbduh, Muḥammad," in *Encyclopaedia of the Qurʾān*, ed. Jane Dammen McAuliffe (Leiden: Brill, 2015), consulted online on 13 March 2022 at http://dx.doi.org/10.1163/1875-3922_q3_EQCOM_050483.

6 Anke Kügelgen, "ʿAbduh, Muḥammad," in *Encyclopaedia of Islam Three Online*, ed. Kate Fleet, Gudrun Krämer, Denis Matringe, John Nawas, and Everett Rowson, consulted online on 13 July 2021 at http://dx.doi.org/10.1163/1573-3912_ei3_COM_0103.

reformist interpretations and engagement with contemporary issues. ʿAbduh's engagement with interreligious discourse and critique of modernity is further evident in his *al-Islām bayna al-ʿilm wa-l-madaniyya* (*Islam between Science and Civilization*), a work written as a refutation of the views of Christian thinker Faraḥ Antūn (d. 1430/1922). In this text, ʿAbduh defends Islam against claims that it is incompatible with scientific progress and modern civilization. Similarly, his work *al-Islām wa-l-radd ʿalā muntaqidīh* (*Islam and the Defense against Its Critics*) critically addresses the arguments of French historian Gabriel Hanotaux (d. 1944), showcasing his efforts to challenge misconceptions and defend the intellectual and moral integrity of Islam. Beyond these major works, ʿAbduh was a prolific writer who contributed numerous articles to *al-Manār* and various Egyptian newspapers. Muḥammad ʿImāra, an influential Egyptian thinker, recognized the significance of ʿAbduh's contributions and compiled his complete works in four volumes under the title *al-Aʿmāl al-kāmila* (*The Complete Works*). This collection, published by Dār al-Shurūq in 1993, includes ʿAbduh's writings alongside ʿImāra's insightful commentary, providing a comprehensive resource for understanding ʿAbduh's ideas and their enduring impact on Islamic reform.

3.1 *The Concept of Reason in the Thought of Muḥammad ʿAbduh*

One of the most defining characteristics of Muḥammad ʿAbduh's reformist religious thought is his emphasis on the pivotal role of reason in addressing various religious issues. He championed reason as a fundamental tool for understanding and interpreting religious rulings, emphasizing the inherent compatibility between Islam and rationality. To this end, ʿAbduh authored several articles addressing the role of reason in comprehending the teachings of Islam. Moreover, he engaged with the concept of reason extensively in his theological discussions and his commentary on the Qurʾān. For ʿAbduh, reason functions as a criterion for discerning interests and benefits and plays a central role in understanding the relationship between humanity and the universe, as well as the connection between the soul and the body. He eloquently described reason as follows:

> Reason is one of the loftiest powers. Moreover, it is the strength and pillar of human power. The whole universe is the document that reason looks at and the book it reads. Indeed, everything that could be read is a guide and a way to God.[7]

7 Muḥammad ʿAbduh, *al-Aʿmāl al-kāmila*, ed. Muḥammad ʿImāra (Cairo: Dār al-Shurūq, 1414/1993), vol. 3, 295.

In his theological treatise *Risālat al-tawḥīd*, ʿAbduh frequently employs a rationalist approach, which in many instances aligns with the methodologies of the Muʿtazila. His reliance on reason in addressing theological issues reflects his commitment to rational speculation as the primary means of understanding the principles of Islam. Two key passages from his works—the Qurʾānic commentary *al-Manār* and *Risālat al-tawḥīd*—illustrate ʿAbduh's vision of reason and its role in human life and the interpretation of legal provisions.

In his commentary on the Qurʾānic verse "They ask you, [O Muḥammad], about the crescent moons ..." (Qurʾān 2:189), ʿAbduh asserts: "What a human can understand by himself, Prophets are not asked to explain."[8] This statement underscores ʿAbduh's belief that reason is the primary source of knowledge, and therefore, individuals should not rely on revelation or the teachings of the Prophets for matters that are within the reach of rational understanding.

This means that reason, according to ʿAbduh, is the first basis of knowledge, and therefore a person should not understand the matters of his religion by means of revelation or the heritage of the Prophets except in matters that reason is unable to perceive. Thus, ʿAbduh states that the first principle of Islam is *al-naẓar al-ʿaqlī* ('rational speculation'). He stresses that turning to external mediation in matters comprehensible to reason neglects the innate talents and intellectual faculties that God has endowed humanity with.[9] This position highlights his broader vision of Islam as a religion deeply rooted in rationality and his belief in the harmonious relationship between reason and revelation, where each complements the other without contradiction.

The second quote refers to the benefit that accrues to man (or humanity) from relying on reason. Muḥammad ʿAbduh here draws a connection between the role of reason, as perceived in Islam, and the ethical values that arise from adopting rationality in practical life. In *Risālat al-tawḥīd*, ʿAbduh says:

> Islamic rationality equips man with two great things he was deprived of for a long time, namely, freedom of will and independence of opinion and thought. Humanity is built on these two and with them man was prepared to reach the happiness God meant for him to reach.[10]

---

8 Muḥammad Rashīd Riḍā and Muḥammad ʿAbduh, *Tafsīr al-Manār* (Cairo: Maṭbaʿat al-Manār, 1350/1931), vol. 2, 204.

9 Cf. Harun Nasution, *The Place of Reason in ʿAbduh's Theology: Its Impact on His Theological System and Views* (McGill University, 1968; PhD thesis), 57, https://escholarship.mcgill.ca/concern/theses/pz50h1458.

10 Muḥammad ʿAbduh, *Risālat al-tawḥīd* (Cairo: al-Maṭbaʿa al-Khayriyya, 1343/1924), 86.

This statement encapsulates ʿAbduh's conviction that freedom of will and independence of thought are fundamental to human completeness and are direct results of employing reason in life. He regards these attributes not as incidental but as essential to humanity's capacity to achieve the divine purpose of happiness and fulfillment. However, his characterization of this rationality as "Islamic" is crucial, as it underscores that he does not promote an unrestrained or absolute reliance on reason. Instead, he conceives of reason as operating within the boundaries of Islamic teachings, where it is harmonized with and governed by the principles of faith. This framework ensures that rationality remains aligned with ethical and spiritual objectives, reflecting the intended balance between human intellectual capability and divine guidance.

ʿAbduh's conception of the role of reason in attaining freedom of opinion and thought is derived primarily from the Qurʾānic verses that exhort individuals to engage in rational speculation and contemplation of the universe as a pathway to belief in God. This freedom, which arises through the use of reason, serves as a foundational influence on ʿAbduh's legal thought, as will be explored further in the second section. In essence, ʿAbduh views human freedom to choose one's actions as the crucial link between his theological positions and his reformist stance on socio-legal issues. This freedom, however, is not unrestricted but remains firmly rooted in the framework of Islamic rationality, closely intertwined with a belief in God and the moral responsibilities that such belief entails.[11]

The question that arises in this context is: What are the boundaries of reason in ʿAbduh's intellectual framework? This inquiry highlights the intersection between ʿAbduh's perspective and the Muʿtazilī approach regarding the interplay of reason and revelation. While ʿAbduh emphasizes the centrality of reason, he acknowledges its limitations in certain legal and metaphysical matters. He contends that human reason, despite its capacity for rational inquiry, requires the guidance of revelation to prevent it from falling into the pitfalls of natural religiosity. Without this divine guidance, reason alone, according to ʿAbduh, is "insufficient to secure human happiness and fulfillment in this world." Revelation thus plays a complementary role, ensuring that reason operates within a framework that aligns with divine wisdom and the ultimate purpose of human existence:[12]

> For the issues that are not possible to be comprehended, that sense and reason fail to perceive, or that are difficult to identify, we need a guide

11 Kügelgen, "ʿAbduh, Muḥammad."

12 Cf. ʿAbduh, *Risālat al-tawḥīd*, 41.

> with a revelation from God Almighty so that we can accept them through faith and submission, which is why I said that the messenger is the mind of the nation.[13]

ʿAbduh's description of the messenger as the "mind" of the nation underscores his recognition of the limitations of individual intellect in discerning legal rulings that are exclusively accessible through revelation. Even in such cases, ʿAbduh intriguingly equates revelation itself with reason, suggesting that divine guidance operates as a higher form of intellect, aligned with but surpassing human reasoning capabilities. This perspective resonates with the Muʿtazilī framework, which differentiates between rulings derived from reason (*aḥkām ʿaqliyya*) and those dependent on revelation (*aḥkām sharʿiyya*). The Muʿtazila emphasized that while revelation provides rulings inaccessible to reason, it must never contradict rational principles. Al-Qāḍī ʿAbd al-Jabbār, a prominent Muʿtazilī scholar, elaborates on this dynamic in *al-Mughnī fī abwāb al-tawḥīd wa al-ʿadl*. He classifies legal provisions into two types: those discernible through reason, referred to as "reason-based provisions," and those reliant on revelation, termed "revelation-based provisions."[14] Among the latter are "acts of worship and other matters that transcend rational comprehension," requiring submission to divine command.[15] Like the Muʿtazila, ʿAbduh maintains that there must be no contradiction between the rulings of revelation and the dictates of reason, thus affirming a harmonious relationship between the two. Harun Nasution indirectly underscores this similarity between ʿAbduh and the Muʿtazila by emphasizing that ʿAbduh views revelation as both a confirmation of the truths discerned by reason and a source of guidance for matters beyond the capacity of human intellect:

> Reason, having a certain power, exerts itself to attain knowledge of God, and revelation having certain functions, comes down to man to confirm the knowledge he has obtained through reason, as well as to inform him of matters which his reason has not been able to discover.[16]

---

13 Riḍā and ʿAbduh, *Tafsīr al-Manār*, vol. 2, 204.

14 al-Qāḍī ʿAbd al-Jabbār al-Hamadhānī, *al-Mughnī fī abwāb al-tawḥīd wa-l-ʿadl*, ed. Ṭāhā Ḥusayn and Amīn al-Khūlī (Cairo: The Egyptian General Institution for Authorship, Translation, Printing and Publishing, 1381/1961), part no. 17, "Legal Matters," 95.

15 Ibid., 101.

16 Nasution, *The Place of Reason in ʿAbduh's Theology*, 52.

What stands out in this context is ʿAbduh's innovative discussion on the limitations of human senses and desires, which can impede reason from fulfilling its intended function. He argues that, in such situations, human beings require revelation to discern the truth about what is morally good or evil. To illustrate this, ʿAbduh presents the example of an individual who abuses narcotic substances. While this person may intellectually recognize the harm such substances cause to others, their own desires, dominated by lust, prevent them from acknowledging the harm these substances inflict upon themselves. Consequently, they prioritize their immediate pleasure over the rational directive to avoid what is harmful. In ʿAbduh's framework, this scenario underscores the necessity of an external guide—revelation—to bolster reason against the dominance of sensory desires. He explains that revelation, conveyed through the messenger, serves as this higher teacher, reinforcing the authority of reason and providing a moral deterrent against the temptations of lust. By doing so, revelation ensures that individuals adhere to the path of righteousness and align their actions with ethical principles.[17]

Several researchers have examined Muḥammad ʿAbduh's rationality, recognizing it as one of the most defining features of his reformist thought. This focus has led scholars to describe his rationality in ways that align with their own interpretative frameworks for analyzing ʿAbduh's intellectual contributions. For instance, Moroccan scholar ʿAmmār bin Ḥammūda,[18] in his work *Athar al-muʿtazila fī al-fikr al-islāmī al-ḥadīth* (*The Impact of the Muʿtazilī School on Modern Islamic Thought*), refers to ʿAbduh's rationality as "Islamic (or believing) rationality."[19] This description emerges in the context of Ḥammūda's discussion on the influence of ʿAbduh's ideas on Muḥammad ʿImāra's reception of Muʿtazilī thought.

Conversely, Tunisian scholar Muḥammad al-Ḥaddād,[20] in his book *Muḥammad ʿAbduh: Qirāʾa jadīda fī khiṭāb al-iṣlāḥ al-dīnī* (*Muḥammad ʿAbduh: A New Reading of the Discourse of Religious Reform*), characterizes ʿAbduh's

---

17 Cf. Riḍā and ʿAbduh, *Tafsīr al-Manār*, vol. 2, 204.

18 Bin Ḥammūda is a Tunisian scholar specializing in Islamic literature and civilization. He holds a PhD and serves as a professor at the Faculty of Arts and Humanities in Sfax, Tunisia. His research focuses on the influence of Muʿtazilī thought on modern Islamic thought.

19 ʿAmmār Bin Ḥammūda, *Athar al-muʿtazila fī al-fikr al-islāmī al-ḥadīth* (Beirut: Arab Cultural Center, 1435/2014), 77.

20 Al-Ḥaddād is a prominent Tunisian scholar and academic. He holds a PhD from the Sorbonne University in Paris and currently serves as a professor of higher education at the University of Manouba, Tunisia. His research interests encompass Islamic studies, with a particular focus on hermeneutics and literary criticism within the Islamic discourse.

approach as "moral rationalism." Al-Ḥaddād argues that ʿAbduh considers reason to be both a criterion for knowledge and a foundation for ethics. This conviction aligns ʿAbduh with certain Muʿtazilī views, particularly the belief that reason has the independent capacity to discern moral good (*al-ḥusn*) and moral wrong (*al-qubḥ*), even in the absence of scripture. According to al-Ḥaddād, ʿAbduh's position stems from his belief in the inherent moral value of reason, which he sees as absolute and transcendent, with revelation serving primarily to affirm this intrinsic value.[21]

Another significant interpretation comes from Egyptian thinker Muḥammad ʿImāra,[22] who, in his book *al-Manhaj al-iṣlāḥī li-l-Imām Muḥammad ʿAbduh* (*The Reformist Approach of Imām Muḥammad ʿAbduh*), describes ʿAbduh's rationality as "moderate rationality." According to ʿImāra, this rationality stands in opposition to two extremes: the literalist Wahhābī–Salafī approach to Sharīʿa interpretation and the materialist perspective that entirely rejects scripture and revelation as sources of knowledge. For ʿImāra, ʿAbduh's rationality seeks a balanced path that integrates reason and revelation without succumbing to the excesses of either extreme.[23]

The diversity in how scholars characterize ʿAbduh's rational approach reflects the plurality of intellectual influences that shaped his thought. These influences include classical Islamic philosophers, theologians, works on logic and ethics, as well as modern Western thinkers such as Jean-Jacques Rousseau (d. 1778), Immanuel Kant (d. 1804), Jules Francois Simon (d. 1896), Ernest Renan (d. 1892), and Herbert Spencer (d. 1903). This scholarly variety, while enriching ʿAbduh's intellectual project, also makes it challenging to ascribe a single, cohesive systematic identity to his body of work, whether in *tafsīr*, *fiqh*, *fatwa*, or his political writings. This lack of a unified methodological framework has drawn criticism from some scholars. Al-Ḥaddād, for example, underscores the complexity of ʿAbduh's intellectual diversity, noting that his engagement extended beyond Islamic texts to include significant works of Western philosophy and social thought. ʿAbduh's translation of Spencer's educational treatise *Education: Intellectual, Moral, and Physical* into Arabic exemplifies

21 Muḥammad al-Ḥaddād, *Muḥammad ʿAbduh: Qirāʾa jadīda fī khiṭāb al-iṣlāḥ al-dīnī* (Beirut: Dār al-Ṭalīʿa, 1424/2003), 133.

22 ʿImāra (d. 1441/2020) was an Egyptian Islamic thinker, author, and editor. He wrote numerous books on the Muʿtazila and Islamic philosophy. In the 1960s, he delved deeply into the political teachings of Averroes, aiming to revitalize Arab thought. ʿImāra held several leading positions at al-Azhar. In addition to his membership in the Academy of Islamic Research, he also served as editor-in-chief of the al-Azhar Magazine.

23 Muḥammad ʿImāra, *al-Manhaj al-iṣlāḥī li-l-Imām Muḥammad ʿAbduh* (Cairo: Dār al-salām, 1430/2009), 63.

this cross-cultural intellectual engagement. Al-Ḥaddād reiterates the difficulty of pinpointing a dominant system within ʿAbduh's rational approach, an observation that reflects both the richness and the ambiguities of his intellectual legacy.[24]

In the following section, this study will undertake a practical analysis of some of ʿAbduh's key theological positions, with a particular focus on his discourse regarding moral valuation (*al-ḥusn wa-l-qubḥ*), which serves as a critical point of comparison between ʿAbduh's rational approach and the principles of the Muʿtazila. As one of the most contentious issues in classical Islamic thought, *al-ḥusn wa-l-qubḥ* carries profound implications, extending beyond theology into the foundational principles of Islamic legal theory (*uṣūl al-fiqh*).

3.2 *The Role of the Reason in Belief*

One of the most significant influences on ʿAbduh's discourse of the role on reason is the theological debate among *kalām*-scholars concerning the relationship between reason and revelation. This discourse profoundly shaped his views, evident both in his treatment of theological issues in *Risālat al-tawḥīd* and in his responses to critics of Islamic teachings. This influence is particularly pronounced in his discussions on the role of reason and the rational foundations of Islam. In his book *al-Islām bayn al-ʿilm wa-l-madaniyya* (*Islam Between Science and Civilization*), written in response to Faraḥ Antūn, ʿAbduh identifies five foundational principles of Islamic faith (theological principles of Islam), namely:[25]
- Rational speculation (*al-naẓar al-ʿaqlī*) for the acquisition of faith;
- Giving precedence to reason over the literal meaning of scripture in case there is a conflict;
- Avoiding *takfīr* (labeling Muslims as disbelievers);
- Considering the divine norms in the universe;
- Getting rid of theocracy.

Although ʿAbduh did not explicitly clarify what he meant by the term *uṣūl* ('principles'), we can still discern the general framework of his reformist

24 Al-Ḥaddād, *Muḥammad ʿAbduh*, 127: "ʿAbduh's discourse does not seem attempting to set standards as much as attempting to justify a set of primary values based on multiple systems in order to confirm the values' absolute nature. It would then be the same either to present the matter in the name of religion or present it in the name of reason, or to rely on Miskawayh or Herbert Spencer. [...] What is important to ʿAbduh is to prove the existence of absolute values."

25 Muḥammad ʿAbduh, *al-Islām bayn al-ʿilm wa-l-madaniyya* (Cairo: Muʾassasat hindāwī li-l-taʿlīm wa-l-thaqāfa, 1433/2012), 78; Mīshāl Juḥā, *al-Munāẓara al-dīniyya bayna al-Shaykh Muḥammad ʿAbduh wa-Faraḥ Anṭūn* (Beirut: Baysān li-l-nashr wa-l-tawzīʿ, 1435/2014), 230.

thought through them. The first and second principles highlight the prominent role reason occupies in this framework, clearly reflecting the significant similarities between his methodology and Muʿtazilī thought. According to ʿAbduh, belief in the existence of God is based solely on reason. It is not the prophets or the revealed scriptures that lead to faith in God and His Oneness, but rather *al-naẓar al-ʿaqlī* ('rational speculation'), which he identifies as the first foundational principle established in Islam. For this reason, Muḥammad ʿAbduh designates rationality as the first theological principle among the five principles he outlines:

> The first foundational principle of Islam is *al-naẓar al-ʿaqlī*. In Islam, rational speculation serves as a means of attaining genuine faith. Islam presents reason as a source of evidence and as an arbiter of truth. He who accepts reason as an arbiter must submit to its judgment.[26]

Although the concept of *al-naẓar al-ʿaqlī* ('rational speculation') has been a significant element in theological discourse since the 4th/10th century among *kalām* scholars, notable differences arose regarding its application to various theological questions. Chief among these debates is the issue of *al-taḥsīn wa-l-taqbīḥ* ('determining what is morally good and what is morally evil'), which I will explore in detail later in the discussion of ʿAbduh's position on this matter.

The Muʿtazilīs championed rational speculation, asserting that knowledge of God can only be achieved through reason. They maintained that other sources of knowledge, including those of *sharīʿa*—such as the Qur'ān, Sunnah, and *ijmāʿ* ('consensus')—are contingent on the rational comprehension of God, His Oneness, and His Justice.[27] Conversely, the other theological schools, while acknowledging reason as a tool for acquiring knowledge, rejected its necessity as a foundational means of attaining such knowledge. For the Ashʿarīs, for instance, knowledge is acquired necessarily and directly through revelation (the Qur'ān and the Sunnah). They argued that reliance on reason alone may lead to doubt, which undermines faith and weakens the certitude upon which belief rests.[28] On this basis, it can be noted that there is a convergence between ʿAbduh's view and the Muʿtazilī perspective, as evidenced by his emphasis on the principle that reason must take precedence over the literal meaning of scripture in cases of apparent conflict. This principle, widely

---

26 ʿAbduh, *al-Islām bayn al-ʿilm wa-l-madaniyya*, 78.

27 Cf. Sulaymān Sālim ʿAlam al-Dīn, *al-Muʿtazila* (Beirut: Nūfal Publications, 1421/2000), 206.

28 Ibid., 202.

associated with the Muʿtazilīs, involves the use of *taʾwīl* ('interpretation') as a rational method to resolve contradictions between the apparent meaning of a text and the conclusions of reason. This approach relies on definitive Qurʾānic verses and established linguistic principles as its foundation.[29] ʿAbduh explicitly referred to this principle in his discussions, alongside other theological positions that reflect his rationalist and reformist stance:

> The scholars of the Islamic tradition, with few exceptions not considered significant, have unanimously agreed that when reason and revelation are in apparent conflict, priority is given to what is established by reason. As for the text of revelation, there are two possible approaches: first, accepting the validity of the transmitted text while acknowledging the inability to comprehend its meaning, and entrusting the matter to God's knowledge; second, interpreting the text (*taʾwīl*) in accordance with the rules of language to align its meaning with what reason has affirmed.[30]

ʿAbduh's belief in this principle prompted him to assert that there is an agreement among all scholars (except for a few) on this principle. However, it is well known that there is no such agreement on this issue. A good number of scholars refused the precedence of reason over revelation on the pretext that there is no conflict between the authentic revelation and explicit reason. Ibn Taymiyya (d. 728/1328), for example, wrote his famous book *Darʾ taʿāruḍ al-ʿaql wa-l-naql* (*Refutation of the Conflict of Reason and Revelation*)[31] to refute this claim. It seems that ʿAbduh was influenced in his view by the Muʿtazilīs and some later Ashʿarīs, such as al-Rāzī (d. 606/1209) and Ibn Rushd (d. 595/1198), in terms of giving precedence to reason over revelation in the case of conflict and resorting to rational reconciliation between proofs to remove this contradiction. ʿAbduh refers to the opponents who doubt reason's ability to realize the belief, "those are the Salafīs, *muḥaddithūn* ('scholars of *ḥadīth*') and *mushabbiha* ('anthropomorphists')."[32] He applied this principle in many issues discussed in his articles, such as the issue of the Oneness of God, human actions, *al-qaḍāʾ wa-l-qadar* ('predestination'), polygamy, and divorce.

---

29 Cf. Zāhid Khalaf Rūsān, "Mawqif al-ʿaql kamā yarāhu al-Imām Muḥammad ʿAbduh min baʿḍ al-mafāhīm allatī ṭaraḥahā al-Islām," *Journal of Damascus University*, 18/3 (1423/2002), 137–67, here 140.

30 ʿAbduh, *al-Islām bayn al-ʿilm wa-l-madaniyya*, 78.

31 Abū al-ʿAbbās Taqīyy al-Dīn Aḥmad Ibn Taymiyya, *Darʾ taʿāruḍ al-ʿaql wa-l-naql*, ed. Muḥammad Rashād Sālim (Riyadh: Imam Muhammad Bin Saud Islamic University, 1411/1991).

32 Rūsān, "Mawqif al-ʿaql kamā yarāhu al-Imām Muḥammad," 140.

Another central aspect of ʿAbduh's rationalist approach concerns the identification of *al-taḥsīn wa-l-taqbīḥ*. This issue has been one of the most debated topics among Muslim theologians, particularly its implications for divine reward, punishment, and human accountability in *uṣūl al-fiqh*. Through an in-depth reading of ʿAbduh works, we can conclude an agreement with the opinion of the Muʿtazilīs on this issue, he asserts that reason independently discerns good and evil without reliance on revelation. For ʿAbduh, human voluntary actions are judged as good or evil based on their inherent outcomes: actions are deemed "good" due to their benefits and "evil" due to their harms. He explains in *Risālat al-tawḥīd*:

> Voluntary actions are good or bad in themselves or by reference to their particular or general consequences. Sense and reason are well able to distinguish the two in the above examples without having to rely on revelation.[33]

Thus, the issue of distinguishing between *ḥasan* and *qabīḥ* is known to human reasoning which differentiates between what is harmful and what is beneficial, labeling the former as "the act of evil" and the latter as "the act of goodness." ʿAbduh rejects the classical statement of Ashʿarīs that "*ḥasan* is what is declared so by the *sharʿ* ('revelation') and *qabīḥ* is what is declared so by the *sharʿ*."[34] Thus, the ability to distinguish between good and evil is not solely dependent, in his view, on the revelation (or the *sharīʿa*), but rather reason precedes the revelation in this, and the revelation comes only to reveal this to us. It is noteworthy that some researchers emphasized this convergence between ʿAbduh's view and the Muʿtazilīs' views regarding the issue of *al-ḥusn wa-l-qubḥ* ('good and evil').[35] Thomas Hildebrandt indicated that Muḥammad ʿAbduh adopted

---

33 ʿAbduh, *Risālat al-tawḥīd*, 37.

34 Al-Qāḍī Abū Bakr Muḥammad Ibn al-Ṭayyib al-Bāqillānī, *al-Taqrīb wa al-irshād*, ed. ʿAbd al-Ḥamīd Ibn ʿAli Abū Zunayd (Beirut: Risālah Foundation, 1419/1998): "The reason itself does not judge something as good […] or evil […]. Rather, the deed of *mukallaf* ('legally responsible person') should be described as good or evil based on God's judgement."

35 Cf. al-Ḥaddād, *Muḥammad ʿAbduh*, 133; Rūsān, *Mawqif al-ʿaql kamā yarāhu al-Imām Muḥammad*, 140; Aḥmad Khamīs Zakī Mirʿī, "Athar al-nazʿa al-ʿaqliyya ʿinda al-Muʿtazila fī ʾārāʾ kull min Jamāl al-Dīn al-Afghānī (t. 1897) wa-Muḥammad ʿAbduh (t. 1905) al-kalāmiyya," *Journal al-baḥth al-ʿilmī fī al-ʾādāb*, 23/5 (1443/2022), 65–83, here 75, https://jssa.journals.ekb.eg/article_268831.html; Muḥammad ʿAbduh and Ṭārik ʿAbd al-Ḥalīm, *al-Muʿtazila bayna al-qadīm wa-l-ḥadīth* (Birmingham: Dār al-Arqam, 1987), 128; Haider Kh. Murad, "al-Muʿtazila wa-atharuhum fī al-fikr al-siyāsī fī al-tārīkh al-islāmī wa-l-muʿāṣir," *Journal Ahl al-Bayt ʿalayhim al-salām*, 21 (1443/2022), 53–74, here 69, https://abu.edu.iq:8081/ar/research/articles/68062.

the Muʿtazilī view on this issue to emphasize the ability of the human reason to realize the inherent moral value of its actions.[36]

The final issue I wish to address in this context is the matter of "the creation of actions." In *Risālat al-tawḥīd*, Imām ʿAbduh assigns an independent role to reason in judging human actions. Through his perspective on this issue, ʿAbduh sought to reconcile the views of various theological schools, rejecting the dogmatic adherence to specific opinions. The question of "the creation of voluntary actions" was a subject of significant debate among the Muʿtazila, the Ashʿarīs, and the Jabarīya. Imām ʿAbduh asserts in *Risālat al-tawḥīd* that humans are

> aware of their voluntary actions, weighing their outcomes with reason, assessing them with their will, and then executing them with an inherent power within themselves. To deny any part of this is equivalent to denying one's own existence, as it contradicts the self-evident truths of reason.[37]

By using the expression "an inherent power," ʿAbduh avoids taking a clear stance in favor of either the Muʿtazilī or the Ashʿarī positions. He rejects the Muʿtazilī view, which attributes full authority to humans over their actions, describing it as "an obvious delusion on their part." At the same time, he critiques the Ashʿarī doctrine of *kasb* ('acquisition'), labeling it as "a negation of accountability and a nullification of the self-evident rulings of reason." ʿAbduh neither defines the concept of *power* he uses as a contingent power acquired

36 Thomas Hildebrandt, "Waren Ǧamāl ad-Dīn al-Afġānī und Muḥammad ʿAbduh Neo-Muʿtaziliten?" ("Were Jamāl ad-Dīn al-Afghānī and Muḥammad ʿAbduh Neo-Muʿtazilī?") *Die Welt des Islams*, 42/2 (2002), 207–62 writes: "Was die Moral betrifft, so erinnert ʿAbduhs Haltung in der Tat stark an die mu'tazilitische Position. [...] Für ʿAbduh kann der Mensch nicht nur die ästhetischen Kategorien „schön" und „hässlich" von allein unterscheiden [...], sondern er sei auch in der Lage, seine frei gewählten Taten (*al-afʿāl al-ikhtiyāriya*) selbständig auf ihren moralischen Wert hin zu beurteilen, denn diese Taten seien in sich selbst (*fī nafsihā*) bzw. im Hinblick auf die durch sie entstehenden Folgen „gut" oder „schlecht". Somit verfüge der Mensch über die Fähigkeit, die Tugenden und die Last durch die bloße Vernunft zu erkennen." ("With regard to morality, ʿAbduh's position indeed strongly recalls the Muʿtazilī stance. [...] For ʿAbduh, humans are not only capable of independently distinguishing between the aesthetic categories of "good" and "evil" by himself [...], but they are also able to assess the moral value of their freely chosen actions (*al-afʿāl al-ikhtiyāriyya*). These actions, he argues, are 'inherently' (*fī nafsihā*) or consequentially "good" or "bad" based on the outcomes they produce. Thus, humans possess the ability to discern virtues and burdens solely through reason."). (See p. 244f.)

37 ʿAbduh, *Risālat al-tawḥīd*, 30.

by humans after intending and resolving to act, as the Ashʿarīs assert, nor does he describe it as created by humans themselves, as the Muʿtazila claim. Instead, he refrains from delving into metaphysical speculations about this power, stating,

> The secret of power is beyond our reach, and we are prohibited from engaging in matters that reason can scarcely grasp.[38]

What is most important in this discussion is ʿAbduh's emphasis on human freedom in choosing their actions and their responsibility for these choices.[39] This affirmation links ʿAbduh's theological thought with his perspective on socio-legal issues, as we will see in the next section. He provides an example of this responsibility and the sense of accountability by describing someone who fails in a task or in saving another person from peril. This individual realizes their misjudgment and reattempts the task with alternative means to achieve success, driven by the belief that they are the agent of their actions and responsible for them. ʿAbduh comments on this, stating that through this understanding,

> Divine Ordinances are effectuated. Whoever denies any part of this denies the very foundation of faith within themselves, which is their reason, honored by God through His commands and prohibitions.[40]

In the following section, I will present examples of how Imām Muḥammad ʿAbduh's rationalist methodology influenced his treatment of certain legal issues, particularly his perspectives on marriage, polygamy, and oral divorce.

---

38 Ibid.

39 Nasution believes that this conclusion makes ʿAbduh's viewpoint quite similar to the Muʿtazilī school of thought, though not identical to it. See Nasution, *The Place of Reason in ʿAbduh's Theology*, 158: "[T]he result of this discussion is that the Muʿtazilah and ʿAbduh, as his *Risālah* reveals, have the same opinion that man has a great degree of free will and free act. Their similar ideas of man's independence and man's power as implied in their mutual ascription of the same powers to reason, have led them to the same conclusion with regard to the question of free will and predestination. The difference between them is that while ʿAbduh believes in the natural power of man, the power that is innately created with him, the Muʿtazilah seem to think that the power is created before the act, i.e. that it is not man's natural power."

40 Ibid., 31.

3.3 *Impact of the Rational Approach on ʿAbduh's Discussion of Legal Issues*

The practical implementation of ʿAbduh's rationalist thought is particularly evident in his treatment of social and legal issues, especially those pertaining to family law, such as the definition of marriage, the permissibility of polygamy, and divorce procedures. Yusra Khreegi's study highlights the centrality of these issues within Imām Muḥammad ʿAbduh's reformist project, attributing his focus on them to four primary reasons.

> First, ʿAbduh's rural upbringing—where family values are sacred and family solidarity is central to social and economic life—certainly influenced his interest in upholding family values and concern about the disintegration of traditional family ties. [Second,] of course, this is inseparable from the traditional Islamic promotion of marriage and family building where the institution of the family is seen as the basic social building block and a bulwark against social discord and disintegration. [Third,] ʿAbduh's focus on education and social reform rather than political change clearly led him to focus on the family as a starting point for reform. Finally, ʿAbduh's professional career, and his participation in fatwa and sharia courts where a large number of cases were related to family law, must have reinforced his belief in the primacy of this area.[41]

This section explores how ʿAbduh's theological principles—especially those emphasizing freedom of thought and human responsibility—shaped his legal approach, with a strong focus on the principles of equality and the freedom of women. These moral principles serve as a key feature linking his theological outlook with his legal interpretations and his broader exegesis of the Qurʾān. ʿAbduh's contributions to the Qurʾānic exegesis in *al-Manār* reflect his commitment to moral guidelines intended to reshape human behavior.[42] This has led some researchers, as noted earlier, to describe ʿAbduh's rationality as "moral rationality." The legal provisions ʿAbduh advocated for family affairs, which were considered reformist in their historical context, stemmed from his theological stance in *Risālat al-tawḥīd*. His emphasis on human freedom to choose actions and accept their consequences underpins these reforms. Central to his framework is the principle of equality between men and women, which he considered foundational to Islamic law and ethics.

---

41 Khreegi, *Women in the Writings of Muhammad ʿAbduh*, 137.

42 Hans Küng, *Der Islam: Wesen und Geschichte* (Munich: Piper Publisher, 2007), 626.

A significant aspect of ʿAbduh's legal methodology is his reliance on the concept of *maṣlaḥa* ('public interest') as a legislative tool to advocate for reformist legal provisions, particularly concerning polygamy. In *uṣūl al-fiqh* ('Islamic legal theory'), *maṣlaḥa* functions as a source of legislation aimed at prioritizing the welfare of society, even if it requires deviating from the literal interpretation of texts. The use of *maṣlaḥa* as a legislative concept dates back to the early development of Islamic legal theory, with theologians emphasizing that God's commands are inherently purposeful, serving both immediate and eternal human interests.[43]

3.3.1 Definition of Marriage

Muḥammad ʿAbduh explicitly critiques the definition of marriage found in classical *fiqh* literature, which overwhelmingly describes it as "a contract through which a man can legally engage in sexual relations with a woman." He laments that such definitions are almost exclusively focused on satisfying physical desires, with little to no reference to the moral responsibilities and higher objectives of marriage. To contrast this narrow legal perspective, ʿAbduh refers to the Qurʾānic verse "And among His Signs is that He created spouses from among yourselves for you to live with in tranquility. He ordained love and kindness between you." (Qurʾān 30:21). For ʿAbduh, this verse captures a more holistic understanding of marriage that prioritizes tranquility, love, and kindness. He argues that the jurists' definitions contributed to a deterioration of women's status in society, which subsequently spread among ordinary Muslims. ʿAbduh states:

> It is not surprising after that to see the low status that marriage has reached as it become just a contract that enables man to enjoy his wife sexually. Moreover, many sub-provisions resulted from this heinous principle.[44]

The definition of marriage as presented by several jurists in classical Islamic legal texts, in Imām ʿAbduh's view, reflects the juristic perception of the marital institution. He critiques this definition for failing to align with the language and ethical dimensions conveyed in the Qurʾān and the Sunnah regarding marriage. However, there are three critical observations that can be made regarding ʿAbduh's critique of this definition.

---

43 Cf. al-Hamadhānī, *al-Sharʿiyyāt*, pp. 13, 35 and 39.

44 Muḥammad ʿAbduh, "al-Zawāj," in *al-Aʿmāl al-kāmila*, vol. 2, 70.

First, ʿAbduh adopts a generalized approach, implying that all jurists defined marriage solely as a contract permitting a man to engage in physical relations with his wife. While this definition is indeed found among some jurists, it is not universally representative. For instance, within the Ḥanafī school of thought, the definition referenced by ʿAbduh aligns with that of Ibn ʿĀbidīn (d. 1252/1836).[45] However, other prominent jurists, such as al-Sarakhsī (d. 483/1090)[46] and al-Mirghiyānī (d. 593/1197),[47] provided alternative definitions that do not explicitly reference physical enjoyment. Second, the definition criticized by ʿAbduh appears in *fiqh* texts, which are primarily focused on legal and contractual matters. These definitions are not intended to capture the full ethical and spiritual dimensions of marriage as highlighted in the Qurʾān. Instead, the Qurʾān's discourse emphasizes moral guidance and the ethical responsibilities inherent in marital life, which are distinct from the technical legal frameworks addressed in *fiqh* literature. Third, ʿAbduh's critique seems heavily influenced by his theological orientation, which emphasizes moral principles. While his criticism is valid to a significant extent, it is also rooted in a framework that prioritizes ethics over legal formalities. Despite the legitimacy of his critique, ʿAbduh does not propose a comprehensive alternative definition to the ones he critiques, leaving a gap in his reformist project.

ʿAbduh continues to discuss some of these aforementioned "sub-provisions," especially the pre-marriage (or engagement) rulings, on which jurists of different *madhāhib* (sg. *madhhab*, 'schools of Islamic Law') approved the permissibility of looking at one's fiancée based on evidence quoted from the Prophet's Sunnah. However, ʿAbduh raises a more fundamental question about women's right to choose their husbands. He rejects the idea that this right should be solely in the hands of male guardians under the guise of preserving modesty and propriety. Although *sharīʿa* grants women this right and jurists have acknowledged that women must be consulted in marriage decisions, ʿAbduh criticizes the jurists for emphasizing men's rights—whether as husbands or guardians—while neglecting to affirm women's equality in this regard.

It is well known in this regard that jurists—other than the Ḥanafīs—agreed that a woman cannot not conclude the marriage contract on her own without having a guardian, and they have devoted a chapter for guardianship to

45 Muḥammad Amīn Ibn ʿUmar Ibn ʿĀbidīn, *Radd al-muḥtār ʿalā al-durr al-mukhtār*, ed. ʿĀdil Aḥmad ʿAbd al-Mawjūd (Riyadh: Dār ʿālam al-kutub, 2003), vol. 4, 59.

46 Shams al-Dīn Muḥammad Ibn Aḥmad al-Sarakhsī, *al-Mabsūṭ fī al-fiqh*, ed. a group of Islamic jurists (Beirut: Dār al-kutub al-ʿilmiyya, n.d.), vol. 4, 192.

47 Burhān al-Dīn Abū al-Ḥasan ʿAlī al-Mirghiyānī, *al-Hidāya: Sharḥ bidāyat al-mubtadī*, ed. Naʿīm Ashraf Nūr Aḥmad (Karachi, Department of Qurʾān and Islamic Sciences, 1417/1996), vol. 3, 3.

identify the order of the woman's male relatives who can assume the position of a guardian.[48] It is only Ḥanafī scholars who opine that a sane and adult woman can conclude her marriage contract herself without having a guardian.[49] ʿAbduh calls for complete equality between men and women with regard to the provisions of engagement. Not only a man who has the right to know about the woman from her guardians, but also women have the same right, ʿAbduh argues, to come to know about the person proposing to her to find out whether he suits her ambitions. ʿAbduh attributes societal customs and traditions that restrict women's rights in this context to the jurists' neglect of the principle of equality. He states:

> Anyone with sound judgment will approve that a woman has the right to choose her husband just as a man has the right to choose his wife, because this matter affects her more than it affects her relatives. […] She has the same right as a man to ensure her expectations are fulfilled.[50]

To support this argument, ʿAbduh cites the Qurʾānic verse "Wives have [rights] similar to their [obligations], according to what is recognized to be fair," (Qurʾān 2, 228), which is a verse that the Qurʾānic exegetes and jurists quote when discussing the provisions of marriage not the issues of engagement. He emphasizes the general meaning of the words of the verse, a matter that indicates the principle of equality. ʿAbduh's approach reflects his broader theological vision, which emphasizes the moral responsibility of individuals before God. He extends his critique beyond juristic definitions and legal frameworks, criticizing the lack of education for women about their rights in the Arab-Islamic context. According to him, if women were properly educated about their societal status and rights, three significant outcomes would follow: (1) marriage would become the natural path to mutual happiness for both men and women; (2) marital relationships would be founded on mutual love and intellectual compatibility; (3) families would recognize women's ability to make sound judgments in selecting a spouse, leading men to respect women's status in society.[51]

The terms used by ʿAbduh, such as "equality," "reason," "education," and "love," hardly appear in the literary or legal articles of his peers, especially

48 ʿAbd al-Raḥmān al-Jazīrī, *al-Fiqh ʿalā al-madhāhib al-arbaʿa* (2nd edition, Beirut: Dār al-kutub al-ʿilmiyya, 1424/2003), vol. 4, 29.

49 Ibid., 35.

50 ʿAbduh, "al-Zawāj," 72–73.

51 Ibid., 74.

the scholars of the al-Azhar, the institution he graduated from and through which he became the Grand Mufti of Egypt. At the end of his speech, ʿAbduh speaks about "men of the new age," who believe in these ideas and refuse to marry except a woman who would be "a friend to have mutual love with, not a maid who is used for any purpose." ʿAbduh also counters accusations of "Westernization" levied against those who support such reformist ideas, urging critics to evaluate these ideas through reason and *sharīʿa*. He argues that these reforms represent "a sound rational renewal."[52]

3.3.2 Polygamy

Muḥammad ʿAbduh's stance on polygamy is one of the most notable examples of his rationalist and reformist approach to legal and social issues. Rejecting the conventional *fiqh*-based view that polygamy is a general legal right simply because it is mentioned in the Qurʾān, ʿAbduh argues that the Qurʾān permits polygamy conditionally and in an exceptionally narrow scope. His views are presented in three significant contexts: his two articles "Taʿaddud al-zawjāt" ("Polygamy"),[53] and "Fatwā fī taʿaddud al-zawjāt" ("Fatwa on Polygamy"),[54] and his commentary on *Sūrat al-Nisāʾ* (Qurʾān 4:3).[55] Tracing ʿAbduh's arguments against polygamy across his writings reveals two key observations.

Firstly, unlike most jurists and Qurʾānic exegetes, ʿAbduh does not primarily rely on direct quotations from the Qurʾān or Sunna in his initial arguments. Instead, he employs rational deduction to highlight the detrimental social consequences of polygamy, describing it as an "old custom" with negative societal impacts. Secondly, ʿAbduh's arguments against polygamy are underpinned by four key concepts: reason, equality, fairness, and *maṣlaḥa*. Both observations confirm the extent to which Muḥammad ʿAbduh was influenced by his theological ideas in *Risālat al-tawḥīd* in which he emphasized the centrality of man, man's reasoning, the freedom of his thought, and the responsibility for his actions, considering these as the pillars that lead to genuine faith. Reflecting these theological underpinnings, ʿAbduh begins his first article against polygamy by addressing the role of human intellect:

> When a husband reaches a state of intellectual perfection that enables him to realize the status of his wife [...] and comes to know that one of

52 Ibid., 75.

53 Muḥammad ʿAbduh, "Taʿaddud a.-zawjāt," in *al-Aʿmāl al-kāmila*, vol. 2, 82.

54 Muḥammad ʿAbduh, "Fatwā fī taʿaddud al-zawjāt," in *al-Aʿmāl al-kāmila*, vol. 2, 88.

55 Riḍā and ʿAbduh, *Tafsīr al-Manār*, vol. 4, 320.

> her rights is to be in the rank she deserves in accordance with *sharīʿa* and humans' natural instinct, he would be satisfied with one wife.[56]

This statement underscores ʿAbduh's belief that intellectual maturity leads to a deeper appreciation of the principles of justice and equality in marital relationships. By framing his arguments within the context of reason and moral responsibility, ʿAbduh not only critiques traditional justifications for polygamy but also advances a vision of marriage rooted in ethical and rational principles.

In another part of the same article, ʿAbduh highlights that the maturity of men's intellects plays a crucial role in eradicating the practice of polygamy. He evaluates polygamy through the lens of rationality, arguing that mature reason must inherently reject this practice, which he frequently refers to as a "custom." Moving further, ʿAbduh asserts that polygamy fundamentally contradicts the principle of human equality. He contends that it is self-evident that polygamy undermines fairness and equality between men and women. Human beings, by their nature, desire exclusivity in marital relationships. Just as a man would dislike another man sharing his wife, a woman would equally find it unbearable to share her husband with another woman.[57] Regarding cases of successful polygamy, which some cite as evidence for its permissibility, ʿAbduh views such instances as rare exceptions that should not serve as the basis for a general rule applicable to society as a whole. Even when jurists cite specific justifications for polygamy, such as a woman suffering from a medical condition that prevents her from conceiving, ʿAbduh regards these as exceptional circumstances. In such cases, he emphasizes the moral obligation of a husband to bear with his wife's suffering, rather than seeking another marriage:

> I say this, and I do not approve of a man marrying another woman even in such cases or similar ones, where the woman is not at fault. Honor and integrity require that he bear with his wife's afflictions, just as she is obligated to bear with any afflictions he might face.[58]

This moral dimension forms the core of ʿAbduh's rejection of polygamy. He argues that polygamy is inherently incompatible with the principle of equality and thus contradicts the essential purpose of marital life, which is founded on

---

56 ʿAbduh, "Taʿaddud al-zawjāt," 82.

57 Ibid., 83.

58 Ibid., 85. In case of lacking these exceptional cases, ʿAbduh considers polygamy "a legal device to satisfy one's bestial lusts and a sign of corruption of morals."

mutual respect and partnership.[59] From an exegetical perspective, ʿAbduh also engages with the Qurʾānic verse that permits polygamy under specific conditions: "If you fear that you will not deal fairly with orphan girls, you may marry whichever [other] women seem good to you, two, three, or four. If you fear that you cannot treat them with equal fairness, then marry only one" (Qurʾān 4: 3). In his *Tafsīr al-Manār*, ʿAbduh emphasizes that the permissibility of polygamy in this verse is strictly conditional upon equitable treatment among wives. He underscores that the Qurʾān itself acknowledges the impossibility of achieving such fairness, as stated later in the same chapter: "You will never be able to treat your wives with equal fairness, no matter how keen you are" (Qurʾān 4: 129).[60]

Although ʿAbduh concurs with other exegetes that the concept of 'fairness' (*ʿadl*) in the Qurʾānic verse regarding polygamy refers to inner feelings, he argues that the Qurʾān frames polygamy as permissible only under the narrowest of circumstances. Despite this, polygamy became a widespread practice and, in ʿAbduh's view, has been accompanied by numerous societal harms, leading to family discord and moral corruption. These include a variety of social ills such as "theft, adultery, lying, unfaithfulness, cowardice, forgery, and murder … all of which are reflected in court cases."[61] Based on his interpretation, ʿAbduh invokes the principle of *maṣlaḥa* ('public interest') to justify the prevention of polygamy due to its harmful consequences. He calls upon jurists to adopt this principle, emphasizing that "religion was revealed for the benefit and welfare of people, and one of its primary objectives is the removal of harm. If something that was once permissible begins to cause harm that it did not previously incur, it becomes necessary to amend the ruling."[62]

In his *fatwā* published in *al-Manār*, ʿAbduh affirms that the Qurʾānic allowance for polygamy is explicitly conditional upon the ability to treat wives equitably. He argues that this condition is inherently unattainable in most cases. While he does not categorically dismiss the possibility of achieving fairness, he describes it as exceedingly rare, stating that it might occur "in one in a million cases" and should therefore not be regarded as the normative basis for polygamy. Moreover, ʿAbduh asserts that the moral corruption prevalent among individuals further diminishes the likelihood of equitable treatment between co-wives. ʿAbduh concludes that the ruler (*waliyy al-amr*) holds the authority

59 Muhammad Sameer Murtaza, *Die Reformer des Islam: Jamāl al-Dīn al-Afghānī, Muḥammad ʿAbduh, Qāsim Amīn, Muḥammad Rashīd Riḍā* (Norderstedt: Book on Demand, 2015), 181.

60 Riḍā and ʿAbduh, *Tafsīr al-Manār*, vol. 4, 348.

61 Ibid., 349.

62 Ibid., 350.

to restrict or prohibit polygamy in accordance with *maṣlaḥa* and prevailing circumstances. Similarly, scholars have the discretion to issue *fatwās* prohibiting polygamy when it serves the greater public interest. By invoking the principle of "consideration of the majority of cases."[63]

ʿAbduh emphasizes the role of *maṣlaḥa* as a legal maxim in Islamic jurisprudence. This principle allows for the suspension or modification of otherwise permissible acts when they result in harm or conflict with public welfare. In another article, ʿAbduh elaborates that the permissibility of polygamy, like all permissible acts, is subject to secondary legal rulings such as 'prohibition' (*taḥrīm*) or 'disapproval' (*karāha*), depending on the resulting harms or benefits.[64] He reinforces this argument by stating:

> In consideration of the public *maṣlaḥa*, the ruler has the authority to prohibit polygamy, with or without conditions, based on what he deems most appropriate for the public good.[65]

3.3.3 Divorce[66]

In his articles about divorce, ʿAbduh maintains his rationalist approach to interpreting *sharīʿa* texts, grounding his analysis in the principle of *maṣlaḥa*. As with other matters of family law, ʿAbduh does not approach divorce solely from a legal standpoint; instead, he integrates socio-ethical considerations, reflecting his holistic understanding of Islamic jurisprudence. He asserts that divorce is fundamentally disapproved of under Islamic *sharīʿa*, supporting his claim with verses from *Sūrat al-Nisāʾ* (Qurʾān 4:19, 35, and 128).[67] According to

---

63 Cf. ʿAbduh, "Fatwā fī taʿaddud al-zawjāt," 88.

64 ʿAbduh, "Taʿaddud al-zawjāt," 86.

65 Ibid.

66 This point is based on a lengthy article that ʿAbduh wrote in Qāsim Amīn (d. 1908), *Taḥrīr al-Marʾa*, published for the first time in 1899, as stated by Muḥammad ʿImāra in the footnote on the article in the second volume of *al-Aʿmāl al-kāmila*. Muḥammad ʿAbduh, "al-Ṭalāq," in *al-Aʿmāl al-kāmila*, vol. 2, 114.

67 "Live with them in accordance with what is fair and kind: if you dislike them, it may well be that you dislike something in which God has put much good." (Qurʾān, 4: 19) "If you [believers] fear that a couple may break up, appoint one arbiter from his family and one from hers. Then, if the couple want to put things right, God will bring about a reconciliation between them: He is All Knowing, All Aware." (Qurʾān, 4: 35) "If a wife fears high-handedness or alienation from her husband, neither of them will be blamed if they come to a peaceful settlement, for peace is best. Although human souls are prone to selfishness, if you do good and are mindful of God, He is well aware of all that you do." (Qurʾān, 4: 128)

ʿAbduh, these verses encourage exhaustive attempts at reconciliation between spouses, with divorce serving as a final and reluctantly permissible solution.

While classical jurists generally adhered to this principle and applied it to specific rulings on divorce, ʿAbduh critiques their excessive focus on the explicit expressions that indicate divorce, even when the husband's intention contradicts his spoken words. His primary criticism is directed at the Ḥanafī school,[68] which holds that a divorce issued under intoxication, coercion, or even as a joke is legally valid. This position, according to ʿAbduh, overlooks foundational principles in Islamic jurisprudence.[69] ʿAbduh argues that such rulings fail to prioritize the role of intention, a principle enshrined in the Prophetic tradition:

> It seems that proponents of this view did not pay much attention to intention, which, in fact, constitutes a very basic principle in Islam as understood in the ḥadīth "*Actions are [determined] by intentions.*" Moreover, they neglect the underlying purpose of *sharīʿa*, which discourages divorce as one of the most detestable permissible acts in the sight of God.[70]

In this light, ʿAbduh—and here lies the central point of his position—questions the wisdom of holding a divorce legally binding based solely on a verbal pronouncement, regardless of the husband's actual intention.

For ʿAbduh, while the spoken word carries legal weight, it cannot exist in isolation from the intention behind it. Divorce, as an act that dissolves a marital bond, must be accompanied by a deliberate intent to separate. This perspective reflects ʿAbduh's broader approach to legal reform, which seeks to harmonize legal rulings with the principles of *maṣlaḥa*. In his critique of those who emphasize the verbal formula of divorce while disregarding intention, ʿAbduh underscores the responsibility of a "reform seeker" to revisit juristic views and identify opinions that align with the public welfare. He stresses

68 Cf. Ibn ʿĀbidīn. *Radd al-Muḥtār*, vol. 4, 438–44.

69 Cf. ʿAbduh, "al-Ṭalāq," 117.

70 Ibid. In another place, ʿAbduh criticizes this common attitude among jurists, saying, "One who reviews their books will be astonished at their excessive focus on expressions and explaining their indications, regardless of the (state of the) person. In their view, once a word is pronounced, the legal effect ensues. This was why they limited their investigation to the words and expressions, and most of their discussions focused on attempting to understand the indications of *ṭallaqtukii* ('I divorce you'), *anti ṭāliq* or *anti muṭallaqa* (both meaning 'you are divorced') ... etc. Thus, the issue turned to be an examination of structures and expressions that may be useful for linguistic purposes but has no avail at all for the science of *fiqh*." 121.

the importance of eliminating rulings that perpetuate harm or moral corruption within society.[71] For instance, ʿAbduh endorses the opinion that a divorce pronounced in a state of anger—where the husband is not fully aware of his actions—should not be considered valid. This scenario, recognized in Islamic jurisprudence as *ighlāq* ('duress' or 'mental constraint'), exemplifies the need to account for the psychological state and intention of the individual.

Afterward, ʿAbduh addresses the prevailing social realities, noting how many husbands abused their authority by frivolously using expressions of divorce. He highlights the moral decay among some men, where divorce was employed casually, either as a joke or as a means to threaten their wives. Drawing from his experiences—likely during his tenure as a judge or mufti—ʿAbduh references numerous cases that reflect this misuse of divorce. Notably, the article in which he discusses these issues was published the same year he assumed the position as mufti and a few years after serving as a judge.

ʿAbduh concludes that the ultimate solution to address this socio-legal challenge lies in adopting the legislative principle of *maṣlaḥa* to eliminate what he describes as "corruption and weakness of minds and the negligence of intentions."[72] He proposes that divorce should only be considered valid if accompanied by witnesses, akin to the requirements for marriage. This view is rooted in the Qurʾānic command regarding witnesses, mentioned after the discussion of divorce and *rajʿa* ('reinstating a divorced wife into the marriage during the waiting period') in the verse: "Call two just witnesses from your people" (Qurʾān 65:2). ʿAbduh reflects on this verse, asking:

> Is this not an explicit command, to have witnesses, that applies to all preceding cases of divorce and *rajʿa*? … Is it not a clear intent of the Lawgiver that divorce should be documented to ensure proof? Why, then, do we not require the presence of witnesses as a fundamental condition for the validity of divorce?[73]

Upon reviewing the rulings of various schools of Islamic law, ʿAbduh notes that none of them stipulate the presence of witnesses as a condition for the validity of divorce. While some jurists consider it a recommended procedure based on the above-quoted verse, this position is not universally upheld. Qurʾānic exegetes, as well as Ḥanafī and Shāfiʿī jurists, have historically treated the

71 Ibid., 118–22.
72 Ibid., 122.
73 Ibid., 123.

requirement of witnesses as non-obligatory.[74] ʿAbduh's perspective, however, represents a novel interpretation driven by his pursuit of social reform and reliance on *maṣlaḥa* as a legal maxim.

It is noteworthy that ʿAbduh drafted specific legal articles to regulate divorce, informed both by his judicial experience and, arguably, his exposure to French legal systems during his residence in France. The following are the five legal provisions he proposed:

> If the government aims to implement measures for the benefit of the nation, it must establish a systematic framework for divorce, adhering to the following procedures:
>
> Art. 1: When a husband intends to divorce his wife, he must first appear before the *sharīʿa* judge or the *maʾdhūn* ('marriage official') in his locality to disclose the causes of discord between him and his wife.
>
> Art. 2: The judge or *maʾdhūn* is required to counsel the husband, based on the teachings of the Qurʾān and Sunna, emphasizing that divorce is deeply disliked in the sight of God. They must also explain the social and personal consequences of divorce and advise the husband to postpone his decision for a period of one week.
>
> Art. 3: If the husband persists after the waiting period, the judge or *maʾdhūn* must appoint two mediators, one from the husband's family and one from the wife's family. If no suitable family members are available, two impartial and just individuals should be designated to attempt reconciliation.
>
> Art. 4: If the mediators fail to reconcile the couple, they must submit a report to the judge or *maʾdhūn*. At this stage, the judge or *maʾdhūn* may authorize the husband to proceed with the divorce.
>
> Art. 5: For the divorce to be valid, it must be pronounced in the presence of the judge or *maʾdhūn*, with two just witnesses present. Furthermore, the divorce must be officially documented for it to be legally recognized.[75]

74 Cf. Fakhr al-Dīn Ibn ʿUmar al-Rāzī, *al-Tafsīr al-kabīr* (Beirut: Dār al-fikr, 1401/1981), vol. 30, 34.

75 ʿAbduh, "al-Ṭalāq," 123.

Divorce is the sole issue for which ʿAbduh proposed a specific legal framework to operationalize his reformist *fiqh* perspective. He believed that implementing this system would significantly reduce divorce cases by reactivating a *sharīʿa* principle that had previously been neglected and never fully applied. Notably, Article 3 of his proposed framework is grounded in a Qurʾānic directive, which recommends seeking the intervention of wise individuals from the families of both the husband and the wife to mediate and attempt reconciliation in cases of marital discord (Qurʾān 4:35).[76] Traditional Muslim jurists have generally interpreted this verse as a moral recommendation rather than a binding requirement for the husband before proceeding with divorce. However, ʿAbduh reframes this ethical guidance from the Qurʾān as a mandatory legal obligation, thereby transforming it into enforceable legislation. This shift underscores the centrality of the ethical dimension in ʿAbduh's rational and reformist approach to family law. For ʿAbduh, this ethical consideration is not merely supplementary but foundational to his vision of family provisions, reflecting his broader commitment to harmonizing the moral objectives of *sharīʿa* with practical legal reforms.

4 Conclusion and Results

Muḥammad ʿAbduh's intellectual legacy underscores the centrality of 'reason' (*ʿaql*) as an indispensable tool for interpreting Islamic teachings and deriving *sharīʿa* rulings that align with 'societal welfare' (*maṣlaḥa*). His approach is distinguished by the integration of rationality and ethical considerations, with *maṣlaḥa* as the ultimate objective and morality serving as the guiding framework that bridges reason with legal and theological outcomes. This intricate interplay between reason, morality, and public welfare reflects a reformist vision that seeks to harmonize Islamic principles with contemporary societal needs. In his seminal works, such as *Risālat al-tawḥīd* and *al-Islām bayn al-ʿilm wa-l-madaniyya*, ʿAbduh applies a rationalist methodology to theological questions, prioritizing reason as the foundation of belief and practice. His rationalist approach has drawn comparisons to the Muʿtazilī school, particularly due to his critical stance on issues such as *al-taḥsīn wa-l-taqbīḥ* ('moral valuation'). Unlike the Ashʿarī position, which emphasizes divine texts as the basis for determining moral good and evil, ʿAbduh asserts that reason holds

---

76 "If you [believers] fear that a couple may break up, appoint one arbiter from his family and one from hers. Then, if the couple want to put things right, God will bring about a reconciliation between them: He is All Knowing, All Aware."

this primary function. This divergence illustrates his broader commitment to grounding theology in principles that resonate with human intellect and ethical values.

Despite his rationalist leanings, ʿAbduh avoided direct alignment with specific theological schools. His writings strategically omit references to the names of scholars or schools, compelling readers to infer the origins and affiliations of the ideas he engages with. This deliberate ambiguity reflects his awareness of the institutional and doctrinal sensitivities of his time, particularly given his association with al-Azhar, which adhered to the Ashʿarī tradition. By navigating these constraints, ʿAbduh crafted a methodology that is at once reformist and cautious, ensuring that his ideas could provoke debate without outright rejection from traditionalist circles. The diversity of sources informing ʿAbduh's thought—ranging from classical Islamic scholarship to modern Western philosophy—has fueled scholarly debate over the scope and nature of his rationalism. Some scholars see his approach as a continuation of Muʿtazilī principles, while others view it as a balanced synthesis that avoids extremes. This diversity underscores the intellectual complexity of his project, which resists simplistic categorization and seeks to reconcile rational inquiry with Islamic orthodoxy.

A central feature of ʿAbduh's thought is the ethical dimension, which permeates both his theological and legal reasoning. In *Risālat al-tawḥīd*, he emphasizes values such as justice, human freedom, and individual accountability, framing these as essential to both faith and jurisprudence. This ethical foundation profoundly influenced his legal thought, particularly in areas of family law, where he advocated for reforms that reflect the moral imperatives of justice and equality. For instance, his views on marriage, polygamy, and divorce reveal a consistent effort to align legal rulings with ethical values, while also addressing the evolving needs of society. On the subject of marriage, ʿAbduh critiques traditional juristic conceptions that, in his view, failed to uphold the Qurʾānic principle of equality between men and women. He highlights the need for a relationship grounded in mutual respect, education, and emotional fulfillment, using terms such as "equality," "friendship," "reason," and "love" to articulate his vision of marital relations. However, his critique remains broad, and he does not provide a comprehensive alternative framework for defining marriage within Islamic jurisprudence. His opposition to male guardianship over women in matters of marriage and engagement represents a broader challenge to patriarchal structures that he viewed as inconsistent with the ethical and spiritual principles of Islam.

ʿAbduh relied on *maṣlaḥa* as a legal maxim to reject the idea of polygamy mentioned in the Qurʾān in view of the societal evils it produced. He calls for applying this maxim to the idea of polygamy since polygamy resembles all lawful things that are subject to other legal provisions including being disliked or prohibited according to the consequent harms and interests. He argued that polygamy, though conditionally permitted in the Qurʾān, inherently undermines the principles of fairness and equality between men and women. Drawing on the Qurʾānic conditions for equitable treatment among wives (Qurʾān 4:3) and the acknowledgment of its practical impossibility (Qurʾān 4:129), ʿAbduh concluded that the societal harms resulting from polygamy outweighed its benefits. These harms, including family discord and moral corruption, led him to advocate for its restriction or prohibition in the interest of public welfare. He asserted that Islamic law allows such legislative adaptations, as the permissibility of polygamy—like other lawful acts—can be curtailed when it contradicts broader ethical objectives or leads to societal harm.

In addressing divorce, ʿAbduh extended his rational and ethical critique to propose substantive reforms aimed at preventing its misuse. He rejected the classical focus on verbal pronouncements as the sole determinant of a valid divorce, arguing instead that intention, accountability, and proper procedure should govern its legitimacy. Citing the Qurʾānic stipulation for witnesses in divorce cases (Qurʾān 65:2), he called for a system requiring judicial oversight, formal documentation, and evidence to validate divorce proceedings. By prioritizing *maṣlaḥa* in his legal reasoning, ʿAbduh sought to curb the rampant abuse of divorce and its detrimental effects on families and society. He set legal regulations that allow discussing the case of divorce with the husband, without accepting divorce except when coupled with evidence or witnesses, and then recording it officially before a judge or a *maʾzūn*. These proposed reforms not only reflected his theological emphasis on human accountability but also demonstrated his commitment to aligning legal practices with ethical values.

Ultimately, ʿAbduh's reformist approach to legal and societal issues reflects a profound integration of his rationalist theological principles with his commitment to social justice. By applying reason and *maṣlaḥa* to reinterpret traditional rulings, he sought to uphold the moral objectives of *sharīʿa* while addressing the evolving needs of his society. His critiques and reformist proposals on marriage, polygamy, and divorce highlights the ethical dimension as a critical link between theology, *fiqh*, and *uṣūl al-fiqh*. This dimension raises important questions for future research, including the extent to which jurists have been influenced by theological doctrines that emphasize human accountability and the primacy of reason. Additionally, it invites an exploration of how these principles might inform the development of new jurisprudential methodologies that address the complexities of modern social realities while remaining faithful to the ethical and spiritual foundations of Islam.

Bibliography

ʿAbd al-Jabbār, al-Qāḍī al-Hamadhānī, *al-Mughnī fī abwāb al-tawḥīd wa-l-ʿadl*, ed. Ṭāhā Ḥusayn and Amīn al-Khūlī (Cairo: The Egyptian General Institution for Authorship, Translation, Printing and Publishing, 1381/1961).

Abdelrahem, Mohammed, "Auswirkung der Theologie auf das rechtsphilosophische Denken der Muʿtazila: Lektüre bei al-Qāḍī ʿAbd al-Ǧabbār," *Zeitschrift für Recht & Islam*, 13/14 (2022), 57–80, http://zri.gair.de/index.php/en/contents/current-issue.

ʿAbduh, Muḥammad, *al-Aʿmāl al-kāmila*, ed. Muḥammad ʿImāra (Cairo: Dār al-Shurūq, 1414/1993).

ʿAbduh, Muḥammad, *al-Islām bayn al-ʿilm wa-l-madaniyya* (Cairo: Muʾassasat hindāwī li-l-taʿlīm wa-l-thaqāfa, 1433/2012).

ʿAbduh, Muḥammad, *Risālat al-tawḥīd* (Cairo: al-Maṭbaʿa al-Khayriyya, 1343/1924).

ʿAbduh, Muḥammad and Ṭārik ʿAbd al-Ḥalīm, *al-Muʿtazila bayna al-qadīm wa-l-ḥadīth* (Birmingham: Dār al-Arqam, 1987).

ʿAlam al-Dīn, Sulaymān Sālim, *al-Muʿtazila* (Beirut: Nūfal Publications, 1421/2000).

al-Bāqillānī, al-Qāḍī Abū Bakr Muḥammad Ibn al-Ṭayyib, *al-Taqrīb wa al-irshād*, ed. ʿAbd al-Ḥamīd Ibn ʿAli Abū Zunayd (Beirut: Risālah Foundation, 1419/1998).

Bin Ḥammūda, ʿAmmār, *Athar al-muʿtazila fī al-fikr al-islāmī al-ḥadīth* (Beirut: Arab Cultural Center, 1435/2014).

al-Ḥaddād, Muḥammad, *Muḥammad ʿAbduh: Qirāʾa jadīda fī khiṭāb al-iṣlāḥ al-dīnī* (Beirut: Dār al-Ṭalīʿa, 1424/2003).

Hildebrandt, Thomas, "Waren Ǧamāl ad-Dīn al-Afġānī und Muḥammad ʿAbduh Neo-Muʿtaziliten?" *Die Welt des Islams*, 42, no. 2 (2002), 207–62.

Ibn ʿĀbidīn, Muḥammad Amīn Ibn ʿUmar, *Radd al-muḥtār ʿalā al-durr al-mukhtār*, ed. ʿĀdil Aḥmad ʿAbd al-Mawjūd (Riyadh: Dār ʿālam al-kutub, 2003).

Ibn Taymiyya, Abū al-ʿAbbās Taqīyy al-Dīn Aḥmad, *Darʾ taʿāruḍ al-ʿaql wa-l-naql*, ed. Muḥammad Rashād Sālim (Riyadh: Imam Muhammad Bin Saud Islamic University, 1411/1991).

ʿImāra, Muḥammad, *al-Manhaj al-iṣlāḥī li-l-Imām Muḥammad ʿAbduh* (Cairo: Dār al-salām, 1430/2009).

al-Jazīrī, ʿAbd al-Raḥmān, *al-Fiqh ʿalā al-madhāhib al-arbaʿa* (2nd edition, Beirut: Dār al-kutub al-ʿilmiyya, 1424/2003).

Juḥā, Mīshāl, *al-Munāẓara al-dīniyya bayna al-Shaykh Muḥammad ʿAbduh wa-Faraḥ Anṭūn* (Beirut: Baysān li-l-nashr wa-l-tawzīʿ, 1435/2014).

Khreegi, Yusra, *Women in the Writings of Muhammad ʿAbduh* (School of Oriental and African Studies, University of London, 2014; PhD thesis), https://eprints.soas.ac.uk/20318/.

Kügelgen, Anke, "'Abduh, Muḥammad," in *Encyclopaedia of Islam Three Online*, ed. Kate Fleet et al., consulted online on 13 July 2021 at http://dx.doi.org/10.1163/1573-3912_ei3_COM_0103.

Küng, Hans, *Der Islam: Wesen und Geschichte* (Munich: Piper Publisher, 2007).

Mirʿī, Aḥmad Khamīs Zakī, "Athar al-nazʿa al-ʿaqliyya ʿinda al-Muʿtazila fī ʾārāʾ kull min Jamāl al-Dīn al-Afghānī (t. 1897) wa-Muḥammad ʿAbduh (t. 1905) al-kalāmiyya," *Journal al-baḥth al-ʿilmī fī al-ʾādāb*, 23, no. 5 (1443/2022), 65–83, https://jssa.journals.ekb.eg/article_268831.html.

al-Mirghiyānī, Burhān al-Dīn Abū al-Ḥasan ʿAlī, *al-Hidāya: Sharḥ bidāyat al-mubtadī*, ed. Naʿīm Ashraf Nūr Aḥmad (Karachi, Department of Qurʾān and Islamic Sciences, 1417/1996).

Murad, Haider Kh., "al-Muʿtazila wa-atharuhum fī al-fikr al-siyāsī fī al-tārīkh al-islāmī wa-l-muʿāṣir," *Journal Ahl al-Bayt ʿalayhim al-salām*, 21 (1443/2022), 53–74, https://abu.edu.iq:8081/ar/research/articles/68062.

Murtaza, Muhammad Sameer, *Die Reformer des Islam: Jamāl al-Dīn al-Afghānī, Muḥammad ʿAbduh, Qāsim Amīn, Muḥammad Rashīd Riḍā* (Norderstedt: Book on Demand, 2015).

Nasution, Harun, *The Place of Reason in ʿAbduh's Theology: Its Impact on His Theological System and Views* (McGill University, 1968; PhD thesis), https://escholarship.mcgill.ca/concern/theses/pz50h1458.

Pink, Johanna, "'Abduh, Muḥammad," in *Encyclopaedia of the Qurʾān*, ed. Jane Dammen McAuliffe (Leiden: Brill, 2015), consulted online on 13 March 2022 at http://dx.doi.org/10.1163/1875-3922_q3_EQCOM_050483.

al-Rāzī, Fakhr al-Dīn Ibn ʿUmar, *al-Tafsīr al-kabīr* (Beirut: Dār al-fikr, 1401/1981).

Riḍā, Muḥammad Rashīd and Muḥammad ʿAbduh, *Tafsīr al-Manār* (Cairo: Maṭbaʿat al-Manār, 1350/1931).

Rūsān, Zāhid Khalaf, "Mawqif al-ʿaql kamā yarāhu al-Imām Muḥammad ʿAbduh min baʿḍ al-mafāhīm allatī ṭaraḥahā al-Islām," *Journal of Damascus University*, 18 no. 3 (1423/2002), 137–67.

al-Sarakhsī, Shams al-Dīn Muḥammad Ibn Aḥmad, *al-Mabsūṭ fī al-fiqh*, ed. a group of Islamic jurists (Beirut: Dār al-kutub al-ʿilmiyya, n.d.).

PART 3

Perspectives

CHAPTER 6

Al-Shāfiʿī, God's Rule (*ḥukm allāh*) and the Turn to Theology

Mohammad Fadel

1 Introduction

1.1 *Al-Shāfiʿī and Theology*

Despite general agreement on the important role that Muḥammad b. Idrīs al-Shāfiʿī played in Islamic law (*fiqh*) and the development of theoretical jurisprudence (*uṣūl al-fiqh*), the relationship of al-Shāfiʿī's legal theory to the theological debates that were current in second/eighth- and third/ninth-century Iraq is undertheorized. George Makdisi, relying on al-Shāfiʿī's alleged distaste for the rationalist theologians (*mutakallimūn*), argued that al-Shāfiʿī intended for his legal theory to function as a counterpoint to the rationalist theology Makdisi claims al-Shāfiʿī vehemently opposed. Accordingly, the *Risāla* from this perspective is an *alternative* to rationalist theology (*kalām*), not *continuous* with it.[1] From Makdisi's perspective, therefore, the subsequent penetration, if not takeover, of theoretical jurisprudence by rationalist theologians and their concerns is at best ironic, and at worst a hostile takeover of al-Shāfiʿī's project, which he had mounted in an attempt to insulate law from theology and its methods. Indeed, Makdisi even suggests that the prominence of theological concerns in post-Shāfiʿī texts of theoretical jurisprudence was an illegitimate product of rationalist Ashʿarī and Muʿtazilī theologians "infiltrating" the Shāfiʿī and Ḥanafī schools of law, respectively.[2]

The most common view of al-Shāfiʿī's contribution to Islamic jurisprudence focuses on his epistemological claims and his articulation of an approach to legal reasoning that mediated between revealed authority and rational authority. Wael Hallaq, for example, speaks of al-Shāfiʿī's achievement as being one of synthesis between "traditionalists" and "rationalists." By this, Hallaq

---

1 George Makdisi, "The Juridical Theology of Shāfiʿī: Origins and Significance of Uṣūl al-Fiqh," *Studia Islamica*, 59 (1984), 5–47, here 12 (describing his legal theory as an "antidote" to *kalām*), https://doi.org/10.2307/1595294.

2 George Makdisi, "Ashʿarī and the Ashʿarites in Islamic Religious History I," *Studia Islamica*, 17 (1962), 37–80, here 46, https://doi.org/10.2307/1595001.

 | DOI:10.1163/9789004746886_008

is pointing to al-Shāfiʿī's contribution to legal hermeneutics, in particular, al-Shāfiʿī's method for reconciling Prophetic reports with the Quran and the legitimate role he assigns to legal analogy (*qiyās*) in the juristic enterprise. While Hallaq recognizes that al-Shāfiʿī had important connections with the Muʿtazilīs, however, Hallaq does not suggest that either the formal structure of rationalist theology or its substantive concerns played a meaningful role in al-Shāfiʿī's legal theory.[3]

Joseph Lowry, by contrast, identifies al-Shāfiʿī's greatest theoretical contribution as laying out a theory of law that is founded exclusively in divine communication, *bayān*. This means that in al-Shāfiʿī's theory, *all* rules of Islamic law are ultimately derived from the Quran and are the effects of divine speech.[4] While Lowry observes that the ultimate purpose of al-Shāfiʿī's theory was to disclose how the law, its "structures, texts, and techniques ... reflected the numinous aspects of the Divinity," he makes no attempt to unpack the theological dimension of al-Shāfiʿī's legal theory.[5] Accordingly, while Lowry hints at the existence of a larger theological project that animated al-Shāfiʿī's legal theory, his analysis is limited to the epistemological consequences of al-Shāfiʿī's divine-communication theory of Islamic law.

Ahmed El Shamsy interprets al-Shāfiʿī's accomplishment largely from the perspective of the sociology of Islamic law. Al-Shāfiʿī's theoretical contribution was crucial because it mediated the transformation of Islamic law from a "community of tradition" to a "community of interpretation." Islamic law could become a "community of interpretation" in al-Shāfiʿī's generation because of the profound social transformations taking place in third/ninth-century Muslim society: the recording and widespread dissemination of Prophetic reports, the establishment of Baghdad as a cosmopolitan center of Muslim learning, the adoption and spread of a book culture, and the rise of non-Arab Muslims into positions of prominence within the ʿAbbāsid caliphate.[6] These factors led to what he terms the "canonization" of Islamic law. Canonization in turn allowed al-Shāfiʿī to imagine Islamic law as an object of knowledge akin to other sciences that were being developed in second-century Islamdom—primarily

3 Wael B. Hallaq, "Was al-Shāfiʿī the Master Architect of Islamic Jurisprudence?" *International Journal of Middle East Studies*, 25 (1993), 592–93.

4 Joseph Lowry, *Early Islamic Legal Theory: The Risāla of Muḥammad Ibn Idrīs al-Shāfiʿī* (Leiden: Brill, 2007), 23, http://brill.com/view/title/13822. Lowry also published an English translation of al-Shāfiʿī's work: al-Shāfiʿī, *The Epistle on Legal Theory: A Translation of al-Shāfiʿī's Risālah*, trans. Joseph E. Lowry (New York, NY: New York University Press, 2013).

5 Lowry, *Early Islamic Legal Theory*, 1.

6 Ahmed El Shamsy, *The Canonization of Early Islamic Law: A Social and Intellectual History* (Cambridge, UK: Cambridge University Press, 2013), 5–6.

Iraq—at the same time, such as rationalist theology, speculative jurisprudence (*raʾy*)[7] and grammar.[8] The *Risāla*, and al-Shāfiʿī's other theoretical works, on this view, should be seen as part of his effort to make Islamic law a transparent, "verifiable," science.[9] El Shamsy seems to suggest that the systematic quality of theological reasoning had a profound impact on al-Shāfiʿī's legal theory but, like Lowry, he does not consider whether, in addition to the influence the formal structure of theological debate had on how al-Shāfiʿī envisioned legal argument should proceed, whether he also had in mind a grander theological project.

Other scholarship, working on post-Shāfiʿī Muslim jurists, by contrast, has expressly considered the impact (or lack thereof) of rationalist theology on the development of theoretical jurisprudence in the post-Shāfiʿī era. The late Aron Zysow has drawn attention to the centrality of theological controversies to a proper understanding of Central Asian Ḥanafī debates on theoretical jurisprudence.[10] Murteza Bedir, in his dissertation, *The Early Development of Ḥanafī* Uṣūl al-Fiqh, gives a brief overview of how theology impacted the later development of theoretical jurisprudence.[11] David Vishanoff's *The Formation of Islamic Hermeneutics*, expressly explores different theological theories of divine speech and how they impact different theoretical conceptions of Islamic law among a representative sample of jurist-theologians who came after al-Shāfiʿī.[12] The more recent work of Mohamed Eisa, *The Jurist and the Theologian*, gives a useful overview of the state of the field with respect to the relationship of rationalist theology to theoretical jurisprudence and a careful study of a handful of theologically contentious issues within the post-Shāfiʿī, classical tradition of theoretical jurisprudence.[13] Bernard Weiss' magisterial *The Search for God's Law*, systematically explores how the Shāfiʿī jurist Sayf al-Dīn al-Āmidī's Ashʿarī theological commitments shaped his arguments in

7 El Shamsy, *The Canonization of Early Islamic Law*, 44.

8 Hassaan Shahawy, *How Subjectivity Became Wrong: Early Hanafism and the Scandal of Istihsan in the Formative Period of Islamic Law* (750–1000 CE) (PhD diss., University of Oxford, 2019), 43, https://ora.ox.ac.uk/objects/uuid:2f210fie-a598-455f-a2cc-853ad402a35b.

9 El Shamsy, *The Canonization of Early Islamic Law*, 70.

10 Aron Zysow, *The Economy of Certainty: An Introduction to the Typology of Islamic Legal Theory* (Atlanta, GA: Lockwood Press, 2013).

11 Murteza Bedir, *The Early Development of Ḥanafī* Uṣūl al-Fiqh (PhD diss., The University of Manchester, 1999), 12–18, https://hawramani.com/wp-content/uploads/2017/11/bedir_early_development_of_hanafi_usul_al_fiqh.pdf.

12 David R. Vishanoff, *The Formation of Islamic Hermeneutics: How Sunni Legal Theorists Imagined Revealed Law* (New Haven, CT: American Oriental Society, 2011).

13 Mohamed Abdelrahman Eissa, *The Jurist and the Theologian: Speculative Theology in Shāfiʿī Legal Theory* (Piscataway, NJ: Gorgias Press, 2017).

theoretical jurisprudence.[14] None of these scholars, however, explore the links, if any, between al-Shāfiʿī's substantive theological commitments and the epistemological claims he advances in his legal theory.

1.2 *Al-Shāfiʿī's Theological Conception of Law:* ḥukm allāh *versus* ḥukm al-muslimīn

Scholars' relative inattention to al-Shāfiʿī's substantive theological assumptions is surprising, given the importance theological debates would subsequently have in the history of Islamic legal theory. Perhaps this inattention is because his theological assumptions, with the benefit of hindsight at least, seem *obvious*. But such an assumption would not have been obvious to his contemporaries: it is my claim that al-Shāfiʿī was the first jurist of note to make theology central to the law. His central theological argument—that all legal rules are internal to divine speech—is but one of numerous theological premises he introduces into his legal theory. His express incorporation of theological premises in law represents an important departure from pre-Shāfiʿī Islamic law. Al-Shāfiʿī's success in establishing his central claim that conflated legal rules with divine speech was so complete and thorough that we hardly recognize it as an innovation today. We just assume that his formulation of Islamic law as centered in the quest to discover God's rule or law (*ḥukm allāh*) is the "natural" or "obvious" understanding of what constitutes rules in Islamic law. Accordingly, we assume that Muslim jurists prior to al-Shāfiʿī, such as Mālik, Abū Ḥanīfa, Abū Yūsuf, and others, also believed that their task was to discover God's rule, but that their methods for doing so were simply inchoate, primitive or even ad hoc when compared to al-Shāfiʿī's systematic reasoning. We assume it was al-Shāfiʿī's destiny to place systematic order on what had been prior to him a disorganized theoretical discipline, but one that nevertheless had been united in a common aim, despite the disparate methods and authorities recognized by jurists—to discover God's rule for each and every case.

If Islamic law is nothing other than God's law, *and* if God's law is communicated through the divine speech act of revelation, it follows that the task of the jurist is nothing more than determining the legal implications of divine speech. A careful reading of the *Muwaṭṭaʾ* and other early Mālikī texts, however, raises doubts that Mālik shared al-Shāfiʿī's view that Islamic law is wholly *internal* to divine speech. Mālik does not articulate a formal theory of what constitutes a proper rule, but based on his practice as a jurist, we can propose as a working hypothesis that for Mālik Islamic law was nothing other than the law of the

14 Bernard G. Weiss, *The Search for God's Law: Islamic Jurisprudence in the Writings of Sayf al-Dīn al-Āmidī* (Salt Lake City, UT: University of Utah Press, 1992).

Muslims. Perhaps the most important component of that law was communicated through revelation and thus was divine speech, but it was, nevertheless, only a *part* of Muslim law. On Mālik's conception of Islamic law, divine speech (i.e., revealed law) was *internal* to Muslim law in the sense that some, but not all rules of Muslim law derived from revelation. In other words, the Quran and Prophetic teachings, while they were constitutive elements of Muslim law, did not exhaust the rules of Islamic law. The stark difference between al-Shāfiʿī's view of the juristic enterprise and those of his predecessors is evidenced linguistically in the relative paucity of pre-Shāfiʿī juristic use of the term *ḥukm allāh* compared to al-Shāfiʿī's ubiquitous use of that term.[15]

But the concept of *ḥukm allāh* is not merely an epistemological debate between al-Shāfiʿī and his fellow jurists about the proper sources of law; it is also a theological debate about the nature of God. For al-Shāfiʿī, the kind of immanent reasoning used by Medinese and Iraqi jurists was sinful, perhaps even blasphemous, because according to al-Shāfiʿī, it assumed, even if only by implication, that revelation was deficient. The Medinese and Iraqi tools of legal reasoning that al-Shāfiʿī called *istiḥsān* were problematic not only because they introduced subjectivity into legal reasoning,[16] but also because such techniques were an impious attempt to usurp divine authority.[17] Prior to al-Shāfiʿī, legal disputes could be characterized as epistemological disputes about authority. After al-Shāfiʿī, however, his theoretical claims about

15 I ran a search for *ḥukm allāh* using the Shamela database (https://shamela.ws) of the Mālikī texts *al-Muwaṭṭaʾ*, *al-Mudawwana*, *al-Nawādir wa-l-ziyādāt* and *al-Bayān wa-l-taḥṣīl* and the early Ḥanafī texts *al-Aṣl* and *al-Siyar al-ṣaghīr* and obtained 18 hits. Six of those results, however, are part of Ibn Rushd's commentary on the *Bayān*, not from the base text that reflects early juristic language. The expression *ḥukm allāh* does not appear even once in either the *Muwaṭṭaʾ* or the *Mudawwana*. By contrast, the same search in al-Shāfiʿī's *al-Umm* produced 112 hits.

16 See, for example, Shahawy, *How Subjectivity Became Wrong*.

17 See, for example, Muḥammad ibn Idrīs al-Shāfiʿī, *al-Risāla*, ed. Aḥmad Muḥammad Shākir (Cairo: Dār al-kutub al-ʿilmiyya, 1358/1939), 25, 69–70; Muhammad ibn Idrīs al-Shāfiʿī, *al-Umm*, ed. Muḥammad Zahrī Najjār (Beirut: Dār al-maʿrifa, 1393/1973), vol. 7, 298 (al-Shāfiʿī citing, among other Quranic texts, *al-Qiyāma*, 75:36, "Does man believe that he has been left to his own devices (*sudā*)?" as proof that *istiḥsān*, insofar as it is derived from personal reasoning and not textual inference, is an impious usurpation by the jurist of God's role as Lawgiver; and al-Shāfiʿī, *The Epistle on Legal Theory*, 13 ("Thus did He inform them of His decree: 'Does Man think he will be without guidance?' 'Without guidance' means to be neither commanded to do something nor prohibited from doing something. This all indicates that no one other than God's Emissary may pronounce on the law except by means of inference ... Neither may anyone express opinions based on subjective interpretation, since to do so is to pronounce according to mere preference, something that is simply invented and not based on a prior example.").

the status of legal rules as "rules of God" (*aḥkām allāh*) transformed what had been low-stakes, ordinary disputes about quotidian rules of law into sites of potential heresy.

The difference between pre-Shāfiʿī jurists and post-Shāfiʿī jurists is not that the former were indifferent to revelation but rather that there was an important difference in how pre-Shāfiʿī jurists deployed revelation in their arguments. Rather than using revelation to establish the existence of a rule as part of divine speech, citations to revelation for pre-Shāfiʿī jurists functioned to show that a particular rule was part of Muslim law. To put the difference starkly, a jurist like Mālik held an *immanent* conception of Islamic (or perhaps more accurately, Muslim) law in contrast to al-Shāfiʿī, who adopted a *transcendent* conception of Islamic law. To the extent al-Shāfiʿī's conception of Islamic law became hegemonic among later generations of Muslim jurists, Islamic law became a branch of theology because it was inseparable from divine speech, regardless of the consistency or lack thereof between particularly theological and jurisprudential doctrines.[18]

1.3 *Post-Shāfiʿī Responses to the Dogmatic Implications of al-Shāfiʿī's Theory of God's Rule*

On the positive side of the ledger, al-Shāfiʿī's recasting of law as a science along the lines of theology played a crucial role in systematizing and rationalizing legal thought among later generations of jurists. On the negative side of the ledger, however, al-Shāfiʿī's conception of Islamic law as aiming for knowledge of a transcendent ontological reality had the real potential to transform law into a dogmatic enterprise. Post-Shāfiʾī Muslim jurists adopted two strategies to resist the risk that the theologizing implications of al-Shāfiʿī's theory of the law would produce dogmatic conflicts about the law.

The first was to relativize the conclusions (*ijtihād*) of jurists by questioning the ontological status of rules that derived from legal reasoning. Some jurists such as al-Ghazālī and al-Bāqillānī, went so far as to deny that these rules had any ontological reality. For them and scholars who accepted their arguments (*al-muṣawwibūn*), legal rules originating in legal reasoning only "existed" in the minds of the jurists who derived them. Most jurists after al-Ghazālī and al-Bāqillānī, however, distanced themselves from their radical relativism in favor of a theory that (1) affirmed that these legal rules did have an ontological

18 One example of the dissonance between theology and jurisprudence in later centuries is the Ashʿarī doctrine denying that God is obliged to pursue the best interests of His creatures (*wujūb al-aṣlaḥ*) and their adoption of the doctrine of *maqāṣid al-sharīʿa* and the presumption that the revealed law exists to further *maṣlaḥa*.

reality independent of the interpreter's subjective mental state but (2) in cases where legal interpreters disagreed, it was impossible to know which of the different opinions was correct (*al-mukhaṭṭiʾa*). Some jurists favored an intermediate position known as the "most appropriate opinion" (*al-qawl bi-l-ashbah*).[19]

The second strategy was through the regime of deference (*taqlīd*). While the position of radical relativism (*taṣwīb*) seemed to have lost popularity among jurists after al-Bāqillānī and al-Ghazālī, the triumph of deference mooted debates as a practical matter about the ontology of legal rules and their relationship to divine speech by requiring legal officials to adhere to pre-existing rules.[20] The result was that, despite the increasing intellectual prestige of theoretical jurisprudence, law in the age of *taqlīd* again became a thoroughly immanent science, albeit in the guise of a transcendent law. This was not quite a restoration, however: instead of Islamic law being the law of the Muslim community as it arguably had been in the pre-Shāfiʿī era, Muslim law in the era of *taqlīd* was transformed into the law of the Muslim jurists. In this transition, the idea of the Muslim community as self-governing through its own law lost importance in favor of a legal culture monopolized by legal specialists and supplemented by periodic legislative decisions of rulers (*siyāsa*).

The rest of this chapter proceeds as follows. First, it will provide an interpretation of pre-Shāfiʿī Islamic law based on a close reading of selected cases from the *Muwaṭṭaʾ* with the aim of demonstrating that pre-Shāfiʿī jurists held an immanent understanding of law. This is most clearly evidenced in rules that Mālik and other pre-Shāfiʿī Muslim jurists attributed directly to the Muslim community rather than divine speech, implying that for those jurists, the Muslim community enjoyed a legitimate power to legislate for itself. Second, it will consider how al-Shāfiʿī's conception of law transformed Islamic law from a practice that was immanent in the Muslim community to the study of a transcendent object that had both a phenomenal aspect (*ẓāhir*) expressed in revelation, and a noumenal one (*bāṭin*) present with God, thus making Muslim practice, opinion or decisions of public officials, in principle, irrelevant to the constitution of the law. Third, it will consider how this new understanding of Islamic law as a transcendent object transformed understandings of practice (*ʿamal*), from the normative practice of the Muslim community (or some portion of it), to a phenomenon indicative of a noumenal reality, i.e., *ʿamal* comes

---

19 On the controversies regarding the ontological status of the conclusions of legal reasoning, see generally Zysow, *The Economy of Certainty*, 259–72.

20 For a general overview of the role of deference in the legal system of post-Shāfiʿī Muslim societies, see Mohammed Fadel, "The Social Logic of *Taqlīd* and the Rise of the Mukhataṣar," *Islamic Law and Society*, 3 (1996), 193–233, https://doi.org/10.1163/1568519962599122.

to be understood as a kind of consensus (*ijmāʿ*) rather than a decision. Fourth, it will consider debates about the ontological status of legal rules derived from *ijtihād* and argue that the effect of these debates was to moot, from a practical perspective, the transcendent element that al-Shāfiʿī had introduced into the law and restore law to an immanent practice focused on the integrity of legal reasoning rather than the substantive correctness of its conclusions. Finally, it concludes with a discussion of the rise of deference as a response to al-Shāfiʿī's conflation of a jurist's legal judgment with an interpretation of divine speech.

2 The Immanent Structure of Islamic Law Through the Lens of the *Muwaṭṭaʾ*

Muslim jurists, even before al-Shāfiʿī, appealed to the authority of revealed texts, but they did not assume that their law was limited to revealed sources. The most obvious fact which confirms this belief is the role played by public officials as lawmakers in the *Muwaṭṭaʾ*. This feature of that text confirms that for Mālik at least, the Muslim community had its own legislative authority that existed in addition to divine law. Muslim self-government in the *Muwaṭṭaʿ* is exercised under abstract principles that find their origins in revelation, but which are specified through the decisions (*qaḍāʾ*) of public officials—caliphs, governors and judges—and the legal reasoning of legal experts to the extent their opinions find substantial support in the community and become practical norms (*amr*). Despite the obvious authority both the Quran and statements and decisions of the Prophet enjoy in the *Muwaṭṭaʾ*, legal doctrine is regularly defended or criticized on immanent grounds, rather than transcendent claims of accurately representing divine law.

This section is divided into three subparts. The first gives an overview of the role that Umayyad-era public officials played in the *Muwaṭṭaʾ* as lawmakers to dispel the notion that only public officials who enjoyed an independent reputation for outstanding religious piety or legal expertise could legitimately make law. The second subsection will discuss the role of legal experts in rule-making, and Mālik's implicitly positivist approach to law. The third subsection will give examples of immanent critique as the primary tool for defending and criticizing legal rules.

2.1 *Umayyads as Lawmakers in the* Muwaṭṭaʾ

Mālik accepted numerous decisions of Umayyads as authoritative precedents, most prominently Muʿāwiya b. Abī Sufyān, Marwān b. al-Ḥakam, and ʿAbd al-Malik b. Marwān.[21] Contrary to the argument of Crone and Hinds, who asserted that Umayyad caliphs, by virtue of the charismatic authority associated with their office, also held sway over the law,[22] Mālik's recognition of Umayyad law making activities is not because he attributed to them *religious* authority.[23] The most straightforward explanation for the inclusion of their precedential decisions is simply that Mālik believed that public officials played a constitutive rule in Muslim law-making and were not simply "enforcers" of a pre-existing law.

Mālik cites Muʿāwiya for the following rules:

- No retaliation against an intentional murderer if he is insane (*majnūn*).[24]
- Drunkenness does not preclude the punishment for intentional murder.[25]

Mālik cites ʿAbd al-Malik b. Marwān for the following rules:

- Someone who beats another to death using a club (*ʿaṣā*) is subject to retaliation.[26]
- When a slave who is a party to a manumission contract (*mukātab*) dies, leaving a living daughter and property, but he has not paid the balance due to his master and he owes debts to third parties, his property first goes to satisfy the claims of his creditors, then to the balance of the manumission contract, and the remainder is split between the master and the decedent slave's daughter.[27]
- A man who rapes a free woman is liable to her for her dower.[28]

Mālik cites Marwān b. al-Ḥakam for the following rules:

- A slave who is a party to a manumission contract, if his master refuses to accept payment prior to the agreed term, may pay what he owes to the treasury and be immediately manumitted.[29]

---

21 Mālik also identifies other Umayyad-era governors of Medina as sources of law, such as Abān b. ʿUthmān and Hishām b. Ismāʿīl.

22 Patricia Crone, *God's Caliph: Religious Authority in the First Centuries of Islam* (Cambridge, UK: Cambridge University Press, 1986).

23 Umar F. Abd-Allah, *Mālik and Medina: Islamic Legal Reasoning in the Formative Period* (Leiden: Brill, 2013), 79–80 (denying that Mālik adhered to a charismatic theory of the law but was instead committed to legal rationalism).

24 Mālik ibn Anas, *al-Muwaṭṭaʾ: The Recension of Yaḥyā b. Yaḥyā al-Laythī (d. 234/848)*, trans. Mohammad H. Fadel and Connell Monette (Cambridge, MA: Program in Islamic Law, Harvard Law School, 2019), 678, hadith no. 2342.

25 Mālik ibn Anas, *al-Muwaṭṭaʾ*, 697, hadith no. 2434.

26 Mālik ibn Anas, *al-Muwaṭṭaʾ*, 697, hadith no. 2430.

27 Mālik ibn Anas, *al-Muwaṭṭaʾ*, 435–36, hadith no. 1545.

28 Mālik ibn Anas, *al-Muwaṭṭaʾ*, 613, hadith no. 2152.

29 Mālik ibn Anas, *al-Muwaṭṭaʾ*, 449–50, hadith no. 1580.

- A man who divorces his wife 'absolutely' (*al-battata*) effects a triple divorce.[30]
- A man who delegates to his wife the authority (*tamlīk*) of divorce may resume married life with her, even if she claims that she effected a triple divorce, if he takes an oath that he only delegated to her one divorce.[31]
- That whoever injured a slave was liable for any diminution in the slave's fair market value.[32]
- That theft of a date sapling is exempt from the punishment of amputation for theft.[33]

Mālik also provides evidence that Umayyad officials made general rules that applied prospectively. Muʿāwiya, for example, deducted *zakāt* obligations directly from state pensions, and not just to discharge pre-existing *zakāt* obligations.[34] Mālik also reported that Abān b. ʿUthmān and Hishām b. Ismāʿīl, two governors of Medina during the era of ʿAbd al-Malik b. Marwān, made a point to mention in their Friday sermons the special rules regarding warranties of fitness that applied to the sale of a slave (*ʿuhdat al-raqīq*).[35] Abū al-Walīd al-Bājī, commenting on this report in his *al-Muntaqā sharḥ* al-Muwaṭṭa, claimed that Medina's rulers would only promulgate a rule in the Friday sermon after consultation with, and the approval of, the legal experts among the Companions and Successors who lived in Medina.[36]

Mālik also shows that the juristic community of Medina, prior to and including Mālik, were not passive recipients of the decisions of public officials, sometimes contesting decisions as being contrary to the law, or being incoherent. Public officials would either defend their decision or revise it in light of this criticism. One example involves a case of a divorcee who did not observe her waiting period in her husband's home. According to Mālik, when ʿĀʾisha came to know of this, she criticized Marwān b. al-Ḥakam for permitting her to leave the marital home. Marwān replied, citing the precedent case of a woman named Fāṭima bt. Qays and arguing to ʿĀʾisha that just as in that prior case, where conflict in the household had justified an exception to the ordinarily applicable rule, there was sufficient conflict in this case to justify allowing the divorcee to leave her home and observe her waiting period in

30 Mālik ibn Anas, *al-Muwaṭṭa'*, 494, hadith no. 1725.
31 Mālik ibn Anas, *al-Muwaṭṭa'*, 496, hadith no. 1735.
32 Mālik ibn Anas, *al-Muwaṭṭa'*, 689, hadith no. 2393.
33 Mālik ibn Anas, *al-Muwaṭṭa'*, 725, hadith no. 2520.
34 Mālik ibn Anas, *al-Muwaṭṭa'*, 222, hadith no. 661.
35 Mālik ibn Anas, *al-Muwaṭṭa'*, 540, hadith no. 1928.
36 Sulaymān ibn Khalaf al-Bājī, *Kitāb al-muntaqā sharḥ* Muwaṭṭa' *Imām dār al-hijra sayyidinā Mālik ibn Anas* (Cairo: Dār al-kitāb al-islāmī, 1322/1904), vol. 4, 173.

her own family's home.[37] In another case, Marwān is portrayed as intervening quickly to bring to an end an informal futures market in foodstuffs when he was informed that those dealings involved *ribā*.[38] Mālik reported an example of an early Medinese jurist who criticized the rulings of two caliphs, ʿUmar b. al-Khaṭṭāb and Muʿāwiya b. Abī Sufyān, regarding compensation for the loss of teeth, and who suggested his own solution, which he believed to be more coherent.[39] Mālik himself rejected a ruling that he attributes to either ʿUmar b. al-Khaṭṭāb or ʿUthmān b. ʿAffān on the grounds that his proposed solution was fairer (*aʿdal*).[40] Finally, Mālik portrays public officials as regularly consulting with other public officials and persons known to have legal expertise when faced with difficult cases.[41] In the legal system Mālik portrays in the *Muwaṭṭaʾ*, public officials make law, enforce it and are bound by it.

2.2 *Jurists as Lawmakers in the* Muwaṭṭaʾ

Mālik's willingness to recognize the normative status of at least some of the decisions of public officials as constitutive of the law is consistent with the technical terms he uses to describe Medinese legal doctrines. Unlike later generations of scholars who use the term *ḥukm* (judgment) to describe the outcome of juristic activity, he instead uses the term *amr* to describe a rule developed by the jurists reasoning in common. This term bears the connotation of a decision rooted in will and, in the early Islamic context, it is likely the result of a consultative process (*shūrā* or *mushāwara*).[42] This contrasts

37 Mālik ibn Anas, *al-Muwaṭṭaʾ*, 515, hadith no. 1833.

38 Mālik ibn Anas, *al-Muwaṭṭaʾ*, 562, hadith no. 1998.

39 Mālik ibn Anas, *al-Muwaṭṭaʾ*, 687, hadith no. 2387.

40 Mālik ibn Anas, *al-Muwaṭṭaʾ*, 618, hadith no. 2167. The case concerns an enslaved woman who marries a free man while misrepresenting herself as free. In such a case, the children born to the marriage are slaves of the mother's owner. The solution Mālik attributed to either ʿUmar or ʿUthmān was that the father of the children would provide the owner with a number of slaves equivalent to the number of his children. Mālik instead argued that the father need only compensate the owner for the value of his minor children, on the assumption they were slaves.

41 See, for example, Mālik ibn Anas, *al-Muwaṭṭaʾ*, 407, hadith no. 1458 (Muʿāwiya writing to Zayd b. Thābit for guidance regarding the inheritance share of the grandfather); Mālik ibn Anas, *al-Muwaṭṭaʾ*, 435, hadith no. 1545 (the governor of Mecca writing to ʿAbd al-Malik b. Marwān about how to divide the estate of a deceased slave); Mālik ibn Anas, *al-Muwaṭṭaʾ*, 616, hadith no. 2161 (Muʿāwiya writing to Abū Mūsa al-Ashʿarī to get ʿAlī b. Abī Ṭālib's opinion on a difficult homicide case); and, Mālik ibn Anas, *al-Muwaṭṭaʾ*, 678, hadith no. 2342 (Marwān b. al-Ḥakam writing to Muʿāwiya to obtain his opinion regarding the treatment of a murderer who was insane).

42 See, for example, Quran 28:20, where the verb *iʾtamara* is used to describe the process by which the leaders of a community come together to make a decision. For the role

with the more common post-Shāfiʿī term that jurists use to describe their activities, *ḥukm*. This latter term implies a determinate judgment rooted in an individual's exercise of rational judgment.

A legal opinion becomes a rule, an *amr*, in the sense that Mālik uses it, only when it garners sufficient support among the legal community that it takes on a tangible existence in the life of the community. The greater the support for the rule, the more authority the rule gains, a feature of Mālik's reasoning that leads him to grade different rules by virtue of the extent to which they enjoy effective support in the legal community.[43] A rule, a *ḥukm*, in the post-Shāfiʿī sense, by contrast, gains its validity by the extent to which it can be justified by certain formal features of reasoning that produce the rule, regardless of the degree to which it enjoys assent within the legal community.

Mālik from this perspective can be accurately described as adopting a positivist methodology toward the legal reasoning of jurists in his *Muwaṭṭaʾ*: the law is just what is reflected in social practice and jurists make law by successfully marshalling adherence to their views.[44] Only when a position obtains a critical mass of support, which at a minimum seems to be a majority of legal experts, does it become law, an *amr*.

More generally, however, Islamic law is known through a close study of the accepted practices of Muslims regarding their own legal practices. There are of course hard cases that require the reasoning of legal specialists, the decisions of public officials, or a combination of both, but their decisions and answers only become law to the extent that the community accepts them as consistent with the law and the community manifests their proposed solutions to legal problems in their lived social experience.[45] *ʿAmal*, allegedly the distinc-

---

of consultation in connection with legal deliberation, see Muḥammad ibn Aḥmad al-Sarakhsī, *Uṣūl al-Sarakhsī*, ed. Abū al-Wafāʾ al-Afghānī (Cairo: Maṭābiʿ dār al-kitāb al-ʿarabī, 1372/1953), vol. 2, 131 (explaining that consultation [*mushāwara*] in Islamic law applies to everything which requires judgment [*iʿmāl al-raʾy*] and not just matters of war). See also ʿAllāl al-Fāsī, *Maqāṣid al-sharīʿa al-islāmīya wa-makārimuhā* (5th edition, Beirut: Dār al-gharb al-islāmī, 1413/1993), 121–22 (explaining the role of deliberation and mutual consultation in lawmaking during the Rāshidūn period).

43 Mālik ibn Anas, *al-Muwaṭṭaʾ*, 28. Thus, when Mālik describes a rule with the qualifier *al-amr ʿindanā*, he is indicating that it commands the support of a majority of the legal community, but there remains a number of dissenters. A rule described with the qualifier as *al-mujtamaʿ ʿalahyi ʿindanā* is one that has *nearly* universal support. If he adds the qualifier *alladhī lā ikhtilāfa fihī ʿindanā*, it signifies a rule that enjoys universal support among the legal community.

44 Scott Shapiro, *Legality* (Cambridge, MA: Belknap Press, 2011), 47.

45 See, for example, Mālik ibn Anas, *al-Muwaṭṭaʾ*, 505, hadith no. 1778 (explaining that a woman who was pressured into paying money to her husband in exchange for a divorce

tive feature of Mālikī jurisprudence, from the perspective of Mālik, is simply the practical effect of the self-governing nature of the Muslim community in Medina. It takes on its universal normative status not because their lawmaking satisfies some external criteria of rational validity, but because of Medina's pre-eminent place in Islam. As Mālik explains to the Egyptian jurist Saʿd b. al-Layth, "the people are subordinate to Medina (*innamā al-nās tabaʿ li-ahl al-madīna*)."[46]

Both public officials and jurists make law on Mālik's account, but they do so interstitially, *within* the law, by elaborating and giving more precise content to otherwise abstract principles of law that undoubtedly find support in revelation. There is no sense in Mālik's writings, however, that in doing so they are communicating a rule that has an ontological existence separate and prior from their own decision to recognize it as a rule.

2.3 *Legal Reasoning and Immanent Critique*

As argued above, the *Muwaṭṭa'* is written primarily as a positivist elaboration of the law: it purports to record what the law is based on the social reality of the Muslim community of Madina and generally eschews any type of foundationalist defense of its rules other than simply the social fact of their status as rules. At the same time, there is an inescapable normative dimension to the law, and as some of the examples discussed above suggest, the possibility that legal officials can make legal mistakes, either through ignorance, misapplication, or confusion. Indeed, Mālik himself "corrected" an earlier decision of either ʿUmar b. al-Khaṭṭāb or ʿUthmān on the grounds that cash compensation rather than compensation in kind is more "just" when a man is deceived into marrying an enslaved woman and is forced to liberate his own children from slavery.[47]

In this subsection, I provide examples of what I call immanent critiques of legal rules where the objection or defense is based on the internal features of the law rather than its correspondence (or lack thereof) to an external norm, e.g., text of revelation. One particularly illuminating example is found in Mālik's presentation of the evidentiary rule authorizing a judge to rule on the basis of the testimony of a single witness along with the oath of the claimant

---

could recover that property later in accordance with "the rule of our people" [*alladhī ʿalayhi amr al-nās ʿindanā*]).

46 ʿAbd al-Salām Muḥammad ʿUmar ʿAllūsh, *Taqrīb al-madārik: bi-sharḥ risālatay al-Layth ibn Saʿd wa-l-Imām Mālik* (Beirut: al-Maktab al-islāmī, 1415/1995), 37.

47 The rule Mālik proposes in this case is that the master of the enslaved woman be obligated to sell the children to his father for their fair market value rather than having the father deliver to the master an equivalent number of slaves.

(*al-shāhid wa-l-yamīn*).[48] The formal authority for the rule is weak: a hadith attributed to the great-greatgrandson of the Prophet Muḥammad and fifth Imām of the Shīʿa, Muḥammad al-Bāqir, that "the Messenger of God (pbuh) decided cases on the basis of the testimony of a single witness and the claimant's oath." Mālik also reported that ʿUmar b. ʿAbd al-ʿAzīz ordered his governor in Kūfa to rule based on the evidence of a single witness along with the plaintiff's oath and that two of Medina's well-known jurists also endorsed that rule. Mālik claims, however, that this rule, despite its counter-analogical nature, is of ancient vintage (*maḍat al-sunna*) in Medina.[49] After explaining the various contours of the rule, including that its use is limited to matters of property and explaining how it interacts with non-monetary claims, such as claims of manumission and divorce, he turns to the defense of the rule against unnamed (but obviously Iraqi) detractors, whom he quotes as criticizing the rule for being contrary to the Quran.

Mālik does not defend the rule based on the pedigree of its sources; rather, he argues that the Iraqi criticism, i.e., that the rule is contrary to the Quran, makes no sense considering the Iraqis' own positions on two other issues concerning the law of evidence. First, both the Medinese and the Iraqis agree that if a plaintiff makes a claim against a defendant, and the plaintiff lacks any witnesses, the defendant wins the case simply by swearing an oath denying the plaintiff's claim. Second, both the Medinese and the Iraqis agree that if, in the previous case, the defendant refuses to swear an oath denying the plaintiff's claim, and the plaintiff then swears an oath in support of his claim, the plaintiff wins. Indeed, according to Mālik, this rule is accepted in all Muslim towns. Yet, neither rule is in the Quran. The fact that the Iraqis accept these two other rules should lead them to accept the Medinese rule regarding the witness and an oath, even though it is not mentioned in the Quran. The ancient vintage of the rule in Madina ought to be enough for them.[50]

Another example of immanent critique that Mālik presents is the controversy regarding the compensation due for destruction of another person's molar tooth. The background to the controversy is as follows: the Prophet established that the compensation due for causing the death of a free Muslim male was 100 camels, and compensation due for the loss of a tooth (*sinn*)

---

48 Mālik ibn Anas, *al-Muwaṭṭaʾ*, 601–4, hadith nos. 2125–32.

49 When Mālik describes a rule using the term *sunna* as opposed to the term *amr*, he is indicating that the rule is not based on juristic deliberation but is rather based on binding historical authority. Mālik ibn Anas, *al-Muwaṭṭaʾ*, 28.

50 Mālik ibn Anas, *al-Muwaṭṭaʾ*, 604, hadith no. 2132.

was five camels.[51] The amount of compensation granted for the loss of other body parts in the Prophet's declaration, e.g., eyes, hands, feet and fingers, were such that if a person lost both eyes, both feet or all ten fingers, the total compensation due would be equal to that due upon the death of a free Muslim male—100 camels.[52] That did not hold true, however, if someone caused another to lose all 32 of his teeth, in which case the compensation due would be 160 camels, a sum well in excess of the amount due for the loss of a life. Mālik reports that ʿUmar b. al-Khaṭṭāb resolved this apparent anomaly by distinguishing the incisors and the canines (the 12 frontal teeth) from the molars and premolars (the 20 rear teeth), awarding five camels for losses of the frontal teeth and only one for the loss of a rear tooth. Muʿāwiya, by contrast, upheld the plain sense of the rule, and awarded five for each tooth, whether frontal or in the rear. Mālik quotes Saʿīd b. al-Musayyab as criticizing both approaches: ʿUmar's rule results in undercompensation, insofar as a person who lost all his teeth under ʿUmar's rule would receive only 80 camels, while Muʿāwiya's solution leads to overcompensation, insofar as a person would receive 160 camels if he lost all his tooth. Saʿīd instead proposed to award two camels for each of the rear tooth, a solution which would result in an award of 100 camels if a person were to lose all his teeth.[53]

Despite the elegance of the solution, however, Saʿīd's resolution of the problem did not find currency in Medina, and according to Mālik, the prevailing rule (*al-amr ʿindanā*), but not the unanimous rule, was to award five camels for the loss of a tooth, regardless of whether it was a frontal tooth or a rear tooth. He explained this approach by noting its consistency with the plain meaning of the Prophet's use of the term 'tooth' (*sinn*): "Molars are also teeth. No tooth is more valuable than another."[54] In the end, Mālik's positivism trumped the elegance of Saʿīd's solution to the apparent anomaly in the rule. What is interesting for our purposes here is that Saʿīd's approach to the problem is not based on anything more than an attempt to provide the best understanding of the rule on the assumption that is part and parcel of a comprehensive and intelligible set of rules regulating compensation for injuries. The interpretive assumption of the law's coherence, of course, is a non-positivist stance, but not one that requires the assumption that the proper object of legal inquiry is a noumenal reality found only in divine speech.

---

51 Mālik ibn Anas, *al-Muwaṭṭa'*, 677, hadith no. 2337.

52 In other words, the compensation due for the loss of an eye, foot or hand was 50 camels, and for the loss of a finger 10 camels.

53 Mālik ibn Anas, *al-Muwaṭṭa'*, 687, hadith no. 2387.

54 Mālik ibn Anas, *al-Muwaṭṭa'*, 688, hadith no. 2391.

2.4 Conclusion

As shown above, the *Muwaṭṭa'* reflects a legal system that assumes that the Muslim community is a self-governing community, one that gives itself its own laws. Divine law is a part of Muslim law, and provides for the Muslim law its foundational principles, but it does not exhaust that law. Public officials regularly make law by exercising the authority given to them to specify more abstract principles of law, usually on a case-by-case basis, but sometimes by promulgating general rules, such as providing for withholding of *zakāt* from state pensions and introducing a special warranty of fitness applicable to the sale of slaves (*ʿuhdat al-raqīq*). Jurists also play a role in rulemaking, but only by proposing solutions to legal problems and successfully persuading a critical mass of the legal community to accept that solution as the applicable rule (*amr*). Legal critique is generally immanent in character, rather than transcendent, with no hint that the aim of legal inquiry is to identify, correctly, a norm that exists in the noumenal realm.[55]

3 Al-Shāfiʿī and the Theologization of Juristic Reasoning

It is not exactly clear why theology came to dominate law in the latter half of the second hijri century, but it is clear that al-Shāfiʿī was not the first to recognize the potentially theological dimension of law. Indeed, we know that al-Shāfiʿī engaged in extensive debates with theologians whose criticisms of Prophetic reports that had been transmitted only by a small number of the Prophet's companions (known as *aḥādīth āḥād* in Arabic or 'solitary traditions' or 'unit-traditions' in English) were derivative of their larger theological concerns, including, the nature of the Quran.[56] It is also likely that emerging second/eighth-century Shīʿī theological doctrines regarding the concept of

55 These features were also present in pre-Shāfiʿī Iraqi legal discourse. Al-Shaybānī, for example, in criticizing the Medinese for holding that the amount due for the unintentional killing of a free Muslim male was 12,000 silver coins rather than the 10,000 the Iraqis held, criticized them for the inconsistency of adopting a 1:12 gold to silver exchange ratio in the case of compensation (*al-diya*) for wrongful death when everyone applies a 1:10 gold to silver exchange ratio in other areas of the law. Moreover, he explicitly attributes to the "Muslims" these monetary conversion rates, asking rhetorically "What exchange rate would the Muslims establish for compensation for wrongful death, one gold dinar for ten silver dirhams or one gold dinar for twelve dirhams?" Muḥammad ibn al-Ḥasan al-Shaybānī, *Kitāb al-ḥujja ʿalā ahl al-Madīna*, ed. Ḥasan Mahdī al-Kalyānī (Beirut: ʿĀlam al-kutub, 1403/1983), vol. 4, 262.

56 El Shamsy, *The Canonization of Early Islamic Law*, 56–59.

naṣṣ as an incontrovertible element of religion had a formative impact on al-Shāfiʿī's thought.[57] Even if al-Shāfiʿī exhibited reticence toward certain aspects of rationalist theology, his interactions with rationalist theologians in Iraq at a minimum influenced his concerns with the epistemological foundations of the law and drove him to construct a legal theory in which every rule of law could find its origin, directly or indirectly, in the Quran.[58]

While we are generally familiar with al-Shāfiʿī's *epistemological* contribution to the sources of Islamic law, and his insistence on the authoritativeness of the unit-tradition that has been transmitted by an unbroken chain of reliable transmitters, less attention has been paid to his claim that God commanded a particular method of legal interpretation. Just as God commands a judge to rule based on the testimony of upright witnesses, despite the possibility that they may lie or be mistaken, so too, God commands Muslims to obey the Prophet. Indeed, al-Shāfiʿī explains this duty using language that clearly reflects second/eighth-century theological debates:

> And He informed them that his (i.e., the Messenger's) decision is His rule, insofar as He obliged submission to his ruling and because of God's foreknowledge, glorious is His praise, that he (i.e., the Messenger) is blessed with infallibility and succor (*wa mā sabaqa fī ʿilmihi jalla thanāʾuhu min isʿādihi bi-ʿiṣmatihi wa-tawfīqihi*).[59]

After the Prophet's death, this duty may only be discharged through adherence to reports about the Prophet, transmitted across the generations by reliable reporters. The possibility that they might err or even lie no less undermines the obligation to obey the Prophet than does the possibility that a witness may lie entitle a judge to discard the witness's testimony.

The Quran also commands Muslims to use their reason (*ʿaql*) as part of applying the law, in cases such as determining the direction of prayer, the proper domesticated ruminant (*naʿam*) to be offered in sacrifice as the equivalent (*mithl*) of a wild animal killed by a person in the consecrated state (*muḥrim*) for Pilgrimage or ʿUmra, and to determine whether a man is, or is not, upright (*ʿadl*). In all these cases, reason is fallible, but nevertheless the

---

57 Rodrigo Adem, "Classical *Naṣṣ* Doctrines in Imāmī Shīʿism: On the Usage of an Expository Term," *Shii Studies Review*, 1 (2017), 42–71, https://doi.org/10.1163/24682470-12340002.

58 One reason to do so was that rationalist theologians gave epistemological primacy to the Quran, and so the Quran's text served as a point of common reference between them and their adversaries.

59 Al-Shāfiʿī, *al-Risāla*, 84.

law obligates us to use it despite its fallibility. In each one of these examples, al-Shāfiʿī argues, use of reason requires the use of analogy to discharge the legal obligation: to find the direction of prayer, a person must use natural signs to determine his actual position relative to the location of the Kaʿba; in determining the proper ruminant to be sacrificed, he must compare the species of the wild animal killed with different ruminants to determine which of the latter most resembles (*ashbah*) the former; and in determining whether a man is upright, the judge must compare the man's observed behavior to the standards of uprightness.

God commands us to engage in these practices of judgment (*ijtihād*) as part of the law despite the possibility of error, and despite the *possibility* that sometimes, a more accurate decision could have been had by following an alternative procedure, a risk that judges face every day. Even though an unauthorized source might provide superior evidence of the underlying facts, God nevertheless prohibited the Prophet, and therefore, Muslim judges who succeed him, from taking that evidence into account in many cases.[60] *Ijtihād* is lawful even if fallible, while *istiḥsān* is illegal, and therefore sinful, because it entails using a procedure to derive a rule that the Quran did not authorize. For al-Shāfiʿī, the legal interpreter that engages in *istiḥsān* is just as blameworthy as a judge who decides a case outside the applicable rules of evidence.[61]

4 Al-Shāfiʿī's Use of *Ijtihād* and Right and Wrong Answers in Legal Reasoning

Al-Shāfiʿī was not the first jurist to use the term *ijtihād*; indeed, Mālik uses the term at least nine times in the *Muwaṭṭaʾ*, but never in connection with the labors of jurists; rather, Mālik used it, with one exception, in connection with rules which delegate to the ruler or another public official discretion to make

60 Al-Shāfiʿī gives several examples in *Kitāb ibṭāl al-istiḥsān* of cases where the Prophet knew the truth of a case, e.g., the hypocrisy of the hypocrites, and the guilt of some accused adulterers, but nevertheless ruled in accordance with the external evidence (*al-ẓāhir*) that God made relevant to earthly applications of the law (outward adherence to Islam in the case of the hypocrites, and the sworn denial of adultery in the case of a spouse accused of adultery), leaving a true judgment (*al-bāṭin*) of their affairs to God in the next life.

61 From this perspective, the problem with *istiḥsān* is not its subjectivity, an objection that can also be raised against legal reasoning generally. Cf. Shahawy, *How Subjectivity Became Wrong*.

a determination based on the public interest,[62] or a judge to determine the amount of compensation due for injuries whose compensation was not specified in the law.[63] Mālik seems to use *ijtihād* non-technically to mean 'judgment' or 'decision', (e.g., *'alā wajh ijtihād al-wālī ... bi-qadr mā yarā al-wālī*), but he would presumably agree that it is not *standardless discretion*. In the case of the distribution of *zakāt* revenue, for example, Mālik provides the ruler with standards to guide his discretion, i.e., relative need and relative number of the beneficiaries. Nothing in the *Muwaṭṭaʾ*, however, suggests that Mālik believed a "right" answer existed for these questions.

The one example Mālik gives that uses the notion of *ijtihād* in connection with an error involved ʿUmar b. al-Khaṭṭāb mistakenly breaking his fast *before* sunset on a cloudy day.[64] After being informed of his mistake, ʿUmar reportedly told the man who informed him of his error, "Calm down; this is not a big deal. We certainly acted in accordance with our best judgment" (*al-khaṭb yasīr wa-qad ijtahadnā*). Mālik explains ʿUmar's calm reaction by noting that there is no serious consequence to this mistake because the broken fast can be made up (*qaḍāʾ*) on another day. Nothing in Mālik's description of this case, however, implies that ʿUmar will be rewarded for his attempt to follow the rule, as al-Shāfiʿī asserts to be true for someone who makes a mistake in determining the direction of prayer.

Most of al-Shāfiʿī's examples of *ijtihād* and *qiyās* (which is the only kind of legitimate *ijtihād* because it is always based on a settled rule or settled fact) involve fact-finding of the type that by its nature bears only one correct answer, e.g., the direction of prayer, or whether a particular is properly included in a universal, e.g., whether a person is upright or not, or whether a ram is the closest ruminant "equivalent" to a hyena. He does, however, also use *ijtihād* and *qiyās* to refer to analogy for the deduction of new legal rules. Thus, in novel cases it might be that more than one precedent rule (*aṣl*) could apply, with the result that two different jurists reach two different conclusions using analogy. It is not clear, however, whether al-Shāfiʿī believes that there is a "right" answer in such cases. Some of his language implies that he does so believe because he states that after the different solutions to the novel case are articulated, it is possible to take a second look at the case and determine which of the two

62 Mālik ibn Anas, *al-Muwaṭṭaʾ*, 238–39, hadith no. 722 (the imam distributes *zakāt* revenues based on his *ijtihād* in light of relative need); *al-Muwaṭṭaʾ*, 365–66, hadith nos. 1314 and 1316 (the imam may award individual soldiers an excess share of booty out of the share given to the imam based on his *ijtihād*).

63 Mālik ibn Anas, *al-Muwaṭṭaʾ*, 684–86, hadith nos. 2373, 2374, 2381 and 2382.

64 Mālik ibn Anas, *al-Muwaṭṭaʾ*, 264, hadith no. 840.

original rules the novel case resembles *more*, and if it is determined that the novel case bears a greater resemblance to one rather than the other, than it is governed by *that* rule, not the other one.[65]

I could find no examples illustrating this kind of *ijtihād* in either the *Risāla* or *Ibṭāl al-istiḥsān*, but al-Shāfi'ī's treatment of a transaction known as *quṭāʿa* in the *Umm* illustrates his approach. This transaction involves an amendment to a manumission contract between the master and the slave (*mukātab*) who is a party to the contract with the master: in this transaction the master waives a portion of the future instalments owed to him by the slave and renders the manumission immediately effective in exchange for the slave paying some lesser amount immediately. Al-Shāfiʿī confidently asserts that the *mukātaba* contract is a species of a contract of sale or hire, and so its validity is governed by the same rules that govern contracts of sale and employment contracts.[66] Yet, al-Shāfiʿī must have known that Mālik expressly denies that the *mukātaba* contract is a kind of sale and therefore is *not* subject it to the same conditions that apply to a contract of sale. Accordingly, Mālik validates such amendments to a manumission contract,[67] while al-Shāfiʿī refuses to do so on the ground that a waiver of the obligation, combined with immediate manumission, amounts to a kind of *ribā*, and therefore is void.[68] Ironically, while al-Shāfiʿī does not explain to us *why* he believes the principles governing sales and employment contracts are applicable to a manumission contract, Mālik explains that a manumission contract is fundamentally dissimilar to a contract of sale because the former involves status while the latter involves property and so is better understood as a reward contract (*juʿl*) rather than a sale.[69]

We are thus left at a loss as to how to compare the conclusions of Mālik and al-Shāfiʿī in this case where the transaction could plausibly be governed by two different legal regimes: the law of contracts, or the law of unilateral rewards. Perhaps this is an indication that al-Shāfiʿī's view is that in such cases there is no right answer and both solutions are permissible cases of *ijtihād*.

Al-Shāfiʿī, by contrast, has clear examples of what constitutes *illegitimate* legal reasoning because it goes beyond what *qiyās* would legitimately authorize. One example from the *Risāla* is compensation due for nonlethal injuries. He noted that all jurists agree that in the case of an unintentional killing, the perpetrator's next of kin (*ʿāqila*) shares the burden of providing compensation

65 Al-Shāfiʿī, *al-Umm*, vol. 7, 318.
66 Al-Shāfiʿī, *al-Umm*, vol. 8, 46.
67 Mālik ibn Anas, *al-Muwaṭṭa'*, 443–44, hadith no. 1566.
68 Al-Shāfiʿī, *al-Umm*, vol. 8, 63.
69 Mālik ibn Anas, *al-Muwaṭṭa'*, 443–44, hadith no. 1566.

to the deceased's family. Cases of intentional killing or intentional nonlethal injuries, by contrast, place the compensation burden entirely on the perpetrator, that is, if retaliation is foregone. But in contrast to the case involving unintentional killing, there is no Prophetic precedent on point with respect to unintentional nonlethal injuries.

According to al-Shāfiʿī, the absence of text covering this case could be rationally interpreted in one of two ways: that the next of kin shares liability with the perpetrator *only* in the case of the victim's death, treating this rule as an exception to the basic principle of individual responsibility, *or* it can be understood as requiring the next of kin to share financial responsibility with the perpetrator on the theory that if it is fair that they should help defray the costs of the loss of a life, it is fair to expect them to contribute to lesser amounts. Yet the Medinese and the Iraqis impose a minimum value on the compensation due for the nonlethal injury before the next of kin becomes responsible to help defray the costs of injury. In the case of the Medinese, the next of kin bears no financial responsibility unless the compensation due is a third or more of the compensation due for a free male, while the Iraqis did not impose liability on the next of kin for injuries whose compensation was less than 1/20 of that due for the loss of a life. Moreover, according to al-Shāfiʿī, because all jurists agree that the next of kin is liable for amounts in excess of a third of that due for loss of life, a consensus to extend the original case—that next of kin must contribute to help defray the costs incurred from a unintentional killing—to the novel case of whether the next of kin must also contribute to the cost of compensating nonlethal injuries exists. In light of this consensus, it becomes *arbitrary* for both the Hijazis and the Iraqis to limit the analogy, whether to injuries in excess of one-third of that for a life, or in excess of 1/20 of a life.[70] If we are to take al-Shāfiʿī seriously, the Medinese and Iraqi jurists are not just committing an error in reasoning; they are also committing a *sin* by doing so.[71] The proper method of reasoning, therefore, is itself determined by his theological conception of the law and disagreements about how to resolve silences in the law become elevated, or are at least potentially elevated, to questions of religious dogma.

70 Al-Shāfiʿī, *al-Risāla*, 529–36.

71 Indeed, al-Shāfiʿī makes clear that the jurists who use what he calls *istiḥsān* to qualify or make exceptions to analogy are more blameworthy than the bureaucrats (*ahl al-ʿuqūl*) around the ʿAbbāsids who make appeals to unaided reason to govern in such situations. Al-Shāfiʿī, *al-Umm*, vol. 7, 316.

5 The Reception of al-Shāfiʿī's Thought as Reflected in Debates on the Ontological Status of *ijtihād*-Derived Rules

Al-Shāfiʿī's powerful theory of the law not only made the Quran the pivot of all substantive rules of Islamic law, it also made it the source of all rules for its own interpretation. And because of the universal agreement among Muslims that the Quran is divine speech, his theory meant that all law had its source in divine speech. On the Ashʿarī theory of divine speech, the Quran only existed in the noumenal realm, while the Arabic language used to recite it audibly or the script used to record it in writing was merely an expression (*ʿibāra*) of the noumenal Quran. The tangible, linguistic manifestation of the Quran in the Arabic language was the *phenomenal* (*ẓāhir*) counterpart to the noumenal reality of divine speech, to which it was related by virtue of its function as indicants (*adilla*, sg. *dalīl*) of God's eternal, noumenal speech.[72] It was God's noumenal eternal speech, particularly as this idea was further developed in post-Shāfiʿī Ashʿarī rationalist theology, that served as the situs of the divine law. Al-Juwaynī sums up these points succinctly in his definition of 'the sources of the law' (*uṣūl al-fiqh*):

> Were one to ask, "What are the sources of jurisprudence (*uṣūl al-fiqh*)?" we would say, "They are its indicants (*hiya adillatuhu*), and the indicants of the law are linguistic (*al-samʿiyya*), and they are divided into the categories of (1) a clear text of the Quran (*naṣṣ al-kitāb*), (2) a clear text of concurrent and widespread Prophetic report (*naṣṣ al-sunna al-mutawātira*), and (3) consensus (*al-ijmāʿ*), and the foundation of all of these is the speech of God (*mustanad jamīʿihā qawl allāh taʿālā*), Elevated is He."[73]

But to say that the fundamental sources of the law are that part of God's speech which is clear to us does not tell us about the ontological status of the conclusions reached by jurists in interpreting divine speech. This is a fundamental question insofar as the jurist qua jurist is distinguished from other Muslims by his claim to be able to derive rules from revelation that are *not* based on clear text, *naṣṣ*, through his mastery of the techniques of legal interpretation (*istidlāl*) and reasoning (*ijtihād*). Al-Shāfiʿī's discussion of this problem in his many writings pointed in opposite directions, and the various strands in his analysis of the problem of determining the legal status of rules derived from *ijtihād* led

72 Vishanoff, *The Formation of Islamic Hermeneutics*, 179–90.

73 Imām al-Ḥaramayn Abū al-Maʿālī ʿAbd al-Malik b. ʿAbd Allāh al-Juwaynī, *al-Burhān fī uṣūl al-fiqh*, ed. ʿAbdul ʿAẓām al-Dīb (3rd edition, Manṣūra: Dār al-wafāʾ, 412/1992), vol. 1, 78–79.

later jurists to engage in extensive discussions about a series of related questions, e.g., Is a *mujtahid* under an obligation to engage in *ijtihād* whenever he faces a novel question, or may he follow the view of another scholar? If he is under an obligation to perform *ijtihād*, is it plausible to describe the results of his reasoning as being 'correct' (*muṣīb*) or 'mistaken' (*mukhṭiʾ*), and if so, in what sense? Do the legal rules derived through *ijtihād* correspond to a noumenal reality in divine speech, or is their existence solely in the mental conception of the *mujtahid* engaging in the act of *ijtihād*? Even assuming that derived rules lack an ontologically 'real' rule within divine speech, is *ijtihād* itself rule-governed, as al-Shāfiʿī seems to suggest, or is a *mujtahid* free to judge using whatever means he finds appropriate in order to reach a conclusion regarding the novel case that is presented to him? If the former, it may be the case that many opinions of jurists do not 'count' as legal rules because they were not the product of legitimate *ijtihād* as much as they were the product of arbitrary thought.[74]

Space limitations preclude a systematic exploration of these various questions.[75] Recent scholars have read al-Shāfiʿī as subscribing to a version of metaphysical realism, i.e., the belief that derived rules have a 'real' existence in the external world independent of the jurist's mind,[76] but it is sufficient to point out that al-Shāfiʿī's writings on the topic of *ijtihād* were rich enough to support different stances on these questions. Later scholars took essentially three different stances toward the question of the ontological status of derived rules: the first position, and the one that seems to have gained greater adherence over time, was the view that God has a singular rule for every event (*li-llāhi taʿālā ḥukm fī kull nāzila*), and it is the duty of the *mujtahid* to discover what that rule-in-itself is. If, after engaging in diligent inquiry, his conclusion happens to coincide with the content of the rule of God for that case, then the jurist's conclusion is 'correct' (*ṣawāb*). This position is known as *takhṭiʾa* and those who hold it are called the *mukhaṭṭiʾa*.

The *mukhaṭṭiʾa* justified their position on the grounds that the *mujtahid*, by definition, is seeking 'something', and it would be absurd to charge the *mujtahid* for seeking something that did not have an independent existence. This position was known as the 'fallibilist' position because it assumed that the *mujtahid*'s conclusion, while it was binding upon him and his followers, and

---

74 Zysow, *The Economy of Certainty*, 276.

75 For an overview of these debates within theoretical jurisprudence, see Zysow, *The Economy of Certainty*, chapter 5.

76 Lowry, *Early Islamic Legal Theory*, 247; El Shamsy, *The Canonization of Early Islamic Law*, 80–81.

was a correct judgment from the phenomenological perspective (*fī al-ẓāhir*), insofar as it corresponded to the jurist's good faith belief, it might not correspond with the noumenal rule as it existed in divine speech (*al-ḥukm fī nafs al-amr*).

Al-Shāfiʿī's conceptual vocabulary supports attributing to him the fallibilist position: on the assumption that the jurist followed a proper method of reasoning, he held that every derived rule is outwardly correct (*fī al-ẓāhir*) but might not be correct-in-itself (*fī al-bāṭin*). In this latter case the jurist's opinion 'does not encompass' (*ghayr iḥāṭa*) the true rule. Where there is correspondence between the *mujtahid*'s derived rule (*al-ẓāhir*) and the rule-in-itself (*al-bāṭin*), he describes the *mujtahid*'s judgment as 'encompassing' (*iḥāṭa*) the true rule.[77]

There is yet another way to understand al-Shāfiʿī as endorsing the notion that there is a correct answer for all problems of legal reasoning, however, *without* ascribing to him the belief that derived legal rules have a real noumenal existence in divine speech. Because al-Shāfiʿī argues that the process of *ijtihād* is itself rule-governed, like the rules of evidence that a judge must follow, a jurist's *ijtihād* about a derived rule is 'correct' only if the *mujtahid* followed the correct procedure. Accordingly, even if, for example, the *mujtahid* relied on a Prophetic report that, despite its indicia of reliability, was wrongfully attributed to him, the *mujtahid*'s answer is still correct, while the answer of the *mujtahid* who rejected that same hadith using impermissible reasons would be wrong.

From this perspective, al-Shāfiʿī could be read as advocating a conception of correctness based entirely on the jurist's fidelity to the correct procedure God imposed on the jurist for undertaking *ijtihād*, not because his conclusion corresponds to an actual rule existing in divine speech. Fakhr al-Dīn al-Rāzī gives a comprehensive overview of the debates surrounding the position that there is one correct answer for each derived question of law and vigorously defends the position that there must be one correct answer for questions of law, but his analysis implies an understanding of correctness that is procedural, not one that necessitates the noumenal existence of an actual rule outside the mind of the jurist.[78]

On the other hand, theologians such as al-Bāqillānī read al-Shāfiʿī as advocating the view that there is no such thing as a substantively correct answer

77 See, for example, al-Shāfiʿī, *al-Risāla*, 477, 478, 480, 485, 1327, 1329, 1335–38, 1368.

78 Fakhr al-Dīn Muḥammad b. ʿUmar al-Rāzī, *al-Maḥṣūl fī ʿilm al-uṣūl* (Beirut: Dār al-kutub al-ʿilmiyya, 1408/1988), vol. 2, 503–22.

to derived questions of law, and therefore the conclusions of all *mujtahid*s, by definition, are correct (*taṣwīb* or *muṣawwiba*).[79]

> [Al-Shāfiʿī said:] "When those who are qualified to engage in legal reasoning [*qiyās*] do so, and they disagree, each one is free to hold the view that is in accordance with his own reasoning, and he may not follow a view based on the reasoning of another."… [Al-Bāqillānī said:] "How can it be that he may not follow the reasoning of another when it very well might be the case—according to those who hold there is a single right answer—that the correct opinion is that of another jurist? It is as though—from this perspective—he is obliging him to hold fast to an opinion that is erroneous before God while obliging him to hold a correct opinion. This is implausible and a manifest contradiction."

For the *muṣawwiba*, it is clear that derived rules have no noumenal reality; the only reality is the probable belief that exists in the mind of the jurist (*al-ẓann*), and therefore the goal of the *mujtahid*, in their view, is not to identify the rule-in-itself that exists within God's speech in the noumenal realm, but rather to achieve a probable opinion regarding what the derived rule ought to be in light of what the jurist *knows* about God's revelation. Indeed, al-Ghazālī holds that the belief that God has a single correct answer for every legal question is based on a fundamental misunderstanding of the reality of the legal rule (*ḥukm*) as a product exclusively of divine address (*khiṭāb*). Because *ijtihād* takes place, by definition, in a context where there is no divine address, it follows that positing the existence of a divine rule (*ḥukm*) for such cases is inconceivable.[80] He even goes so far as to mock his fellow Shāfiʿī jurist, Abū Isḥāq al-Isfarāyīnī, who had condemned the views of the *muṣawwiba* as leading to heretical sophistry, calling him a "simple-minded jurist, [who is] ignorant of jurisprudence, the definition of a contradiction, and the definition of a rule [of God] (*ḥukm*)."[81]

But, the same proceduralist interpretation of al-Shāfiʿī mentioned above could be applied to the infallibilist argument to produce, paradoxically, a single answer for every derived legal issue *if* it is taken for granted there is only one

79 Abū Bakr Muḥammad b. al-Ṭayyib al-Bāqillānī, *al-Taqrīb al-irshād fī uṣūl al-fiqh*, ed. Muḥammad b. ʿAbd al-Razzāq b. Aḥmad al-Darwīsh (Kuwait: Wizārat al-awqāf wa-l-shuʾūn al-islāmiyya, 1436/2015), 61–62.

80 Abū Ḥāmid Muḥammad b. Muḥammad b. Muḥammad al-Ghazālī, *al-Mustaṣfā fī ʿilm al-uṣūl*, ed. Muḥammad ʿAbdul Salām ʿAbdul Shāfī (Beirut: Dār al-kutub al-ʿilmiyya, 1413/1993), 362.

81 Al-Ghazālī, *al-Mustaṣfā fī ʿilm al-uṣūl*, 355.

prescribed method for engaging in *ijtihād*.[82] Al-Ghazālī, perhaps to preclude this line of argumentation, denies outright that the evidence used by *mujtahids* is in any meaningful sense objective. He instead argues that the persuasiveness of the evidence used in *ijtihād*—which he calls 'signs' (*amārāt*) rather than 'indicants' (*adilla*) to emphasize the equivocal nature of the former—is not an objective feature of the 'signs', but is rather a product of the psychological features of the interpreter. The fact that some jurists are attracted to some signs, but not others reflect their different personal natures (*ṭabāʾiʿ*), not anything inhering in the sign.[83]

Fallibilism, based on its belief in the objective existence of a divine rule for each legal case, posed the risk of dogmatism. It risked turning every legal dispute into a doctrinal question, with all the risks that entailed for parties to a legal debate.[84] Infallibilism, however, came with the opposite risk of licentiousness, an invitation for legal subjects to act as they pleased in situations where no express rule governed their conduct.[85]

The unease which these two arguments produced among jurists in turn help lead to the formulation of a third position which tried to hew a median position between the two extremes of fallibilism and infallibilism. This median position was called "the most appropriate rule (*al-asbhah*)," and was described as the rule that God would have established, had He established a rule for that case.[86] This position tried to satisfy certain elements of the fallibilist position as well as the infallibilist position.[87] Insofar as this position denied that God had established a unique rule for each particular event, it agreed with the infallibilists that the rules derived by jurists using *ijtihād* were not right or wrong in the sense of correspondence with an objectively existing rule in the noumenal realm. Insofar as this position asserted the existence of one unique rule that

---

82 Zysow, *The Economy of Certainty*, 276.

83 Al-Ghazālī, *al-Mustaṣfā fī ʿilm al-uṣūl*, 353–54.

84 Indeed, one of the objections raised by al-Rāzī's hypothetical interlocutor on the question of fallibilism/infallibilism is that if al-Rāzī is correct, it would mean that all dissenters are either licentious sinners (*fussāq*) or non-believers (*kuffār*). See al-Rāzī, *al-Maḥṣūl fī ʿilm al-uṣūl*, vol. 2, 511, 519.

85 Mohammad Fadel, "'*Istafti qalbaka wa in aftāka al-nasu wa aftūka*': The Ethical Obligations of the *Muqallid* between Autonomy and Trust," in *Islamic Law in Theory: Studies on Jurisprudence in Honor of Bernard Weiss*, ed. A. Kevin Reinhart and Robert Gleave (Leiden: Brill, 2014), 114–16, https://doi.org/10.1163/9789004265196_006.

86 Al-Rāzī, *al-Maḥṣūl fī ʿilm al-uṣūl*, 503; al-Ghazālī, *al-Mustaṣfā fī ʿilm al-uṣūl*, 362.

87 Aḥmad ibn Idrīs al-Qarāfī, *Nafāʾis al-uṣūl fī sharḥ al-Maḥṣūl*, ed. ʿAlī Muḥammad Muʿawwaḍ, Fakhr al-Dīn Muḥammad ibn ʿUmar Rāzī, and ʿĀdil Aḥmad ʿAbd al-Mawjūd (2nd edition, Mecca: Maktabat Nizār Muṣṭafā al-Bāz, 1418/1997), vol. 9, 3877.

could be described as the rule that God would have legislated, this group of scholars agreed with the fallibilists, however, that *ijtihād*, to be non-arbitrary, had to aim at a substantive result that went beyond the jurist reaching a probable conclusion, whatever that may be.

Despite the seeming attractiveness of this position, it seems that it did not win many adherents. Al-Ghazālī dismissed it as articulating nothing more than what a 'potential rule' (*ḥukm bi-l-quwwa*) might be, and for him a potential rule was no rule at all.[88] Fakhr al-Dīn al-Rāzī, meanwhile, argued that this doctrine either was in accordance with his position as a fallibilist, if it meant that the *mujtahid* was required to follow the strongest sign available, or if it meant something other than giving effect to the strongest sign, it was nonsensical,[89] or violated one or another theological principle.[90]

The controversy over whether each legal case had a correct answer was, in my opinion, driven largely by a desire to restore the immanent aspect of legal reasoning that al-Shāfiʿī's theologized conception of Islamic law threatened to obscure. The scholars who supported infallibilism sought to do this by emphasizing the subjective nature of *ijtihād*, whether they were absolute in their infallibilism like al-Ghazālī, or accepted a qualified form of infallibilism by endorsing the idea of 'the most appropriate rule'.

The best argument against a strong reading of al-Shāfiʿī's theological interpretation of Islamic law, however, came from the consensus (*ijmāʿ*) that the opinions of *mujtahid*s represented God's law.[91] This argument had the advantage of being both a theological argument, and a reflection of the social practice of the Muslim community. Al-Bāqillānī already pointed out the theological argument: everyone is in agreement that *mujtahid*s, paradoxically perhaps, assert simultaneously two things: first, that their determination of the applicable rule is binding upon everyone, but that other *mujtahid*s are bound to follow their own opinion regarding the content of the law. Because there is universal agreement that a *mujtahid* is obliged to follow the results of his own reasoning and is prohibited from following the reasoning of another *mujtahid*, it follows that every *mujtahid* is correct in following *that* rule, i.e., following his own judgment rather than the judgment of another *mujtahid*. Whether there

88 Al-Ghazālī, *al-Mustaṣfā fī ʿilm al-uṣūl*, 363.

89 Al-Rāzī, *al-Maḥṣūl fī ʿilm al-uṣūl*, vol. 2, 522.

90 Al-Rāzī, *al-Maḥṣūl fī ʿilm al-uṣūl*, vol. 2, 521.

91 Al-Qarāfī, *Nafāʾis al-uṣūl fī sharḥ* al-Maḥṣūl, vol. 9, 3876 (*al-ijmāʿ munʿaqid ʿalā anna mā ẓahara ʿalā alsinat al-mujtahidīn huwa ḥukm allāh*).

is an objective rule-in-itself in the noumenal realm is a separate question.[92] From the perspective of social practice, it was also true that consensus immunized a judge's ruling against being overturned based on a difference of opinion regarding the correct rule to be applied in the case.[93]

This meant that judgments could only be overturned on factual grounds, e.g., if the judge convicted Zayd of murder, but it was actually ʿAmr who was the guilty party, or if the judge committed a clear legal error by applying a rule with no plausible basis in revelation, either because it contradicted consensus, a general principle of the law (*al-qawāʿid al-fiqhiyya*), an express text (*naṣṣ*) or an a fortiori analogy (*al-qiyās al-jalī*).[94] From the perspective of the sociology of Islamic law, then, the doctrine of the infallibility of *ijtihād* triumphed, not because of theological reasons, but because that was the rule that the Muslim community adopted in its universal social practice.

The consensus against overturning a judicial ruling on account of a disagreement over the content of the rule—despite the growing ascendancy of the belief that each case had one unique solution before God—was further buttressed by the spread and consolidation of the regime of *taqlīd* that effectively mooted controversies regarding the legitimacy of the opinions of the different opinions of the founding era *mujtahid*s, and instead focused attention on the correctness of legal decisions from the internal perspective of the established doctrines of the legal school to which the deciding judge was affiliated.[95] The institutionalization of *taqlīd*, moreover, through the literary form of the *mukhtaṣar* and the guild-like organization of the legal school, lent itself to the production of unique answers to legal questions, at least within the boundaries of each school of law.[96] This feature of *taqlīd* not only gave it a tremendous practical advantage over decision-making by *ijtihād*, it also made judicial review for legal error practical, in contrast to an *ijtihād*-based system which could only offer very limited grounds for appeal.[97]

92 Al-Qarāfī, *Nafāʾis al-uṣūl fī sharḥ* al-Maḥṣūl, vol. 9, 3876.

93 Al-Qarāfī, *Nafāʾis al-uṣūl fī sharḥ* al-Maḥṣūl, vol. 9, 3908–9.

94 Al-Qarāfī, *Nafāʾis al-uṣūl fī sharḥ* al-Maḥṣūl, vol. 9, 3911.

95 Aḥmad ibn Idrīs al-Qarāfī, *The Criterion for Distinguishing Legal Opinions from Judicial Rulings and the Administrative Acts of Judges and Rulers = Al-Iḥkām Fī Tamyīz al-Fatāwā ʿan al-Aḥkām Wa-Taṣarrufāt al-Qāḍī Waʾl-Imām*, trans. Mohammad H. Fadel (New Haven, CT: Yale University Press, 2017).

96 Fadel, "The Social Logic of *Taqlīd* and the Rise of the *Mukhtaṣar*."

97 Ibid., 228–32.

6 Conclusion

Ironically, perhaps, al-Shāfiʿī succeeded in making law derivative of theology, but by the thirteenth century CE, the regime of *taqlīd* had restored a positivist outlook to Islamic law insofar as legitimacy of legal decisions was determined by conformity to extant legal doctrine, not the transcendent concerns of fidelity to divine speech. This was true even for the Shāfiʿī school, where the norm of *taqlīd* applied with the same rigor as it did for the followers of other legal schools. Nevertheless, the internalization of al-Shāfiʿī's theory of Islamic law being entirely contained within divine speech was not without its consequences. Post-formative Ḥanafīs were forced to denounce *istiḥsān*, even though it had been a distinguishing feature of their founder's approach to the law, after al-Shāfiʿī's critique of *istiḥsān* rendered it increasingly controversial, if not quite illegitimate.[98] In post-Shāfiʿī Mālikism, too, the concept of *ʿamal* became transformed, with the result that something that had been a reflection of the dynamic and self-governing nature of the early community in Medina came to be treated as either a universally transmitted report (*khabar mutawātir*) in the case of matters related to ritual, e.g., the call to prayer (*adhān*) or standard weights and measures, and in other areas of the law, the nonbinding legal opinions of Medinese scholars derived from their subjective exercise of *ijtihād*, or a universal, ahistorical indicant of divine law (*ijmāʿ*).[99]

The relationship between theology and law calls for both a careful reconstruction of debates in the *uṣūl al-fiqh* literature alongside a careful analysis of the kinds of arguments jurists were advancing in works of positive law. Al-Shāfiʿī played a decisive role in the development of Islamic law not only for making explicit epistemological considerations central to legal reasoning, but also by placing legal reasoning under the shadow of theological claims of divine sovereignty and omniscience. For al-Shāfiʿī, therefore, jurists who exercised erroneous methods of reasoning were not simply mistaken, they were also potentially impious insofar as such techniques could not plausibly be claimed to be relevant in understanding divine speech. The juristic task, however, was nothing other than interpreting divine speech. Despite theoretical jurisprudence's general acceptance of al-Shāfiʿī's transcendent framing of the jurist's task, however, jurists were reluctant to accept the dogmatic implications of al-Shāfiʿī's theological interpretation of Islamic law. Instead of the transcendent reasoning al-Shāfiʿī advocated for, jurists, acting under the

98 Shahawy, *How Subjectivity Became Wrong*.

99 Sulaymān ibn Khalaf al-Bājī, *Iḥkām al-fuṣūl fī aḥkām al-uṣūl*, ed. ʿAbd Allāh Muḥammad Jubūrī (2nd edition, Damascus: Dār al-risāla al-ʿālamīya, 1433/2012), 415–18.

norm of deference, largely advanced arguments based on the internal values of pre-existing legal rules. They also relativized the conclusions of legal reasoning such that even conclusions they viewed to be wrong could not be condemned as sinful. Al-Shāfiʿī's theological quest for the rule-in-itself as it existed in the noumenal realm had become, as a practical matter, irrelevant to legal practice.

Bibliography

Abd-Allah, Umar F., *Mālik and Medina: Islamic Legal Reasoning in the Formative Period* (Leiden: Brill, 2013).

Adem, Rodrigo, "Classical *Naṣṣ* Doctrines in Imāmī Shīʿism: On the Usage of an Expository Term," *Shii Studies Review*, 1 (2017), 42–71, https://doi.org/10.1163/24682470-12340002.

al-Bājī, Sulaymān ibn Khalaf, *Kitāb al-muntaqā sharḥ* Muwaṭṭaʾ *Imām dār al-hijra sayyidinā Mālik ibn Anas* (Cairo: Dār al-kitāb al-islāmī, 1322/1904).

al-Bājī, Sulaymān ibn Khalaf, *Iḥkām al-fuṣūl fī aḥkām al-uṣūl*, ed. ʿAbd Allāh Muḥammad Jubūrī (2nd edition, Damascus: Dār al-risāla al-ʿālamīya, 1433/2012).

al-Bāqillānī, Abū Bakr Muḥammad b. al-Ṭayyib, *al-Taqrīb al-irshād fī uṣūl al-fiqh*, ed. Muḥammad b. ʿAbd al-Razzāq b. Aḥmad al-Darwīsh (Kuwait: Wizārat al-awqāf wa-l-shuʾūn al-islāmiyya, 1436/2015).

Bedir, Murteza, *The Early Development of Ḥanafī* Uṣūl al-Fiqh (PhD diss., The University of Manchester, 1999), https://hawramani.com/wp-content/uploads/2017/11/bedir_early_development_of_hanafi_usul_al_fiqh.pdf.

Crone, Patricia, *God's Caliph: Religious Authority in the First Centuries of Islam* (Cambridge, UK: Cambridge University Press, 1986).

El Shamsy, Ahmed, *The Canonization of Early Islamic Law: A Social and Intellectual History* (Cambridge, UK: Cambridge University Press, 2013).

Eissa, Mohamed Abdelrahman, *The Jurist and the Theologian: Speculative Theology in Shāfiʿī Legal Theory* (Piscataway, NJ: Gorgias Press, 2017).

Fadel, Mohammad, "'*Istafti qalbaka wa in aftāka al-nasu wa aftūka'*: The Ethical Obligations of the *Muqallid* between Autonomy and Trust," in *Islamic Law in Theory: Studies on Jurisprudence in Honor of Bernard Weiss*, ed. A. Kevin Reinhart and Robert Gleave (Leiden: Brill, 2014), 105–26, https://doi.org/10.1163/9789004265196_006.

Fadel, Mohammad, "The Social Logic of *Taqlīd* and the Rise of the Mukhataṣar," *Islamic Law and Society*, 3 (1996), 193–233, https://doi.org/10.1163/1568519962599122.

al-Fāsī, ʿAllāl, *Maqāṣid al-sharīʿa al-islāmīya wa-makārimuhā* (5th edition, Beirut: Dār al-gharb al-islāmī, 1413/1993).

al-Ghazālī, Abū Ḥāmid Muḥammad b. Muḥammad b. Muḥammad, *al-Mustaṣfā fī ʿilm al-uṣūl*, ed. Muḥammad ʿAbdul Salām ʿAbdul Shāfī (Beirut: Dār al-kutub al-ʿilmiyya, 1413/1993).

Hallaq, Wael B., "Was al-Shāfiʿī the Master Architect of Islamic Jurisprudence?" *International Journal of Middle East Studies*, 25 (1993), 592–93.

al-Juwaynī, Imām al-Ḥaramayn Abū al-Maʿālī ʿAbd al-Malik b. ʿAbd Allāh, *al-Burhān fī uṣūl al-fiqh*, ed. ʿAbdul ʿAẓām al-Dīb (3rd edition, Manṣūra: Dār al-wafāʾ, 412/1992).

Lowry, Joseph, *Early Islamic Legal Theory: The Risāla of Muḥammad Ibn Idrīs al-Shāfiʿī* (Leiden: Brill, 2007), http://brill.com/view/title/13822.

Makdisi, George, "The Juridical Theology of Shāfiʿī: Origins and Significance of Uṣūl al-Fiqh," *Studia Islamica*, 59 (1984), 5–47, https://doi.org/10.2307/1595294.

Makdisi, George, "Ashʿarī and the Ashʿarites in Islamic Religious History I," *Studia Islamica*, 17 (1962), 37–80, https://doi.org/10.2307/1595001.

Mālik ibn Anas, *al-Muwaṭṭaʾ: The Recension of Yaḥyā b. Yaḥyā al-Laythī (d. 234/848)*, trans. Mohammad H. Fadel and Connell Monette (Cambridge, MA: Program in Islamic Law, Harvard Law School, 2019).

ʿAllūsh, ʿAbd al-Salām Muḥammad ʿUmar, *Taqrīb al-madārik: bi-sharḥ risālatay al-Layth ibn Saʿd wa-l-Imām Mālik* (Beirut: al-Maktab al-islāmī, 1415/1995).

al-Qarāfī, Aḥmad ibn Idrīs, *Nafāʾis al-uṣūl fī sharḥ al-Maḥṣūl*, ed. ʿAlī Muḥammad Muʿawwaḍ, Fakhr al-Dīn Muḥammad ibn ʿUmar Rāzī, and ʿĀdil Aḥmad ʿAbd al-Mawjūd (2nd edition, Mecca: Maktabat Nizār Muṣṭafā al-Bāz, 1418/1997).

al-Qarāfī, Aḥmad ibn Idrīs, *The Criterion for Distinguishing Legal Opinions from Judicial Rulings and the Administrative Acts of Judges and Rulers = Al-Iḥkām Fī Tamyīz al-Fatāwā ʿan al-Aḥkām Wa-Taṣarrufāt al-Qāḍī Waʾl-Imām*, trans. Mohammad H. Fadel (New Haven, CT: Yale University Press, 2017).

al-Rāzī, Fakhr al-Dīn Muḥammad b. ʿUmar, *al-Maḥṣūl fī ʿilm al-uṣūl* (Beirut: Dār al-kutub al-ʿilmiyya, 1408/1988).

al-Sarakhsī, Muḥammad ibn Aḥmad, *Uṣūl al-Sarakhsī*, ed. Abū al-Wafāʾ al-Afghānī (Cairo: Maṭābiʿ dār al-kitāb al-ʿarabī, 1372/1953).

al-Shāfiʿī, Muḥammad ibn Idrīs, *al-Risāla*, ed. Aḥmad Muḥammad Shākir (Cairo: Dār al-kutub al-ʿilmiyya, 1358/1939).

al-Shāfiʿī, Muḥammad ibn Idrīs, *al-Umm*, ed. Muḥammad Zahrī Najjār (Beirut: Dār al-maʿrifa, 1393/1973).

al-Shāfiʿī, *The Epistle on Legal Theory: A Translation of al-Shāfiʿī's Risālah*, trans. Joseph E. Lowry (New York, NY: New York University Press, 2013).

Shahawy, Hassaan, *How Subjectivity Became Wrong: Early Hanafism and the Scandal of Istihsan in the Formative Period of Islamic Law (750–1000 CE)* (PhD diss., University of Oxford, 2019), https://ora.ox.ac.uk/objects/uuid:2f210f1e-a598-455f-a2cc-853ad402a35b.

Shapiro, Scott, *Legality* (Cambridge, MA: Belknap Press, 2011).

al-Shaybānī, Muḥammad ibn al-Ḥasan, *Kitāb al-ḥujja ʿalā ahl al-Madīna*, ed. Ḥasan Mahdī al-Kalyānī (Beirut: ʿĀlam al-kutub, 1403/1983).

Vishanoff, David R., *The Formation of Islamic Hermeneutics: How Sunni Legal Theorists Imagined Revealed Law* (New Haven, CT: American Oriental Society, 2011).
Weiss, Bernard G., *The Search for God's Law: Islamic Jurisprudence in the Writings of Sayf al-Dīn al-Āmidī* (Salt Lake City, UT: University of Utah Press, 1992).
Zysow, Aron, *The Economy of Certainty: An Introduction to the Typology of Islamic Legal Theory* (Atlanta, GA: Lockwood Press, 2013).

CHAPTER 7

Al-Māturīdī on the Cause (*sabab*) and Human Action between *Kalām* and *Uṣūl al-Fiqh*

Ramon Harvey

1 Introduction

Abū Manṣūr al-Māturīdī (d. 333/944) was an influential Ḥanafī scholar from Samarqand in Transoxiana. He is best known for his theological work—he gives his name to one of the two major schools of Sunnī *kalām*—as well as his Qur'anic exegesis. Corresponding to this, only two of his works seemingly survive: his theological summa, *Kitāb al-tawḥīd*, and his *tafsīr*, *Ta'wīlāt al-qur'ān*. Yet these two disciplines did not exhaust al-Māturīdī's repertoire. From his terse use of legal theoretical concepts within his *tafsīr*[1] and from the writing of ʿAlā' al-Dīn al-Samarqandī (d. 539/1144) who takes him as the exemplar of a distinct Samarqandī tradition within the discipline, we know that he also theorised in *uṣūl al-fiqh*.[2] Al-Samarqandī mentions that his two main books in this field are *Kitāb ma'ākhidh al-sharā'iʿ fī uṣūl al-fiqh*[3] and *Kitāb al-jadal fī uṣūl al-fiqh*.[4] Although both are lost to us, they were still in circulation in al-Samarqandī's time, and he takes the opportunity to regularly cite and quote

1 For example, see the discussion of his approach to *naskh* ('abrogation') in Ramon Harvey, "Al-Māturīdī on the Abrogation of the *Sharīʿa* in the Qur'an and Previous Scriptures," in *İmâm Mâtürîdî ve Te'vîlâtü'l-Kur'ân*, ed. Hatice K. Arpaguş, Mehmet Umit and Bilal Kır (Istanbul: M. U. İlahiyat Fakultesi Vakfı Yayınları, 2019), 511–24, esp. 517–22.

2 See Aron Zysow, *The Economy of Certainty: An Introduction to the Typology of Islamic Legal Theory* (Atlanta, GA: Lockwood Press, 2013), 66, 75; Aron Zysow, "Muʿtazilism and Māturīdism in Ḥanafī Legal Theory," in *Studies in Islamic Legal Theory*, ed. Bernard G. Weiss (Leiden: Brill, 2002), 223–65, esp. 238.

3 On this reading of the title, see Zysow, "Muʿtazilism and Māturīdism in Ḥanafī Legal Theory," 238–39, n. 14.

4 ʿAlā' al-Dīn al-Samarqandī, *Mīzān al-uṣūl fī natā'ij al-ʿuqūl*, ed. ʿAbd al-Malik ʿAbd al-Raḥmān al-Saʿdī, 2 vols (Mecca: Jāmiʿat Umm al-Qurā, 1984), vol. 1, 2–3. Other books ascribed to him in this genre are probably either alternative titles for the above, such as *Kitāb ma'ākhidh al-sharā'iʿ fī l-fiqh*, or mistaken attributions, such as *Uṣūl al-dīn*. See Mustafa Cerić, *Roots of Synthetic Theology in Islam: A Study of the Theology of Abū Manṣūr al-Māturīdī (d. 333/944)* (Kuala Lumpur: International Institute of Islamic Thought and Civilization, 1995), 36–37. On the latter text, see Ramon Harvey, *Transcendent God, Rational World: A Māturīdī Theology* (Edinburgh: Edinburgh University Press, 2021), 12, n. 10.

 | DOI:10.1163/9789004746886_009

from them. This means that, as demonstrated by Aron Zysow, there is enough extant material on al-Māturīdī's views about legal theory to make connections to his theological work and to draw conclusions on the continuity between the two.[5]

My objective in this chapter is to excavate al-Māturīdī's use of the term *sabab* (cause) within his surviving *kalām* and *uṣūl* materials as it is used for theorising human action. In the first section I will introduce the main features of the term *sabab* before the time of al-Māturīdī. In the second section I will explore the way that he uses it to underpin the metaphysics of free choice (*ikhtiyār*) in his *kalām* system. Here I will also show that al-Māturīdī develops a concurrentist rather than occasionalist theory of causality. I will then turn in the third section to a specific function that the *sabab* plays in the normative fulfilment of God's commands within his *uṣūl* work.[6] In the fourth section I will examine applications of this *uṣūl* principle in his *tafsīr*. Finally, I will reflect on what this topic can tell us about the systematic intentions of al-Māturīdī on human action in these genres.

2 Use of *Sabab* in Theology and Law up to the Fourth/Tenth Century

The Arabic word *sabab* (pl. *asbāb*) means 'a rope' and specifically one that is used to achieve some end, such as climbing up palm trees, or accessing water. By extension, *sabab* became used for anything that is a means, occasion or cause for another thing.[7] In the field of *kalām*, *sabab* was a common term for discussion of the causal relationship between human actors and their actions,

5 See Zysow, *The Economy of Certainty*, 66–72, 75–86, 271–72; Zysow, "Muʿtazilism and Māturīdism in Ḥanafī Legal Theory."

6 Mohamed Eissa makes a sustained comparison between four Shāfiʿī jurists on what he calls natural causality, the 'cause' (*sabab*) of natural human actions, and juridical causality, the 'cause' (*ʿilla*) of 'deontic qualifications', i.e., rulings of the *sharīʿa*, in the context of *qiyās* (legal analogy). See Mohamed Eissa, *The Jurist and the Theologian: Speculative Theology in Shāfiʿī Legal Theory* (Piscataway, NJ: Gorgias Press, 2017), 95–120. On the *uṣūl* side, this concerns a related, albeit slightly different question than the present study, which (using what is quoted from al-Māturīdī's legal writings) looks instead at actions as the 'deontic cause' of the fulfilment of God's obligations.

7 E. W. Lane, *Arabic–English Lexicon*, 2 vols (Cambridge: Islamic Texts Society, 2003), vol. 1, p. 1285. Al-Māturīdī gives the definition of 'rope' (*ḥabl*) for *sabab*, which he attributes to the dialect of Hudhayl. Abū Manṣūr al-Māturīdī, *Taʾwīlāt al-qurʾān*, ed. Ertuğrul Boynukalın and Bekir Topaloğlu, 18 vols (Istanbul: Dār al-Mīzān, 2006), vol. 9, 354.

although in the early period *ʿilla* was often used interchangeably with it.[8] *Sabab* makes an appearance in this context in the works of the Imāmī Shīʿī theologian Hishām b. al-Ḥakam (d. 179/795–6) and also in those of Ḍirār b. ʿAmr (d. 200/815), an independent thinker with links both to the circle of Abū Ḥanīfa and the early Muʿtazila.[9]

With respect to al-Māturīdī's specific theological milieu, we should consider his reception of philosophical ideas from the circle around Abū Yūsuf al-Kindī (d. ca 259/873),[10] as well as his selective appropriation of some concepts associated with the Muʿtazila. Al-Kindī takes up the four kinds of causes recognised by Aristotle, a distinction not associated with *kalām* proponents in the early period.[11] He also makes use of both the terms *ʿilla* and *sabab*. For instance, al-Kindī writes:

> It has been shown that all things have a first cause (*ʿilla*), which does not share with them a genus, shape, similarity, or association. Rather [the cause] is higher and nobler than they, and prior to them, and it is the cause (*sabab*) of their coming-to-be and their stability.[12]

A philosophical doctrine relevant to causation held in common by the *falāsifa* and several Muʿtazilī theologians concerns the action of natures (*ṭabāʾiʿ*). In the thought of al-Kindī and some of the Muʿtazila, including the Transoxianan Abū l-Qāsim al-Kaʿbī (al-Balkhī) (d. 319/931), these are the primary qualities of heat, cold, moisture and dryness that comprise bodies.[13] Despite some differences in the way that these figures theorised about the causal operation of

---

8 See L. Gardet, "ʿIlla," in *The Encyclopaedia of Islam, New Edition*, ed. P. Bearman, T. Bianquis, C. E. Bosworth, E. Van Donzel, and W. P. Heinrichs, 12 vols (Leiden: Brill, 1986–2004); Özgür Koca, *Islam, Causality, and Freedom: From the Medieval to the Modern Era* (Cambridge: Cambridge University Press, 2020), 2, n. 1.

9 See Josef van Ess, *Theology and Society in the Second and Third Centuries of the Hijra, Volume 1*, trans. John O'Kane (Leiden: Brill, 2017), 433–34 for Hishām, and Josef van Ess, *Theology and Society in the Second and Third Centuries of the Hijra, Volume 3*, trans. Gwendolin Goldbloom (Leiden: Brill, 2018), 37 and 50 for Ḍirār.

10 See Ramon Harvey, "Philosopher of Samarqand: Abū Manṣūr al-Māturīdī's Theory of Properties," in *Pluralizing Philosophy's Past*, ed. Amber L. Griffioen and Marius Backmann (London: Palgrave, 2023), 77–90, at 78–79.

11 Josef van Ess, *Theology and Society in the Second and Third Centuries of the Hijra, Volume 4*, trans. Gwendolin Goldbloom (Leiden: Brill, 2018), 545.

12 Peter Adamson and Peter E. Pormann, *The Philosophical Works of al-Kindī* (Karachi: Oxford University Press, 2012), 40. Also see 182 and 237, n. 73.

13 Adamson and Pormann, *The Philosophical Works of al-Kindī*, 188; Racha El Omari, *The Theology of Abū l-Qāsim al-Balkhī/al-Kaʿbī (d. 319/931)* (Leiden: Brill, 2016), 176.

natures, the common feature was that a given nature would always result in the production of characteristic effects, for instance the burning of objects exposed to fire.[14] I will discuss al-Māturīdī's own doctrine of natures and how it fits into his theory of human action below.

The use of *sabab* within legal writing in the sense of the cause or occasion for a certain ruling (*ḥukm*) was in place by the fourth/tenth century, although again some authors preferred *ʿilla*. As well as in al-Māturīdī's texts, the term can be found in *al-Fuṣūl fī l-uṣūl* by Abū Bakr al-Jaṣṣāṣ (d. 370/981), which is the earliest surviving comprehensive Ḥanafī text of *uṣūl al-fiqh*. For instance, al-Jaṣṣāṣ writes: "the occasioning factor (*ʿilla*)[15] is a cause (*sabab*) for what is based on it."[16] Nevertheless, the origin and early history of the *sabab* remains obscure.[17] The question is made especially difficult by the parallel non-technical use of *sabab* for a reason or means, combined with the fragmentary sources available for works of legal theory in the third/ninth and fourth/tenth centuries.[18] It therefore remains a desideratum for wider research in the field.

3 The Metaphysics of *Sabab* in al-Māturīdī's *Kalām*

Al-Māturīdī deploys the term *sabab* (pl. *asbāb*) in several ways within *Kitāb al-tawḥīd*. For instance, he prominently uses it to discuss three "means" of knowledge in his epistemological introduction,[19] as well as relying on its common linguistic meaning. Here, I am only considering his technical use of it as "cause". This specific sense of *sabab* is intimately connected to his discussion of the accident of power (*qudra*).

---

14 El Omari, *The Theology of Abū l-Qāsim al-Balkhī/al-Kaʿbī (d. 319/931)*, 179–81. This general point was also upheld by al-Kaʿbī, albeit unlike some earlier Muʿtazilīs he did not think that natures were directly causally active, but rather that they defined the natural characteristic (*khāṣṣiyya*) to which a body characteristically reacts (see 179).

15 For this translation, see Bernard G. Weiss, *The Search for God's Law: Islamic Jurisprudence in the Writings of Sayf al-Dīn al-Āmidī* (revised edition, Salt Lake City, UT: University of Utah Press, 2010), 546.

16 Aḥmad b. ʿAlī al-Jaṣṣāṣ, *al-Fuṣūl fī l-uṣūl*, ed. ʿUjayl Jāsim al-Nashamī, 4 vols (Kuwait: Wizārat al-Awqāf wa-l-Shuʾūn al-Islāmiyya, 1994), vol. 4, 9.

17 See Zysow, *The Economy of Certainty*, 232, n. 447.

18 See Ahmed El Shamsy, "Bridging the Gap: Two Early Texts of Islamic Legal Theory," *Journal of the American Oriental Society*, 137, no. 3 (2017), 505–36, esp. 505–6.

19 Abū Manṣūr al-Māturīdī, *Kitāb al-tawḥīd*, ed. Bekir Topaloğlu and Muḥammad Aruçi (second edition, Istanbul: Maktabat al-Irshād, 2010), 69.

Before studying relevant passages in greater detail, I will briefly summarise al-Māturīdī's divine action model. Al-Māturīdī demonstrates a simultaneous commitment to divine omnipotence and creative agency over every aspect of the world and to the reality of causes, whether compelled by the natures of things or chosen by humankind. The former aspect of divine activity is well-known and documented, but the latter aspect of worldly activity has been subject to some debate.[20] My treatment of al-Māturīdī's causal theory below reflects my understanding that al-Māturīdī does not see his system as occasionalist. This is because he identifies causes (*asbāb*) with metaphysically efficacious aspects of the created world: the accident of volitional power (*qudra*) in human voluntary choice and the interaction of involuntary natures (*ṭabāʾiʿ*). It is in this context that he secures the place for human moral actions in terms of his notion of free choice (*ikhtiyār*), to do an act of obedience or an opposite act of disobedience.

Al-Māturīdī's divine action model can, therefore, be understood as concurrentist. Unlike occasionalism, which arrogates causal participation in the effects seen within the world to God alone, concurrentism upholds causal participation for both God and created entities.[21] For al-Māturīdī, this can be framed through the following propositions:

1. God timelessly creates every aspect of the spatiotemporal world, including all accidents constituting bodies.[22]
2. Accidents constituting bodies (as spatiotemporal loci for the outcome of God's creative activity) are nothing but powers that necessarily cause their effects under the right conditions.[23]

---

20 See Nazif Muhtaroglu, "Al-Māturīdī's View of Causality," in *Occasionalism Revisited: New Essays from the Islamic and Western Philosophical Traditions*, ed. Nazif Muhtaroglu (Abu Dhabi: Kalam Research & Media, 2017), 3–21, esp. 12–16. In my view, Muhtaroglu errs in not considering all the texts in *Kitāb al-tawḥīd* discussing the *sabab* and related matters, as well as al-Māturīdī's polemical engagement with the Muʿtazilī position exemplified by al-Kaʿbī. This leads him to dismiss the possibility that al-Māturīdī understands created things to act with causal efficacy based on incorrect assumptions about his metaphysical position.

21 Concurrentist divine action models often receive criticism for an alleged instability, which leads to their collapse into occasionalism. For further detailed discussion on al-Māturīdī's model and a defence against this charge, see Ramon Harvey and David Solomon Jalajel, "Al-Māturīdī's Divine Action Model: A Distinctive Concurrentist Account of Causality," *Journal of Islamic Philosophy*, 16, no. 1 (2025), 63–106.

22 See al-Māturīdī, *Kitāb al-tawḥīd*, 110–13.

23 See al-Māturīdī, *Kitāb al-tawḥīd*, 83–84, 348–49.

Therefore:

> 3. Bodies have their aggregate causal powers necessarily from the cumulative created outcomes of their constituent accidents.

To see how his overall stance is expressed within the technical debates of *kalām*, I shall turn to a section mainly concerned with an analysis of divinely granted human volitional power.[24] In this section, al-Māturīdī addresses the position that an accident of volitional power (*qudra*) for an act of obedience (*ṭāʿa*) could have equally been "spent" in an act of disobedience (*maʿṣiya*), as opposed to requiring another distinct accident of *qudra*. He mentions that this is the view of Abū Ḥanīfa and a group of the Muʿtazila, whereas it is opposed to the Basran theologian al-Ḥusayn al-Najjār (d. ca 230/845) and other unnamed proponents.[25] Al-Māturīdī argues that this position is used by the Muʿtazila as the basis for their well-known doctrine that power precedes the act.[26] It would seem that he has in mind an argument that if divinely granted power is suitable for acts that either enact obedience or disobedience, then it must

24 The section is just marked as *Masʾala* ('Enquiry') in the manuscript and runs continuously until *Masāʾil fī l-irāda* ('Enquiries on the Will'). See Abū Manṣūr al-Māturīdī, "Kitāb al-tawḥīd," Cambridge University Library, Cambridge, MS Add.3651, 137v; 150v. The editors of the printed edition have subdivided it into several shorter subsections. Al-Māturīdī, *Kitāb al-tawḥīd*, 349–75.

25 Al-Māturīdī, *Kitāb al-tawḥīd*, 349. The subsequent Ḥanafī Māturīdī Abū l-Yusr al-Bazdawī (d. 493/1097) adds the Ḥanafī al-Bishr al-Marīsī (d. 218/833) and Abū l-Ḥasan al-Ashʿarī (d. 324/935–36) to those opposed to Abū Ḥanīfa's position and ʿAbd Allāh b. Kullāb (d. ca 240/854–55) to its supporters. Abū l-Yusr al-Bazdawī, *Al-Muyassar fī l-kalām al-musammā uṣūl al-dīn*, ed. ʿAbd Allāh Muḥammad Ismāʿīl and Muḥammad Ḍarghām (Cairo: Dār Nūr al-Yaqīn, 2024), 435. That this doctrine can be reliably traced to Abū Ḥanīfa is confirmed by its quotation in the creed *al-Fiqh al-akbar* by Abū Ḥanīfa's student Abū Muṭīʿ al-Balkhī (d. 199/814), though the term used is *istiṭāʿa* ('capacity'). Abū Ḥanīfa al-Nuʿmān b. Thābit, *al-ʿĀlim wa-l-mutaʿallim riwāyat Abī Muqātil ʿan Abī Ḥanīfa raḍiya Allāhu ʿanhumā wa-yalīhi risālat Abī Ḥanīfa ilā ʿUthmān al-Battī thumma al-fiqh al-absaṭ: Riwāyat Abī Muṭīʿ ʿan Abī Ḥanīfa raḥimahumā Allāh*, ed. Muḥammad Zāhid al-Kawtharī (Cairo: Maṭbaʿat al-Anwār, 1949), 43. For an account of the Ashʿarī position in comparison with the Muʿtazilī one, see Weiss, *The Search for God's Law*, 62.

26 Al-Māturīdī, *Kitāb al-tawḥīd*, 349. Al-Māturīdī draws a distinction between use of the term *qudra* for sound means (*salāmat al-asbāb*) and healthy organs (*ṣiḥḥat al-ālāt*), which are blessings from God that precede the action, and for the power that is only with the act (*li-l-fiʿl*). Al-Māturīdī, *Kitāb al-tawḥīd*, 342. For further analysis of this passage, see J. Meric Pessagno, "Irāda, Ikhtiyār, Qudra, Kasb: The View of Abū Manṣūr al-Māturīdī," *Journal of the American Oriental Society*, 104/1 (1984), 177–91, esp. 184–85; and Ulrich Rudolph, *Al-Māturīdī and the Development of Sunnī Theology in Samarqand*, trans. Rodrigo Adem (Leiden: Brill, 2015), 305–6.

be given (and used) in advance of the moment of action so that the act itself takes place independently of God. The Muʿtazila were especially concerned with this point to avoid, as they saw it, the attribution of evil and unjust actions to God. Al-Māturīdī rejects this inference and instead argues for the coherence of volitional power given at the moment of action for either of the two possible outcomes.[27]

To understand how this discussion connects to causation and the concept of *sabab*, it is useful to jump to a later part of the same section. Here, al-Māturīdī records al-Kaʿbī attempting to draw a distinction between *qudra* and *sabab* with the proposition that whereas an action must be simultaneous with its cause (*sabab*), it does not need to be simultaneous with its accident of power.[28] The picture is thus one in which the actor "spends" the accident of power prior to causing the instantiation of the action as an effect.[29] Rather than the concurrentism that al-Māturīdī upholds, this would free the human being to act as a secondary cause independently of divine causal participation.

Al-Māturīdī responds to this stance by denying that such a gap can be opened between the concept of *qudra* and *sabab*:

> The summary of [the position] is that the action has a time of non-existence, which is before [its realisation], a time of cessation, which is after it, and a time of existence, which is during it. God must see it with its states, as [al-Kaʿbī] mentioned, and nothing else. Likewise, this is the case for the times and places in which actions occur and also for causes (*asbāb*). Power (*al-quwwa*) is the same as this, He sees it as non-existent before [its realisation in the action], cessated after it, and existent with it.[30]

From this we can conclude that at least as far as the analysis of human action goes, al-Māturīdī understands volitional power and cause to be coextensive notions. Further remarks in *Kitāb al-tawḥīd* support this reading. He states: "volitional power, which is the cause of the action in reality … (*al-qudra allatī hiya sabab al-fiʿl fī l-ḥaqiqa*)."[31] In another place, he frames the relationship

---

27 He makes several metaphysical arguments against the Muʿtazilī doctrine that power precedes the action. See Al-Māturīdī, *Kitāb al-tawḥīd*, 346–48; Pessagno, "Irāda, Ikhtiyār, Qudra, Kasb," 186–87.

28 Al-Māturīdī, *Kitāb al-tawḥīd*, 357.

29 See Richard M. Frank, "The Structure of Created Causality, according to al-Ashʿarī: An Analysis of the *Kitāb al-Lumaʿ*, §§ 82–164," *Studia Islamica*, 104 (1966), 13–75, esp. 19, n. 4.

30 Al-Māturīdī, *Kitāb al-tawḥīd*, 359.

31 Al-Māturīdī, *Kitāb al-tawḥīd*, 412. Also see al-Māturīdī, *Taʾwīlāt al-qurʾān*, vol. 16, 115.

as follows: "volitional power (*al-qudra*) is created for the action and it is the cause (*sabab*) of it being freely chosen (*mukhtāran*) and not compelled (*muḍṭarran*)."[32]

This leads neatly back to the initial passage that I cited on the use of power for either obedience or disobedience. Here, al-Māturīdī goes on to mention that "the foundational principle is that everything that is suitable for something, but not suitable for its opposite, occurs by nature (*bi-l-ṭabʿ*), not by choice (*bi-l-ikhtiyār*). Were power not suitable for them both it would be something that operates by nature, not by choice."[33]

Al-Māturīdī is mainly focused on theological questions, such as the relationship between divine and human action, so his physical ontology must be inferred from indications throughout his work. Given my focus in this chapter, I will not provide a detailed reconstruction of this aspect of his thought. To advance the present discussion, however, it is important to recognise that he understands bodies as bundles of causally powerful accidents of various kinds. What he refers to as natures (*ṭabāʾiʿ*) are accidents that act with specific dispositional powers to cause effects within the makeup of their bundle and to cause aggregate effects on other bodies.[34]

The distinction that al-Māturīdī draws in the present context is that volitional power, a momentary accident granted to human beings that can be used for obedience or disobedience, underpins free moral choice, whereas the dispositional natures of entities lead to their characteristic actions, for instance "we find heat rises by its nature and cold descends."[35] He even sees the human body as composed of natures that will tend to compel a person to certain involuntary or habitual acts, such that it is only reason (*ʿaql*) that allows one to instead make truly conscious choices.[36]

Al-Māturīdī thus applies his causal account to two kinds of entities. First, there are natural entities that causally act without any aspect of choice according to the aggregate dispositional powers of their constituent accidents. Of course, such natures are not held by him to lie in any respect outside of

32 Al-Māturīdī, *Kitāb al-tawḥīd*, 321.

33 Al-Māturīdī, *Kitāb al-tawḥīd*, 349.

34 See Harvey, *Transcendent God, Rational World*, 89, and further discussion on 90–93. This builds on the view of Rudolph. See Rudolph, *Al-Māturīdī and the Development of Sunnī Theology in Samarqand*, 259–60. I argue, *pace* Rudolph, that al-Māturīdī does not restrict the concept of natures to the four elemental qualities. For further detailed reconstruction of al-Māturīdī's physical ontology, see Harvey and Jalajel, "Al-Māturīdī's Divine Action Model," 74–78.

35 Al-Māturīdī, *Kitāb al-tawḥīd*, 184.

36 Al-Māturīdī, *Kitāb al-tawḥīd*, 67, 76.

God's power. Like everything else, God creates them with His timeless creative action—it is just that what He thereby creates are the very causally active powers that comprise worldly entities.[37] For al-Māturīdī, such natures cannot receive *qudra*, as this is not suitable for their "compelled" action. Rather, once the bundle of accidents that makes up a body are exposed to a certain causal condition, the effect described by their aggregate dispositional powers necessarily occurs.[38] For example, the bundle of accidents that makes up a body of glass has the disposition to shatter once hit by a sufficiently strong force. When a stone is thrown at a window and the causal condition is met, the aggregate natures of the bundles involved must act to realise the resultant effect of shattering. This may result in the body being split into several smaller bodies. Note that under this account of causality, the bodies in question undergo substantial change over time; there is not a mere seamless replacement of intact glass with shattered pieces, as an occasionalist picture would understand it.[39] Rather, stability and change can be accounted for by persistence and flux in the accidents comprising the bodies.[40] This also puts al-Māturīdī at odds with later figures within his tradition who would not only adopt atomism, but would forcefully insist on the momentary existence of all accidents.[41]

Second, created volitional agents, human beings and other entities with free will, which includes the *jinn* at least,[42] possess a degree of choice in causing effects. Al-Māturīdī points to our intuitive certainty that we freely choose our actions as evidence for this distinction.[43] Ontologically, this is accounted for by God's creation of an accident of *qudra* that is the *sabab* ('cause'), of one act rather than an alternative at the same moment that it is given. The human being's use of *qudra* as a choice function for the causal result of the chosen act is termed 'free choice' (*ikhtiyār*).[44] Although it is perfectly possible, and even likely, for a person to have an intention that precedes a given action, freedom

37 See Harvey, *Transcendent God, Rational World*, 176–79.

38 Al-Māturīdī, *Kitāb al-tawḥīd*, 349. This necessity comes from God's creation of any given nature. Within the context of al-Māturīdī's wider theological system it is ultimately underpinned by the concept of divine wisdom. As al-Māturīdī discusses elsewhere, even miraculous events are understood through the idea of specific, rare natures. See Ramon Harvey and Kayhan Özaykal, "Abū Manṣūr al-Māturīdī," in *Seven Classical Perspectives for Islam and Science*, ed. Shoaib Ahmed Malik (Abingdon: Routledge) (forthcoming).

39 See Ulrich Rudolph, "Occasionalism," in *The Oxford Handbook of Islamic Theology*, ed. Sabine Schmidtke (Oxford: Oxford University Press, 2016), 347–63, esp. 355–56.

40 Al-Māturīdī, *Kitāb al-tawḥīd*, 211.

41 See al-Bazdawī, *Uṣūl al-dīn*, 24–26.

42 See Al-Māturīdī, *Ta'wīlāt al-qur'ān*, vol. 14, 285.

43 Al-Māturīdī, *Kitāb al-tawḥīd*, 307.

44 See Pessagno, "Irāda, Ikhtiyār, Qudra, Kasb," 183.

is ultimately the immediate selection of the specific act that the accident of *qudra* is to cause.[45] This means that, unlike accidents classified as natures, the causal result of the accident of *qudra* is not fully determined by the prior interactions of accident bundles.

With an understanding of the metaphysics of al-Māturīdī's causal theory in place, it is now possible to address how he uses it to underpin his ethics. In the same passage that has been my primary focus in this section, he writes:

> The foundational principle of [the present question] is that as every cause of action (*sabab min asbāb al-fiʿl*) is suitable for something and its opposite, so is volitional power (*al-qudra*). In addition, if the power is not suitable for both matters [i.e., either something or its opposite], the power to do the opposite action would be missing. One is sometimes ordered to do something and at other times prohibited from it. So, it is necessary that [one] power serves for something and its opposite. This means that command and prohibition are based on capacity (*al-wusʿ*) and power.[46]

In other words, the significance of human obedience to the divine command is secured by the fact that the volitional power granted by God, which is used to fulfil it, could be used to flaunt it. Moreover, just as a single accident of power cannot be simultaneously the cause of two opposite actions, it can never be the case that something is both commanded and prohibited at the same time. In some cases, however, the same action is alternately commanded and prohibited. For instance, fasting is commanded on the last day of Ramadan but prohibited on the day of Eid. Moreover, each moment one fasts, the power that could be used to eat is spent in the choice to refrain from it. The two options are mutually exclusive, because volitional power is conceived as an accident that can only act as the cause for one performed action at any given moment. This binary aspect of commands and prohibitions will be developed further below.

---

45 This is contrary to the interpretation offered in Philip Dorroll, "Māturīdī Theology in the Ottoman Empire: Debating Human Choice and Divine Power," in *Osmanlı'da İlm-i Kelâm: Âlimler, Eserler, Meseleler*, ed. O. Demir, V. Kaya, K. Gombeyaz and U. M. Kılavuz (Istanbul: İSAR Yayınları, 2016), 219–38, esp. 225. Dorroll suggests that al-Māturīdī argues for the precedence of *ikhtiyār* to the creation of power on the basis of a passage in al-Māturīdī, *Kitāb al-tawḥīd*, 352. But what al-Māturīdī points to in the cited location is the possibility of the successive renewal of a certain choice instead of its alternatives. For a translation of the passage and detailed discussion of this point, see Pessagno, "Irāda, Ikhtiyār, Qudra, Kasb," 183–84, 187.

46 Al-Māturīdī, *Kitāb al-tawḥīd*, 349.

When al-Māturīdī touches on commands and prohibitions in his *kalām* it is usually to provide the underlying theological reasoning for why God gives them and how human beings can choose to obey or disobey them. This is because the discipline of *kalām* looks at the metaphysical conditions that enable human beings to act with choice in response to divine obligations, of which the most important is the pairing of obedience and disobedience. This leads to the framing adopted by al-Māturīdī in which he typically writes of using volitional power to realise a given action or its opposite, by which he means those acts related in general to these two kinds of response to divine commands. What matters for underpinning *ikhtiyār* in a more specific normative sense, however, is that the same accident of volitional power would have been effective for any alternative action. It is not as if one is always confronted by a pair of options. As his *uṣūl* discussion clarifies, when the focus turns to the value of acts themselves, the multiple possibilities in any given scenario become important in accounting for the rich variety of ethical responses available to the human being. It is also crucially within the discipline of *uṣūl al-fiqh* that one can explain in detail how God's commands and prohibitions can be expressed as statements of legal value, such as obligations, which actions "cause" to be fulfilled or violated.

4 The Normativity of the *Sabab* in al-Māturīdī's *Uṣūl*

Unlike *kalām*, in which we can draw from the entire text of al-Māturīdī's *Kitāb al-tawḥīd*, when it comes to his own views on *uṣūl* we are reliant on the few texts preserved by ʿAlāʾ al-Dīn al-Samarqandī in his *Mīzān al-uṣūl*, as well as specific principles that he brings to his exegesis. For the present investigation into the *sabab*, there are three relevant passages in this text, all drawn from the section on *amr* ('command'), which record, or paraphrase, al-Māturīdī's words. What is preserved is only a fraction of the typical coverage of this section within works of *uṣūl*, and so only a partial picture can emerge of what al-Māturīdī may have thought. Nevertheless, fragmentary reconstruction is better than no reconstruction at all.

Before looking at these materials, it is useful to articulate what scholars of *uṣūl al-fiqh* were attempting to do when theorising about commands. As pointed out by David Vishanoff, they typically saw their role as providing rubrics for performing legal translation of the divine address, especially as found within the Qurʾan. This means that commands in the imperative need to be expressed as indicative statements of "act *a* by person *p* under circumstance *c* has the legal value *v*."[47] The specific topic that al-Māturīdī addresses in the surviving materials concerns what can be called a reciprocity rule between commands and prohibitions. Simply put, any divine command that can be expressed as one performing a certain act *a* to fulfil an obligation *o* is necessarily equivalent to refraining from a corresponding act *not-a* by which one would have otherwise fulfilled a forbiddance *f*, and vice versa. For instance, the command to fast in Ramadan is expressed by the obligation to perform the act of fasting, and this is equivalent to refraining from eating, drinking and sexual relations, which are forbidden. In order to further explore the implications of this theoretical construct, I will present a translation of the aforementioned source materials:[48]

> 1. Shaykh Abū Manṣūr, may God have mercy on him, unrestrictedly treated the prohibition of something as a command to refrain from it—as a command for [an act] refraining from and preventing [that act][49]—and there are [multiple] causes (*asbāb*) for refraining from it, which are for ease (*musāhala*) and facilitation (*tawassuʿ*).[50]
>
> 2. The correct view is what Shaykh Abū Manṣūr al-Māturīdī, may God have mercy on him, says: "the opposite of something is refraining from [that act], but refraining can be due to a single cause (*sabab*) or due to causes (*asbāb*). The command is a prohibition of refraining from [that act], and the prohibition from something is the command to refrain from it. Then, if it is refrained from due to a single cause, that cause is described with obligation and forbiddance. And if it is refrained from due to causes, each of them is described individually according to its state."[51]
>
> 3. Shakyh Abū Manṣūr al-Māturīdī, may God have mercy on him, says: "there is no distinction between the command and the prohibition, as each of them has an opposite in reality, which is refraining from [that act]. So, the command to do an action is a prohibition of its opposite (and

47 David R. Vishanoff, "The Ethical Structure of Imām al-Ḥaramayn al-Juwaynī's Legal Theory," in *Islamic Law and Ethics*, ed. David R. Vishanoff (Herndon, VA: IIIT, 2020), 1–33, at 19–20. The letters have been italicised.

48 I have put these passages in the most useful order for introducing their ideas, rather than the order that they appear in al-Samarqandī's book.

49 This parenthetical remark comes after the phrase mentioning causes (*asbāb*) in the text, but it makes better syntactical sense to translate it here.

50 Al-Samarqandī, *Mīzān al-uṣūl fī natāʾij al-ʿuqūl*, vol. 1, 224.

51 Al-Samarqandī, *Mīzān al-uṣūl fī natāʾij al-ʿuqūl*, vol. 1, 222.

> its opposite is refraining from it). [It is] not that [one performs] the act of refraining from it by a single specific action, like motion is refrained from by a single specific action, which is stillness. Refraining from it can be by many actions, such as the command to stand is a prohibition of its opposite, which is refraining from it. That can be by many actions, such as sitting, reclining, lying down and more. In the same way, the prohibition of an action is the command to do its opposite, which is refraining from it, and that [is performed] by the kinds of actions that we have mentioned."[52]

The first point to draw from these passages is that al-Māturīdī holds the view, also associated with Abū Bakr al-Bāqillānī (d. 403/1013) in his *uṣūl* work *al-Taqrīb wa-l-irshād*, that commands and prohibitions are two sides of the same coin.[53] That is, any command immediately and automatically expresses a corresponding prohibition and vice versa. Vishanoff connects this to al-Bāqillānī's Ashʿarī position of God's speech as a single *maʿnā* ('meaning, attribute').[54] I would suggest that there is a difficulty in this line of reasoning due to the position held by al-Bāqillānī and Ashʿarīs after him, such as Abū l-Maʿālī al-Juwaynī (d. 478/1085). This difficulty is that, while they understood divine speech as a single attribute, they referred to differentiated meanings and commands within it.[55] Al-Māturīdī treats divine speech as a class of divine action and openly discusses its plural meanings.[56] Nevertheless, since the *uṣūl* texts that we have from him, as quoted above, do not draw a connection to his theology of God's speech, I will not discuss this question further here.

The second point, and the main subject of my inquiry, derives from the reciprocity rule that has already been outlined. The fact that every command or prohibition corresponds to refraining from an opposite act has an interesting consequence. Whereas the commanded or prohibited act is defined by the

52 Al-Samarqandī, *Mīzān al-uṣūl fī natāʾij al-ʿuqūl*, vol. 1, 208–9.

53 David R. Vishanoff, *The Formation of Islamic Hermeneutics: How Sunni Legal Theorists Imagined a Revealed Law* (New Haven, CT: American Oriental Society, 2011), 174. In his later work, al-Bāqillānī apparently modified his view to the command logically entailing but not constituting a prohibition of what is opposite to it. See Vishanoff, *The Formation of Islamic Hermeneutics*, 174, n. 114. Al-Māturīdī seems to have shared the earlier view found in his *al-Taqrīb*. On this point, see Weiss, *The Search for God's Law*, 378.

54 Vishanoff, *The Formation of Islamic Hermeneutics*, 174–75.

55 Omar Farahat, *The Foundation of Norms in Islamic Jurisprudence and Theology* (Cambridge: Cambridge University Press, 2019), 111–12.

56 Al-Māturīdī, *Kitāb al-tawḥīd*, 116–17, 121. See Harvey, *Transcendent God, Rational World*, 197, 200–1, 209.

specific linguistic form within revelation, its opposite is left unrestricted. This leads to two kinds of cases. Sometimes, there is only a single way to refrain from the opposite act, and therefore only one action can be the 'cause' (*sabab*) to refrain from it and thereby fulfil the obligation. An example of this is motion, which is left by stillness. This binary metaphysical scenario is one familiar from al-Māturīdī's *kalām*.[57] In other cases, and it seems from his treatment that al-Māturīdī considered this common, several actions are available as causes. He explains that the reason there are several ways to fulfil the command is due to divinely granted ease. Hence, by formally defining fulfilment of commands and prohibitions through the action of refraining from their opposites and by not restricting the different possible ways to do so, he builds a degree of inherent flexibility into his treatment of the legal implications of the divine address.

Moreover, the selection by human beings of which of these various possibilities to perform is metaphysically grounded in their *ikhtiyār*. This means that, as well as the basic choice to obey or disobey the command or prohibition, there is a further "normative choice" between a range of acts to fulfil the legal obligation. The implication is that al-Māturīdī does not merely understand the divine address to tell human beings precisely what to do but dignifies them with selecting the means to "cause" their compliance with the Law. This also gives theoretical space for other ethical frameworks, such as an account of the cultivation of the virtues, to be layered upon the core account of obligation towards God's commands.[58] To return once more to the example of fasting in Ramadan, a believer fulfils the prohibition of eating (and so on) by refraining from it with the free selection between a range of other acts. While sleeping through most of the day will fulfil the obligation of fasting, it does so in an inferior way in terms of virtue and reward to reciting the Qur'an. What is important for the present study is that, springing from al-Māturīdī's concurrentist divine action model, these are genuine choices that are causally efficacious in realising the attendant legal obligations. This amounts to a consistent system that vouchsafes human responsibility in normative engagement with God's commands and prohibitions.

The key point that al-Māturīdī draws from this analysis is that by recasting the relationship of the human agent to acts of legal value in terms of refraining from corresponding acts, it becomes possible to account for how the actions performed instead are the 'cause' (*sabab*) for this refraining and thereby the

57 Al-Māturīdī, *Kitāb al-tawḥīd*, 79–80.

58 See Ramon Harvey, "Whose Justice? When Māturīdī Meets MacIntyre," in *Justice in Islam: New Ethical Perspectives*, ed. Ramon Harvey and Daniel Tutt (Herndon, VA: IIT, 2023), 50–76, at 64–65.

fulfilment of the obligation. Al-Māturīdī's discussion within the discourse of *uṣūl al-fiqh*, then, does not look at the metaphysical dynamics of how freely willed decisions play out as aggregates of the created accidents that constitute volitional agents, as is the case within *kalām*. Rather, the focus within *uṣūl* is strictly upon the normative actions that result from that process and how they are, in turn, causes for the introduction of fulfilled accidents of obedience or disobedience into the volitional agent bundle. Though this deontic effect of human acts of obedience and disobedience is invisible, according to al-Māturīdī's ontology it must be a real aspect of each person's accident bundle—the way that one participates in the normative goodness and badness within the world.

5 Normative Human Action within *Uṣūlī* Discourses in al-Māturīdī's *Tafsīr*

The above points can be further elaborated with reference to material found in al-Māturīdī's *Ta'wīlat al-qur'ān*. It is in his *tafsīr* that al-Māturīdī both justifies the studied *uṣūl* principle through the Qur'anic text and applies it as part of his exegetical repertoire.

Commenting on Q. 8:45, "Believers, when you meet a force in battle, stand firm …," he refers back to the earlier verse Q. 8:15, "When you meet the disbelievers in battle, do not turn and flee …" He observes that in Q. 8:45 the phrase 'stand firm' (*fa-thbutū*) lets it be known that in the prohibition of turning and fleeing there is a command to stand firm and vice versa. Here he implies that the context of the preceding verse and use of the particle *fā'* to connote an already received instruction establishes the general principle that in the prohibition of something there is a command for its opposite and vice versa.[59] In this case, the obligation can only be fulfilled by a single *sabab*: standing firm, which is taken as identical to refraining from fleeing.

Al-Māturīdī approaches several other Qur'anic texts in a similar way. One of these is Q. 55:9: "Weigh with justice and do not fall short in the balance." Here he mentions the principle that commanding something prohibits its opposite and then states that the verse's explicit combination of the command and the prohibition is for emphasis on the topic of weighing fairly.[60] On Q. 2:16, "Their trade did not profit," he says that the negation of something obligates

---

59 Al-Māturīdī, *Ta'wīlāt al-qur'ān*, vol. 6, 237.
60 Al-Māturīdī, *Ta'wīlāt al-qur'ān*, vol. 14, 258.

affirming its opposite—that is, the hypocrite's trade of guidance for error is loss-making.[61] Again, on Q. 93:10, "Do not turn away the beggar," al-Māturīdī considers that what is meant is that such a prohibition is a command for the opposite, whereupon he refers to Q. 2:16.[62] Reading these cases in light of the greater technical elaboration in the quotations preserved from his works of *uṣūl al-fiqh*, it is implicit that when the choice is made to perform (or refrain from the opposite of) any of these normative actions, that act becomes the cause for deontic fulfilment of a specific obligation expressed by the divine address.

6 Conclusion

In this chapter, I have explored al-Māturīdī's concept of 'cause' (*sabab*) in two main genres, *kalām* and *uṣūl* (though this latter includes *uṣūlī* comments within his *tafsīr*). In his *kalām*, the focus was on his theological elaboration of the Ḥanafī doctrine that God creates an accident of volitional power that is "spent" at the very moment that the human being acts for one of two opposite kinds of result, obedience or disobedience. This volitional power (*qudra*) is the concurrent cause (*sabab*) of the action's created existence. He contrasts this distinctive account of human choice (*ikhtiyār*) with an analysis of divinely created natural causality, in which the nature (*ṭabʿ*) of things compels their action. Whereas the first aspect of his treatment bequeathed an important legacy within the subsequent Māturīdī tradition,[63] albeit often reinterpreted through the lens of occasionalism, his approach to natures was quickly abandoned and replaced with atomism.[64]

Turning to al-Māturīdī's contributions to *uṣūl al-fiqh*, of which we have only limited sources, I showed that though the *sabab* in *uṣūl* has an analogous function in terms of being a kind of cause, it is identified with the human act, rather

61 Al-Māturīdī, *Taʾwīlāt al-qurʾān*, vol. 2, 43.

62 Al-Māturīdī, *Taʾwīlāt al-qurʾān*, vol. 17, 250.

63 This point goes beyond the scope of the current chapter. For further discussion, see Rudolph, *Al-Māturīdī and the Development of Sunnī Theology in Samarqand*, 305, n. 347; Dorroll, "Māturīdī Theology in the Ottoman Empire," 229–30; Nazif Muhtaroglu, "An Occasionalist Defence of Free Will," in *Classic Issues in Islamic Philosophy and Theology Today*, ed. Anna-Teresa Tymieniecka and Nazif Muhtaroglu (Dordrecht: Springer, 2010), 45–62, esp. 49; Philipp Bruckmayr, "The Particular Will (*al-irādat al-juzʾiyya*): Excavations Regarding a Latecomer in *Kalām* Terminology on Human Agency and Its Position in Naqshbandi Discourse," *European Journal of Turkish Studies*, 13 (2011), 1–24, esp. 3, 12.

64 Rudolph, *Al-Māturīdī and the Development of Sunnī Theology in Samarqand*, 248–9; Harvey, *Transcendent God, Rational World*, 93.

than the volitional power that makes it possible. Hence, al-Māturīdī uses the concept of *sabab* to articulate how human actions are the normative or deontic causes for the fulfilment of obligations derived from the divine address, especially in terms of whichever action is used to refrain from the opposite of a command or prohibition.

This lets us better understand the purpose of each of these genres to our theologian. Al-Māturīdī concentrates in his *kalām* on the metaphysical conditions for the human being to freely choose obedience or disobedience without compromising his commitment to God's creation of human volitional power as cause and the performed action as effect. His *uṣūl* picks up the account from this point to treat the action as a deontic cause for the fulfilment of a divinely stipulated obligation or forbiddance as derived from a divine command or prohibition. This means that he takes *uṣūl al-fiqh* to be concerned with the normative standings of divine obligations, rather than their metaphysical possibility as genuine choices. Moreover, by equating the fulfilment of each command to an act of refraining from its converse prohibition and vice versa, and by arguing that in most cases there are various ways to cause this deontic effect, he embeds a "normative choice" into the human response to the divine address. At a deeper level, we can see that al-Māturīdī's dual role for the *sabab* is what makes the test of command and prohibition meaningful and wise. According to his system, a choice to obey God is to cause an act by which one selects how to refrain from disobedience to Him. And each such choice could have genuinely been otherwise. God's power and creative activity are absolute, but human power within its proper scope is sufficient for us to freely make the existential choices that constitute our destinies.

Acknowledgements

I extend my gratitude to the organisers and participants of the Dynamics of Tradition conference, where I first presented this chapter as a paper, to Kayhan Özaykal and David Jalajel who read earlier drafts and constructively engaged with me on the contents, and to the two anonymous reviewers.

Bibliography

Abū Ḥanīfa al-Nuʿmān b. Thābit, *al-ʿĀlim wa-l-mutaʿallim riwāyat Abī Muqātil ʿan Abī Ḥanīfa raḍiya Allāhu ʿanhumā wa-yalīhi risālat Abī Ḥanīfa ilā ʿUthmān al-Battī thumma al-fiqh al-absaṭ: Riwāyat Abī Muṭīʿ ʿan Abī Ḥanīfa raḥimahumā Allāh*, ed. Muḥammad Zāhid al-Kawtharī (Cairo: Maṭbaʿat al-Anwār, 1949).

Adamson, Peter and Peter E. Pormann, *The Philosophical Works of al-Kindī* (Karachi: Oxford University Press, 2012).

al-Bazdawī, Abū l-Yusr, *Al-Muyassar fī l-kalām al-musammā uṣūl al-dīn*, ed. ʿAbd Allāh Muḥammad Ismāʿīl and Muḥammad Ḍarghām (Cairo: Dār Nūr al-Yaqīn, 2024).

Bruckmayr, Philipp, "The Particular Will (*al-irādat al-juz'iyya*): Excavations Regarding a Latecomer in *Kalām* Terminology on Human Agency and Its Position in Naqshbandi Discourse," *European Journal of Turkish Studies*, 13 (2011), 1–24.

Cerić, Mustafa, *Roots of Synthetic Theology in Islam: A Study of the Theology of Abū Manṣūr al-Māturīdī (d. 333/944)* (Kuala Lumpur: International Institute of Islamic Thought and Civilization, 1995).

Dorroll, Philip, "Māturīdī Theology in the Ottoman Empire: Debating Human Choice and Divine Power," in *Osmanlı'da İlm-i Kelâm: Âlimler, Eserler, Meseleler*, ed. O. Demir, V. Kaya, K. Gombeyaz and U. M. Kılavuz (Istanbul: İSAR Yayınları, 2016), 219–38.

Eissa, Mohamed, *The Jurist and the Theologian: Speculative Theology in Shāfiʿī Legal Theory* (Piscataway, NJ: Gorgias Press, 2017).

El Omari, Racha, *The Theology of Abū l-Qāsim al-Balkhī/al-Kaʿbī (d. 319/931)* (Leiden: Brill, 2016).

El Shamsy, Ahmed, "Bridging the Gap: Two Early Texts of Islamic Legal Theory," *Journal of the American Oriental Society*, 137, no. 3 (2017), 505–36.

Farahat, Omar, *The Foundation of Norms in Islamic Jurisprudence and Theology* (Cambridge: Cambridge University Press, 2019).

Frank, Richard M., "The Structure of Created Causality, according to al-Ashʿarī: An Analysis of the *Kitāb al-Lumaʿ*, §§ 82–164," *Studia Islamica*, 104 (1966), 13–75.

Gardet, Louis, "ʿIlla," in *The Encyclopaedia of Islam, New Edition*, ed. P. Bearman et al. (Leiden: Brill, 1986–2004).

Harvey, Ramon, "Philosopher of Samarqand: Abū Manṣūr al-Māturīdī's Theory of Properties," in *Pluralizing Philosophy's Past*, ed. Amber L. Griffioen and Marius Backmann (London: Palgrave, 2023), 77–90.

Harvey, Ramon, "Whose Justice? When Māturīdī Meets MacIntyre," in *Justice in Islam: New Ethical Perspectives*, ed. Ramon Harvey and Daniel Tutt (Herndon, VA: IIT, 2023), 50–76.

Harvey, Ramon, *Transcendent God, Rational World: A Māturīdī Theology* (Edinburgh: Edinburgh University Press, 2021).

Harvey, Ramon, "Al-Māturīdī on the Abrogation of the *Sharīʿa* in the Qur'an and Previous Scriptures," in *İmâm Mâtürîdî ve Te'vîlâtü'l-Kur'ân*, ed. Hatice K. Arpaguş, Mehmet Umit and Bilal Kır (Istanbul: M. U. İlahiyat Fakultesi Vakfı Yayınları, 2019), 511–24.

Harvey, Ramon and David Solomon Jalajel, "Al-Māturīdī's Divine Action Model: A Distinctive Concurrentist Account of Causality," *Journal of Islamic Philosophy*, 16, no. 1 (2025), 63–106.

Harvey, Ramon and Kayhan Özaykal, "Abū Manṣūr al-Māturīdī," in *Seven Classical Perspectives for Islam and Science*, ed. Shoaib Ahmed Malik (Abingdon: Routledge) (forthcoming).

al-Jaṣṣāṣ, Aḥmad b. ʿAlī, *al-Fuṣūl fī l-uṣūl*, ed. ʿUjayl Jāsim al-Nashamī, 4 vols (Kuwait: Wizārat al-Awqāf wa-l-Shuʾūn al-Islāmiyya, 1994).

Koca, Özgür, *Islam, Causality, and Freedom: From the Medieval to the Modern Era* (Cambridge: Cambridge University Press, 2020).

Lane, E. W., *Arabic–English Lexicon*, 2 vols (Cambridge: Islamic Texts Society, 2003).

al-Māturīdī, Abū Manṣūr, "Kitāb al-tawḥīd," Cambridge University Library, Cambridge, MS Add. 3651.

al-Māturīdī, Abū Manṣūr, *Kitāb al-tawḥīd*, ed. Bekir Topaloğlu and Muḥammad Aruçi (second edition, Istanbul: Maktabat al-Irshād, 2010).

al-Māturīdī, Abū Manṣūr, *Taʾwīlāt al-qurʾān*, ed. Ertuğrul Boynukalın and Bekir Topaloğlu, 18 vols (Istanbul: Dār al-Mīzān, 2006).

Muhtaroglu, Nazif, "Al-Māturīdī's View of Causality," in *Occasionalism Revisited: New Essays from the Islamic and Western Philosophical Traditions*, ed. Nazif Muhtaroglu (Abu Dhabi: Kalam Research & Media, 2017), 3–21.

Muhtaroglu, Nazif, "An Occasionalist Defence of Free Will," in *Classic Issues in Islamic Philosophy and Theology Today*, ed. Anna-Teresa Tymieniecka and Nazif Muhtaroglu (Dordrecht: Springer, 2010), 45–62.

Pessagno, J. Meric, "Irāda, Ikhtiyār, Qudra, Kasb: The View of Abū Manṣūr al-Māturīdī," *Journal of the American Oriental Society*, 104, no. 1 (1984), 177–91.

Rudolph, Ulrich, "Occasionalism," in *The Oxford Handbook of Islamic Theology*, ed. Sabine Schmidtke (Oxford: Oxford University Press, 2016), 347–63.

Rudolph, Ulrich, *Al-Māturīdī and the Development of Sunnī Theology in Samarqand*, trans. Rodrigo Adem (Leiden: Brill, 2015).

al-Samarqandī, ʿAlāʾ al-Dīn, *Mīzān al-uṣūl fī natāʾij al-ʿuqūl*, ed. ʿAbd al-Malik ʿAbd al-Raḥmān al-Saʿdī, 2 vols (Mecca: Jāmiʿat Umm al-Qurā, 1984).

van Ess, Josef, *Theology and Society in the Second and Third Centuries of the Hijra, Volume 1*, trans. John O'Kane (Leiden: Brill, 2017).

van Ess, Josef, *Theology and Society in the Second and Third Centuries of the Hijra, Volume 3*, trans. Gwendolin Goldbloom (Leiden: Brill, 2018).

van Ess, Josef, *Theology and Society in the Second and Third Centuries of the Hijra, Volume 4*, trans. Gwendolin Goldbloom (Leiden: Brill, 2018).

Vishanoff, David R., "The Ethical Structure of Imām al-Ḥaramayn al-Juwaynī's Legal Theory," in *Islamic Law and Ethics*, ed. David R. Vishanoff (Herndon, VA: IIIT, 2020), 1–33.

Vishanoff, David R., *The Formation of Islamic Hermeneutics: How Sunni Legal Theorists Imagined a Revealed Law* (New Haven, CT: American Oriental Society, 2011).

Weiss, Bernard G., *The Search for God's Law: Islamic Jurisprudence in the Writings of Sayf al-Dīn al-Āmidī* (revised edition, Salt Lake City, UT: University of Utah Press, 2010).

Zysow, Aron, "Muʿtazilism and Māturīdism in Ḥanafī Legal Theory," in *Studies in Islamic Legal Theory*, ed. Bernard G. Weiss (Leiden: Brill, 2002).

Zysow, Aron, *The Economy of Certainty: An Introduction to the Typology of Islamic Legal Theory* (Atlanta, GA: Lockwood Press, 2013).

CHAPTER 8

ʿAbd al-Jabbār on Good and Evil, and the Divine Law *taklīf*

Maha El Kaisy-Friemuth

Trustworthy biographical details of the life of ʿAbd al-Jabbār are difficult to ascertain; his full name was Abū al-Ḥasan ʿAbd al-Jabbār Ibn Aḥmad al-Hamadhānī.[1] He was born in the region of Hamadhān about 320/932. He started his theological studies in Iṣfahān under the Ashʿarite school, but in Baṣra he was soon impressed by the Muʿtazilite teaching and studied their sciences under the famous theologian Abū Isḥāq Ibn ʿAyyāsh (d. 359/970). He also studied in Baghdad under the Muʿtazilite theologian Abū ʿAbdullāh al-Baṣrī (d. 366/977). The famous wazir al-Ṣāḥib Ibn ʿAbbād appointed ʿAbd al-Jabbār as the chief judge of Rayy at about 361/972. He remained in this office until the death of al-Ṣāḥib in 387/997, afterwards devoting himself to teaching and writing until his death at Rayy in 415/1024 or 1025.[2]

The most important works of ʿAbd al-Jabbār which concern the theme of good and evil are *Sharḥ al-Uṣūl al-khamsa*, *al-Muḥīṭ bi-l-taklīf*, and *al-Mughnī*.

1. *Sharḥ al-Uṣūl al-khamsa*. This work was not dictated by ʿAbd al-Jabbār; it is more a commentary by the Zaydite Mankadīm.[3] *Sharḥ* presents ʿAbd al-Jabbār's discussion in an uncomplicated manner and a summary form, suggesting that it is based on lectures he delivered to public and private students, later compiled by Aḥmad Ibn al-Ḥusayn, known as Mankadīm.[4]

---

1 Johannes R. T. Maria Peters, *God's Created Speech: A Study in the Speculative Theology of the Muʿtazilī Qāḍī al-Qudāt Abū al-Ḥasan ʿAbd al-Jabbār Ibn Aḥmad al-Hamadhānī* (Leiden: Brill, 1976), 8.

2 Ibid.; see also the commentary of ʿAbd al-Karīm ʿUthmān on Abū al-Ḥasan ʿAbd al-Jabbār, *Sharḥ al-Uṣūl al-khamsa*, ed. ʿAbd al-Karīm ʿUthmān (Cairo: Maktabat Wahba, 1416/1996), 13–16.

3 Ibid., pp. 26–28.

4 Ibid. ʿAbd al-Karīm ʿUthmān describes this book as written in a clear and easy manner which aims to challenge the public and students (see *Sharḥ*, 31). The importance of this book, beside explaining ʿAbd al-Jabbār's theology in a simpler language than that of *al-Mughnī* and *al-Muḥīṭ*, is that it preserves the parts missing in *al-Mughnī*: the attributes of God, the promise and punishment and the commandment to do good, prohibiting evil—sections that had not yet been published in *al-Muḥīṭ*.

 | DOI:10.1163/9789004746886_010

2. *Al-Majmūʿ fī al-muḥīṭ bi-l-taklīf*[5] was probably written after ʿAbd al-Jabbār completed his long work *al-Mughnī* in about 382/992.[6] It exists only in the version of his disciple Abū Muḥammad al-Ḥasan Ibn Aḥmad Ibn Mattawiyya (d. 468/1076).

3. The most important work of ʿAbd al-Jabbār is *al-Mughnī*.[7] It consists of twenty volumes, sixteen of which were found in Yemen in 1951. The first three volumes and volumes 18–20 are lost. Peters explains that ʿAbd al-Jabbār dictated this work over a period of twenty years between 361/972 and 382/992.[8]

ʿAbd al-Jabbār in *al-Mughnī* presents the Muʿtazilite theology in a coherent and systematic arrangement in order to form a unity of ideas very closely related to each other. Although ʿAbd al-Jabbār in *al-Mughnī* does not introduce a theology of his own but rather compiles a theology of the Basran school under Abū ʿAlī and Abū Hāshim al-Jubbāʾī, he presents his own reflections on their works and arranges the different theological issues in order to lead to a specific theological concept.[9]

The *Mughnī* can be structured in various ways; however, issues concerning God's *tawḥīd* and *ʿadl* are covered in volumes 1–7.

---

5 This work was published by two scholars in 1965: J. J. Houben in Beirut, and Sayid ʿAzmi in Cairo; see Peters, *Created Speech*, 14. ʿAzmi explains that the problem with this work is that Ibn al-Murtaḍā refers in *al-Munya wa-l-ʿamal* only to *al-Muḥīṭ* as a work of ʿAbd al-Jabbār, but ʿAbd al-Jabbār also has another work in *tafsīr* which is called *al-Muḥīṭ*. This work is mentioned in *Mutashābih al-Qurʾān*. But Ibn al-Murtaḍā also mentions in the same book that Aḥmad Ibn Mattawiyya, the collector of *al-Majmūʿ fī al-muḥīṭ bi-l-taklīf*, has a book with the title *al-Muḥīṭ fī uṣūl al-dīn*. Thus the question here is whether the *Muḥīṭ bi-l-taklīf* is the book of ʿAbd al-Jabbār or not. ʿAzmi, however, is convinced that this book includes all the ideas and theology of ʿAbd al-Jabbār but it is not his dictation, which suggests that it is a secondary source. See Abū al-Ḥasan ʿAbd al-Jabbār, *al-Majmūʿ fī al-Muḥīṭ bi-l-taklīf*, ed. J. J. Houben (Beirut: al-Maṭbaʿa al-Kāthūlikiya, 1965), 7–9; Abū al-Ḥasan ʿAbd al-Jabbār, *al-Muḥīṭ bi-l-taklīf*, compiled by al-Ḥasan b. Aḥmad b. Mattawiyya, ed. ʿUmar Sayid ʿAzmī (Cairo: al-Dār al-Miṣriyya li-l-Taʾlīf wa-l-Tarjama, n.d), 7–10.

6 Peters, *Created Speech*, 14.

7 Abū al-Ḥasan ʿAbd al-Jabbār, *al-Mughnī fī abwāb al-tawḥīd wa-l-ʿadl*, ed. Ibrāhīm Madkūr and Ṭaha Ḥussain (Cairo: Wizārat al-thaqāfa wa-l-irshād al-qawmī, al-Idāra al-ʿāmma li-l-thaqāfah, 1960–68).

8 Ibid.

9 Peters, *Created Speech*, 15. Peters refers here to ʿAbd al-Jabbār's own statement against one of his opponents: "Maybe some will say: what this book contains is only a compilation of what was known from the other books. (In answer): The question is not as he assumes; if you study it, there is no doubt that in every chapter of it nothing is left out: [there is] a wide-spread collection and a miscellaneous compilation, the explanation of the correct issue and the warning against sophism, (the argument of the opponents), the study of the condition of the indication and the definition of those things upon which the point and the correct issues are built." See also *al-Mughnī*, vol. 20/2, 225.

The features of humans are treated in volumes 8–10. Volume 11 is devoted to the subject of *taklīf* and volume 12 to rational knowledge. *Mughnī* 13–17 explain the relationship between God and humans under the titles of God's assistance, *lutf*, prophecy and 'legal matters', *shar'iyyāt*.[10]

Thus, 'Abd al-Jabbār's modification of Mu'tazilite theology in *al-Mughnī* represents a shift from its earlier structure, which was probably arranged primarily according to the five principles before his time.[11]

The understanding of good and evil in the theology of 'Abd al-Jabbār is scattered in many parts of *al-Mughnī*. Good and evil are attributed to human and divine acts in the same way; thus we need first to explain 'Abd al-Jabbār's concept of 'acts' (*af'āl*).

'Abd al-Jabbār analyses the meaning of the word 'to act' in *al-Mughnī* 6, part 1,[12] and defines it as "what comes into existence from someone who has been capable of it." This means that an act is completely related to the one who performed it (*ta'alluq al-fi'l bi-l-fā'il*). This definition already contains the famous Mu'tazilite belief of free will. That the act belongs to the person who performs it declares the agent as the creator of his/her own act.[13] 'Abd al-Jabbār divides acts into two kinds: 1. acts which have an attribute and are performed intentionally and 2. acts which are not attributed but performed unintentionally, such as acts performed by sleeping persons or those unconscious of acting, by children or by someone acting under an obligation.[14] Only intended acts can be judged as good or evil because humans, according to 'Abd al-Jabbār, have the free ability to choose their acts and they therefore deserve either praise or blame. Acts with certain intention, to his mind, depend mainly on two important elements: 1. being capable of it and 2. being not obliged to perform it in a particular way. Thus, *will and ability* are important elements which bring the purposed acts into existence.[15] In judging an act as good or evil, Hourani points out, 'Abd al-Jabbār adopts an objective view of ethics, which means that judgement falls on the act without consideration of who performed this act, whether it was God, a prophet or an ordinary human

10 See the list of topics of all the volumes of *al-Mughnī* supplied by Peters, *Created Speech*, 34–35.

11 The five principles of the Mu'tazilites are 1. *tawḥīd*, 2. *'adl*, 3. *al-manzila bayn al-manzilatayn*, 4. *al-amr bi-l-ma'rūf wa-l-nahy 'an al-munkar* and 5. *al-wa'd wa-l-wa'īd*.

12 'Abd al-Jabbār devotes *al-Mughnī*, vol. 6/1 to a study of the basis for acts; the topic is also mentioned in *Sharḥ*, 324–63 and the sixth chapter of *al-Muḥīṭ*, 229–66.

13 Maha El Kaisy-Friemuth, *God and Humans in Islamic Thought: Abd al-Jabbār, Ibn Sīnā and al-Ghazālī* (London: Routledge, 2006), 47.

14 'Abd al-Jabbār, *al-Muḥīṭ*, 230–32.

15 'Abd al-Jabbār, *al-Muḥīṭ*, 231.

being. Hence the judgement of the act does not depend on whether people or scripture command or prohibit it but only on the nature of the act itself. Wrongdoing and lying, for example, are always recognised as evil even when commanded or performed by a wise person.[16]

The judgement of the act can be made through 1. the inner content of the act *li-ʾamr yukhtaṣṣu bihi* ('for a matter specific to it'), known through necessary knowledge and 2. the result or the consequence of the act which is known through acquired knowledge.[17] The act can be evil because of its inherent nature, as lying is evil because it is lying and wrongdoing is evil because it is wrongdoing, where the content of the act is recognised as necessarily evil. The result or the consequence of the act is an important element of revealing its attribute; to cause evil, the act itself must be considered evil. ʿAbd al-Jabbār devotes a whole chapter to listing the different acts which are considered necessarily evil and the other kinds of evil acts which are judged through acquired knowledge. The same criterion can be used for recognising good acts, but for him a good act is considered good when 'all aspects of evilness' (*kull wujūh al-qubḥ*) are absent, because even an act which has some good aspects may still be considered evil; lying or stealing may have some good consequences but nevertheless they are necessarily known as evil.[18] Thus good and evil are attributed to the act according to a certain cause (*maʿnā*), which has to be either in the content of the act or in the result which the act leads to.

ʿAbd al-Jabbār concludes that since all intended acts have to be judged good or evil, God's acts must fall under the same judgement. The question here is the following: does God in fact do good and evil?

---

16 George F. Hourani, *Islamic Rationalism* (Oxford: Oxford University Press, 1971), 30. See also ʿAbd al-Jabbār, *al-Mughnī*, vol. 6/1, 87–101. See also El Kaisy-Friemuth, *God and Humans*, 48.

17 ʿAbd al-Jabbār, *al-Mughnī*, vol. 6/1, 58.

18 Ibid., pp. 61–69. Both God's gracious acts, however, are closely attached to God's will because God as 'self-sufficient' (*ghanīy*) by His nature does not need the world. His creation and the gift of His guidance are pure grace and therefore must have been given according to a divine will. God must be 'willing' in ʿAbd al-Jabbār's theology because whoever performs an act either wills it or is obliged to do it. The main difficulty with this attribute is that some theologians and philosophers consider that 'will' causes a change in the essence of God, since He would have willed after not willing. In *al-Muḥīṭ* ʿAbd al-Jabbār explains that change means things being transformed through an attribute or an accident into others to cause a new state, such as the transformation of black into white. But if a thing gets a new attribute which it lacked before, this should not be regarded as change because nothing has changed, but instead a new attribute has been gained. See ʿAbd al-Jabbār, *al-Muḥīṭ*, 147–48.

ʿAbd al-Jabbār explains that good and evil belong to the same species of 'acts' and, when God's ability is unlimited, He must be able to do good and evil as well. Nevertheless, ʿAbd al-Jabbār, like all the Muʿtazilites, has the full conviction that although God could perform evil, He actually never does so. This conviction is grounded in two main arguments: 1. since God's eternal knowledge circumscribes all that can be known, He must know the evilness of evil and its consequences, and therefore He neither chooses to do evil nor guides anyone to it; 2. God is self-sufficient and is not in need of any benefit from an evil act. In addition, since God's will is temporal and connected to His acts, He chooses some acts and rejects others. Therefore, one of the most important qualities and criteria of God's acts is that they are free from evil both in their content and in their goals.[19]

1 Are Pain and Suffering Evil?

In the above section I explained the main features of good and evil as human or divine product in ʿAbd al-Jabbār's theology. We reckoned that good can be accomplished by both God and humans. In contrast, evil can only happen under the intention and will of humans. They are able to distinguish between good and evil through necessary and rational knowledge, and thus they are responsible for the increasing of good and evil in the human world.

In this section we ask the question of who is responsible for the pain and suffering which result from illness or natural disasters? To answer this question, we will examine the definitions of pain and suffering and how ʿAbd al-Jabbār evaluates them.

ʿAbd al-Jabbār, in dealing with this problem, starts by declaring that pain and suffering are perceived in a direct immediate way which does not need inquiry; only their causes must be acquired.[20] His main argument here is that pain should be considered under the heading of taste and smell, which are necessarily perceived and therefore it is possible to distinguish between different

19 ʿAbd al-Jabbār, *al-Mughnī*, vol. 6/1, 177. See also El Kaisy-Friemuth, *God and Humans*, 49–50.

20 He devotes about 40 pages to this under the heading *ithbāt al-ālām* ('the proofs of pain'). His discussion is not easy to follow but in general he is arguing against groups who consider pain not perceivable but known only by necessity. In this case it is not easy or even possible to identify a certain pain and distinguish between different pains, especially for someone who is in poor health. They also consider that pain could be neither sent from God nor from man but is simply the absence of good health (*intifāʾ al-ṣiḥḥa*). See ʿAbd al-Jabbār, *al-Mughnī*, vol. 13, 229–71.

kinds of pain just as we distinguish different kinds of taste and smell. In this way pain should be considered as a temporal aspect (*maʿnā ḥādith*), which is caused by someone, either a human or God.[21] He establishes the idea that pain is a generated action and not a primary one; for example, when someone hits another, the blow is a primary action and the pain which is caused by it is a generated one. In other words, pain always comes in connection with reasons, either from a blow or torture or sickness or something else.[22] However, pain and suffering are considered by many to be evil because they cause injury to the one who receives them. ʿAbd al-Jabbār argues here against the opinion of the *thanawiyya* group[23] who hold that pain and suffering can only be regarded evil as being in themselves evil.[24] He argues that it is necessarily known that there are different kinds of pain conceded to be good, such as the pain which results from hard work and which will be rewarded, or deserved pain and the like.[25] First of all, he divides evil into two different kinds: evil because of being evil in itself, and evil because it contains different aspects of evilness, the absence of which could transform the act to good from being regarded as evil. Suffering, which is of the second kind, ʿAbd al-Jabbār explains, has aspects of evil which can be reversed.[26] Therefore it is important here to examine the concept of evil according to ʿAbd al-Jabbār in order to understand how suffering and pain can lead to good acts. He defines wrongdoing (*ẓulm*)[27] as 'any injury without

21 ʿAbd al-Jabbār discusses this point in much detail perhaps because he thinks it important to be able to distinguish between the different kinds of pain to be able to acknowledge the reasons for a specific pain, whether caused by human or by God. Ibid.

22 ʿAbd al-Jabbār, *al-Mughnī*, vol. 13, 272–76.

23 Ritter considers this group to be *ahl al-thanawiyya*, see Abū al-Ḥasan al-Ashʿarī, *Maqālāt al-islāmiyyīn: Die dogmatischen Lehren der Anhänger des Islam*, ed. Hellmut Ritter (Wiesbaden: F. Steiner, 1963), 671. They are mentioned by al-Ashʿarī in *Maqālāt* as the group who believe that the two sources of the world are light and darkness (ibid., p. 308).

24 This was most probably the strongest view, for he devotes later on a separate section to the topic "pain is not evil because it is pain as the *thanawiyya* believe." His main aim is to prove that there are kinds of pain which should not come under the species of evil. See ʿAbd al-Jabbār, *al-Mughnī*, vol. 13, 279–92.

25 Ibid., p. 279.

26 ʿAbd al-Jabbār, *al-Mughnī*, vol. 13, 279. But *aṣḥāb al-tanāsukh* (probably *al-barāhima*) consider pain and suffering good when they are deserved. The *mujabbira* believed that if suffering and pain are caused by humankind, they are evil but if they are caused by God they are good. See also El Kaisy-Friemuth, *God and Humans*, 69–70.

27 The word *ẓulm* is difficult to translate for it should not be limited to the Arabic philologist's narrow meaning of 'unjust act', ʿAbd al-Jabbār explains, because this would mainly describe the agent rather than the act. G. Hourani translates it as 'wrongdoing' in order to include all kinds of wrong action, although it does not express the strong meaning of *ẓulm*. In this section we will use both words, *ẓulm* and 'wrongdoing', side by side. See Hourani, *Rationalism*, 50.

benefit exceeding it or repulsion of harm greater than it which is not deserved or thought to have any of these (good-resulting) aspects'.[28] Thus pain and suffering are considered *ẓulm* ('wrongdoing') when a. they confer no benefit; b. they do not avoid greater harm; c. they are not deserved; and d. there is no doubt about a, b and c. In other words, it contains only aspects of evil. Thus an injury is evil when it lacks all good aspects, just as something good is regarded as such when 'all evil aspects are absent' (*intifāʿ kull wujūh al-qubḥ*).[29] But when these same four reasons which make pain and suffering *ẓulm* are reversed—viz. a. when they confer benefit; b. when they avoid a greater injury; c. when they are deserved; or d. when there is doubt of their evilness—they should not be considered evil. This reversal simply removes the evil aspects of pain and suffering and transforms them from being evil to be accepted as acts which deserve no blame. Thus, when an agent causes pain to others in order to benefit them or in order to let them avoid a greater harm or because it is deserved, then this pain cannot be considered 'evil' (*ẓulm*). 'Abd al-Jabbār explains the four beneficent aspects of pain and suffering as follows:

> *a. Pain and suffering are good because they confer benefit.* When the good or evil aspects of the act change or disappear, the judgement of the act must change, though the injury and the pain remain. Thus, pain which aims to benefit others cannot be deemed evil nor its agent as 'unjust' (*ẓālim*). However, the question here is how to tell whether the pain is inflicted with good or evil intentions. 'Abd al-Jabbār explains that the moral result of the pain and suffering must provide evidence which is known through necessary or acquired knowledge. In addition, this knowledge about the benefit of the injury should be known to the sufferer while (s)he is still suffering in order to be appreciated.[30] The benefit should be identified as the intention of the agent responsible for the suffering, 'Abd al-Jabbār

---

28 Hourani, *Rationalism*, 71. 'Abd al-Jabbār criticises the philologists' understanding of *ẓulm* which for them is the opposite of *ʿadl* ('justice') because it stresses mainly the *ẓālim*, the one who performed the *ẓulm* rather than looking to *ẓulm* as an objective act. See 'Abd al-Jabbār, *al-Mughnī*, vol. 13, 299.

29 The knowledge that 'wrongdoing' (*ẓulm*) is evil comes through our necessary knowledge, 'Abd al-Jabbār explains. Thus, when we do *ẓulm* without any aspect of good in it, we recognise it immediately to be evil. He asserts once more that the problem is not to identify *ẓulm* in general (*mujmal*) as evil, but to identify a particular action as *ẓulm*. (*al-Mughnī*, vol. 13, 301). He proceeds to explain that 'wrongdoing' (*ẓulm*) is evil whether it is intended or not, because the aspects of evilness remain in both cases. See *al-Mughnī*, vol. 13, 308–9.

30 'Abd al-Jabbār, *al-Mughnī*, vol. 13, 319–20.

asserts, and it must also be greater than the injury to allow the sufferer to bear the pain caused by it.

b. Pain is good when it avoids a greater injury. ʿAbd al-Jabbār considers that this reason is known to us through necessary knowledge, such as running across thorns to escape from a lion, and numerous other examples. Also, performing one's obligations is hard, yet good because it avoids a greater punishment.[31] However, a condition is given here that the harm faced has to be recognised by every person as greater than the pain endured, and this should be known through necessary knowledge.[32]

c. Deserved injury. ʿAbd al-Jabbār considers deserved pain a type of punishment, and the appreciation of punishment is recognised by necessary knowledge for it is admitted prima facie that evil actions deserve punishment and pain.[33]

d. Injury is considered good on the basis of doubt. The knowledge about these three aspects above, however, is not always clearly approached and may sometimes come under doubt. Nevertheless, ʿAbd al-Jabbār recognises this as valid for bearing the injury.[34]

The aim of the discussion above is mainly to influence judgements about pain and suffering when they are meant to cause benefit rather than injury and 'wrong' (*ẓulm*). However, ʿAbd al-Jabbār's intention here is primarily to provide arguments which will allow suffering and pain to be regarded as effects which are sent with a view to the benefit. His goal is to give the ground which allows them to be sent from God without regarding God 'unjust' (*ẓālim*). Therefore, we now examine ʿAbd al-Jabbār's grounds for justifying the pains and suffering sent from God.

First of all, ʿAbd al-Jabbār explains that God is able to cause pain to human beings because, if we can cause it, God as eternally able can do so too. However, to distinguish between these two kinds of pain, ʿAbd al-Jabbār explains, we simply have to realise that all pains which do not come to us from any other being or which we could not have avoided, must be caused by God.[35] But if God does not do evil because He understands the evilness of evil, this pain and

31 Ibid., p. 335.

32 Ibid., p. 342.

33 Ibid., p. 346.

34 Ibid., p. 350. See also El Kaisy-Friemuth, *God and Humans*, 70.

35 ʿAbd al-Jabbār, *al-Mughnī*, vol. 13, 267. We realise that a certain pain is from God, in the same way as we realise that colours of things and their movement can only be from God and in the way we know that what we or others with our abilities did not bring into existence must come from God.

suffering which He sends must be deemed good. On this basis ʿAbd al-Jabbār builds his concept of the pain sent from God.[36]

He begins by examining the reasons for God to cause pain and suffering. God does not cause suffering in order for us to avoid greater pain, ʿAbd al-Jabbār explains, because He could protect us from this greater harm without our having to suffer. This, indeed, means that ʿAbd al-Jabbār believes that God never decides to use suffering in order to confer benefit except when it is the only or the best way to do so.[37] God, therefore, causes suffering either because of a benefit or because it is a deserved punishment.[38] Here ʿAbd al-Jabbār argues against the theory of *aṣḥāb al-tanāsukh* ('the proponents of reincarnation'), probably *al-barāhima*, who asserted that pain is always deserved and imagined that it was punishment earned in another, previous life.[39] ʿAbd al-Jabbār argues here that the pain which God causes because it is deserved must only be inflicted at the last judgement, otherwise everyone who suffers pain must also be accused of sin. This is impossible for ʿAbd al-Jabbār because the Qurʾān mentions many prophets who suffered pain in their sickness.[40] In addition, all sick or suffering children would be regarded as sinners, which is impossible because they are not rationally responsible for any of their deeds. Therefore, the only possible way to distinguish between the sickness and suffering which God causes in order for the sufferer to benefit, and pain sent from God as punishment is to consider that deserved pain will be inflicted *only* at the last judgement.[41]

Thus, God causes pain only because it confers benefit. ʿAbd al-Jabbār regards this benefit as 'an admonition' (*iʿtibār*), or 'a lesson' (*miḥna*), which leads to reflection on the reasons for this pain and its warning of danger.[42] This pain, however, should be compensated for, ʿAbd al-Jabbār writes, by some reward in the life to come, in order to remove all its evil aspects. ʿAbd al-Jabbār explains that if someone destroys another person's robe, even for a good

36 ʿAbd al-Jabbār, *al-Mughnī*, vol. 13, 368.

37 Ibid., pp. 369–76.

38 Ibid., pp. 377–81.

39 They also raised the possibility that God causes pain because it is deserved and to confer benefit at the same time. But ʿAbd al-Jabbār argues that if God causes pain for these two reasons, He must cause two different kinds of pain separately, one kind because it is deserved and the other for the sake of benefit. The main objection to the possibility, then, is that causing both at the same time would create confusion and the sufferer would not be able to distinguish the benefit from the punishment. See *al-Mughnī*, vol. 13, 378.

40 ʿAbd al-Jabbār, *al-Mughnī*, vol. 13, 379.

41 Ibid., pp. 377–86, 405–8.

42 Ibid., pp. 405–30.

reason, he ought to replace the destroyed robe.[43] Here he argues against Abū ʿAlī al-Jubbāʾī who considers that God could cause pain only if the sufferer were rewarded with something better. ʿAbd al-Jabbār here asks how God can reward someone by causing him to suffer. Compensation can only here be regarded, to his mind, as removing all aspects of evil from God's act of causing pain and suffering to others, even though His intention was to benefit them. Thus, his aim here is not to think in terms of compensation, but rather to remove all aspects of evil which might be attributed to God's act.[44]

Thus, pain and suffering are sent by God only as an admonition and a lesson which warn the sufferer of his/her present situation and motivate him/her to reflect. ʿAbd al-Jabbār also regards the suffering of children and the suffering caused through disasters as trials and warnings probably to others influenced by this disaster or to the parents of these children.

To conclude, pain and suffering for ʿAbd al-Jabbār are perceivable temporal aspects which always have different reasons. The reasons for this suffering can be good or evil. When pain and suffering are caused by God, they must have good reasons, for God does not cause any evil nor does he lead us to it. God causes pain either as 'admonition' (*iʿtibār*) or because it is deserved, but the deserved punishments are mainly realised in life after death.

However, the treatment of this problem here is not satisfactory because there are innumerable situations in which pain and suffering are not the result of anyone's action, and therefore must be caused by God, but still cannot be accepted as a trial or lesson. Thus, it seems here that ʿAbd al-Jabbār has simplified this problem and limited the meaning of pain to that of warning for

43 Ibid., pp. 387–88.

44 ʿAbd al-Jabbār, *al-Mughnī*, vol. 13, 391. An objection is raised here to the idea of comparing compensation and reward: as the *taklīf* ('responsibility') was given in order to reward people so pain is also given in order to have both compensation and reward. ʿAbd al-Jabbār devotes a long discussion to this problem but the important point for him is that reward is given for those who obey the *taklīf* and this is in itself a good thing because *taklīf* benefits the life of those who obey it and guides them to good acts. In this sense, reward is a praiseworthy action in response to the obedience of these people. But compensation is not a praiseworthy response to the bearing of pain; for pain is something which people have to accept. See *al-Mughnī*, vol. 13, 392–95. Another possibility is raised here: to consider that pain is only caused for the sake of its compensation. Is it possible to consider that pain, with its compensation, is a gracious act of God like *taklīf* because it means rewarding someone who does not deserve to be rewarded in the form of compensation for the pain which he has had to bear? ʿAbd al-Jabbār answers this with a question: if God wanted to act graciously would he choose to give pain? (Can there be a better example of 'uselessness' [*ʿabath*] than that? he comments). This, for him, is just like someone who wants to give something to help another person pouring the water of one river into another. See *al-Mughnī*, vol. 13, 395.

the sake of reflection. Nevertheless, for our purpose here, pain and suffering express God's distinct ways of reaching different persons and urging them to reflect, which, for 'Abd al-Jabbār, is the main consideration. This concept expresses 'Abd al-Jabbār's deep belief in the ability of God to know the circumstances of all people and use effective ways of helping them. God here for 'Abd al-Jabbār acts not only in history but also in each person's life.

2 The Importance of the Divine Law *taklīf* ('Responsibility') for the Problem of Good and Evil

As we have seen above, God's acts come also under good and evil, but they are mainly attributed as all good, even punishment or sending pain and suffering are considered good in 'Abd al-Jabbār's theology. However, God's acts are recognized in two main categories: gracious acts and obligatory acts.

Gracious acts are acts which deserve praise, though omitting them does not deserve blame. Gracious acts are mainly those which aim to benefit someone else and are intended to be good. It is an act of volunteering beyond the bounds of duty.[45] These latter kinds of act are attributed to God and express His gracious acts of creating the world and demonstrating His law, which benefits humans.[46] Obligatory acts, on the other hand, are acts which deserve praise for doing them and blame for omitting them.[47] Obligation can be conferred either because of a command or logical necessity. This last condition is demonstrated in repaying debts, which results from the logical necessity of justice.

The gracious acts of God are discussed in detail in volume 11 of *al-Mughnī*, with a brief summary in *Sharḥ al-Uṣūl al-khamsa* under the title 'grace' (*ni'ma*). 'Abd al-Jabbār starts his discussion by confirming that both God's gracious acts and acts of duty are acts directed towards goodness.[48] Both types aim to assist and benefit others and consequently merit praise.[49]

The first gracious act of God is creation. Creation for 'Abd al-Jabbār must have a certain purpose and wisdom, and cannot fall into the class of purposeless acts, as allowed or useless acts do. He devotes a long argument to the theologians who consider creation an act which does not demand a certain

45 El Kaisy-Friemuth, *God and Humans*, 50.
46 Ibid. See also 'Abd al-Jabbār, *al-Muḥīṭ*, 231.
47 'Abd al-Jabbār, *al-Mughnī*, vol. 6/1, 7–8, and Hourani, *Rationalism*, 39.
48 'Abd al-Jabbār, *al-Mughnī*, vol. 11, 58–60.
49 Ibid., p. 68.

reason.[50] He divides purposeless acts into three kinds: 1. acts of which the agent is unaware of; 2. permissible acts such as eating or breathing; or 3. 'useless acts' (*'abath*) which are done intentionally without meaning and are therefore considered evil.[51] Creating the world, he insists, can neither be the act of someone who does not know what he is doing nor can it be a useless act, because God has eternal wisdom and all His acts are intended towards goodness. Thus, God cannot act unwisely nor can the act of creation be classed as a permissible act which cannot be attributed. Therefore creation must have been performed for certain reasons and can either be an act of duty or an act of grace.[52] While the Baghdadi Muʿtazilites consider that all God's acts have a logical necessity and is classed as His duty, ʿAbd al-Jabbār considers that the act of creating the world was not necessitated through any other precedent act and therefore is an act of grace[53] which has the purpose of benefiting others. God also granted the divine law as the second act of grace to humans. ʿAbd al-Jabbār considers the granting of the divine law to all humans is opening the way for them to obtain deserved rewards which can only be obtained through hard work.[54]

It seems here that the deserved benefits, which are the consequences of adhering to the divine law, play an important role in ʿAbd al-Jabbār's theology. They direct the human interest to the divine law and show the importance of obeying God's commands. God also, according to ʿAbd al-Jabbār, has created humans with certain qualities, all of which are directed to make humans rationally responsible. The first qualities which God created in humans were passion and perception. He also provides them with self-evident and necessary knowledge; and rational capacity which allows them to think and reflect in order to distinguish between good and evil. Thus, when God creates humans with these particular qualities, His aim must be to provide them with the possibility of acquiring the deserved benefit in addition to benefits of His grace.[55]

ʿAbd al-Jabbār believes that God prepares humans for the task of accomplishing the divine law which leads them to deserved rewards; he discusses the obligation of the divine law *taklīf* in full detail in *al-Mughnī* 11.[56] *Kallafa* means to command an inferior to do a certain act which costs him effort.[57] Commanding someone to do something, he explains, discloses the will of the

50 ʿAbd al-Jabbār, *al-Mughnī*, vol. 11, 61–68.
51 Ibid., p. 68.
52 Ibid., pp. 64–67, 86.
53 ʿAbd al-Jabbār, *al-Mughnī*, vol. 13, 7.
54 ʿAbd al-Jabbār, *al-Mughnī*, vol. 11, 81.
55 El Kaisy-Friemuth, *God and Humans*, 50–52.
56 ʿUthmān, *Sharḥ*, 509–11.
57 ʿAbd al-Jabbār, *al-Mughnī*, vol. 11, 293.

commander, therefore the commandments of God indeed disclose His will. The commanding part of the commandments, however, is only a consequence of the disclosure of God's will.[58] So 'Abd al-Jabbār wants to make clear here that God's *taklīf* is a demonstration of His will that certain things should be done (or refrained from), rather than His imposing a burden. But in order to convey the importance of His will, 'Abd al-Jabbār explains, He gives it in the form of a command.

The wisdom of *taklīf* is discussed in a long separate section. 'Abd al-Jabbār argues here against the groups who consider *taklīf* to be evil; their main criticism is that God could have given the reward which we get from *taklīf* without the hard work. 'Abd al-Jabbār argues that the restriction of benefits to the gracious one limits the profits God wishes to grant humans. If there are other kinds of rewards, higher than the gracious ones and can be gained through hard work, he insists, then God should either give us the possibility of gaining them or create us in Paradise.[59] Therefore, *taklīf*, for 'Abd al-Jabbār, demonstrates God's intention from His creation. This is what distinguishes responsible humans from animals or irresponsible persons, for it makes humans responsible for doing righteous acts and it demonstrates that humans can do something and also its opposite. It also demonstrates the free will humans possess, because God, for 'Abd al-Jabbār, does not command us to accomplish what we cannot choose but are compelled to do.[60]

'Abd al-Jabbār defines *taklīf*, therefore, as commanding and informing responsible people of the good acts which they should perform and warning them against the evil deeds which they must avoid. Performing the divine law will cost effort and consequently reward or punishment must follow. This information about good and evil is transmitted through general clues (*mujmal*, 'concise' or 'summary knowledge') from the necessary knowledge, which is created in all responsible persons, but its details must be gained through acquired knowledge. Thus, every adult, for 'Abd al-Jabbār, is responsible not only for doing good and avoiding evil, but also for understanding the reasons for these obligations through knowing the lawgiver, with His attributes.[61] Consequently this *taklīf* has two sides, ethical and theological. 'Abd al-Jabbār calls this kind of obligation *taklīf 'aqlī* ('rational responsibility') which is disclosed to the human

58 Ibid., pp. 295–300.

59 Ibid., p. 137. See also Maha El Kaisy-Friemuth, "The Human and the Prophet in 'Abd al-Jabbār's Theology," in *Rationalität in der Islamische Theologie*, Band 1 *Die Klassische Periode*, ed. Maha El Kaisy-Friemuth, Reza Hajatpour, and Mohammed Abdel Rahem (Berlin: De Gruyter, 2019), 236–37.

60 'Abd al-Jabbār, *al-Muḥīṭ*, 2–3.

61 Ibid., pp. 11–12.

mind at the beginning of creation for every responsible person. The revealed divine law *taklīf samʿī* ('revealed responsibility') is what is granted through prophets to assist people to fulfil their rational obligations and to confirm what is rationally obligatory.[62]

Bibliography

ʿAbd al-Jabbār, Abū al-Ḥasan, *Sharḥ al-Uṣūl al-khamsa*, ed. ʿAbd al-Karīm ʿUthmān (Cairo: Maktabat Wahba, 1416/1996).

ʿAbd al-Jabbār, Abū al-Ḥasan, *al-Mughnī fī abwāb al-tawḥīd wa-l-ʿadl*, ed. Ibrāhīm Madkūr and Ṭaha Ḥusayn (Cairo: Wizārat al-thaqāfa wa-l-irshād al-qawmī, al-Idāra al-ʿāmma li-l-thaqāfah, 1960–68).

ʿAbd al-Jabbār, Abū al-Ḥasan, *al-Majmūʿ fī al-Muḥīṭ bi-l-taklīf*, ed. J. J. Houben (Beirut: al-Maṭbaʿa al-Kāthūlikiya, 1965).

ʿAbd al-Jabbār, Abū al-Ḥasan, *al-Muḥīṭ bi-l-taklīf*, compiled by al-Ḥasan b. Aḥmad b. Mattawiyya, ed. ʿUmar Sayid ʿAzmī (Cairo: al-Dār al-Miṣriyya li-l-Taʾlīf wa-l-Tarjama, n.d).

al-Ashʿarī, Abū al-Ḥasan, *Maqālāt al-islāmiyyīn: Die dogmatischen Lehren der Anhänger des Islam*, ed. Hellmut Ritter (Wiesbaden: F. Steiner, 1963).

El Kaisy-Friemuth, Maha, *God and Humans in Islamic Thought: Abd al-Jabbār, Ibn Sīnā and al-Ghazālī* (London: Routledge, 2006).

El Kaisy-Friemuth, "The Human and the Prophet in ʿAbd al-Jabbār's Theology," in *Rationalität in der Islamische Theologie*, Band 1 *Die Klassische Periode*, ed. Maha El Kaisy-Friemuth, Reza Hajatpour, and Mohammed Abdel Rahem (Berlin: De Gruyter, 2019), 226–41.

Hourani, George F., *Islamic Rationalism* (Oxford: Oxford University Press, 1971).

Peters, Johannes R. T. Maria, *God's Created Speech: A Study in the Speculative Theology of the Muʿtazilī Qāḍī al-Qudāt Abū al-Ḥasan ʿAbd al-Jabbār Ibn Aḥmad al-Hamadhānī* (Leiden: Brill, 1976).

62 Ibid., p. 23.

CHAPTER 9

Failure Becomes the Law

Abdul Rahman Mustafa

The *miʿrāj*, the Prophet's ascent to heaven, is widely narrated in the canonical *ḥadīth* collections and commemorated exuberantly in Muslim prayers, songs and poetry. Asleep in Mecca, the Prophet is awakened by two angels, transported on a winged creature to the farthest mosque in Jerusalem, and from there to the seventh heaven. At the climax of this night journey, the Prophet reaches the super-terrestrial limit of the lote tree. The stage is now set for one of the most dramatic theological juxtapositions of divine love and human debility in the Islamic tradition. Standing at a distance of what the Qurʾān calls "two bow lengths or nearer," the Prophet is addressed by God and told that God has commanded the believers to offer fifty canonical prayers every day. As he descends to earth, however, the Prophet encounters Moses who advises the Prophet to seek a reduction of this obligation, which, Moses says, will prove too burdensome. The Prophet returns to God and pleads for a dispensation, which is granted, only for Moses to recommend a further dispensation. And so, over the course of repeated pleas to God, the Prophet is granted a succession of dispensations until the number of prayers is reduced to five. Finally, the Prophet declares himself too embarrassed to seek a further dispensation. But the word—and will of God—triumphs. God announces that God's word (*qawl*)[1] does not change: those who offer five daily prayers will still obtain a reward equal to that of fifty prayers.[2]

Theologically, what might it mean for God to say that God's word does not change when in fact the command of God has actually changed? One way of interpreting the exchange is to posit that God's real word, the *qawl*, which undergoes no change, is an eternal reality that transcends particular linguistic forms such as the imperative, or juridical ones such as the command. The real

1 The inalterability of God's word is also asserted in the Qurʾān, using both *qawl* and *kalima*. Q. Qāf 50:29, "With Me the Word (*al-qawl*) is not changed, and I do not wrong My servants," with Q. al-Anʿām 6:115, "The Word (*kalima*) of thy Lord is fulfilled in truth and justice. None alters His Words (*kalimātihi*), and He is the Hearing, the Knowing." (Translation: *The Study Quran*).

2 For a fuller account of the *miʿrāj* event, see Muzaffar Iqbal, "The Prophet Muhammad: The Meccan Period," in *The Different Aspects of Islamic Culture: Vol. 1: Foundations of Islam*, ed. Ismail I. Nawwab and Zafar Ishaq Ansari (Paris: UNESCO, 2016), 217–60, at 252.

 | DOI:10.1163/9789004746886_011

qawl of God, the above exchange suggests, is God's will to reward creatures beyond their just deserts. Those who only offer five prayers will still be given the reward of performing fifty prayers. God's word then is at once what conveys the legal command—thereby instituting the law—while also anticipating and responding to the human inability to abide by the command—the failure to live up to demands of the law but to receive divine mercy nonetheless. In this way the *miʿrāj* becomes a story about the capacity of the law to become a site where human fantasies of triumph, success and sovereignty are pierced and where, in their brokenness, humans encounter divine love.

Through a contrapuntal reading of a series of debates in classical Islamic theology, this chapter will show how premodern Islamic theology and legal theory conceived of this capacity of the law to both give form to—and undo—sovereign life. The imbrications of Islamic theology and legal theory are considered here not only through an archaeological excavation of their porous and unsettled borders in jurisprudential or theological texts, but also through reflection on the discussions, within these texts and elsewhere, on the nature of law, punishment and grace, verbal forms such as the command, and how love might be obtained in, yet not contained within, the law.

1 Word, Command and Law

The *miʿrāj* journey suggests that there is a distinction between God's word and the expression of that word in the form of a legal command. Yet Muslim legal theorists of the classical period who regularly insist on this distinction, and conceive of the command (*amr*) as the quintessence of law, rarely refer to this event in support of their view, or to attack the views of their opponents.[3] The command, for many theologians and jurists, is also signified by a specific verbal form—the imperative, the Arabic term *amr* conveying both command and the imperative form.[4] Muʿtazilī thinkers, such as ʿAbd al-Jabbār, and Ashʿarīs, such as al-Ghazālī, also agreed that a command or obligation, which is to say the law, since the command was its quintessence, only exists

3 Abū Isḥāq al-Shīrāzī, *al-Ṭabṣira fī uṣūl al-fiqh*, ed. Muḥammad Ḥasan Haytu (Damascus Dār al-Fikr, 1403/1983), 17; ʿAlī b. Muḥammad al-Bazdawī, *Kanz al-wuṣūl ilā maʿrifat al-uṣūl* (Karachi: Mīr Muḥammad Kutub Khāna, n.d), 19; al-Khabbāzī, *al-Mughnī fī uṣūl al-fiqh*, ed. Muḥammad Baqā (Makka: Jāmiʿat Umm al-Qurā, 1403/1983), 27; Āl Taymiyya, *al-Musawwada*, ed. Aḥmad b. Ibrāhīm b. ʿAbbās al-Dharūrī (Riyadh: Dār al-Faḍīla li-l-Nashr wa-l-Tawzīʿ, 1422/2001), 81.

4 See Abdul Rahman Mustafa, *From God's Nature to God's Law: Theology, Law and Legal Theory in Islam* (Berlin: de Gruyter, 2025), 45–69.

if it is accompanied with a threat of some evil, injury or punishment for not complying with it.[5] For prominent Ashʿarīs such as al-Rāzī, all divine speech is ultimately a declaration (*bayān*)—with legal commands being a declaration of the reward or punishment associated with compliance or failure to comply with the command.[6] Ashʿarī theologians sometimes also adopted a maximalist understanding of the command as containing within it a prohibition. A command to do X, they reasoned, necessarily entails the prohibition of continuing to do not-X.[7] A prohibition too, for many jurists, was properly defined as an act that was accompanied by the threat of injury, sanction or punishment.[8] Making the threat of injury, if not its deliverance, the consequence of legal non-compliance, and treating this as central to law might suggest that legal compliance delivers immunity and protection from injury. But what if compliance with the law offers neither escape nor repair from injury but, instead, a regime of treatment for abiding with the incurability of human affliction and abjection?

This possibility is certainly entertained in Ashʿarī theology. For the philosopher, theologian and legal theorist al-Rāzī, the 'Pride of the Faith', the law is far from being a modality of divine love and grace that rescues humans from injury. Rather, al-Rāzī argues, it is the law that injures and diminishes us in the first place. Al-Rāzī had available to him a number of Ashʿarī theological assertions that could justify his view that compliance to the law cannot secure humans from the threat of injury. The Ashʿarīs, along with the traditionalists,

5 al-Qāḍī Abū al-Ḥasan ʿAbd al-Jabbār, *al-Mughnī fī abwāb al-tawḥīd wa-l-ʿadl*, ed. Muhammad ʿAlī al-Najjār and ʿAbd al-Ḥalīm al-Najjār (Cairo: Wizārat al-Thaqāfa wa-l-Irshād al-Qawmī, 1379–1388/1960–1968), 17: 105, 108; Abū Ḥāmid al-Ghazālī, *al-Mustaṣfā min ʿilm al-uṣūl*, ed. Muḥammad Sulaymān al-Ashqar (Beirut: al-Risāla al-ʿĀlamiyya, 1418/1997), 1:157–58; Mustafa, *From God's Nature*, 54.

6 Abū Bakr al-Bāqillānī, *al-Taqrīb wa-l-irshād*, ed. ʿAbd al-Ḥamīd b. ʿAlī (Beirut: Mu'assasat al-Risāla, 1418/1998), 1:280, 2:31; Fakhr al-Dīn al-Rāzī, *al-Maḥṣūl fī ʿilm uṣūl al-fiqh*, ed. Tāhā Jābir al-ʿAlwānī (Beirut: Mu'assasat al-Risāla, 1412/1992), 2:257; idem, *al-Arbaʿīn fī uṣūl al-dīn*, ed. Aḥmad al-Saqā (Cairo: Maktabat al-Kulliyāt al-Azhariyya, 1406/1986), 1:252; idem, *Muḥaṣṣal afkār al-mutaqaddimīm wa-l-muta'akhkhirīn*, ed. Ṭāhā ʿAbd al-Ra'ūf Saʿd (Cairo: Maktabat al-Kulliyāt al-Azhariyya, n.d.), 185; Sirāj al-Dīn al-Armawī, *al-Taḥṣīl min al-maḥṣūl*, ed. ʿAbd al-Ḥamīd ʿAlī Abū Zunaid (Beirut: Mu'assasat al-Risāla, 1408/1988), 1:329; Ṣafī al-Dīn al-Hindī, *Nihāyat al-wuṣūl ilā dirāyat al-uṣūl*, ed. Ṣāliḥ al-Yūsuf and Saʿīd al-Shuwayḥ (Makka: al-Maktaba al-Tijāriyya, n.d.), 3:1131; Sayf al-Dīn al-Āmidī, *Muntahā al-sūl fī ʿilm al-uṣūl*, ed. Aḥmad Farīd al-Mazīdī (Beirut: Dār al-Kutub al-ʿIlmiyya, 1424/2003), 99; al-Qarāfī, *Nafā'is al-uṣūl fī sharḥ al-maḥṣūl*, ed. ʿĀdil Aḥmad ʿAbd al-Mawjūd (Makka: Maktabat Nizār Muṣṭafā al-Bāz, 1997), 4:1618.

7 Abū al-Maʿālī al-Juwaynī, *al-Burhān fī uṣūl al-fiqh*, ed. ʿAbd al-ʿAẓīm al-Dīb (Qatar: n.p, 1399/1979), 1:250; Mustafa, *From God's Nature*, 59.

8 Mustafa, *From God's Nature*, 155–57.

opposed the Muʿtazilīs who held that God's justice bound God to reward compliance to the law and punish its violation. Divine grace, in the Muʿtazilī view, would unjustly tip the balance, allowing those who have violated God's commands and prohibitions to escape punishment and depriving of their just reward those who had faithfully abided by God's commands and prohibitions.[9] But for the Ashʿarīs and traditionalists, righteous actions alone, without divine mercy and grace, were not a cause of salvation. The Ashʿarī denial of causality delivers a further reason for questioning whether compliance with the law can actually deliver salvation in this world or the next.[10]

Al-Rāzī's view goes further than most Ashʿarī accounts, however, as he invites us to view the law itself as an injury and affront to human dignity and power. Human flourishing and fullness, he says, are diminished when one become an object of a love that makes one less than what one might be. Divine grace, for al-Rāzī, is one such form of love. It diminishes the creatures upon whom it is bestowed. It must be granted, al-Rāzī says at the outset, that God cannot bestow divine grace on those who are self-sufficient and have no need of this gift. Such an act would be futile and unbecoming of God. Therefore, to bestow grace upon creatures, God must first impose a form of abjection on them, debilitating them so that they become dependent on God's grace and favors. For al-Rāzī, it is manifestly evil for creatures to be placed in such a state of abjection, debility and dependency on another.[11] The law cannot, therefore, be a form of God's grace.

What then might it mean for al-Rāzī to say that God's law is good? As an Ashʿarī dialectical theologian and philosopher, it is clear that for al-Rāzī the statement that God's law is good is definitionally true. God's law is good because it proceeds from God who is necessarily good, not because the law necessarily procures the good of creatures. This was a conclusion echoed by many other Ashʿarī theologians who had also remarked that God's act of creation can bring no benefit to God or to ourselves. God cannot possibly obtain any benefit from creatures, while the latter wish that they did not exist with the burden of an existence that imposes moral demands on them, even the most basic

9 Mustafa, *From God's Nature*, 156.

10 Abū Bakr al-Bāqillānī, *al-Inṣāf*, ed. Muḥammad Zāhid al-Kawtharī (Cairo: al-Maktaba al-Azhar li-l-Turāth, 1421/2000), 46; Abū al-Maʿālī al-Juwaynī, *al-Irshād*, ed. Muḥammad Mūsā and ʿAlī ʿAbd al-Ḥamīd (Cairo: Maktabat al-Khānjī, 1369/1950), 381.

11 Fakhr al-Dīn Al-Rāzī, *al-Maṭālib al-ʿāliya min al-ʿilm al-ilāhī*, ed. Aḥmad al-Saqā (Beirut: Dār al-Kitāb al-ʿArabī, 1407/1987), 3:291–92.

of which—gratitude for the gift of existence—they find themselves unable to fulfil.[12]

2 Legal Words and Life

The theologians who expressed these views were, in effect, echoing the advice given by Moses to the Prophet during the latter's night journey to heaven. Moses foretold that the Prophet's community would not be able to fulfil the obligations being imposed on them by God and advised the Prophet to have this heavy burden reduced. The burden was in fact lightened by God announcing a reduction in the obligation to pray fifty times a day, while announcing that God's word does not change. This account lends support to the Ashʿarī view that the speech of God is not to be associated with any particular grammatical forms. The Arabic Qurʾān, in Ashʿarī theology, came to refer to the rendering (*ʿibāra*) or narration (*ḥikāya*) of the real speech or word (*kalām*) of God that subsists in the divine essence.[13] As an attribute of a formless, eternal and indivisible God, the inner speech (*kalām nafsī*) of God shares these qualities.[14] This also makes divine speech an inner meaning (*maʿnā*)—identical to God's eternal will and knowledge.[15] At the same time, however, the Ashʿarī distinction between the *maʿnā*, the real divine speech that subsists in God, and its subsequent clothing in the letters and words that forms its 'body'—the Qurʾān[16]—potentially allows further distinctions to be made between God's speech or will and God's law.

Opening a space between God's timeless word and the command of God expressed in a form assumed in time (such as the Arabic of the Prophet's time)

12 Abū Ḥāmid al-Ghazālī, *al-Iqtiṣād fī al-iʿtiqād*, ed. Hüseyin Atay and Ibrahim A. Çubukçu (Ankara, 1381/1962), 156, 163; al-Rāzī, *al-Maṭālib*, 3:299, 300–1; al-Hindī, *Nihāyat*, 2:741. See also Abdul Rahman Mustafa, "Supernatural, Unnatural, Queer: Gratitude and Nature in Islamic Political Theology," *Political Theology*, 22.8 (2021), 699–719.

13 Taqiyy al-Dīn Ibn Taymiyya, *al-Tisʿīniyya*, ed. Muḥammad b. Ibrāhīm al-ʿAjlān (Riyadh: Maktabat al-Maʿārif li-l-Nashr wa-l-Tawzīʿ, 1420/1999), 2:438, 3:879; ʿAbd al-Jabbār, *al-Mughnī*, 7:92, Abū Bakr al-Bāqillānī, *al-Tamhīd*, ed. Richard Joseph McCarthy (Beirut: al-Maktaba al-Sharqiyya, 1376/1957), 153; idem, *al-Inṣāf*, 26, 67, 105; Abū al-Qāsim al-Iṣbahānī, *al-Ḥujja fī bayān al-maḥajja wa-sharḥ ʿaqīdat ahl al-sunna*, ed. Muḥammad b. Rabīʿ al-Madkhalī and Muḥammad Abū Raḥīm (Amman: Dār al-Rāya, n.d), 2:189, 192.

14 Al-Iṣbahānī, *al-Ḥujja*, 2:189, 192.

15 Al-Bāqillānī, *al-Inṣāf*, 75–76; al-Juwaynī, *al-Irshād*, 118; Taqiyy al-Dīn Ibn Taymiyya, *al-Baʿalbakiyya*, ed. Maryam al-Ṣāʿidī (Riyadh: Dār al-Faḍīla, 1424/2004), 215; Saʿd al-Dīn al-Taftāzānī, *Sharḥ al-maqāṣid*, ed. ʿAbd al-Raḥmān ʿAmīra (Beirut: ʿĀlam al-Kutub, 1419/1998), 4:130.

16 See Key, *Language*; Mustafa, *From God's Nature*, 25.

potentially leads, however, to antinomian conclusions that do not sit well with the doctrines developed in Sunni legal theory. For what the Ashʿarī doctrine on divine speech suggests is that just as the various verbal forms of the Qurʾān constitute one indivisible divine meaning (*maʿnā*), so too do all divine addresses to Prophets such as Moses and Jesus. The Qurʾān, the Torah and the divine revelation to Jesus, the *Injīl*, therefore constitute different renderings of a single, eternal, indivisible meaning.[17] This meaning, when deciphered in Arabic, becomes the Qurʾān, and when deciphered in Hebrew becomes the Torah.[18] This also means, as pointed out by the fiercely anti-Ashʿarī traditionalist Ibn Qudāma, that the commands and prohibitions uttered by God and found in the Torah do not, in reality, differ from those uttered by God and found in the Qurʾān, since both the Torah and the Qurʾān are renderings of the same eternal and indivisible word.[19] It is perhaps too much to say that the Ashʿarī position on the distinction between the non-temporal, eternal and inner speech of God and its temporal, finite and contextual rendering in a particular historical and cultural medium (such as the Arabic or Hebrew spoken in a particular time and region) can be used to construct a more robust account of the secular in premodern Islam than has hitherto been thought available.[20] Nevertheless, an argument along these lines is not entirely implausible. For once it is conceded that there is a distinction between an inner speech that abides in God forever and the changing forms in which this speech is rendered in particular circumstances, it becomes possible to seek the real divine speech by going beyond the forms in which it is expressed.[21]

---

17 Al-Bāqillānī, *al-Inṣāf*, 97–98.

18 Ibn Taymiyya, *al-Baʿalbakiyya*, 156–57; idem, *Darʾ taʿāruḍ al-ʿaql wa-l-naql*, ed. Muḥammad R. Sālim (Cairo: Maṭbaʿat Dār al-Kutub, 1391/1971), 2:114, 6:288; al-Bāqillānī, *al-Inṣāf*, 101; Abū Manṣūr al-Baghdādī, *Uṣūl al-dīn* (Istanbul: Maṭbaʿat al-Dawla, 1346/1928), 108; ʿAlī Ibn Abī al-ʿIzz, *Sharḥ al-ʿaqīda al-Ṭaḥāwiyya*, ed. a group of scholars (Beirut: al-Maktab al-Islāmī 1404/1984), 168–69.

19 Muwaffaq al-Dīn Ibn Qudāma, *Ḥikāyat al-munāẓara fī al-Qurʾān*, ed. ʿAbd Allāh al-Judayʿ (Riyadh: Maktabat al-Rushd, 1418/1997), 20.

20 Jeffry R. Halverson, *Theology and Creed in Sunni Islam: The Muslim Brotherhood, Ashʿarism and Political Sunnism* (New York: Palgrave Macmillan, 2010).

21 On Islamic accounts of the secular, see Mustafa, "Religion;" Rushain Abbasi, "Did Premodern Muslims Distinguish the Religious and Secular? The *Dīn–Dunyā* Binary in Medieval Islamic Thought," *Journal of Islamic Studies*, 31.2 (2020): 185–225; Sherman Jackson, *The Islamic Secular* (Oxford: Oxford University Press, 2024).

3 On Sovereign Love

Theologians and jurists of the classical period regularly engaged theology and law to arrive at an understanding of the attribute of divine love and its relation to divine law by considering the following questions. First, is it proper to attribute love and mercy—in a veridical and not just a tropical or metaphorical sense—to God?[22] Second, does the law—both in the sense of specific legal obligations but also in the more general sense of the imposition of legal obligations—constitute a form of human flourishing and welfare (*maṣlaḥa*)? Third, is the procurement of human welfare an operative objective in all legal norms including—and primarily—ritual worship? A survey of these debates shows how the law becomes a way to think through the entanglements of human debility and divine power that inform classical legal theory. As one would expect, irreconcilably divergent conceptions of divine love do lead to divergent legal verdicts (*fatāwā*) and modes of legal reasoning. But more than that, varying accounts of divine love also become a way to think through sovereign life as experienced and encountered only in paradox. That is to say, reflection on legal sovereignty and love raises questions about how the subject and the sovereign relate to each other. Does the subject enjoy sovereignty when the law subjects them to the sovereignty of another? When the law of the sovereign is subjected to the sovereign's love, what remains of legal sovereignty?

For all their differences, Muʿtazilī and Ashʿarī theologians largely agreed that the *simplicity* of God's unity necessarily meant that God could not experience sensations such as love. A God who experienced such emotions would not only be subject to partiality and inner division, but would also be subject to change and temporality—and would thus not be God.[23] But even in works of theology, to say nothing of disciplines such as legal theory or spirituality, these same Ashʿarī and Muʿtazilī figures would often insist that God's love for mankind is manifested in God's act of instituting a law that procures humanity's flourishing, welfare and best interests (*maṣlaḥa*).[24] This tension is not capable

22 Abdul Rahman Mustafa, "Ibn Taymiyyah & Wittgenstein on Language," *The Muslim World*, 108.3 (2018), 465–91.

23 Mustafa, *From God's Nature*; Abū Bakr Ibn Fūrak, *Kitāb mushkil al-ḥadīth*, ed. Daniel Gimaret (Damascus: al-Maʿhad al-Faransī li-l-Dirāsāt al-ʿArabiyya bi-Dimashq, 1424/2003), 332; al-Bāqillānī, *al-Inṣāf*, 38, 156; idem, *al-Tamhīd*, 27; al-Juwaynī, *al-Irshād*, 239; al-Ghazālī, *al-Iqtiṣād*, 67.

24 On *maṣlaḥa*, see Felicitas Opwis, *Maṣlaḥa and the Purpose of the Law: Islamic Discourse on Legal Change from the 4th/10th to 8th/14th Century* (Leiden: Brill, 2010); idem, "Islamic Law and Legal Change: The Concept of *Maṣlaḥa* in Classical and Contemporary Islamic Legal

of easy resolution, despite the adoption of a hermeneutic in which scriptural accounts of love mean one thing when applied to God and something quite different when applied to human beings—an interpretive strategy adopted by many prominent Ashʿarī scholars.[25]

Another strategy of reconciliation advanced by some Ashʿarīs was to acknowledge that God's actions could—and did—accord with love and grace but not because God desired the fulfilment of a purpose such as human flourishing. It is impossible for God to act for a purpose, these Ashʿarīs had argued, because doing so necessarily makes the perfection of God, which is eternal, subject to the attainment of contingent purposes. This was just one of a host of arguments advanced by al-Rāzī in support of his view on the impossibility of God acting for a purpose.[26]

Notwithstanding the best efforts of the dialectical theologians, the tension between these two tendencies, God's intimate immanence and lofty transcendence, abides in legal theory and is reflected in efforts to explain the dualistic nature of legal obligations. The law seemed, at one and the same time, to inflict a form of debility on humans by subjecting them to legal obligations which were far beyond their ability to perform. Consider, for instance, God commanding that believers offer fifty prayers a day during the Prophet's *miʿrāj* journey. Yet the law also relieves humans of burdens that the law itself imposes. Consider, now, not only God's successive lifting of the burden of offering fifty prayers a day but also God's declaration that the reward of offering five prayers would be multiplied to fifty prayers. Faced with this back and forth, it is hardly surprising that scholars such as al-Rāzī adopt, within the space of a few lines, two diametrically opposed positions on the possibility of God's law being purposive and having as its purpose the flourishing of humans. As has been recalled elsewhere, al-Rāzī recounts that the theologians are agreed on the impropriety of ascribing purposes to God's acts or commands. The jurists

---

Theory," in *Shari'a: Islamic Law in the Contemporary Context*, ed. Abbas Amanat and Frank Griffel (Stanford, CA: Stanford University Press, 2007), 62–82.

25 William C. Chittick, *Divine Love: Islamic Literature and the Path to God* (New Haven, CT: Yale University Press, 2013), 24; Mustafa, *From God's Nature*.

26 Al-Rāzī, *al-Arbaʿīn*, 1:350–54; idem, *al-Masāʾil al-khamsūn fī uṣūl al-dīn*, ed. Aḥmad Saqqā (Cairo: al-Maktaba al-Thaqāfiyya, 1409/1989), 62; idem, *al-Mabāḥith al-mashriqiyya* (*al-Masāʾil al-mashriqiyya*), ed. Muḥammad al-Muʿtaṣim billāh al-Baghdādī, (n.p: n.p, 1343/1924), 1:542–43; idem, *Muḥaṣṣal*, 205; idem, *al-Maṭālib*, 3:289–90. See also Mustafa, *From God's Nature*; 110; Ayman Shihadeh, *The Teleological Ethics of Fakhr al-Dīn al-Rāzī* (Leiden: Brill, 2006), 97–98, https://brill.com/display/title/11560; Opwis, *Maṣlaḥa*, 113–21.

on the other hand are in agreement, says al-Rāzī, on the propriety of ascribing ratiocination to God's commands.[27]

In one of his rare criticisms of al-Rāzī, al-Qarāfī criticizes the former's tactic of mustering Qur'ānic proclamations of God's mercy and God's desire to create ease for creatures to prove that God's institutes laws *for* the *maṣlaḥa* of humanity.[28] For al-Qarāfī, the meaning of language necessarily changes when it moves from describing humans to describing God. Terms such as wisdom and love, al-Qarāfī says, are to be interpreted contrary to their conventional meaning when used in relation to God. One errs if one thinks that being wise or merciful compels God to act in a way that secures human flourishing.[29] For al-Qarāfī, the Qur'ānic proclamation that God desires ease for God's creation (Q., al-Baqara, 2:185), that God has imposed mercy upon God's self and that God's mercy extends over everything (Q., al-Aʿrāf, 6: 56), do not warrant the conclusion that God is bound to act in what is understood to be a merciful manner. It is actually impossible for a quality such as mercy to inhere in God, says, al-Qarāfī, because being merciful involves succumbing to a softness in one's nature, which is impossible for God. Mercy, as a form of tenderness, is actually unbecoming of God, says al-Qarāfī. Hence, God's name 'The Merciful' is to be understood in a tropical or metaphorical, rather than a veridical, sense.[30] Alongside a number of other dialectical theologians, al-Qarāfī thus objects to the idea that God experiences love, bestows grace on creatures out of love and issue commands on the basis of what God loves and abhors.[31]

While Muʿtazilī theologians such as ʿAbd al-Jabbār argued that God is bound to command that which is most perfect and beneficial for humanity,[32] Ashʿarīs such as al-Rāzī insisted that it makes no sense to say that God is obliged to do what is good. For al-Rāzī, as we have seen, the imposition of legal obligations is itself rationally abhorrent and evil rather than beneficial.[33] Al-Rāzī has at his disposal a range of arguments to disprove the proposition that God's commands correspond to what is considered good. He points out, for instance, that God creates people who have been predestined for eternal torment in this world and the next and compels them to exist in a world of tests and suffering

27 Abdul Rahman Mustafa, "Innovation in Premodern Islam: Between Non-Religion, Irreligion and the Secular," *Journal of Islamic Studies*, 34/1 (2023), 1–41, https://doi.org/10.1093/jis/etac029, here 24.

28 Al-Qarāfī, *Nafāʾis*, 9:4082.

29 Al-Qarāfī, *Nafāʾis*, 7:3310–11.

30 Al-Qarāfī, *Nafāʾis*, 7:3310.

31 See al-Qarāfī, *Nafāʾis*, 1:276.

32 ʿAbd al-Jabbār, *al-Mughnī*, 6:48–49, 11:58–133, 14:110–37.

33 Al-Rāzī, *al-Maṭālib*, 3:299, 300–1; Mustafa, *From God's Nature*, 162–63.

while having the power to allow everyone to abide in heaven eternally.[34] Even the procurement of benefits involves effort, exertion and hardship, al-Rāzī says, all of which are unpleasant and evil, although God could have created things in a way that eliminated their capacity for evil. Fire for instance, could have been created so as to only burn when it was beneficial and not when it was harmful.[35] Since God has chosen not to make this a quality of fire, one may conclude that God does not—at least consistently—desire to uphold the *maṣlaḥa*. Al-Ghazālī also summons the jurisprudential distinctions between ritual laws of worship (*taʿabbud*) and non-ritual areas of the law to prove that God's law cannot be said to be based on *maṣlaḥa*. The procurement of *maṣlaḥa* can only be said to be the norm in non-ritual areas of the law, says al-Ghazālī.[36] By contrast, areas of law concerned with ritual worship, as well as punishments and dispensations, are either not based on any apparent *maṣlaḥa*—or stand in stark opposition to the dictates of *maṣlaḥa*.[37]

For jurists such as Ibn Taymiyya, on the other hand, the primary purpose behind all legal regulations, including acts of ritual worship, is the cultivation of attitudes and sensibilities such as devotion, reverence and gratitude to God.[38] Such attitudes were arguably cultivated most perfectly in response to the concessions (*rukhṣa*, pl. *rukhaṣ*) by which God substituted a heavier or more burdensome obligation for a lighter or less burdensome one. The substitution of the command to perform fifty prayers a day by the command to perform five could be read as analogous to, although perhaps not strictly falling within, the category of a concession. The large number of concessions in ritual law justified, for many scholars, the conclusion that ritual law was enacted to deliver legal subjects from the undue burdens which the law itself places on them.[39] Ibn Taymiyya, for instance, argues that humanity recognizes the goodness of God in God's will and desire to promote their flourishing, which moves

34 Al-Rāzī, *al-Maḥṣūl*, 5:182, 192; idem, *al-Maṭālib*, 3:291–92; al-Hindī, *Nihāyat*, 8:3330; al-Āmidī, *Muntahā al-sūl*, 215; Sharaf al-Dīn ʿAbd Allāh ibn Muḥammad Ibn al-Tilimsānī, *Sharḥ al-maʿālim fī uṣūl al-fiqh*, ed. ʿĀdil Aḥmad ʿAbd al-Mawjūd and ʿAlī Muḥammad Muʿawwaḍ (Beirut: ʿĀlam al-Kutub li-l-Ṭibāʿa wa-l-Nashr wa-l-Tawzīʿ), 2:294; al-Juwaynī, *al-Irshād*, 204–5; Mustafa, *From God's Nature*, 162–63.

35 Al-Rāzī, *al-Maṭālib*, 3:282; Mustafa, *From God's Nature*, 162–63.

36 Al-Ghazālī, *al-Mustaṣfā*, 2:312.

37 Al-Ghazālī, *al-Mustaṣfā*, 2:320, 322, 340–341; idem, *Shifāʾ al-ghalīl*, ed. Ḥamad al-Kubaysī (Baghdad: Maṭbaʿat al-Irshād, 1391/1971), 318–29.

38 Abdul Rahman Mustafa, "Ritual and Rationality in Islam: A Case Study on Nail Polish," *Islamic Law and Society*, 27.3 (2019), 240–84, here 268.

39 Ibid., 264.

creatures to respond to God with love, adoration, reverence and obedient servitude towards the One who acts to secure their flourishing.[40]

4 Love, Sovereignty and Failure

In the traditionalist thought of Ibn Taymiyya and Ibn al-Qayyim, we encounter the view that it is entirely proper for love to bind God and creatures into a relationship of difference and dependency. Law here becomes the modality in which God and humans inhabit their relationship of mutual desire and difference. It is unimaginable that the love between God and creatures could ever be a love between equals, says Ibn al-Qayyim.[41] For Ibn al-Qayyim, the imposition of legal responsibility procures human flourishing by forming the proper relationship that ought to exist between God and creatures. To desire being in a position where one is not seeking and expressing gratitude for divine grace and favor is, according to Ibn al-Qayyim, to desire an impossibility—the end to one's own existence as a creature with the capacity to desire and love.[42]

Gratitude, it should be recalled, is for scholars such as Ibn al-Qayyim the ultimate site of human ethical failure and divine grace. As has been elaborated elsewhere, Islamic theological and ethical thought considers gratitude to God as both necessary and impossible. The obligation to be grateful for the gift of life can never be fulfilled, because life itself is the gift that makes it possible to experience and express gratitude. The very ability to experience and express gratitude for the gift is therefore itself a gift for which one would be obliged to express gratitude, and so forth. This tension is kept alive in an aporia: gratitude is an obligation discharged in the recognition of one's incapacity to perform it.[43] It is thus by cultivating "dependency, limitation, self-surrender and the renunciation of personal and political freedom and sovereign autonomy"[44] that one can discharge the obligation of gratitude and find a way to flourish in the debility of creaturely existence.

How would love enact this difference between God and God's creatures while at the same time overcoming the separation that keeps the two apart? In

40 Taqiyy al-Dīn Ibn Taymiyya, *Majmūʿat al-rasāʾil al-kubrā* (Beirut: Dār Iḥyāʾ al-Turāth al-ʿArabī, 1392/1972), 1:332.

41 Ibn al-Qayyim al-Jawziyya, *Miftāḥ dār al-saʿāda*, ed. ʿAbd al-Raḥmān Qāʾid (Makka: Dār ʿĀlam al-Fawāʾid, 1432/2011), 2: 854, 1058, 1066; Taqiyy al-Dīn Ibn Taymiyya, *Majmūʿ al-fatāwā*, eds. ʿĀmir Jazzār and Anwar Bāz (al-Manṣūra: Dār al-Wafāʾ, 1419/1998), 10:37.

42 al-Jawziyya, 2:995–96, 1066.

43 See Mustafa, "Supernatural."

44 Mustafa, "Supernatural."

the linguistic philosophy adopted by the traditionalists, as we recall, the term love does not primarily denote the core of an abstracted universal concept which then comes to be used tropically with greater imprecision the further one moves from the core concept. On the contrary, it is the individual and particular instances of love that possess a reality and relationality which are then aggregated so that we arrive at a sense of the core abstracted universal which has no real existence except in our minds.[45] Love is such a term that expresses what is shared between God and creatures and what makes them capable of loving each other precisely in their difference. Bound together in law and desire, God and creature nevertheless remain distinct, each lover more fully themselves in their love of the other. As the law is an expression of love, it also becomes an inhabitation of difference in sovereign life. Human sovereignty is realized in its subjection to God's love. God's own sovereignty is also realized in the love and mercy by which God's self is bound by God's own love, a love that God has "inscribed upon" God, as the Qur'ān expresses it. The law, then, is the inhabitation of difference in desire.

But if the difference between divine and human subjectivity is expressed in human servitude and divine sovereignty, in the difference between God and creatures, then failure is also a necessary and inescapable aspect of the human experience of love and servitude. This is not the case for God. For as al-Ghazālī argues in his controversial theodicy, even the seeming imperfections in God's acts allow for things more perfect to exist. The world could not be better than it is, al-Ghazālī says, because God, being perfect, necessarily creates the cosmos in the most perfect way, such that even its imperfections allow for that which is more perfect to come forth.[46] Ibn Taymiyya's legal theodicy expresses a similar optimism. The law, according to Ibn Taymiyya, often brings about superior benefits by letting go of inferior ones and eliminates greater evils by allowing ones that are smaller by comparison.[47] For Ibn Taymiyya, God's law procures the *maṣlaḥa* not just by each and every one of its particular commands but also because it diminishes the overall scale of evil through the exercise of its universal moral and coercive power.[48] Just as the natural order of things, could not, for al-Ghazālī, be other than it is, so too for Ibn Taymiyya, God's commands

45 Mustafa, "Ibn Taymiyyah & Wittgenstein on Language."

46 Eric L. Ormsby, *Theodicy in Islamic Thought: The Dispute Over al-Ghazālī's "Best of All Possible Worlds"* (Princeton: Princeton University Press, 1984).

47 Ibn Taymiyya, *Majmūʿ*, 20:30–32; 28:75.

48 Ibn Taymiyya, *Majmūʿat al-rasāʾil*, 1:335–36.

could not enjoin injustice or oppression for, if they did, they would cease to procure the flourishing that God brings about through the law.[49]

For Ibn Taymiyya, this view of divine perfection serves as an argument against the dialectical theologians for whom ritual law does not serve as an instance of God's desire to procure *maṣlaḥa.* Concessions (such as the one granted to the Prophet on his *miʿrāj* journey) once again become the crux of the debate because they reveal the different conceptions of divine power and human debility and failure at play in theological and legal thought. For according to the theologians such as al-Ghazālī, the rules of ritual law were often either not amenable to rational explication or were set aside by other rules that served as dispensations or concessions so that one could no longer say that the procurement of an aim secured by the original rule was desired by the law. Al-Ghazālī, for instance, says that ritual laws come with so many exceptions and dispensations that any ostensibly purpose these laws might have served becomes impossible to secure. Al-Ghazālī considers the dispensation allowing a traveler to wipe over their socks as a substitute for washing their feet in ritual ablutions. Wiping over a barrier that covers parts of one's body cannot, in al-Ghazālī's view, bring about actual purification. This is something only washing can achieve. Therefore, the availability of the dispensation allowing one to substitute washing one's limb with the act of wiping over it means that purification cannot have been the aim or *maṣlaḥa* intended by the ritual laws of purification. The command to wash one's limbs in ritual ablution therefore cannot serve a rational purpose or procure a rational benefit. There is still, al-Ghazālī says, a benefit in dispensations, namely that they prevent people from becoming utterly lax about their ritual obligations and abandoning them altogether.[50] Al-Ghazālī also considers the example of legal dispensations permitting the traveler to shorten and combine their daily prayers and wipe over their socks as a substitute for washing their feet during ritual ablutions, even if the travel does not entail hardship. However, the same dispensations have not been made available for those who might not be travelers but for whom the ritual obligation of praying on time and washing their limbs in ablutions might entail hardship.[51] This shows, al-Ghazālī says, that ritual laws do no uphold a consistent *maṣlaḥa* such as the alleviation of hardship.

---

49 Taqiyy al-Dīn Ibn Taymiyya, *Jāmiʿ al-rasāʾil*, ed. Muḥammad R. Sālim (Jedda: Dār al-Madanī,1405/1984), 1:130–31. For al-Ghazālī's view, see Ormsby, *Theodicy*.

50 Al-Ghazālī, *al-Mustaṣfā*, 2:320; idem, *Shifāʾ al-ghalīl*, 318–29.

51 Al-Ghazālī, *al-Mustaṣfā*, 2:341, 351.

For Ibn Taymiyya, by contrast, every area of law upholds the *maṣlaḥa*, including the rules pertaining to ritual worship and penal law.[52] In fact, Ibn Taymiyya says, the law's aims of procuring the *maṣlaḥa* of alleviating hardship and facilitating ease are most fully realized in the issuance of legal dispensations of the sort which the dialectical theologians dismiss for serving no discernible rational *maṣlaḥa* and for being devoid of a ratio. Ibn Taymiyya, in fact, sees ritual law as the primary arena for the operation of *maṣlaḥa*. Acts of worship, together with their relevant dispensations, come together to cultivate affective states of loving devotion on the part of legal subjects who are moved to adore a merciful lawgiver and lord. The hardship accompanying legal acts is not in itself desired by God.[53] It is precisely because dispensations serve an eminently rational purpose for Ibn Taymiyya that he allows extending the scope of such dispensations analogically, and rejects many of the strict preconditions which, according to many jurists, had to be met by anyone availing themselves of a dispensation. The imposition of such preconditions on these dispensations is not just scripturally unwarranted in Ibn Taymiyya's view, it also undermines their *raison d'être*: the removal of hardship and the facilitation of ease. To take one example, Ibn Taymiyya opposes jurists who insist that the dispensation of wiping over one's sock rather than washing one's foot during a ritual ablution is not available to someone whose foot is not fully covered by their sock. The purpose of a legal concession, Ibn Taymiyya says, is to remove hardship and create ease. It would be quite contrary to the spirit and rationale of a concession to withhold it from travelers and the poor who are compelled to wear socks that are worn out and torn. This consideration, coupled with the absence of a specific *ḥadīth* prohibiting the act of wiping over torn socks suffices, in Ibn Taymiyya's view, to establish that the legal concession of wiping over socks extends to torn socks that expose parts of the foot.[54]

Ibn Taymiyya thus not only centers ritual law as the primary arena for the operation of *maṣlaḥa*; he also insists that dispensations overturning the regular rules of ritual law are the primary expression of God's loving lordship and humanity's grateful servitude. Rejecting the Ashʿarī view that the word of God is single, indivisible and formless, Ibn Taymiyya insists that parts of God's word—those that uphold the *maṣlaḥa* of facilitating ease and removing

52 Ibn Taymiyya, *Majmūʿ*, 8:57; 11:189–90; 14:149; Taqiyy al-Dīn Ibn Taymiyya, *Minhāj al-sunna al-nabawiyya*, ed. Muḥammad R. Sālim (Riyadh: n.p., 1406/1986), 3:14, 28. Compare al-Ghazālī, *al-Mustaṣfā*, 2:341; al-Juwaynī, *al-Burhān*, 2:602–3.

53 Ibn Taymiyya, *Majmūʿ*, 25:151, 20:89–90, 10:300.

54 Ibn Taymiyya, *Majmūʿ*, 19:131; 21:101–7, 122–24; Taqiyy al-Dīn Ibn Taymiyya, *al-Fatāwā al-kubrā*, ed. Muḥammad ʿAbd al-Qādir ʿAṭā (Beirut: Dār al-Kutub al-ʿIlmiyya, 1407/1987), 1:319; Mustafa, *From God's Nature*, 190.

hardship—are better than others, a view for which he also finds scriptural support in the form of the Qur'ānic verse that speaks of those who hear God's word and follow the best of it.[55]

Ibn Taymiyya's account of *maṣlaḥa* is thus very different from that of scholars such as al-Rāzī and al-Ghazālī. To say that Ibn Taymiyya's views on *maṣlaḥa* appear to be aligned to the textualist view of welfare commonly identified with al-Ghazālī[56] is to ignore the fact that the purposive contours of Ibn Taymiyya's account of *maṣlaḥa* allow him to wield much more change—even in ritual law—than al-Ghazālī is willing to entertain. Ibn Taymiyya's views on *maṣlaḥa* also make him do away with many legal rules that he regarded as too onerous, as we saw in the example of the conditions under which wiping over socks could substitute for the obligation of washing one's foot in ritual ablutions. Consider also Ibn Taymiyya's controversial verdict allowing a menstruating woman to circumambulate (*ṭawāf*) the Kaʿba during her pilgrimage if she fears that waiting for the end of her menstruation would prevent her from journeying back to her home in safety, a verdict Ibn Taymiyya justifies by reference to the law's aim of alleviating hardship.[57] Similar to this are the cases of a menstruating woman who needs to recite the Qur'ān or to enter a mosque, both of which Ibn Taymiyya controversially allows her to do on the grounds that withholding permission for such acts would be contrary to the *maṣlaḥa* procured by the law.[58] Yet even as he calls for many rules in ritual law to be set aside for the sake of *maṣlaḥa*, Ibn Taymiyya's view of *maṣlaḥa* ultimately sees submission to God's law as a supreme *maṣlaḥa* without which human flourishing is impossible. Notwithstanding his willingness to suspend the operation of legal rules that appear to contravene *maṣlaḥa*, Ibn Taymiyya's understanding of *maṣlaḥa* has little to offer a theory of *maṣlaḥa* built on a view of human autonomy that operates independently of divine commands and the law.

5 Conclusion

We are thus brought back to the account of the *miʿrāj* and its staging of the extended drama of the Prophet's repeated appeal to God to reduce the number

55 Ibn Taymiyya, *Majmūʿ*, 17:11, 29, 32; 16:7; Muḥammad Abū al-Ḥusayn al-Baṣrī, *Kitāb al-muʿtamad fī uṣūl al-fiqh*, ed. Muḥammad Ḥamīdullāh (Damascus: al-Maʿhad al-ʿIlmī al-Faransī li-l-Dirāsāt al-ʿArabīya bi-Dimashq, 1384/1964), 1:427.

56 Sophia Vasalou, *Ibn Taymiyya's Theological Ethics* (New York: Oxford University Press, 2016), 210.

57 Ibn Taymiyya, *Majmūʿ*, 26:98, 100.

58 Ibn Taymiyya, *Majmūʿ*, 26:98.

of obligatory prayers that his nation had been commanded to perform. One of the possibilities suggested in the account is that the law is not just what brings human failure into being by making sinners of those who fail to live up to its demands, but that it is also the site of the sovereignty of love that responds to human failure to live up to the law's demands. This sovereignty of love is realized in a succession of legal forms: the command, the dispensation and, finally and ultimately, in the operation of divine mercy. The circuitous route of commanding stricter obligations that are set aside in response to human incapacity thus becomes part of the human flourishing that the law seeks to procure. This flourishing consists not of human triumph and success, the values so often pursued in the calculus of *maṣlaḥa* deployed in traditional *uṣūl al-fiqh*. Rather, the realization by humanity of its own failure, debility and incapacity turns out to be one of the main aims procured and realized through the successive imposition and suspension of legal commands. Human flourishing, *maṣlaḥa*, is one's realization of one's debility and dependence on God. This knowledge of one's limitation, incapacity and failure in living up to the commands of the law is also what allows for a love of the divine to proceed from creatures towards God. The law is the medium for this exchange of love between the divine and the human.

Bibliography

Abbasi, Rushain, "Did Premodern Muslims Distinguish the Religious and Secular? The *Dīn–Dunyā* Binary in Medieval Islamic Thought," *Journal of Islamic Studies*, 31, no. 2 (2020), 185–225.

ʿAbd al-Jabbār, al-Qāḍī Abū al-Ḥasan, *al-Mughnī fī abwāb al-tawḥīd wa-l-ʿadl*, ed. Muhammad ʿAlī al-Najjār and ʿAbd al-Ḥalīm al-Najjār (Cairo: Wizārat al-Thaqāfa wa-l-Irshād al-Qawmī, 1379–1388/1960–1968).

al-Āmidī, Sayf al-Dīn, *Muntahā al-sūl fī ʿilm al-uṣūl*, ed. Aḥmad Farīd al-Mazīdī (Beirut: Dār al-Kutub al-ʿIlmiyya, 1424/2003).

al-Armawī, Sirāj al-Dīn, *al-Taḥṣīl min al-maḥṣūl*, ed. ʿAbd al-Ḥamīd ʿAlī Abū Zunaid (Beirut: Muʾassasat al-Risāla, 1408/1988).

Āl Taymiyya, *al-Musawwada*, ed. Aḥmad b. Ibrāhīm b. ʿAbbās al-Dharūrī (Riyadh: Dār al-Faḍīla li-l-Nashr wa-l-Tawzīʿ, 1422/2001).

al-Baghdādī, Abū Manṣūr, *Uṣūl al-dīn* (Istanbul: Maṭbaʿat al-Dawla, 1346/1928).

al-Bāqillānī, Abū Bakr, *al-Inṣāf*, ed. Muḥammad Zāhid al-Kawtharī (Cairo: al-Maktaba al-Azhar li-l-Turāth, 1421/2000).

al-Bāqillānī, Abū Bakr, *al-Tamhīd*, ed. Richard Joseph McCarthy (Beirut: al-Maktaba al-Sharqiyya, 1376/1957).

al-Bāqillānī, Abū Bakr, *al-Taqrīb wa-l-irshād*, ed. ʿAbd al-Ḥamīd b. ʿAlī (Beirut: Muʾassasat al-Risāla, 1418/1998).

al-Baṣrī, Muḥammad Abū al-Ḥusayn, *Kitāb al-muʿtamad fī uṣūl al-fiqh*, ed. Muḥammad Ḥamīdullāh (Damascus: al-Maʿhad al-ʿIlmī al-Faransī li-l-Dirāsāt al-ʿArabīya bi-Dimashq, 1384/1964).

al-Bazdawī, ʿAlī b. Muḥammad, *Kanz al-wuṣūl ilā maʿrifat al-uṣūl* (Karachi: Mīr Muḥammad Kutub Khāna, n.d).

Chittick, William C., *Divine Love: Islamic Literature and the Path to God* (New Haven, CT: Yale University Press, 2013).

al-Ghazālī, Abū Ḥāmid, *al-Iqtiṣād fī al-iʿtiqād*, ed. Hüseyin Atay and Ibrahim A. Çubukçu (Ankara, 1381/1962).

al-Ghazālī, Abū Ḥāmid, *al-Mustaṣfā min ʿilm al-uṣūl*, ed. Muḥammad Sulaymān al-Ashqar (Beirut: al-Risāla al-ʿĀlamiyya, 1418/1997).

al-Ghazālī, Abū Ḥāmid, *Shifāʾ al-ghalīl*, ed. Ḥamad al-Kubaysī (Baghdad: Maṭbaʿat al-Irshād, 1391/1971).

Halverson, Jeffry R., *Theology and Creed in Sunni Islam: The Muslim Brotherhood, Ashʿarism and Political Sunnism* (New York: Palgrave Macmillan, 2010).

al-Hindī, Ṣafī al-Dīn, *Nihāyat al-wuṣūl ilā dirāyat al-uṣūl*, ed. Ṣāliḥ al-Yūsuf and Saʿīd al-Shuwayḥ (Makka: al-Maktaba al-Tijāriyya, n.d.).

Ibn Abī al-ʿIzz, *Sharḥ al-ʿaqīda al-Ṭaḥāwiyya*, ed. a group of scholars (Beirut: al-Maktab al-Islāmī 1404/1984).

Ibn al-Qayyim al-Jawziyya, *Miftāḥ dār al-saʿāda*, ed. ʿAbd al-Raḥmān Qāʾid (Makka: Dār ʿĀlam al-Fawāʾid, 1432/2011).

Ibn al-Tilimsānī, Sharaf al-Dīn ʿAbd Allāh ibn Muḥammad, *Sharḥ al-maʿālim fī uṣūl al-fiqh*, ed. ʿĀdil Aḥmad ʿAbd al-Mawjūd and ʿAlī Muḥammad Muʿawwaḍ (Beirut: ʿĀlam al-Kutub li-l-Ṭibāʿa wa-l-Nashr wa-l-Tawzīʿ).

Ibn Fūrak, Abū Bakr, *Kitāb mushkil al-ḥadīth*, ed. Daniel Gimaret (Damascus: al-Maʿhad al-Faransī li-l-Dirāsāt al-ʿArabiyya bi-Dimashq, 1424/2003).

Ibn Qudāma, Muwaffaq al-Dīn, *Ḥikāyat al-munāẓara fī al-Qurʾān*, ed. ʿAbd Allāh al-Judayʿ (Riyadh: Maktabat al-Rushd, 1418/1997).

Ibn Taymiyya, Taqiyy al-Dīn, *Darʾ taʿāruḍ al-ʿaql wa-l-naql*, ed. Muḥammad R. Sālim (Cairo: Maṭbaʿat Dār al-Kutub, 1391/1971).

Ibn Taymiyya, Taqiyy al-Dīn, *al-Baʿalbakiyya*, ed. Maryam al-Ṣāʿidī (Riyadh: Dār al-Faḍīla, 1424/2004).

Ibn Taymiyya, Taqiyy al-Dīn, *al-Fatāwā al-kubrā*, ed. Muḥammad ʿAbd al-Qādir ʿAṭā (Beirut: Dār al-Kutub al-ʿIlmiyya, 1407/1987).

Ibn Taymiyya, Taqiyy al-Dīn, *al-Tisʿīniyya*, ed. Muḥammad b. Ibrāhīm al-ʿAjlān (Riyadh: Maktabat al-Maʿārif li-l-Nashr wa-l-Tawzīʿ, 1420/1999).

Ibn Taymiyya, Taqiyy al-Dīn, *Jāmiʿ al-rasāʾil*, ed. Muḥammad R. Sālim (Jedda: Dār al-Madanī, 1405/1984).

Ibn Taymiyya, Taqiyy al-Dīn, *Majmūʿ al-fatāwā*, ed. ʿĀmir Jazzār and Anwar Bāz (al-Manṣūra: Dār al-Wafāʾ, 1419/1998).

Ibn Taymiyya, Taqiyy al-Dīn, *Minhāj al-sunna al-nabawiyya*, ed. Muḥammad R. Sālim (Riyadh: n.p., 1406/1986).

Ibn Taymiyya, Taqiyy al-Dīn, *Majmūʿat al-rasāʾil al-kubrā* (Beirut: Dār Iḥyāʾ al-Turāth al-ʿArabī, 1392/1972).

Iqbal, Muzaffar, "The Prophet Muhammad: The Meccan Period," in *The Different Aspects of Islamic Culture: Vol. 1: Foundations of Islam*, ed. Ismail I. Nawwab and Zafar Ishaq Ansari (Paris: UNESCO, 2016), 217–60.

al-Iṣbahānī, Abū al-Qāsim, *al-Ḥujja fī bayān al-maḥajja wa-sharḥ ʿaqīdat ahl al-sunna*, ed. Muḥammad b. Rabīʿ al-Madkhalī and Muḥammad Abū Raḥīm (Amman: Dār al-Rāya, n.d).

Jackson, Sherman, *The Islamic Secular* (Oxford: Oxford University Press, 2024).

al-Juwaynī, Abū al-Maʿālī, *al-Burhān fī uṣūl al-fiqh*, ed. ʿAbd al-ʿAẓīm al-Dīb (Qatar: n.p, 1399/1979).

al-Juwaynī, Abū al-Maʿālī, *al-Irshād*, ed. Muḥammad Mūsā and ʿAlī ʿAbd al-Ḥamīd (Cairo: Maktabat al-Khānjī, 1369/1950).

al-Khabbāzī, *al-Mughnī fī uṣūl al-fiqh*, ed. Muḥammad Baqā (Makka: Jāmiʿat Umm al-Qurā, 1403/1983).

Mustafa, Abdul Rahman, "Ibn Taymiyyah & Wittgenstein on Language," *The Muslim World*, 108, no. 3 (2018), 465–91.

Mustafa, Abdul Rahman, "Innovation in Premodern Islam: Between Non-Religion, Irreligion and the Secular," *Journal of Islamic Studies*, 34, no. 1 (2023), 1–41, https://doi.org/10.1093/jis/etac029.

Mustafa, Abdul Rahman, "Ritual and Rationality in Islam: A Case Study on Nail Polish," *Islamic Law and Society*, 27, no. 3 (2019), 240–84.

Mustafa, Abdul Rahman, "Supernatural, Unnatural, Queer: Gratitude and Nature in Islamic Political Theology," *Political Theology*, 22, no. 8 (2021), 699–719.

Mustafa, Abdul Rahman, *From God's Nature to God's Law: Theology, Law and Legal Theory in Islam* (Berlin: de Gruyter, 2025).

Opwis, Felicitas, "Islamic Law and Legal Change: The Concept of *Maṣlaḥa* in Classical and Contemporary Islamic Legal Theory," in *Shari'a: Islamic Law in the Contemporary Context*, ed. Abbas Amanat and Frank Griffel (Stanford, CA: Stanford University Press, 2007), 62–82.

Opwis, Felicitas, *Maṣlaḥa and the Purpose of the Law: Islamic Discourse on Legal Change from the 4th/10th to 8th/14th Century* (Leiden: Brill, 2010).

Ormsby, Eric L., *Theodicy in Islamic Thought: The Dispute Over al-Ghazālī's "Best of All Possible Worlds"* (Princeton: Princeton University Press, 1984).

al-Qarāfī, *Nafāʾis al-uṣūl fī sharḥ al-maḥṣūl*, ed. ʿĀdil Aḥmad ʿAbd al-Mawjūd (Makka: Maktabat Nizār Muṣṭafā al-Bāz, 1997).

al-Rāzī, Fakhr al-Dīn, *Muḥaṣṣal afkār al-mutaqaddimīm wa-l-muta'akhkhirīn*, ed. Ṭāhā 'Abd al-Ra'ūf Sa'd (Cairo: Maktabat al-Kulliyāt al-Azhariyya, n.d.).

al-Rāzī, Fakhr al-Dīn, *al-Arba'īn fī uṣūl al-dīn*, ed. Aḥmad al-Saqā (Cairo: Maktabat al-Kulliyāt al-Azhariyya, 1406/1986).

al-Rāzī, Fakhr al-Dīn, *al-Mabāḥith al-mashriqiyya* (*al-Masā'il al-mashriqiyya*), ed. Muḥammad al-Mu'taṣim billāh al-Baghdādī, (n.p: n.p, 1343/1924).

al-Rāzī, Fakhr al-Dīn, *al-Masā'il al-khamsūn fī uṣūl al-dīn*, ed. Aḥmad Saqqā (Cairo: al-Maktaba al-Thaqāfiyya, 1409/1989).

al-Rāzī, Fakhr al-Dīn, *al-Maḥṣūl fī 'ilm uṣūl al-fiqh*, ed. Tāhā Jābir al-'Alwānī (Beirut: Mu'assasat al-Risāla, 1412/1992).

al-Rāzī, Fakhr al-Dīn, *al-Maṭālib al-'āliya min al-'ilm al-ilāhī*, ed. Aḥmad al-Saqā (Beirut: Dār al-Kitāb al-'Arabī, 1407/1987).

Shihadeh, Ayman, *The Teleological Ethics of Fakhr al-Dīn al-Rāzī* (Leiden: Brill, 2006), https://brill.com/display/title/11560.

al-Shīrāzī, Abū Isḥāq, *al-Ṭabṣira fī uṣūl al-fiqh*, ed. Muḥammad Ḥasan Haytu (Damascus Dār al-Fikr, 1403/1983).

al-Taftāzānī, Sa'd al-Dīn, *Sharḥ al-maqāṣid*, ed. 'Abd al-Raḥmān 'Amīra (Beirut: 'Ālam al-Kutub, 1419/1998).

Vasalou, Sophia, *Ibn Taymiyya's Theological Ethics* (New York: Oxford University Press, 2016).

Index

www.ingramcontent.com/pod-product-compliance
Lightning Source LLC
Chambersburg PA
CBHW071333230926
51849CB00002B/384
9789004530874